GLORY
DAYS

GLORY
DAYS

365 Inspired Moments in African-American History

For Diana —

May all your days be
Glory Days —

Janus Adams

Janus Adams
16 nov. 1995

HarperCollins*Publishers*

HarperCollins books may be purchased for educational, business, or sales promotional use. For information please write: Special Markets Department, HarperCollins Publishers, Inc., 10 East 53rd Street, New York, NY 10022.

FIRST EDITION

Designed by Caitlin Daniels

Library of Congress Cataloging-in-Publication Data

Adams, Janus.
    Glory days : 365 inspired moments in African-American history / Janus Adams. — 1st ed.
        p.   cm.
    Includes index.
    ISBN 0-06-017262-2
    1.   Afro-Americans — History — Chronology.   2.   Afro-Americans History — Miscellanea. I. Title.
    E185.A234   1995
    973'.0496073'00202 — dc20   95-31434

95 96 97 98 99 ❖/HC 10 9 8 7 6 5 4 3 2 1

For
my mother

a driving force

ACKNOWLEDGMENTS

As this book evolved, my family, friends, and the strangers I've come to know as friends encouraged me through troubled waters. With their help and by their insistence, I have had the privilege of writing *Glory Days*.

For making this book possible, I thank these loving friends: Hattie Winston, Harold Wheeler, and Samantha Diana; Gail Hamilton and James Stovall; my lawyer and special treasure, Richard Spooner; my agent and my faith-healer, Marie Brown.

For their years of sisterhood, I am ever indebted to my Underground Railway: Johnnetta B. Cole, Camille O. Cosby, and Sonia Sanchez.

For their joy, I am ever grateful for the gifts of Frances Bernat, Joel Brokaw, Roberto Hunter, Betty and Stan Katz, Linda and James Keeler, Evelyn Neal, and Adrianne and Lenzy Wallace.

For their faith, Nicki Brown and colleagues.

For their midnight oil–burning searches, thanks are due to a network of librarians in Wilton, Westport, and Stamford, Connecticut; at Fisk University and the New York Public Library's Schomburg Center for Research in Black Culture.

For her spirit, insight, scrawl, and tenacity, I thank my editor, Peternelle van Arsdale.

And because they continue to enrich my life and give me hope, I owe the greatest thanks to my mother, Muriel Landsmark Tuitt; my daughters, Ayo and Dara Roach; my aunts, Marjorie deLewis and Rubye Wright; all those who know me and love me anyway; and to those who were once so near and are now with the ancestors and angels: my father and grandparents.

INTRODUCTION

Over the years I've heard writers say that they write the books they need to read. For me, *Glory Days* is that book. It has willed itself to life out of the conversations and context of the late twentieth century. My friends wanted it. My children, their friends, and the times demanded it.

All of us were feeling the earth quake under us with the eruption of hard-core racial hatreds and of renewed hardship. Regardless of our occupations, hometowns, or income brackets, we were feeling the kind of hardship that comes when words like *dark* and *black* creep back into the vocabulary to stand for all things negative and threatening; the kind of hardship that throughout history has arrived on the coattails of demagogues and demigods; the kind that penetrates to the bone and destroys a nation's soul. But it is also the kind of hardship over which our people have triumphed many times before. This much we knew. We had heard it in the spirituals, we had seen it in the faces of our elders, we had read it in the eyes of our newest born. What we didn't know was how this triumph had taken place, day by day; how had we done it? Because I grew up under the tutelage of a family steeped in Garveyism (the Pan-Africanist philosophy of Marcus Garvey)—with all its yearning and its celebration of the Pan-African diaspora and heritage—I learned to look to history for answers. And thus the idea for *Glory Days: 365 Inspired Moments in African-American History* was born.

Rooted in three specific events, *Glory Days* pays homage to three specific gifts: history, heritage, and hope.

One day a group of my friends were discussing the growing racism, possible ways to overcome it, the problems of how to achieve in spite of it and of how to survive it. I watched as our host's father began to hang his head in sorrow, mourning the notion that, as he said, his generation had "done so little" to ensure that our generation would not have to suffer this pain. We tried to tell him that this wasn't so, tried to soothe his pain as he had wished to soothe ours, but Mr. Bailey didn't and couldn't know all that his generation had really done. He had never had the privilege of studying African-American history; in a very real sense, he did not know what he was missing. He is a man who enjoys building things, but he did not know to what extent Blacks had built this very country. He did not know that the term *slave labor*, for example, must be translated: what it really refers to are the inventions, the skills, and the craft of people who were enslaved. Because Blacks were not considered American citizens until the passage of the Fourteenth Amendment to the U.S. Constitution in 1868, the courts held that Black people could not enter into contracts; thus, for 250 years of invention, knowledge, and skill, we could not legally take credit for our accomplishments. But that doesn't mean that we did not make those contributions or accomplish a great deal. Instead, it means that Eli Whitney's slave did not get the credit he or she deserved for working on the cotton gin in 1794. Cyrus McCormick did acknowledge that his slave Jo Anderson "helped" to build the reaper in 1831, but Anderson's name could not appear on the patent. Because these contributions are not recognized to this day, and because the denial of ongoing Black achievement still plagues our contemporary world, Mr. Bailey did not know all that his peers and their forebears had really done. Thus, *Glory Days* was written to recognize this unrecognized history, honoring women inventors on March 8, the unknown enslaved collaborator on the invention of the cotton gin on March 14, and Jo Anderson on October 9; it honors all those whose gifts of spirit and invention have bettered our lives every day of the year.

Glory Days also owes a debt to the eternal question posed by a line from a spiritual: *How we got ovah.* How did we do it, how did we *get ovah*? For answers, this book turns to the history that centuries of fathers (and mothers) of invention—in every field from business to religion, literature, and sport—have provided for us.

The second event that inspired *Glory Days* occurred when

my mother and I were talking about what her parents had endured during the Great Depression as they raised their three daughters. We spoke about how they had come to the United States as immigrants, eager to build new lives. We spoke about the joys and disappointments that they and others from the Caribbean had experienced. As we spoke, something gnawed at the back of my mind: How did centuries of parents make it? As a mother, and as a daughter, I needed to know, needed to be able to say "how they got ovah." Researching their stories, I found that at a time when insurance companies would only underwrite a Black life if it was owned by a slave master, a group of Philadelphians in 1787 had formed the Free African Society, and this group had not only insured the individuals involved but had also ensured the cohesion of a community. Within a few years that community founded one of the nation's earliest public libraries — "spreading the wealth," so to speak. Those were the Glory Days: February 20 and April 12. Providing further food for thought, there was Mary McLeod Bethune with her recipes for success and sweet-potato pie. With them she founded a college, Bethune-Cookman Institute, as you'll find on October 5.

How we got ovah, indeed. We have a long, deep heritage — and what it produced was pure gold, like the world our ancestors had built in a distant time and home called the Gold Coast, Ghana. There, the ancient leader Tenkamenin held court in the year 1067 (as you'll discover on March 9), four hundred years before Europe invaded Africa. Gold was the standard set then and forever by the brilliant achievements of Africans throughout the diaspora. As African-Americans we have known what it means to be lost, but because of our rich heritage, we have never lost our sense of direction.

And the third event: at a speech to an historical society, I shared an authentic slave ledger with the predominantly African-American audience, and I watched them sink, dejected. But then a miracle happened: for the first time, they, as a body, seemed to realize that their ancestors had not been

slaves; rather, their ancestors had been *en*-slaved. And as that
recognition dawned, I watched the group *rise*. And basking in
their response, I, too, felt my spirit soar. Together we had
come to a wondrous truth. Ours was a mighty people who had
gone through so much, endured so much, and yet we were
here to tell the tale. *How we got ovah,* it says in the spiritual. *My
soul looks back in wonder, how we got ovah.*

And that's when I knew that I would write this book—for
my friend's father (Louis Alexander Bailey), for my grandparents, for that audience, for me, and for readers, for all of us.
For who among us does not need encouragement? Especially
in such times, who would not appreciate a reminder of *how we
got ovah*? We did it day by day. We did it because we never lost
hope. Aesop, an enslaved man in Aethiop (Ethiopia), did it
with his fabled teaching on May 20. Michael Jackson, Quincy
Jones, and Lionel Richie did it when they opened their hearts
and raised their voices for Aesop's descendants over two thousand years later on March 6 with "We Are the World." Mary
Hamilton did it on September 26 when she spent five days in
jail for the dignity of African-American womanhood, refusing
to allow "the authorities" to disrespect her. Harriet Tubman
and Frederick Douglass did it when they turned their backs
on slavery, escaped to freedom, determined to rescue others—
and did! On Christmas Day, December 25, we celebrate the
fact that Solomon and Anne Northup *got ovah,* too. Solomon
struggled for twelve years to rejoin his family in freedom,
while Anne never gave up hope. For twelve years she
watched, waited, and worked for his return. And there are so
many more proofs everywhere we turn. I could go on for 365
days—and more. Because of the depth of our history, our heritage, and our hope, even if I were to write ten such books, we
would never see the end of our Glory Days.

For centuries, African-Americans have been portrayed as
"slaves," as though the shame of those who would enslave us
could take the measure of our lives. We have been segregated
and villainized as though the blindness of those who would

mock us could share the vision of all we survey. We have known the depths of despair, yet we have lifted ourselves and our world up through the legacies of our past and the promise of our future. We have infused our world with the wonder of all our Glory Days. When our ongoing story of accomplishment is revealed through *365 Inspired Moments in African-American History*, we rejoice in the knowledge of all we have done. And the fruits of these vast achievements can now help us to build better worlds for ourselves and others. Congratulations!

A Note on the Text

Glory Days: 365 Inspired Moments in African-American History can be enjoyed as a fully documented work of history, a reference volume, and a book of daily inspirations. As such, the bottom of each page references the exact day and date of the event, its location, the subject matter (e.g., education, architecture, law) and the inspirational theme (e.g., courage, roots, self-determination). For your convenience each entry has been indexed by the name of the featured person, event, location, subject, and theme. Also included is an extensive suggested bibliography.

JANUARY

Building More Stately Mansions (1944). Aaron Douglas. Oil on canvas (54" x 42"). Permanent collection, Fisk University Department of Art. For more information, see May 29.

JANUARY 1

January 1, a day of beginnings and endings. Imani, Kwanza's seventh and final day: time to renew our faith in the future while savoring the last candle's flickering glow.

A ritual rooted in wisdoms and traditions centuries old, Kwanza was first celebrated thirty years ago. But long before Dr. Maulana Ron Karenga claimed this day for Imani (see December 26) and fifty-six years before it was declared Emancipation Proclamation Day in 1863, January 1 was a day of thanksgiving.

For the two hundred years of our American sojourn, from 1619 to 1808, we had slaved for freedom. Our men had fought in the Revolutionary War, only to see their sacrifices betrayed by American colonists who reveled in their freedoms at the expense of ours. The first bend in the long road to freedom finally neared in 1807 as Congress banned the torturous importation of Africans that was the slave trade. Speaking for the millions of lives consumed by its evils, Absalom Jones, an ex-slave and cofounder of the African Methodist Episcopal (AME) Church, preached this first African-American Thanksgiving Day sermon the day the ban went into effect — January 1, 1808:

> Let the first of January, the day of the abolition of the slave trade in our country, be set apart in every year, as a day of publick thanksgiving for that mercy. Let the history of the sufferings of our brethren, and of their deliverance, descend by this means to our children to the remotest generations; and when they shall ask, in time to come, saying, What mean the lessons, the psalms, the prayers and the praises in the worship of this day? let us answer them by saying, the Lord, on the day of which this is the anniversary, abolished the trade which dragged your fathers from their native country, and sold them as bondmen in the United States of America.

Friday, January 1, 1808, Pennsylvania, U.S.A.

Celebrations   **Faith**

JANUARY 2

January 2 marks a milepost in theater history. By the early 1960s, a decade of African-American activism had taken hold of imaginations nationwide. In New York, the nation's theater capital, Broadway producers were hiring all-Black casts to extend the run of successful white shows, but the original plays and ideas of Black playwrights and their ideas were rarely found. The situation made Langston Hughes's twenty-year-old poem "Note on the Commercial Theatre" seem sadly contemporary.

"You've taken my blues and gone," protested Hughes. "You sing 'em on Broadway, and you mixed 'em up with symphonies, and you fixed 'em so they don't sound like me. . . . But someday somebody'll stand up and write about me, black and beautiful, and put on plays about me! I reckon it'll be me myself! Yes, it'll be me." And it was.

Standing up on January 2, 1967, was the vibrant new Negro Ensemble Company (NEC) with an opening production of Peter Weiss's *Song of the Lusitania Bogey.* Founded by actor Robert Hooks, producer Gerald Krone, and playwright Douglas Turner Ward, the NEC was different from the start. It dated its roots to Ward's 1966 *New York Times* article, "American Theatre: For Whites Only?" (see August 14). Encouraged by a Ford Foundation start-up grant, the NEC was launched as a repertory company where actors could develop their skills and their range through full-time devotion to their craft; new plays by unknown Black playwrights were nurtured and mounted without the budgetary demands of the commercial Broadway stage.

At its peak, NEC was home to such talents as Rosalind Cash, Laurence Fishburne, Phylicia Rashad, and Hattie Winston. It nurtured teleplaywright Samm-Art Williams of *Frank's Place* and Pulitzer Prize–winner Charles Fuller, whose NEC-produced play-turned-film *A Soldier's Story* brought another alumnus, Denzel Washington, to the screen.

Monday, January 2, 1967, New York, U.S.A.

Theater   **Vision**

JANUARY 3

On January 3, 1900, the gift of music underscored the promise of a new century. In 1900, Lincoln's birthday was a treasured annual opportunity for slavery's children and grandchildren to celebrate their freedom. As each new Jim Crow law eroded that hard-won freedom, people needed a major celebration in order to renew their spirits and energies for the battles ahead. In Jacksonville, Florida, two brothers—James Weldon and J. Rosamond Johnson—decided to compose a hymn for the occasion. With the premiere fast approaching, they had finished the first two stanzas:

> *Lift ev'ry voice and sing,*
> *Till earth and heaven ring,*
> *Ring with the harmonies of liberty. . . .*
> *Stony the road we trod,*
> *Bitter the chastening rod*
> *Felt in the days when hope unborn had died.*

But James Weldon Johnson, the lyricist, was having a hard time with the third verse. He said, "I paced back and forth on the front porch repeating the lines over and over to myself, going through all the agony and ecstasy of creating. As I worked through the opening and middle lines of the last stanza I could not keep back the tears, and made no effort to do so:

> *God of our weary years, God of our silent tears,*
> *Thou who hast brought us thus far on our way,*
> *Thou who hast by thy might, led us into the light,*
> *Keep us forever in the path, we pray,*
> *Lest our feet stray from the places, our God, where we met Thee,*
> *Lest our hearts drunk with the wine of the world, we forget Thee.*

A month later their hymn, "Lift Ev'ry Voice," was performed by a chorus of five hundred children to overwhelming acclaim. Nearly a century later, it has inspired generations as our "Black National Anthem."

Wednesday, January 3, 1900, Florida, U.S.A.

Music   **Racial Dignity**

JANUARY 4

January 4, 1971, provided tangible proof that the voter registration campaigns of the 1950s and 1960s were finally bearing fruit. A century after the Fifteenth Amendment had guaranteed our voting rights, this year marked the first time that the number of African-Americans in Congress exceeded the level achieved in the post–Civil War days of Reconstruction: twelve African-American members of Congress were taking their seats—eleven men and one woman. We'd come this far by faith, courage, ambition, and skill. Running a century-long gauntlet of racist Black codes, grandfather clauses, illegal censures, and outright terror in states North and South, we had emerged on the other side with a healthy respect for our own power.

A moment of reflective rejoicing was definitely due. But no one could ignore the harsh reality. In a nation arguably more than 15 percent Black, only 2 percent of the Congress represented this population. Each African-American congressperson was well aware that his or her presence on Capitol Hill required loyalty and homage to an ideal far mightier than mere politics. Each representative had been swept into Congress on a wave of people who had literally flooded the streets with their bodies and their blood.

Rising to national prominence on that wave, the twelve linked arms and egos on January 4, 1971, to form the Congressional Black Caucus. Because they comprised only 2 percent of the legislature, voting as a block would clearly be their least successful strategy. But as catalysts, they could build awareness and alliances across racial, political, social, and geographical lines. Over the years, the number of Blacks in the House and Senate has grown to thirty-one—still just 6 percent. But the reason and the need for the Caucus have changed little.

As Congressman William Clay once put it, "we have no permanent friends, no permanent enemies—only permanent interests."

Monday, January 4, 1971, Washington, D.C., U.S.A.

Politics   **Respect for Use of Power**

JANUARY 5

People travel the world seeking cures. But before January 5, 1849, who could have guessed that one magic dose would cure a young man of multiple ailments in just minutes! It was a miracle that made history.

From the cut of his clothes to his first-class accommodations, it was clear that the fashionable young gentleman had everything as he boarded a train in Georgia with his trusted slave—everything, that is, except good health. With his face inflamed by a bad tooth, his right arm in a sling, his eyes so sensitive to light that he shaded them with green glasses, and his hearing so bad that his slave had to interpret and answer for him, hotel clerks took pity and spared him the ritual of signing in. Only in Baltimore did a ticket agent challenge the slave's impudence in speaking for his master—until, that is, he took a look at the wretched young man in such dire need of sympathy.

But when the pair got off in Philadelphia, the true nature of the young man's dis-ease became evident, as every ailment was healed by the soothing balm of freedom. Hearing returned. Glasses and bandages became unnecessary. Truth revealed the young white man and his slave to be, in fact, two escaped slaves—Ellen and William Craft, a light-skinned woman and her dark-skinned husband.

When their daring escape was publicized in *The Liberator*, an abolitionist newspaper, the shock was felt nationwide. Northern abolitionists rushed to hear the Crafts' lectures, and southern planters pushed for the most repressive fugitive slave law ever passed. Although the Crafts settled first in Boston, they later fled to England to avoid recapture. After the Civil War they returned to Georgia, bought a plantation, and founded an industrial school for Black children.

Of their heroic escape and future life together, we may not be able to say that "love conquers *all*," but it certainly did "make a way."

Friday, January 5, 1849, Georgia–Pennsylvania, U.S.A.
Freedom   **Love**

JANUARY 6

Rarely has the bridge between cause and effect borne greater weight and reward than it did when it spanned the century from January 6, 1869—the first day of classes at Howard University's new law school—to the day in 1967 when Thurgood Marshall was confirmed as the first African-American justice of the U.S. Supreme Court.

In 1869, John Mercer Langston was the perfect choice to be the founding dean of the law school. Not only was he one of the few Black attorneys during the slavery era but he was also one of slavery's most ardent foes. His leadership as dean helped to set the law school on its course, so that today it continues to produce major societal gains through the Black legal talent it nurtures. Charlotte Ray, who was the first Black woman to ever graduate from law school (1872) and the first woman to qualify to practice before the Supreme Court, was among his early students. So was William Houston, a member of the Washington, D.C., bar who inspired his son Charles to follow him into law.

Years later, as the law school's head librarian and vice dean, Charles Houston improved the curriculum and achieved full American Bar Association accreditation for the school. The quality of his legal research led to his appointment as founding attorney of the NAACP Legal Defense team, where he strategized an attack on segregation via education and the courts.

After Houston's untimely death, the NAACP team was led by a Howard Law School graduate he had mentored, Thurgood Marshall. Carrying forward Houston's strategic assault, the team won the landmark *Brown v. Board of Education* Supreme Court decision in 1954 that ended "lawful" segregation. When a vacancy gave President Lyndon Johnson his opportunity to make a lifetime appointment to the nation's highest court, Marshall—a national symbol of heroic proportions, thanks to *Brown*—was named the first African-American justice.

Wednesday, January 6, 1869, Washington, D.C., U.S.A.
Institution-Building   **Legacies**

JANUARY 7

On January 7, 1904, the rift between two rival giants—Booker T. Washington and W. E. B. Du Bois—was bridged. For years the two had vied for Black followers and white funds. Washington had vital support for his Tuskegee Institute, which educated thousands in the practical fields of industry and technology. Du Bois's concept of the "talented tenth," a strategic elite, yielded coups in academic scholarship, the arts, and culture. Washington had boosted himself "up from slavery," as the title of his autobiography proclaimed. Harvard's first Black Ph.D., Du Bois was born in Massachusetts to a Haitian-born Creole father and freeborn Black mother three years after slavery had ended, and he had studied abroad in Europe. For these two men to get along would require a miracle. But when they met on this January day, their common concern over escalating anti-Black brutality provided just that miracle.

With Jim Crow laws undermining abolition, the constitutional amendments passed in the name of freedom by now had little meaning. The times demanded unity. Washington initiated the call to share the platform with his longtime tactical adversary. They disagreed about everything—even the list of leaders to be invited to the summit at New York City's Carnegie Hall—and up to the last moment Du Bois maintained the suspense about whether he would attend at all. But when the megamillionaire industrialist and philanthropist Andrew Carnegie welcomed the audience to his hall, Du Bois was indeed seated among the stars on the stage.

Washington and Du Bois would never get along, but "for the good of the race," as people said in those days, they learned to accommodate themselves to each other's perspective and existence.

Thursday, January 7, 1904, New York, U.S.A.

Events   Leadership

JANUARY 8

The story that led to the events of January 8, 1912, in South Africa began with the plans and dreams that a young Zulu student formed while he was attending Columbia University in New York City and Oxford Univesity's Jesus College. Going home after years at school, Pixley Ka Izaka Seme, now a proud young Zulu attorney, was in for a terrible shock. Not only was European colonialism ravaging his native land, but a violent white supremacist minority government had now erected the walls of apartheid. Laws that had been imposed by the Dutch 250 years before and rescinded by British colonists as "repugnant and unnecessary" had now been resurrected. Africans were not allowed to walk on city sidewalks. Their hats had to be removed when passing whites. By law, Black schooling ended at a rudimentary level. Openly racist taxes ensured that Blacks were exploited as a severely underpaid workforce—and there was much more.

At first Pixley Ka Izaka Seme thought that his educated status might insulate him from the humiliations his countrymen faced, but it did not. He sought counsel among his friends Alfred Mangena (South Africa's first Black barrister), Richard Msimang (son of the founder of the Independent Methodist Church), and George Dixon Montsioa (a descendant of the Barolong paramount chief in Mafeking). But although they banded together, they could find no means of redress.

These men could have fled to the relative security they had known as foreigners abroad. But they did not. They decided to reclaim their homeland with a strategy based on unity among South Africa's indigenous peoples. On January 8, 1912, delegates from every traditional South African regional nation arrived for the first meeting of the African National Congress (ANC). Enoch Songonga composed an anthem for the event, "Nkosi Sikelel' i-Afrika"— the same anthem sung in 1994 when ANC leader Nelson Mandela was inaugurated as South Africa's first indigenous president, and it is sung whenever we honor that nation's resurrection from colonial oppression.

Monday, January 8, 1912, Zululand, South Africa
Pan-African World   **Responsibility**

JANUARY 9

One of the first schools to open within months of the Civil War's end, Fisk University was founded on January 9, 1866, with aid from the Freedmen's Bureau. But just as quickly as its opening had occurred, the funds seemed to disappear. With poverty and necessity mothering their invention, the Fisk Jubilee Singers were established as part of a fund-raising campaign. For repertoire, the singers would turn to songs they all knew: the spirituals.

With the reverence we feel for the spirituals today, it's hard to understand the furor that the idea of singing them evoked back then. For some, the painful "sorrow songs" were a relic best left behind with slavery. Others could not fathom that anyone would appreciate what they cruelly demeaned as "darky songs." Others simply did not recognize the unique richness of the music with its distinctive African-based pentatonic (five-tone) melodies. Rejecting the songs in pursuit of so-called sophistication, many ignored the fact that they were thus trying to emulate the cultural values of the very people who had once bartered their lives as chattel. Then, too, there were others whose deep love for the music would not let them accept the commercialization of a precious musical heritage—the voice of slaves.

With a deaf ear to their critics and a firm grip on the gravity of their financial state, the Fisk Jubilee Singers began their first of many successful European and American tours in 1871. Their fund-raising efforts saved Fisk, allowing the university to break ground on the first campus building, Jubilee Hall, and they established a tradition of Black college singing groups.

Of lasting import, the singers' choice of repertoire resulted in the documentation of a musical legacy that might otherwise have died out with the slaves. Because of their inspired success, the messages of our slave ancestors, deeply embedded in their lyric and melodic codes of survival, teach and encourage us, offering benefits we continue to reap to this day.

Tuesday, January 9, 1866, Tennessee, U.S.A.

Education   **Wealth**

JANUARY 10

In a test of Black voting strength in 1965, the charismatic young activist Julian Bond ran for a seat in the Georgia state legislature. Winning the election was a proud first step for the communications director of the Student Nonviolent Coordinating Committee (SNCC, pronounced "Snick"), the group that had popularized lunch counter sit-ins and outspoken opposition to the Vietnam War. Once Bond was seated, Georgia's power brokers could have simply outvoted and ignored him. Instead, they chose to embark on a foolish and fortuitous campaign that literally made Bond's election into a federal case.

On January 10, 1966, Georgia barred Bond from taking his seat. Knowing it was not wise to deny him his seat on racial grounds, officials cited Bond's war opposition. Violating his First Amendment rights of free speech as well as his district's right to the qualified representative of its choice, Bond's foes underestimated the situation. Among Bond's constituents were people who had risked their lives for the right to vote. His foes were also barking up the wrong family tree: although Bond had earned respect on his own merits, he was also the son of noted educator Horace Mann Bond and the heir to a proud family tradition of service in the cause of Black liberation.

As SNCC's communications chief, Julian Bond knew how to handle himself and the press. He challenged Georgia to "show cause," just as he had shown commitment to his cause — human and civil rights. For a year, Georgia prevailed until a Supreme Court decision and national public opinion forced the legislators to back down.

Firmly wedded to his principles, Bond's cause made him such a public figure that he was nominated for vice president at the 1968 Democratic National Convention. He was forced to decline the honor, however. Not yet thirty-five years old, he was not eligible for the job.

Monday, January 10, 1966, Georgia, U.S.A.

Politics

Principles

JANUARY 11

The who and when of the first African conversion to American Christianity are unknown, but the why is found in Virginia's court records from the early seventeenth century. Brought to colonial Jamestown in 1619, the first Africans were called "indentures," the same term used for whites working off prison time, debt, apprenticeship, or transatlantic passage with years of servitude. As the African indentures neared the end of their term, usually a period of five to seven years, they petitioned the courts for freedom, as was the custom. However, in the years since their kidnapping and importation, the planters had learned a key lesson. The main benefit of Black indentures was that their skin color prevented them from escaping or disappearing into the general white population. Thus, judges now gladly granted wealthy planters the boon of free labor by creating a crime of which Africans could be found guilty—heathenism. As "non-Christians" their crime was punishable by extended servitude. To avoid punishment, Africans began converting to American Christianity, and they began to baptize their newborn babies in order to release them from the hold of indenture.

On January 11, 1626, it was nearly seven years after the first boatload had landed, months since the promised freedom for which they had worked had been ripped from them, and just days since their New Year's wish had been betrayed. The hope of ever seeing home again was fast disappearing. It was Sunday and at least one of the first converts must have cried "Mercy!" on this day.

From the depths of despair, that unnamed, pragmatic forefather or foremother must have experienced a surging triumph of spirit as he or she turned from the gods and ways of home to walk toward Christianity and survive.

Sunday, January 11, 1626, Virginia, U.S.A.

Religion   **Survival**

JANUARY 12

On January 12, 1865, an amazing thing happened: the United States government asked Black men to speak for themselves.

In 1619, the fate of "twenty and odd negars" brought to Jamestown, Virginia, determined the future of American slavery. Now, 246 years later, the same symbolic "twenty" gathered in Savannah, Georgia, to determine the future of freedom. No one knows who the first twenty were. The second were men ages twenty-six to seventy-two. Three had been freed by their masters, three had bought themselves, five were freeborn, and nine had been freed by the Union Army three years before. They were ministers or lay leaders of enslaved and freeborn congregations ranging from 200 to 1,900 members.

The government, in the persons of War Secretary Edwin M. Stanton and General William T. Sherman, invited the men to Union headquarters. Theirs was a one-time opportunity to define the terms of freedom for millions of African-Americans. The government asked: What is slavery? Do you know how to care for yourselves? How can you aid in maintaining your freedom? Would you rather live among whites or by yourselves? The men responded:

> Slavery is receiving by irresistible power the work of another man, and not by his consent. Freedom is taking us from under the yoke of bondage and placing us where we could reap the fruit of our own labor. The way we can best care for ourselves is to have land and . . . by our own labor . . . maintain ourselves and have something to spare. To assist the Government, the young men should enlist. . . . We would rather live by ourselves, for there is prejudice against us that will take years to get over.

Four days later General Sherman issued Special Field Order Number Fifteen, which set aside a tract of coastal land from South Carolina to Florida in order to provide "forty acres of tillable ground" for each family; today this order provides the legal grounds on which the claims for reparations to be paid African-Americans are based.

Thursday, January 12, 1865, South Carolina–Florida, U.S.A.
Reparations   **Vision**

JANUARY 13

On January 13, 1913, few African-American women were lucky enough to be attending college. For those who were, the privilege brought unique responsibilities and opportunities. As Jim Crow threatened every individual of color, the repression of women heaped further burdens on Black families. Yet in these strained and challenging times, there was still hope.

People were fighting for their rights. The NAACP was four years old. Women's rights activists were planning a mass demonstration in Washington, D.C., that would take place in March and focus on suffrage, birth control, and the right to work outside the home. And although most Black men saw the needs of women as secondary—and often antagonistic—to those of race, there were an enlightened few. Among them, Dr. W. E. B. Du Bois acknowledged that extending the vote to women meant that Black women would also have the vote. This, in turn, would increase the strength of Black family voting.

On the Howard University campus, young Black women were feeling the pull and the possibilities of all these complications: race versus gender, caste versus class. For support, they sought to establish bonds based on understanding and friendship that would help them address their needs as women. Thus, while the "Greek" movement was growing on white campuses, the Black sorority movement was born.

Although united by race and gender, Howard's women faced another reality: the growing numbers of students brought with them growing diversity. On January 13, 1913, these visionary women chose healthy rivalry over self-annihilation. Out of their strength, they gave birth to the twin sisters of service, success, and political activism that now act on a global stage: Alpha Kappa Alpha and Delta Sigma Theta—the "Alphas" and the "Deltas."

JANUARY 14

In 1779, January 14 was a day of epiphany. With the disparities that exist between what is practiced and what is preached in American Christianity, it has long been a cause of amazement that the slaves embraced Christianity so profoundly. But slaves didn't actually *adopt* the Christianity of their slave owners—rather, they *adapted* it. Or, as theologian Delores Williams has observed, Blacks bridged the gaps in racist preaching by knowing that "your Christ is not my Jesus!" Church implied both heaven and haven. It was the only time when slaves could gather without the presence of suspicious slave owners and overseers. It provided the opportunity to "steal away" to the comfort and strength that congregants could provide for one another. Its prophet was a spokesman for the oppressed.

The story of the first African-American church makes the point in its own special way. The Silver Bluff Baptist Church was founded in South Carolina by David George, a slave, sometime between 1773 and 1775. Using biblical texts to fire the imaginations of parishioners, George strategized a historic mass flight from slavery. If God had saved Daniel in the lion's den, He (or She) could save them, too. As God had delivered Israel out of bondage in Egypt, He would deliver them, too. The story of an oppressed people's deliverance struck deep chords. And in the winter of 1778, so, too, did the tales of a shepherd and his flock.

Virginia's loyalist governor had declared that any slaves who fled their owners to side with the British would be granted immediate freedom. By January 14, 1779, David George had safely delivered his flock out of bondage to freedom behind British lines. The now ex-slaves knew they had been divinely guided. Their Jesus had walked with them and suffered with them. Together, they had found a route to the promised land.

From the legacy of David George and his followers has come a movement of faith, conscience, consistency, and independence that still empowers us more than two hundred years later.

Thursday, January 14, 1779, South Carolina, U.S.A.

Religion   **Roots**

JANUARY 15

On January 15, 1992, film lovers had an opportunity to see what they had been missing throughout a century of filmmaking—a Black woman's image of herself and her people. In the early 1970s, Maya Angelou had written the screenplay for *Georgia, Georgia,* but her directorial duties had been reassigned and her images changed. In the 1980s, Kathleen Collins wrote, directed, and produced feature films, but none had achieved commercial recognition. Then came the 1990s and Julie Dash.

From the moment that rumors of the plot began to leak out during the early funding and casting efforts, hope swept the cultural community. With a script extensively researched, written, and to be directed by an African-American woman, Julie Dash, this film was bound to be "different." It told of a turn-of-the-century Gullah family's decision to leave their Sea Island home for the mainland. It called up the oral history of Ibo Landing. It came as close to capturing the meaning of "African-plus-American" as we may ever see on film. Beautifully, passionately it spoke of real women, not stereotypical icons used (in every sense of the word) to advance alien white ideas about race. These women were in full color; the depth of characterization demonstrated that Black women have emotional lives all their own.

In 1991, *Daughters of the Dust* was screened at Robert Redford's prestigious Sundance Film Festival, taking top honors for cinematography. Several festivals and numerous honors later, it opened at New York's Film Forum on January 15, 1992, leaving its first commercial audiences breathless and well rewarded. Their stunned nonstop buzz became the word-of-mouth whoosh of energy needed to push the film onto screens nationwide. Julie Dash's *Daughters of the Dust* became the first film by a Black woman filmmaker to achieve national commercial distribution.

Wednesday, January 15, 1992, Utah–New York, U.S.A.
Film   **Cultural Continuity**

JANUARY 16

On January 16, 1978, the National Aeronautics and Space Administration (NASA) named the first three African-American astronauts: Major Guion S. Bluford, Major Frederick D. Gregory, and Dr. Ronald E. McNair. Their appointments marked a breakthrough that had been seventeen years—and a millennium—in the making. NASA's announcement finally acknowledged the fact that men and women of all cultural traditions have contributed to the eternal human quest for the stars.

To predict future coming floods, Africans were the first to divide the year into twelve months sometime before 4000 B.C. Africans have been space scientists for 6,000 years. Egyptians first linked the appearance of a star, Sirius, to the flooding of the Nile in 1700 B.C. A miniature glider dating to Egypt's third century B.C. signals the earliest known aircraft experimentation. The Dogon of Mali first sighted Sirius B sometime between the thirteenth and fourteenth centuries A.D. Even with the aid of the telescope, the tiny star would not be seen by Western astronomers until the twentieth century. At the world's first university, Timbuktu, founded in the fourteenth century, scholars dated the use of astronomy in navigation to at least 600 B.C.

Space science offers incredible stories. These are only the start of what we must resurrect for the benefit of our children's education—and for ourselves.

Monday, January 16, 1978, Florida, U.S.A.

Space/Science   **Knowledge**

JANUARY 17

January 17, 1970, marks what filmmaker and historian Ken Burns called the "end of slavery" in baseball. From the way baseball's story is told, one might think that race as an issue ended with Jackie Robinson in 1956. Not so. As Robinson exited, Curt Flood arrived on a still-racist playing field. And in 1969, after years of proven talent and tenacity, one callous phone call informed Flood of his trade and changed his life. Unlike Robinson's exit, Flood's was hardly graceful. When the axe of the trade fell on him, Flood used his anger to fight for players' rights. On January 17, 1970, he sued the baseball establishment.

For Flood, the straw that moved him to risk all was one more insult. It was being traded to Philadelphia where the fans were notorious for their racist ballpark manners. The trade jeopardized his family life and business interests. And it was the principle of the thing. Baseball was the only industry exempt from antitrust law. Only in "the nation's pastime" could management own its players. Due to the long-contested "reserve clause" in every team's contract, players had no voice in determining their career path. Owners could trade a player, play him, or let him rot. Players had no recourse.

Flood attempted to work with management, the league, and the baseball commissioner to achieve an amicable resolution. All these attempts failed. But the Players' Association was grateful for his initiative. With the players' union leader and ex–Supreme Court Justice Arthur Goldberg in his corner, Flood sued baseball.

Flood's case went to the Supreme Court, where he lost and left the game. In the wake of his loss, however, management agreed to make minor concessions. Ironically, a victory for Flood might have averted the unprecedented baseball strike and management-player standoff of 1994–95.

Saturday, January 17, 1970, Missouri, U.S.A.

Sports   **Convictions**

JANUARY 18

By January 18, 1837, slavery had been abolished in New York for over ten years, but the state had a long way to go in meeting the minimum standards of justice for freemen and ex-slaves. In 1835, a courageous group committed to sabotaging slavery formed the New York Vigilance Committee. The annual report that was circulated secretly among them on January 18, 1837, proudly asserted that "the total number of persons protected from slavery by the Committee [was] 335." Their actions were not just the result of philosophical beliefs and brotherly conscience; they also had personal ramifications—especially for the self-emancipated members of the committee like one Mr. Reymond.

At a New York meeting of Blacks five years before, Reymond had offered news of a colony of escaped slaves and freeborn Blacks. Slave catchers' spies had reported his name and remarks in a newspaper, a copy of which was sent to the mayor of Norfolk, Virginia, his hometown. Seeing his name, the mayor had issued a warrant for Reymond's immediate arrest. Upon his return to Norfolk, he was asked if he had been out of the state for over a year. It was a trick question meant to establish the fact that he had once lived in Virginia and was therefore most likely an escaped slave. Reymond unsuspectingly answered yes and was imprisoned with no chance to defend himself. Luckily he was not claimed by an owner. Twenty-four hours later, he was released and forever banished from the state. All this because he had spoken at a meeting in a free state!

As America's insatiable appetite for slaves grew, even free Blacks found their liberty meaning less in the face of dubious warrants "proving" their status as slaves. To speak in public, sign a petition, sign a church notice, enroll a child in school, or advertise a business was to face the very realistic threat of being seized. Yet these freemen and freewomen did it. And their constant, unrelenting, courageous agitation ultimately dismantled slavery.

Wednesday, January 18, 1837, New York, U.S.A.

Freedom   **Responsibility**

JANUARY 19

With the debut of his *Chicago Defender* column, "From Here to Yonder," during World War II, Langston Hughes had a forum from which to write about the big, important topics of the day—the war, discrimination, the famous, and the infamous—and how those events and people affected his readers' lives. But as he drafted his column on January 19, 1943, a different voice came into his head. There were two voices, really—a sophisticated interviewer and a more relaxed, humorously philosophical alter ego he referred to as "My Simple Minded Friend."

This second voice had been inspired—or rather, coaxed out—by his experiences in a Harlem bar. As Hughes sat at the bar, a local character he'd seen before but did not know decided that Hughes should not be drinking alone that night. Inviting Hughes to join him and his girlfriend, Mary, at their table, the character struck up a "Conversation at Midnight," as Hughes later titled the column. It was a rambling, rather useless chat about making cranks in a defense factory. But embedded in it, a quirky undertow of philosophy seemed to pull the conversation along.

The character did not know what the cranks he manufactured were for. Mary thought he ought to know since he was the one making them. The character protested that white folks never told Negroes those kinds of things. "I don't crank with those cranks. I just make 'em." As their banter with its rhythm of familiarity continued, Mary grew more and more exasperated until she finally told the man, "You sound right simple."

Within days, "Simple," Hughes's literary creation and companion, was born. For the next twenty-three years "Jesse B. Semple," as he would be addressed on more formal occasions, filled columns and books to the delight of readers the world over.

Tuesday, January 19, 1943, New York–Illinois, U.S.A.

Literature   **Humor**

JANUARY 20

For his presidential inauguration on January 20, 1993, Bill Clinton asked Maya Angelou to write and recite a poem. A half billion people would be listening in the global village that day—from those who braved Washington's chill on the Capitol steps to those filling the streets and watching via satellite.

After her sad and silent childhood, Maya Angelou not only knew "why the caged bird sings," as her memoir so poignantly told, but she had also discovered that she was not alone in overcoming a childhood of trauma. As the inaugural laureate, she could speak with experience, humility, a slight case of nerves, and justifiable pride in her achievement. Empowered by the wisdom of the ancestors, she spoke her poem with a voice centuries in the making. With literary metaphors that had been preserved in the spirituals informing her lines, she told her story, "On the Pulse of Morning":

> *Lift up your eyes upon*
> *This day breaking for you . . .*
> *Women, children, men . . .*
> *Mold it into the shape of your most*
> *Private need . . . your most public self.*
> *Lift up your hearts*
> *Each new hour holds new chances*
> *For new beginnings*
> *Do not be wedded forever*
> *To fear, yoked eternally*
> *To brutishness.*

"Here, root yourselves beside me—I am that Tree planted by the River—Which will not be moved," she said. But we were moved, for our story was the one called forth to teach the universe a brand-new song.

Wednesday, January 20, 1993, Washington, D.C., U.S.A.
Poetry   **Toward Better Worlds**

JANUARY 21

For Mary Johnson and her son William, January 21, 1820, was a Glory Day two years in the making. Although her former owner, a wealthy planter, had decided to free her son, he was unable to do so by law. The complex laws of the day required Blacks to post bonds guaranteeing their "character" as free persons of color. Slave children could not post the bond, nor could their parents. Because the law required adults of color to be bonded or sponsored themselves, as parents they had insufficient legal standing, or "character," to take custody of their children. But with determination and influence, the planter, William Johnson, got the legislature to pass a special law all his own.

On January 21, 1820, William Johnson certified that he was a state resident with no debts that would invalidate the liquidation of his property (Mary's son). The next day his eloquent petition for the boy's freedom was presented to the Mississippi Assembly's lower house; he asked the legislators to enable the "disposition of his property most agreeable to his feelings & consonant to humanity." Johnson declared that he was acting to give "Liberty to a human being which all are entitled to as a Birthright, & extend the hand of humanity to a rational Creature, on whom unfortunately Complexion Custom & even Law in This Land of freedom, has conspired to rivet the fetters of Slavery." A special bill was passed and was approved by the governor on February 10, freeing young William. As was the custom, the child took his former master's surname, later making a name for them both in business and letters as William Johnson, the "Diarist of Natchez."

For years, the story of the younger William Johnson's literary success has been told to honor freedom and underscore the waste of slavery. But it also raises deeper issues. Johnson's white contemporaries did not have to prove themselves in order to justify their freedom. Are our children being steered toward failure by irrational demands for superlative success?

Friday, January 21, 1820, Mississippi, U.S.A.

Children   **Responsibility to Youth**

JANUARY 22

Civil rights demonstrators used to sing:

I know one thing we did right
Was the day we started to fight
Keep you eyes on the prize
Hold on, hold on.

And because the demonstrators and their film documentarians held on at their respective battlefronts, the story of both victories has survived to inform and reward us all. January 22, 1987, marked the premiere of *Eyes on the Prize*—a six-part public television documentary on the civil rights movement of 1954–1965.

Behind the cameras, in a drama that matched that of the historical footage, the producers surmounted hurdles of their own. To the issue of funding was added a still greater nemesis—those people, at every level, who refused to believe that an audience would want to relive the civil rights movement. To view the footage of children being set upon by dogs and fire hoses, of bodies being dredged from troubled waters, was to gaze on wounds that were still open, they thought. Yet to see children peacefully cross police lines at the start of a new day in schools nationwide, to hear Dr. King speak from pulpits and pit stops, was to feel the triumph of the long march of history that had led people from Selma, Alabama, across the Pettus Bridge to Montgomery twenty-five thousand strong.

Series creator Henry Hampton was among the marchers crossing that bridge in 1965. He had a firsthand view of "segregated America [forced], in a single decade, to take a giant step from a feudal state toward a free and open democracy." By holding on to his dream, he managed to capture the dreams of "farmers and ministers, teachers and students, dishwashers and lawyers [who] joined together to awaken this nation to the pursuit of liberty." Partly because he kept his "eyes on the prize," the legacy forged by thousands of unnamed achievers continues to inspire us to hold on—and move on.

Thursday, January 22, 1987, Regional (South) U.S.A.
Radio and TV   **Human Spirit**

JANUARY 23

January 23, 1940, marked a cultural milestone—a tribute to the art of the critic and to the critical role of the artist as two Harlem Renaissance luminaries, critic Alain Locke and artist Jacob Lawrence, honored each other's work.

As a Harlem child in the 1930s, Jacob Lawrence loved his time at the 135th Street library with its Schomburg Collection on African-American history. As he matured as a visual artist, his knowledge of history and culture informed the narrative of his paintings. *Street Orator* (1936) captured the look of deep concentration on the faces of those listening to Harlem's famous "street-corner philosophers." *Toussaint L'Ouverture* (1938) was a series of forty-one paintings dramatizing Haiti's slave revolution and liberation as the oldest Black nation in the Americas. So impressive was Lawrence's work that he was nominated as a Rosenwald Fellow.

In a letter to the Julius Rosenwald Fund dated January 23, 1940, the preeminent critic Alain Locke assessed Lawrence: "What impresses me about Lawrence is his ability to combine social interest and interpretation (he selects his own episodes from careful library reading and research) with a straight art approach when he comes to work on his drawings." As the first African-American Rhodes Scholar with numerous accomplishments of his own, Locke had made history many times over (see June 5). His kudos, then, were doubly significant.

In taking the time to study the wealth and depth of his heritage and incorporate it into his art, Lawrence was honoring the work of those like Locke who had struggled to preserve that history. In taking the time to enunciate his respect for Lawrence's work, Locke paved the way for a generation of artists to come. This day marked a rare symbiotic tribute indeed.

Tuesday, January 23, 1940, New York, U.S.A.

Art   **Culture**

JANUARY 24

January 24 marks the anniversary of a test of courage for thousands of African-Americans, relating to the American Colonization Society (ACS). With its founding in 1816, unscrupulous whites in the North and South united in an attempt to capitalize on Black Back-to-Africa aspirations (see February 6). The name of the organization itself sounded ominous. How could a nation that had struggled to defeat its own colonizers just forty years earlier call for colonization? The ACS had two arguments: first, that free Blacks represented "a dangerous and useless part of the community," and second, that the removal of free Blacks from the States would remove slavery's greatest opposition. Within weeks of that declaration, thousands of free Blacks gathered to oppose legislative support for the ACS.

On January 24, 1817, Richmond's free people, locked within a slaveholding state, met to assess the impact that the Colonization Society's proposals might have on them. Would going back to Africa against one's will make one more free than being forced to stay? Could a campaign that had at its roots a disrespect for human life offer any hope of freedom? Was freedom possible? At considerable risk to themselves, they passed this resolution: "We respectfully submit to the wisdom of Congress whether it would not be an act of charity to grant us a small portion of their territory, either on the Missouri River, or any place that may seem to them most conducive to the public good and our future welfare."

Even in crisis, African-American minds have been "stayed on" a freedom of our own definition. The colonization movement was seen for what it was—an attempt to achieve further profit at the expense of Black life. Our African-American ancestors recognized that the choice to remain in a slaveholding America or to spread the slaveholders' philosophy to Africa via colonization was no choice at all.

Friday, January 24, 1817, Pennsylvania–Virginia, U.S.A.
Emigration   **Racial Dignity**

JANUARY 25

On January 25, 1995, the lessons of the civil rights movement found new application in the wake of FBI charges against Malcolm X's daughter, Qubilah Shabazz; she was charged with conspiracy to avenge her father's thirty-year-old murder with a plot to assassinate Nation of Islam leader Louis Farrakhan. The FBI's historic lack of credibility on civil rights and its COINTELPRO (Counter-Intelligence Program) network of violence-prone spies (see April 11) quickly came to mind. People were skeptical.

But skepticism didn't make the predicament any less real. Nor could friends retreat in silence, awaiting a verdict that could take years. The Shabazz family needed, and deserved, immediate support. Who better to provide it than those with firsthand knowledge of anti–civil rights government tactics? On January 25, 1995, in a display usually reserved for celebrations, seven daughters of history gathered in support of a tragedy-stricken eighth: Bernice King, daughter of Nobel Peace Prize laureate Martin Luther King, Jr.; Rena Evers, daughter of slain NAACP Mississippi leader Medgar Evers; Santita Jackson, daughter of civil rights hero and presidential candidate Jesse Jackson; Andrea Young, daughter of King aide, former Atlanta mayor, and United Nations delegate Andrew Young; Lisa Jones, daughter of playwright-author-activist LeRoi Jones (Amiri Baraka); Rebecca Walker, daughter of Pulitzer Prize–winning author-activist Alice Walker; and Jewell Jackson McCabe, daughter of broadcast pioneer Hal Jackson and organizer of the event. In the somber and grateful presence of Malcolm's widow and Qubilah's mother, Dr. Betty Shabazz, they gathered at New York's Schomburg Center for Research in Black Culture, the greatest public repository of African-American history.

As daughters of the movement, their assembly drew attention and funds to Qubilah's defense. In an unprecedented move, they defied the forces of "divide and conquer," demonstrating vital lessons of faith and survival garnered in the storm. Perhaps the tragedy that united them was a celebration after all.

Wednesday, January 25, 1995, New York, U.S.A.

Heroes   **Mutual Support**

JANUARY 26

On January 26, 1863, just twenty-five days after the Emancipation Proclamation took effect in the rebel states, the U.S. War Department authorized the governor of Massachusetts to recruit Black troops to fight in the Union Army.

From the start, the Fifty-fourth Massachusetts Colored Regiment was destined for history (see March 2, July 18). Frederick Douglass took a personal interest in rallying this first northern Black regiment with his historic editorial, "Men of Color! To Arms!" Two of his sons were among those who answered the call. By May, the Confederacy had placed the burden of punishment by death or slavery on all Blacks captured in battle. But the members of the Fifty-fourth had to fight not only against being taken as slaves but also to be taken seriously as soldiers. The army denied them proper uniforms and attempted to pay them less than their white counterparts. Unified as men of indomitable character and resolve, for eighteen months every man in the regiment refused partial pay until every man had been guaranteed full pay.

In July, the "Fighting Fifty-fourth" won lasting respect in the now-historic attack on Fort Wagner in Charleston, South Carolina. That battle made a hero of standard-bearer William H. Carney, whose bravery made him the first African-American Congressional Medal of Honor recipient. The courage of this regiment earned them honors for this and other achievements. And a century after the war, the Fifty-fourth's battle to end slavery and the injustice heaped upon them by their own military command was immortalized in the film, *Glory*. For resurrecting their heroism, *Glory* received several Academy Award nominations, including Denzel Washington, who won for best actor in a supporting role.

Monday, January 26, 1863, South Carolina–Massachusetts, U.S.A.

Civil War   **Racial Dignity**

JANUARY 27

By 1963, appropriately black-and-white scenes of unrelenting brutality against nonviolent demonstrators had dominated television news images for a decade. As the civil rights movement redefined the nation, a Black boy coming of age in those hopeful but traumatic days needed help holding on to his dreams and his confidence. For one special boy, that help came in a letter from his namesake and uncle, James Baldwin—a letter that reached the public as a book, *The Fire Next Time*, on January 27, 1963.

Seized by the spectacle of the nation's reluctance to heal—even on the centennial of the Emancipation Proclamation—Baldwin knew what to say. He had the boy's spiritual and emotional emancipation in mind when he wrote, "You know, and I know, that the country is celebrating one hundred years of freedom one hundred years too soon. . . . You can only be destroyed by believing that you really are what the white world calls a nigger. If you know whence you came, there is really no limit to where you can go. . . . You come from sturdy, peasant stock, men who picked cotton and dammed rivers and built railroads, and, in the teeth of the most terrifying odds, achieved an unassailable and monumental dignity. You come from a long line of great poets."

Baldwin's letter was published in *The Fire Next Time*, the title of which was inspired by the lyrics from a spiritual: "God gave Noah the rainbow sign/No more water, the fire next time." True to his self-imposed mission as a "disturber of the peace," Baldwin's book was a warning. But with typical denial, America's reading elite loved the book and ignored its prophecy. Among the thousands consumed in the blaze of fury that was 1963, NAACP leader Medgar Evers was murdered, four girls died in the firebombing of a Birmingham church, and President Kennedy was assassinated. Thirty years later the embers of guilt and hatred are smoldering still.

Sunday, January 27, 1963, New York, U.S.A.

Literature   **Commitment to Self**

JANUARY 28

January 28 marks the rebirth and vindication of a musical spirit. In the 1970s, the hit movie soundtrack of *Butch Cassidy and the Sundance Kid* fueled a revival of Scott Joplin's ragtime music and interest in the composer himself. Rumor spread fast about Joplin's untimely death in 1917. There were stories of his bawdy-house days as a young piano player, a time about which pianist Eubie Blake once quipped: "There were only two places where a Negro musician could play in those days—in a church or a bordello. And you know you couldn't make a living in a church!"

Joplin's music was hot. And even those who couldn't hum his deceptively simple tunes and others who couldn't play his sophisticated syncopation knew that Scott Joplin had died of syphilis. But few wanted to believe that Scott Joplin had given his life for *Treemonisha*—an opera he'd composed in 1911 to honor his mother.

The story of *Treemonisha* passes on the hopeful message that Joplin's mother had given her son in his childhood: through education Blacks would find the road to freedom. But featuring a positive female in the lead role broke the rules. And the fact that the opera was written by a Black composer thoroughly crossed the line—even if he was the composer who had invented ragtime. Even those publishers and producers whose own financial success could be traced directly to Joplin were not supportive. Joplin was deemed audacious for thinking he could write grand opera and for believing anyone would want to see it if he did. After all he'd accomplished, Joplin couldn't accept this humiliating blockade, and his obsessive attempts to find a way to stage his opera broke his spirit and health.

But on January 28, 1972, Scott Joplin's spirit was reborn when *Treemonisha* premiered in Atlanta to critical acclaim. Several other productions have since been mounted, and a national PBS broadcast is still available on video.

Friday, January 28, 1972, Georgia, U.S.A.

Music   **Resurrections**

JANUARY 29

Nature frequently reminds us that she has a way with miracles. Some of her most unusual trees will regenerate themselves in the aftermath of an otherwise totally devastating fire. In like manner, on January 29, 1985, nature bestowed upon us a miraculous regeneration of theatrical history.

For over thirty years, photographer Bert Andrews was the closest thing to a backstage groupie that Black theater had. As actress Cicely Tyson says, he was "obsessively vigilant" about capturing on film some of the most moving moments in theater history—the power, passion, and promise of African-American theater, the fervor that, as Tyson says, "burst onto the stage with such imaginative force that American theater was never the same again."

Andrews loved the theater—the plays, the playwrights, and the players. His recommendation led to Tyson's first television role, and there were others who had Bert to thank for similar breaks—not to mention for preserving their achievements with his pictures. In the course of thirty years, Andrews produced more than forty thousand prints and one hundred thousand negatives from a thousand shows. Not only did he chronicle the theater but he generously shared these pictures with his friends. When a tragic fire destroyed his life's work and his studio on January 29, 1985, the theater he so loved had a unique chance to show how much it loved him back. Actors, directors, dancers, producers assembled—and reassembled: they returned to Bert as many of the pictures he had given them as they could find.

In 1989, this collection became the first photographic treasury of African-American theater ever published. Compiled by Andrews, *In the Shadow of the Great White Way* will inspire the imaginations of theater lovers for generations to come.

Tuesday, January 29, 1985, New York, U.S.A.

Theater/ Photography   **Love**

JANUARY 30

On January 30, 1982, when the news of Mary Johnston's death began to spread, few who had witnessed her final frugal years would have guessed that the ninety-one-year-old subsisting on $4,500 a year was a philanthropist. From 1974 until her death in 1982, Ms. Johnston donated $1,000 of her yearly income to the students of Oberlin College!

Born in 1890, she was slavery's child. Her mother was freed in 1863. Her father's free family were stationmasters for an Underground Railroad post so trusted that it was called the "Antislavery Baptist Church." After her father's untimely death, the family fell into poverty. Yet her mother nurtured a determination in each of her three children to attend college. Mary set about working her way through Oberlin, which gave her a $16 scholarship toward the semester tuition of $37.50 and waived its gym requirement so that she could work weekends. But after two years she still had to take a leave of absence, during which she worked as a domestic and taught at a start-up college where the completion of her own degree was not mandatory. She kept up her course work, however, and after twenty-five years, in 1937, Mary Johnston finally walked across Oberlin's graduation platform.

She loved Oberlin, which "helped me so much when I was within her walls." Upon her retirement from teaching, she wanted others to know similar joy. So firm was her commitment to her $1,000 annual gift that she refused to put in a phone until friends convinced her that at age ninety, she needed one in case of emergency. Her first $1,000 bought Black Studies books for the library. Her second gave a music scholarship to a student who became an opera singer. Her third bought an African sculpture for the museum. Later gifts went to general use, and her estate continues to yield scholarship aid.

Saturday, January 30, 1982, Ohio, U.S.A.

Philanthropy   **Determination**

JANUARY 31

January 31 marks the coming together of hurt and healing. For few events in American history have salted deeper wounds than the case of the Scottsboro Boys: nine Black youths, ranging in age from thirteen to nineteen, falsely accused of raping a Caucasian woman and then sentenced to death.

In 1931 the boys were dragged from a train at Paint Rock, Alabama, near Scottsboro and became the tragic victims of a conspiracy that reached the highest levels of government. Even after the "victim" had recanted her allegations and sworn that no rape had occurred, their ordeal went on. For forty-five years they endured false arrest, lynch mobs, trials, torture, forced confessions, death-row "rape" convictions, Supreme Court reversals, retrials, and pardons for a crime that never happened. For forty-five years their lives were sacrificial symbols—of the "Negro threat," of a "Communist agenda," of legal impotence, and of power gone mad. At times they were a front-page cause célèbre. At other times they were all but forgotten by sincere and frustrated people who didn't know what else to do. Mercifully, death reached out to take them, one by one, to a long-overdue amnesty.

If any inspiration can be derived from a tragedy of this magnitude, perhaps it is this: On January 31, 1989, at a funeral organized by the NAACP, the Reverend Calvin O. Butts—a young minister who was not even born when the ordeal began—took time to eulogize the last "Scottsboro Boy" at New York's Abyssinian Baptist Church, site of so many Scottsboro defense rallies over the years. People remembered. It wasn't an easy thing to do. Revisiting this episode underscored the vulnerability of today's young men. But in that memory might also be found a cleansing balm with which to soothe our anger, forgive our failures, and resurrect ourselves for the sake of today's boys before it is once again too late.

Tuesday, January 31, 1989, Alabama, U.S.A.

Human Rights   **Rising from Defeat**

FEBRUARY

Photo of Jane Van Ter Pool, circa 1915. Photographer unknown. Reprinted courtesy of the author. For more information, see July 22.

FEBRUARY 1

On February 1, 1960, four students took their seats at a lunch counter and their places in history. To some, their youth meant that they had time, that their whole lives were ahead of them. To them, their youth meant that if they did not get segregation out of the way, it would waste the rest of their lives.

As NAACP Youth Chapter members, Ezell Blair, Jr., Franklin McCain, Joseph McNeil, and David Richmond were actively committed to ending segregation. Sitting around on a Sunday night, they came to the conclusion that the best time to act was now. Their strategy would be a sit-in. At Woolworth's the next day, the North Carolina A & T freshmen made a few small purchases around the store before sitting down at the lunch counter. When the waitress refused to serve them, they put forth their challenge: "Why would the store invite us in to serve us at one counter and not another?" A policeman nearby stood stunned and confused, not knowing what to do. He had a gun. He had a stick. But they had been respectful, peaceful, and logical—and that was something to which he had not been trained to respond. They occupied the seats until the store closed, and left.

Said McCain of the event years later, "If it's possible to know what it means to have your soul cleansed, I felt pretty clean that time. I probably felt better on that day than I've ever felt in my life. A lot of feelings of guilt left me. . . . I felt as though the manhood of a number of other Black persons had been restored and had gotten some respect from just that one day."

In truth, the Greensboro sit-in was not the first. But by braving the odds, risking their safety, and acting on their own, these young men inspired similar protests by college students across the South, and they contributed to the student activism of the 1960s and 1970s that culminated in the Black Studies, women's, and antiwar movements.

Monday, February 1, 1960, North Carolina, U.S.A.

Civil Rights   **Dignity**

FEBRUARY 2

The NAACP's coveted Spingarn Medal is awarded each year in recognition of the outstanding achievement of an African-American. But over eighty years ago when the creation of the award itself was first publicized on February 2, 1914, tributes to African-Americans were hard to come by. News about people of color focused on crime, deviant behavior, and the latest rumored racial threat. Anxious for a change, Dr. W. E. B. Du Bois added a top-priority item to the already overcrowded agenda of his four-year-old NAACP: public relations. The NAACP would sponsor a nationally newsworthy annual event to offer a more accurate portrait of Black life. It would honor and publicize African-American achievement, nurture the ambitions of youth, and present its highest tribute, the Spingarn Medal.

The Spingarn Medal honors the commitment of its white namesake, Joel Spingarn, who was elected NAACP board chairman in January 1914. Joel Spingarn, a man of independent means and a Columbia University English professor, worked tirelessly to recruit support, funds, and members for the NAACP. In the era of Jim Crow, his considerable social position allowed him to persuade well-connected friends to use their own power and influence in the court of public opinion.

The first Spingarn Medal was presented in 1915 to Dr. Ernest Just of the Howard University Medical School for distinction in biological research. The next year it was awarded to Colonel Charles Young for his work in Liberia (see July 26). Successive Spingarn medalists have included educator Mary McLeod Bethune, Nobel Peace Prize laureates Ralph Bunche and Martin Luther King, Jr., author Langston Hughes, singer Lena Horne, sports legend Jackie Robinson, labor leader A. Philip Randolph, and over seventy other notables.

Today, as one honor among many, the Spingarn Medal continues to help counteract negative media and affirm our positive self-talk.

Monday, February 2, 1914, New York, U.S.A.

Honors **Greatness**

FEBRUARY 3

On February 3, 1870, Jonathan Jasper Wright was at the start of a new career in South Carolina as the first African-American Superior Court justice.

His appointment honored a life of service. After completing college and reading law, the Pennsylvania native made South Carolina his adopted home. He was eager to maximize his potential in a state where 60 percent of the eligible male voters were Black men. He worked hard for the postwar South as a teacher, lawyer, Freedmen's Bureau advocate for ex-slaves, organizer of the state's newly formed Republican party, and delegate to South Carolina's state constitutional convention. Clearly, Judge J. J. Wright was an exceptional talent, an exceptional man. And with all this, he was just thirty years old on the day of his appointment to the court.

But the more his skill was seen as a symbol of the hopes and pride of Blacks, the more it was also taken as a threat to whites. In retrospect, many historians have viewed the postwar Reconstruction work of Blacks like Wright as a failure—or as one historian put it, a "glorious failure." Whites' irrational fear of Blacks like Wright unleashed a violent backlash that plagued the South for the next hundred years, but this fear was not forged by the actions of Blacks themselves. On the contrary, most Blacks were eager to set aside their anger over slavery in order to contribute to the building of a better world. And in this they were quite successful—too successful. Whites who feared that an equitable "one man, one vote" society would erode their accustomed positions of dominance and power set out to destroy every Civil War gain made by Blacks. With racist distortions and outright lies, they created a climate of fear and precedents that are with us to this day—witness the dismantling of affirmative action.

In short, the only thing wrong with J. J. Wright was that he was good—too good. For the strong base he provided, and on which today's hundreds of Black judges continue to build, his appointment marks a Glory Day.

Thursday, February 3, 1870, South Carolina, U.S.A.

Law   **Possibility**

FEBRUARY 4

On February 4, 1965, Malcolm X came to Selma, Alabama, to deliver his first "civil rights" speech as an independent spokesperson after his resignation from the Nation of Islam. Never an advocate of sit-ins and marches, he saw his role as that of the outsider—at one with the goal of African-American liberation but at odds with an integrationist approach. Now others had reached out to him, and he was eager to meet them halfway. It was a time for alliance. How that reconciliation came about is a story in itself.

Earlier in the year, Juanita Poitier (actor Sidney Poitier's estranged wife) had called for a "movement summit" at her home in New York State. Hoping to diminish the divisiveness of the movement's internal foes, she invited leaders to air their differences away from the public glare and to establish a united platform from which to deal with the life-and-death fight for freedom. Of that high-profile group, only Dr. King was absent, jailed in Selma just weeks after accepting his Nobel Peace Prize.

In the aftermath of that summit, SNCC's Stokely Carmichael (also known as Kwame Touré) invited Malcolm X to speak in Selma. With Dr. King in jail, the movement had to keep up the pressure. Some feared Malcolm's presence might dilute the appeal of nonviolence. Others feared it would threaten Dr. King's leadership.

Arriving in Selma, Malcolm was keenly aware of the politics of the movement and his role. His speech to an overflow crowd provided just the right spark at the right time. "White people should thank Dr. King for holding people in check," said Malcolm. "For there are others who do not believe in [nonviolence]. . . . If the white people realize what the alternative is, perhaps they will be more willing to hear Dr. King." That day, a federal judge ordered Selma's voter registrar to process at least one hundred Black applicants a day.

Thursday, February 4, 1965, Alabama, U.S.A.

Oration   Unity

FEBRUARY 5

Sometimes it's easy to think that so little has changed. Remember February 5, 1994, and think again.

Within days of Medgar Evers's 1963 assassination, his killer was identified as Byron de la Beckwith, an avowed white supremacist with powerful allies and centuries of institutionalized violence on his side. Over the next months, Beckwith was twice charged and twice freed by all-white, all-male hung juries, and the case was dropped. Some charged that Evers, the NAACP's Mississippi Field Secretary, was the real villain for going against the system. Beckwith saw himself as a hero and was proud of the murder he had committed. "Killing that nigger gave me no more inner discomfort than our wives endure when they give birth to our children," he bragged.

For thirty years, Myrlie Evers sought an opportunity to bring her husband's murderer to justice. That chance came when a reporter researching Klan sympathizers found evidence linked to the murder. Reopening the case was a major ordeal. It meant bypassing those in the courts and on the police force who wanted the past to stay in the past. Still she persisted, even when the murder weapon with Beckwith's fingerprints disappeared, even when the transcript and photographs from the first trial were "lost." Some people would never change, it seemed. But some hearts had. Just as mysteriously, the photos were anonymously recovered. The murder weapon, a rifle, resurfaced in the private gun collection of a local judge. An integrated male/female, biracial jury was impaneled. Witnesses once afraid to testify now came forward, including an ex-Klansman.

On February 5, 1994—thirty years after the crime—Byron de la Beckwith was found guilty in the June 1963 murder of Medgar Evers. Said Myrlie Evers, "I was reborn when that jury said, 'Guilty.'" So, too, was the NAACP. A year later, on February 18, 1995, the national board of directors of the NAACP made Myrlie Evers its new chairperson.

Saturday, February 5, 1994, Mississippi, U.S.A.

Law   **Tenacity**

FEBRUARY 6

Leaving the port of New York on February 6, 1820, the passengers of the *Mayflower of Liberia* embarked on a dangerous course. Navigating increasingly hostile waters, their crossing from New York to Liberia in West Africa stirred political waves more ominous than any nature had planned.

With the controversy surrounding African "colonization" at its highest (see January 24, February 24), it was clear that white political support for the "Back-to-Africa" movement was a ploy to dislodge slavery's most active and vocal opponents, free Blacks. With pirate ships traveling international waters loaded with "cargoes" of enslaved Africans, it was also clear that the ban on the importation of slaves was having little effect. Equally clear was that the slave trade was an ongoing risky business for which prices and profits were higher than ever. The higher fees charged for the precious few slaves brought in paid for the "cargo" dumped overboard when a pirate vessel was intercepted at sea for violating the ban.

Free Blacks were caught in a dilemma that pitted family loyalty against individual salvation. The hugely profitable traffic in human flesh had continued for two hundred years, with no true end in sight. As John B. Russwurm, cofounder of the first African-American newspaper (see March 16), said, "It is a waste of words to talk of ever enjoying citizenship in this country."

For the eighty-six men, women, and children on their Back-to-Africa pilgrimage, this day marked the fulfillment of centuries of longing on both sides of the Atlantic—the longing of those who for generations had spoken of the home they had never seen and of those who had, for the same period, spoken of the children lost across the seas. For these pilgrims aboard their *Mayflower*, the best hope was an earnest belief in their ability to forge a new life mindful both of their past and of the responsibilities for their future.

Sunday, February 6, 1820, U.S.A.–Sierra Leone

Emigration **Choices**

FEBRUARY 7

In art, February 7 marks a day of unqualified recognition for James A. Porter, whose insights were often misunderstood but never undervalued.

"Overdramatizing the feeling of separateness from the mainstream of American life because of oversensitiveness to race discrimination is submission," wrote Porter in the 1950s. This was the sound advice of an artist telling his peers and students not to relinquish their own subtle personal vision and authenticity in order to "please the crowd" of high-paying art collectors. It was also the challenge of an historian who hoped that through his work "the prejudice and mistrust that have restricted the [Black] artist and warped his milieu will be abolished." And it was the statement of a master teacher whose chairmanship of Howard University's Art Department nurtured and presented the work of students and professionals too numerous to count.

In his own right, James A. Porter was an award-winning artist of major proportions. As the world-renowned artist Romare Bearden and his collaborator Henry Henderson have written, "no comparable figure exists among American artists. Most art historians have never seriously used a brush, and most artists tend to be unaware of the social forces behind historical shifts in art." Porter was different. But he sacrificed full-time devotion to painting to address what he saw as "the constantly reiterated statement that the American Negro has no pictorial or plastic art—a statement for which white and Negro persons were responsible." Porter was the pioneer chronicler of African-American artists, and his 1943 history book, *Modern Negro Art,* was the only one available on this subject for nearly forty years.

It is for these reasons that people came to the Wilmington state armory on February 7, 1971. In coming to view "Afro-American Images, 1971: A Memorial Exhibition for James A. Porter," they were also honoring the history of African-American art.

Sunday, February 7, 1971, Delaware, U.S.A.

Art   **Knowledge**

FEBRUARY 8

On February 8, 1961, the Senate Banking Committee conducted hearings to confirm President Kennedy's nomination of Robert C. Weaver as head of the Housing and Home Finance Agency. Weaver was the highest-level Black appointee in history, and forces pro and con paid special attention as the government prepared to break its 180-year-old exclusionary rule. Days later, Weaver was sworn in, but not before the following exchange took place.

In a voice oozing the Red-baiting venom of the McCarthy era of the fifties, Senator William Arvis Blakely asked Weaver about Black groups that had been called Communist fronts. Did he know that the National Negro Congress was a subversive group? No, said Weaver. Did he ever join the Washington Cooperative Bookshop? Yes, the shop gave a 20 percent discount. Was Weaver aware that his landmark book, *The Negro Ghetto*, had been reviewed by a Communist bookshop? How would he like it if the shop displayed the book? Weaver admitted that both he and his publisher would appreciate the publicity. What about a Communist magazine review? What about the fact that a Communist magazine had reviewed his book thirteen years ago? Did he read the review thirteen years ago?

"I read about 250 reviews," said Weaver. "Do you know who wrote it?"

"Yes. This seems to be by J. Crow, Realtor." (The review was in fact bylined "J[im] Crow, Realtor," and signed by the noted historian, Herbert Aptheker.)

"Who?"

"J. Crow. . . . Do you know J. Crow?"

"I did not know he wrote book reviews."

To borrow a line from Robert Welch, founder of the vehemently right-wing John Birch Society, "the whole country is one vast insane asylum and they're letting the worst patients run the place." That June, Texas mercifully recalled Mr. Blakely in a special election.

Wednesday, February 8, 1961, Washington, D.C., U.S.A.

Government   **Humor**

FEBRUARY 9

From some time before 1895 until February 9, 1899, a secret society, Invincible Sons and Daughters of Commerce (ISDC), used the notion of life insurance to underwrite the future of Black communities nationwide.

Thirty years into emancipated life, African-Americans had seized upon freedom and used it well in every field—government, science, industry, education, community service. Yet for all they had done right, each day saw a new wrong perpetrated against them. In self-defense, Blacks in states as disparate as California and the Carolinas, Massachusetts and Mississippi, turned their lodges, leagues, and clubs into secret "orders" and "brotherhoods." With passwords, handshakes, masonic degrees, and signs, these groups used the notion of "life insurance" to empower a national network of buyers and merchants committed to Black survival.

Organizations like the ISDC remained secret for good reason. Every dollar a Black business earned was too often seen as a dollar a white business lost. Yet because white companies refused to grant loans to Blacks or to underwrite Black life, the ISDC faced a unique opportunity to strengthen fragile neighborhood economies. In February 1896, the ISDC secretly began to finance lodges. By 1898, over five hundred "family leagues" and "housewives' circles" had pledged to "purchase all goods from colored merchants and shopkeepers . . . and start stores in locations where there are none kept . . . by colored people." The ISDC's first public notice went out with this ad in Black Indiana newspapers on February 9, 1899: "Business, Wealth and Race Unity! The ISDC is [a society] to benefit you while you live. . . . We differ from the old societies. Their motto is: 'We care for the sick and bury the dead.' Our motto: 'We care for the well and raise the living.'"

For Blacks, secrecy was the miracle that helped many through the Great Depression. In hard times, it kept money on hand. In better days, it financed businesses, bought family homes, and put children through college.

Thursday, February 9, 1899, Indiana, U.S.A.

Business   **Creativity**

FEBRUARY 10

Since colonial times, our war for equal treatment under the law has been waged on every front imaginable. But one of the most unusual battles began on February 10, 1780, when seven freemen spoke the Revolutionary War cry, "Taxation without representation is tyranny!" on their own behalf. "Deprived of Injoying the Profits of our Labouer or the advantage of Inheriting Estates from our Parents as our Neighbours the white peopel do," they demanded that they be given their rights as taxpayers or be made tax exempt as men with no rights.

By May the petition had entered Massachusetts's legislative record. But after four years of war, the state was unwilling to reduce the taxes and equally unwilling to openly turn the Blacks down when Britain was offering immediate freedom to slaves who joined its side in the war. The petition was quietly set aside in October and then dropped. Two of the seven men, the brothers John and Paul Cuffe, continued the challenge. This time, they claimed a tax exemption based on their Indian heritage as freeborn sons of a Wampanoag mother and an African father who had been enslaved and later freed. The brothers' persistence angered officials, who jailed them but relented when a respected adviser to the governor filed a writ forcing tax assessors to disprove the brothers' claim or release them.

Over the next months the battles of wits and writs increased taxes and penalties. Then, on June 9, 1781, embarrassed by the scandal, local officials settled the brothers' taxes at less than 5 percent of their original assessment. Within days, the Cuffes dropped their petition, and by 1783, with continued pressure from Black residents, those subject to taxes were allowed to vote on local affairs. Through it all, Paul Cuffe's unflagging will indicated qualities that would make him one of his day's most successful businessmen—an international shipping magnate and African-America's first entrepreneur (see November 12).

Thursday, February 10, 1780, Massachusetts, U.S.A.

Law   **Justice**

FEBRUARY 11

On February 11, 1990, the world watched a seventy-one-year-old man cross the bridge from South Africa's Victor Vorster Prison to take his place in the global pantheon of all-time great men. After twenty-seven years as a political prisoner, Nelson Rolihlahla Mandela was free.

Born to Xhosa royalty, he had gone to college and studied law. As a young activist he met two men who would become his partners for life—Walter Sisulu and Oliver Tambo. As cofounders of the Youth League of the African National Congress (ANC) in 1944, of South Africa's first Black law firm in 1953, and of the ANC's military wing in 1961, they pledged to overthrow apartheid. Then, in 1963, charged with sabotage and treason, Mandela was sentenced to life in prison.

For twenty-seven years, his wife, Winnie, had been the only tangible symbol of the revered political prisoner. In her battle to free him, she, too, endured prison and torture. Then, in 1988, South Africa's pressured leaders offered to release Mandela if he renounced his freedom fight. He refused. His moral stand propelled other countries to enact stiff economic sanctions in order to pressure South Africa to end apartheid and release Mandela unconditionally. It took two more years, but it worked.

On February 9, South Africa's president de Klerk asked for an audience with an "outlaw": his soon-to-be successor Nelson Mandela. The suspense built. On February 10, a photo came over the wires. A new image emerged of a tall, thin, gray elder statesman. On the eleventh, as tension mounted, TV news anchor Ted Koppel summed up the feelings of millions: "If he could wait twenty-seven years, we can wait an hour." Finally a raised fist came into view, a shout went up, Nelson Mandela walked through the gate in the prison wall, and people wept as they cheered, *"Amandla!"* Power!

Sunday, February 11, 1990, South Africa

Heroes

Stature

FEBRUARY 12

On February 12, 1926, African-American history took on new meaning.

As Dr. Carter G. Woodson said in his book, *The Miseducation of the Negro*, "when you control a man's thinking you do not have to worry about his actions. You do not have to tell him not to stand here or go yonder. He will find his 'proper place' and will stay in it. You do not need to send him to the back door, he will cut one for his special benefit. His education makes it necessary." With that statement, Dr. Woodson signaled the responsibility of each of us to gain access to the front door via knowledge and due pride in our history. To launch his campaign directly to the people by way of predominantly Black churches and schools, he cofounded the Association for the Study of Negro Life and History (see September 9). And on February 12, 1926, he proclaimed the first Negro History Week to promote that vision.

Since he intended it to be an annual commemoration, Woodson timed the week to honor two historic births—that of the legendary self-emancipated slave, abolitionist, Underground Railroad conductor, orator, publisher, and diplomat Frederick Douglass; and that of President Abraham Lincoln, the man who issued the Emancipation Proclamation.

A tribute to Woodson's vision, this week turned into African-American History Month. Seventy years after his initiative, however, there is still so little Black history being taught in schools or accurately portrayed in the public media. Yet the more people learn, the more we want to know. And to meet that need, his association is still at work researching, publishing, and disseminating books and journals on African-American history and culture.

FEBRUARY 13

On February 13, 1920, Black baseball hit a grand slam. NAACP cofounder Dr. Du Bois said, "Baseball is the most popular sport in the country. In every hamlet, town and city may be the future Rube Fosters [the Black baseball promoter]. . . romping over corner lots, batting, pitching, and learning how to play the game. Organize your team!" And we did. Professional teams, semipro teams, and just-for-fun teams in cities nationwide gave Blacks a crack at bat.

"Some of these days," wrote one reporter, "a few people with nerve enough to take the chance will form a colored league of about eight cities and pull off a barrel of money." And we did that, too. Rube Foster organized his team, then set out to organize all the others, inviting club owners to gather at the Colored YMCA in Kansas City on February 13, 1920. There, the National Negro League (NNL) was born. For action, fun, and loyalty to the fans, the NNL was it. "They say that we were not organized," said a three-season Kansas City Monarch vet, Sammie Haynes. "We were organized. We had two leagues. We had a 140-game schedule. We played an all-star game every year in Chicago. We had sellouts. We had a World Series at the end of the season. If that's not organized, I don't know what organized is."

In the first league game on May 2, 1920, the Indianapolis ABCs took the Chicago Giants 4–2, in front of eight thousand fans. By July 17, the first Eastern Division game was played at Ebbets Field, a major league stadium and, prophetically enough, home of the Brooklyn Dodgers. Rube Foster had always predicted the majors would one day look to the NNL for action. A quarter century later, the Dodgers would break the major league color bar against Blacks by recruiting Jackie Robinson from the Negro Leagues' Kansas City Monarchs.

Friday, February 13, 1920, Missouri, U.S.A.

Sports/Business   **Enjoyment**

FEBRUARY 14

Never one to be outdone by what others deemed "impossible," Frederick Douglass wanted a birthday and he was going to have one. But first, he'd have to try to find out when it was.

For Blacks born into slavery, a birthday was as hard to come by as justice. Birthdays were sometimes noted in a slave master's farm book or ledger, but that was rare. Slave parents would pass down general information to their children, but for Douglass that was impossible. He presumed his father to be the slave master from whom he had escaped, so he couldn't ask him. And as Douglass once said, his knowledge of his mother, Harriet Bailey, was "scant." Forcibly separated from her son when he was about five years old, she had died on a plantation twelve miles away when he was about eight. But he could remember a few of the stories she had told him. He knew he'd been born on a Talbot County, Maryland, plantation in the teens. He chose 1817 as his year. For the actual day, he could remember his mother calling him her "valentine." He decided on February 14 for the date.

We never know how our children will remember what we tell them or what effect it will have. We never know what will come back to them when they need it most. For Frederick Douglass's mother—a woman who had so little—she gave him a precious gift, the gift of love.

A century and a half after his "birthday," folks were still praising Harriet Bailey's little "valentine." On February 14, 1967, a twenty-five-cent postage stamp was issued that bore his portrait. And on February 14, 1972, the Frederick Douglass home in the Anacostia section near Washington, D.C., was opened to the public as a national historic landmark.

Friday, February 14, 1817, Maryland–Washington, D.C., U.S.A.
Family   **Love**

FEBRUARY 15

February 15 is the anniversary of a highly profitable partnership that is still yielding dividends. "I cannot offer you money, position, or fame," wrote Booker T. Washington to Iowa State University's first Black graduate student and instructor in 1896. "The first two you have; the last, from the place you now occupy, you will no doubt achieve. These things I now ask you to give up. I offer you in their place work—hard, hard work—the task of bringing a people from degradation, poverty, and waste to full manhood."

Who could resist such an invitation! Certainly not the man who spent his childhood "talking to plants" because he was too sick to work the field. As an artist turned botanist, George Washington Carver understood creativity in nature, art, and life. "Of course, it has always been the one great ideal of my life to be of the greatest good to the greatest number of 'my people' possible," he responded to Washington, ". . . feeling as I do that this line of education is the key to unlock the golden door of freedom to our people."

"Your department exists only on paper, and your laboratory will have to be in your head," Washington told Carver upon his arrival at Tuskegee. With no money and a world of resources, Carver defined his mission: to help poor farmers by developing new uses for "ordinary" or "found" objects. With this partnership grounded in a fundamental utilitarianism, Carver and Washington fueled and fulfilled each other's dreams. On February 15, 1897, when the "Branch Agricultural Experiment Station and Agricultural School for the colored race" was funded by a state legislative act, they had their laboratory, and Carver was its director.

True to his mission, Carver found 325 products in peanuts, 108 uses for sweet potatoes, and 75 for pecans; made pinecones into wallboard, sawdust into synthetic marble, and okra stalks into woven rugs. And true to Washington's prediction, his pioneering efforts in chemurgy (the science of utilizing agricultural products in industry), earned him international acclaim.

Monday, February 15, 1897, Alabama–Iowa, U.S.A.

Science   **Creativity**

FEBRUARY 16

The country should certainly have resolved the issue of racism on campus by now and things should certainly be better. But picture the predicament of twenty-one-year-old Jessie Fauset on February 16, 1905:

"Living as I have nearly all my life in a distinctly white neighborhood, and for the past four years as the only colored girl in a college community [Cornell University in Ithaca, New York] of over 3,000 students, I have had to let people know that we too possess some of the best—or else allow my own personality to be submerged."

Somewhere early in life Fauset had learned the value of ringing the bells to celebrate others when they can most enjoy the chime—during their lifetimes. Refusing to dwell on her own isolation, she reached out to thank and encourage W. E. B. Du Bois, at the time a noted essayist.

"It has been with much pleasure that I have pointed to you as an example of the heights to which it is possible for some of us to climb. It is with the same pleasure and sincerity that I tell you this now—in the desire that in the hour when your work—always arduous—grows irksome through apparent lack of appreciation, you may take heart by remembering that somewhere afar off, some one is 'rendering unto Caesar the things which are Caesar's.'"

What inspires one to realize his or her potential greatness? Is it the action a man takes to release racism's stranglehold by cofounding Pan-African congresses (see February 19) and the NAACP? Or might it be a letter received from a precocious student by a father still mourning the loss of a baby son? Whatever it was, it helped Du Bois—and us. And whatever Fauset's loneliness, she had found a friend, a career path, and, years later, a brief love affair. In 1919, after founding the NAACP and its official journal, *The Crisis,* Du Bois invited Fauset to become the magazine's literary editor, a position she held for seven years.

Thursday, February 16, 1905, Georgia–New York, U.S.A.
Literature/Letters   **Friendship**

FEBRUARY 17

February 17, 1919, was a great day for Black folks—a day for which men had given their lives, valiantly fighting abroad for freedoms that they could not enjoy at home. In particular, this was Harlem's day to shine—and shine she did as the Harlem Hellfighters paraded up New York's Fifth Avenue, stepping to the beat of James Reese Europe's ragtime marching band.

Harlem and its regiment had reason to be proud. As the first Allied unit to reach the Rhine in World War I, it had so distinguished itself that 171 of its officers and men were awarded France's Croix de Guerre. But few people knew of that distinction, for U.S. Commander General Pershing had excluded Blacks from the victory parade up the Champs-Elysées, even though Black French and British troops marched.

But this was not a day for lament. This was a day for cheering. Up Fifth Avenue marched the Hellfighting 369th all the way to 110th Street, where they headed north on Harlem's historic Lenox Avenue. As they took the turn, Europe's marching band, ninety strong, swung into a chorus of "Here Comes My Daddy Now," and "the Hellfighters marched between two howling walls of humanity," reported the *New York Age*. "From the rooftops thousands stood and whooped things up . . . . So frantic did many become that they threw pennants and even hats away." Recalled an officer, "Mothers, and wives, and sisters, and sweethearts recognized their boys and their men; and they rushed right out through the ranks to embrace them. For the final mile . . . we marched through Harlem singing and laughing."

Harlem savored its day, and the ever-vigilant "Lift Ev'ry Voice" lyricist, James Weldon Johnson, wrote, "We wonder how many people who are opposed to giving the Negro his full citizenship rights could watch . . . the march up the Avenue and not feel either shame or alarm."

Monday, February 17, 1919, New York, U.S.A.

Celebrations   **Racial Pride**

FEBRUARY 18

The year 1947 was turning out to be a promising one. In sports, Jackie Robinson would desegregate major league baseball. In music, hard-driving solo performers forged a new jazz idiom, and Charlie "Bird" Parker established his legendary quintet. And in art, corporate purchases gave such a boost of recognition to Black artists as had not been experienced since the Harlem Renaissance.

But as a letter dated February 18, 1947, from artist Hale Woodruff to fellow artist Charles Alston demonstrates, while the labeling of "Black art" versus "art" was meant to be "inclusive" as it related to IBM's new acquisitions, it was also reason for concern. "In light of the Negro artist's present achievements in the general framework of American art today, there does not exist the necessity to continue all-Negro exhibitions which tend to isolate him and segregate him from other American artists." IBM was big business, and its collection was big business, too. Woodruff knew that businesses would think twice before sacrificing a budget line item marked "art," but a line item labeled "Black art" could be erased in a snap. As an artist in business for himself, he wanted to ensure the fiscal survival of the artist and his art form. With skillful forecasting, he predicted the arts' funding crises of the early 1980s and mid 1990s.

Hale Woodruff had come of age as an artist when a sense of Black identity was squashed at its inception. In his work and life he was making up for lost images and time with works like *Celestial Gates,* inspired by Ashanti gold weights and Dogon granary doors. He was willing to celebrate a moment of high-profile recognition. But the wisdom informing his art also made him keenly aware of the art business. He saw a need to stand guard at the door that led artists in and out of vogue. And he clearly saw Black identification and the identification of Blacks as two very distinct issues.

Tuesday, February 18, 1947, New York, U.S.A.

Business/Art   **Truth**

FEBRUARY 19

On February 19, 1919, Dr. W. E. B. Du Bois opened the doors of Paris's Grand Hôtel and ushered in a long-held dream. Since the Pan-African Congress of 1900, Du Bois had been gripped by the need to unify the diaspora around a single objective: extinguishing oppression for people of African descent. At first there were the usual impediments of international communications, sponsorship, and financing. Later, with the outbreak of World War I, there were travel restrictions based on race and nationality. But when the 1918 armistice arrived, he knew the chance to convene the congress had come.

As leaders assembled in France for the historic Versailles peace talks, a press boat was due to leave New York, and Du Bois vowed to be on it. The NAACP board was only mildly interested in his congress idea, but what excited them was the chance to have an NAACP representative at Versailles and the opportunity to research and publish a firsthand report on the status of Black soldiers. Du Bois promised both and was on his way.

For three weeks while conducting his soldiers' study, he unsuccessfully scrambled around Paris seeking support, "with the American Secret Service at my heels." His first break came when the only African member of the French Parliament, Senegal's Blaise Diagne, came to his aid, managing to gain authorization for the congress to be held in France. With that, other doors opened.

On February 19, 1919, as the Big Four nations decided "the destinies of mankind for a hundred years to come," fifty-seven delegates from fifteen countries sat in an historic congress that historian David Levering Lewis has called "more 'pan' than African." Less than ten of the delegates had ever seen the African continent. Yet it was at this meeting that the notion of cultural unity for the African diaspora was born. The NAACP provided $750 toward the effort to unite the worldwide movements. As Du Bois optimistically wrote, had Blacks had the necessary staff and personnel, "they could have settled the future of Africa at a cost of less than $10,000."

Wednesday, February 19, 1919, France

FEBRUARY 20

Too often the easiest information to get is the least useful information to have. On February 20, 1833, African-Americans made a decisive move to reclaim a wondrous world of information too long out of reach. With the founding of the Philadelphia Library Company of Colored Persons, they began the process of recovering priceless gifts of knowledge and launched one of the nation's first public libraries.

They wrote, "We the people of color of this city, being deeply impressed with the necessity of promoting among our rising youth, a proper cultivation for literary pursuits and the improvement of the faculties and powers of their minds . . ." In so doing, they advanced a tradition of African reading and writing two thousand years old.

As with most societies before books were mass-produced, African reading and writing had been limited to an intellectual elite—the scribes. When indigenous African nations were conquered, among the first people killed were those entrusted with the keys to knowledge. In this way, civilizations were literally and figuratively "lost." It is not that ancient people had no history and no written language; it is that the griots (oral historians) had been slaughtered and few scholars or scribes survived to decode the ghostly writings on surfaces that the conquerors had not thought to destroy—pyramid walls, sealed temples, caves, and now-excavated ancient tablets. As the cumulative knowledge gained allows us to decode more and more messages, these ancient writings tell us that the tradition of African libraries dates back to that of Egypt's King Osymandyas, circa 1240 B.C. They tell us that much of what is known as "Greek philosophy" was derived from the ancient religious system known as the "Egyptian Mysteries."

What the oldest Black public library's founding tells us is that despite the pain of our relatively recent history, the wealth that is ours need not remain obscured.

Wednesday, February 20, 1833, Pennsylvania, U.S.A.

Libraries   **Empowerment**

FEBRUARY 21

Malcolm X had a line he would say before giving his speeches: "Make it plain!" It was a sign to his lieutenants that it was time to get on with the moment. It was a warning to focus on the facts and avoid long, flowery introductions. It was a reminder for them all that the real stars of the day were the people who needed to escape the flood of racism and find routes to life's higher ground. "Make it plain!" he said to his aides at the Audubon Ballroom on February 21, 1965. Minutes later he was assassinated onstage.

Much about his assassination will never be made plain. But this is clear. One week earlier his home had been firebombed as his family slept inside. It was their last moment of living together as a family, a prophetic moment foreshadowing the ashes from which a woman would raise up her life.

On February 21, 1965, as Betty Shabazz knelt beside her husband's body at the Audubon, what images could be more lasting in her mind than the hail of bullets, the sea of scrambling humanity, and her husband's body shot down before her eyes? What could be more haunting for her children at her side than to see their father lying in a pool of blood? All these things happened that day in the life of Betty Shabazz, a mother of four daughters ages seven, five, three, and three months and of twins who would be born that fall.

From the ashes of her loss, Betty Shabazz's strength of character saved her and her children. Malcolm X was torn from his family at thirty-nine years of age. Betty Shabazz was left a young woman alone, a widow, a single mother with six daughters to raise and no financial assets. Yet she raised her daughters, entered the University of Massachusetts at Amherst's School of Education, completed her doctorate, joined the faculty of Medgar Evers College, and began her philanthropic career with the goal of helping young people. Make it plain!

Sunday, February 21, 1965, New York, U.S.A.

Heroes   **Stature**

FEBRUARY 22

On February 22, 1965, Margaret Walker brought the Civil War to an end. It was in a chapter in *Jubilee*, her landmark novel; upon its completion, she suddenly realized that she'd been writing, living, and enduring that war for forty years.

When she was a child in the 1920s, her parents had scurried her away from "all those harrowing tales"; they didn't want to fill her dreams with the nightmare of slavery. "Nothing but tall tales," they'd say, and her grandmother would reply, "I'm not telling her tales; I'm telling her the naked truth." And it was. Embedded in those stories was a people's history of America, the rare saga of a Black family. Years later, Walker was able to authenticate the details she'd learned from her griot-grandmother. On a trip to their native Georgia, she came to an eerily familiar place—the actual land her freeborn great-grandfather had once owned, complete with the remnants of his smithy and gristmill that she'd heard about for so long.

Her great-grandmother's view of slavery became that of the book's heroine—a woman shaped by life in the Big House and the quarters who seemed powerless to act but who had determined that prayer would deliver what she needed. Her great-grandfather's story was that of a man frustrated by the restrictions placed on free people of color. He worked hard for what he wanted but was cheated out of his manhood in an era when societal forces were beyond his control.

As a graduate student, Walker had learned that truth in America usually comes in three versions—that of the North, of the South, and of Black folks. But the Black version is hardest to find, clouded as it is by the ongoing struggle between efforts to tell it as it needs to be told and pressures to minimize its existence. Were it not for the elders like Walker's grandmother who have passed on the truths of our family legacies, our history would be impoverished indeed.

Monday, February 22, 1965, Mississippi, U.S.A.

Literature

Truth

FEBRUARY 23

What makes February 23 so special is that it tells a story so normal. Early in 1892, Tuskegee Normal asked local businesspeople to attend a conference at which they would share strategies for the betterment of everyday commerce. At first, only seventy-five attendees were expected. But as Tuskegee founder Booker T. Washington called the meeting to order on February 23, 1892, he was delighted to find himself addressing over five hundred people.

The conferees were people getting the job of living done—farmers, mechanics, teachers, general store owners, ministers. They were lured by the growing reputation of the Tuskegee Normal Industrial Institute. With an impoverished student body, Tuskegee relied on benefactors and state contracts, but what kept it growing was the highly skilled craftsmanship of its teachers and student apprentices. In addition to English, science, and math, it offered courses in the raising of livestock, fruit and tree culture, blacksmithing, wheelwrighting, carpentry, printing, shoemaking, construction, and other nation-building skills. Because the conference brought together on-campus expertise with seasoned real-world experience, it was a hit.

Four conferences and years later, these annual meetings resulted in securing homes, building schools, and extending the elementary school year. When crop blight imperiled farmers and cotton prices, the meetings helped provide ideas on how to restructure farms for survival. The Tuskegee conferences were not about petitions to an unwilling government, they were about life. Speaking to their success, Booker T. Washington said, "We have many things to discourage and disappoint us ... but it seems to me that it is best to confine ourselves to conditions within our own power to remedy."

Tuesday, February 23, 1892, Alabama, U.S.A.

Events   **Potential**

FEBRUARY 24

On February 24, 1820, a Black pilgrim en route to Africa wrote these lines: "May He that was with Moses in the wilderness, be with us; then all will be well. This is a great undertaking, and I feel its importance . . . daily."

Daniel Coker was cofounder of the AME Church (see July 17, November 26) and a deeply religious man who believed faith would bring good to Africa. "Oh God! help me to be true to my trust, and to act for the good of my African brethren in all things. . . .Oh, how happy is my soul while I write these lines," he wrote. Grounded in the teachings of his day, he believed that Africa should be "civilized" with the "light" of Christianity. "I offered up a prayer to God for the conversion of Africa, &c. . . . Great God! what darkness reigns here." With the perils of a slave society behind him, he headed to Africa as a missionary with the American Colonization Society (ACS). Days into the voyage, his expedition weathered rough seas while another ship capsized, killing everyone aboard. Seized with guilt and gratitude, he saw survival as God's blessing on the mission. "My soul travails that we may be faithful. And should God spare us to arrive in Africa that we may be useful," he wrote as his boat inched hopefully on.

Why would Coker join the ACS knowing its clearly stated goal to colonize Africa and thwart abolition (see January 24, February 6)? The thought of an African-American blazing trails as a missionary scout for colonial rule in Africa reminds one of the Africans who ferreted out people for Europeans to enslave. It also reminds us that Blacks on both sides of the Atlantic were under siege; dependent on enslavers and colonizers for "news" from the other side. Is it any wonder that neither knew the other's plight nor empathized with a shared lens and bond? While African-Americans struggled against slavery and segregation, indigenous Africans struggled against capture and colonization. Unable to communicate their own truths, to both the grass must have seemed greener on the other side, indeed. For Coker, the voyage to Africa was both resurrection and epiphany.

Thursday, February 24, 1820, U.S.A.–Sierra Leone

Religion   **Aspirations**

FEBRUARY 25

On February 25, 1870, one month before the Fifteenth Amendment to the Constitution granted universal male suffrage, Hiram Revels became the first African-American senator. Ironically, he was elected to the seat vacated by Jefferson Davis, leader of the Rebel South. Revels served his state well. Cautious on Black issues, he nonetheless named a Black cadet to West Point. But what most distinguishes his record is the fact that he had one at all.

Hiram Revels's career in public service as clergyman, Civil War recruiter, educator, and founder of a freedman's school certainly made him a strong candidate. The issue was not his qualifications, it was the principle of "majority rule" in southern states where that majority was Black. The Mississippi census of 1860 showed a majority Black population of 437,000 to 353,000 whites, which resulted in a postwar majority of 60,000 eligible Black voters to 46,000 eligible whites. This ratio was repeated all across the South with chilling consequences. Whites, guilty and fearful of reprisals for centuries of slavery, saw in Revels's election a dangerous precedent. For weeks the campaign against him raged on. Mississippi's state legislature refused to ratify the Fourteenth Amendment granting citizenship to all races, invalidating the Black vote and Revels's eligibility with a move that stalled passage of the amendment for 125 years. In Washington, the Senate voted to deny Revels's seat. Objections such as this one by a Delaware senator were argued for the record: "the advent of a negro or mulatto or octoroon in the Senate of the United States [holds] little hope for my country. I would avert this great calamity." Finally, after a four-week delay, the censure of Revels was voted down by a narrow majority. Two days later, he was sworn in.

The drive by Black Mississippians to finally ratify the Fourteenth Amendment in 1994 was hardly as symbolic a victory as its detractors charged. The real symbolism was the fact that its ratification had been "overlooked" for 125 years while African-Americans were denied human civil rights.

Friday, February 25, 1870, Mississippi, U.S.A.

Government   **Principle**

FEBRUARY 26

When Cassius Clay took up boxing as a four-foot, eighty-seven-pound Kentucky boy, he was determined to change his fate. He wanted to stop older and bigger boys from taking his bicycle. On his first day as Heavyweight Boxing Champion of the world, no one would doubt his ability to fight. But when he made a brief announcement, he was confronted with a fight the magnitude of which he could never have anticipated. "I believe in the religion of Islam. I believe in Allah and in peace. . . .I'm not a Christian anymore." On February 26, 1964, Cassius Clay became Muhammad Ali and quickly found his fights being booked in a brand-new arena— the courts of law and public opinion.

In a land that prides itself on a founding principle of religious freedom, the harassment of Muhammad Ali was one of its greatest contradictions. Yet, with all the pressures stacking up against him, he could still dance into the ring with fists and wit as quick as ever: "Fly like a butterfly, sting like a bee. You can't catch me, I'm Muhammad Ali." The better he was, the more the pressure would build. And wherever bets were being taken, the sure bet was against Ali. For the right to believe in his faith and himself on his own terms, he would face such formidable opponents as the corps of sportscasters and fans, the general press and public, sports promoters, his then wife, even his draft board and the United States Supreme Court (see June 28). Yet, with skill, talent, a lot of pain, and amazing humor, one by one he took each round.

Over thirty years later, he is still remembered as a man of great stature. He has earned the respect and admiration of millions all over the globe. Living the spirit of his name, he is undeniably Muhammad Ali, "one who is worthy of praise."

Wednesday, February 26, 1964, Florida, U.S.A.
Sports/Religion   **Identity**

FEBRUARY 27

It's Carnival today. And in the northern Americas, the biggest Carnival celebration of all is in Trinidad. As a festival, Carnival came to Trinidad around 1783 when France colonized the island. In Europe, it had been celebrated as a pagan ritual on the last two days before Ash Wednesday and the start of Lent. Converts to Catholicism would purify their spirits by throwing off all traces of the devil, wandering the streets in spirited abandon and enjoying every devilish bit of life in them.

From the start of Carnival in Trinidad, where African slaves outnumbered French colonists eight to one, the event became mostly African in style and content. Not only did white planters "masque," or costume, themselves as slaves but they also reveled in slave dances to the beat of African drums. As the island became more prosperous, the festival period lengthened, often starting as early as the end of the autumn harvest. But unique to Trinidad, it always culminated with *cannes brulés*—or as it is now known, *canboulay*—the burning of left-over cane to produce firecrackerlike sparks. For two days each year, the spark of Carnival created harmony in the midst of cultural discord. Whites relished the days of abandon for what they were able to cast off. Blacks gravitated to those days for what they could retain. In Carnival, Black people had one unguarded moment of opportunity each year to experience the otherwise-banned possession of African ceremonial rituals.

Interestingly, since Africans ruled parts of Europe during the so-called Dark Ages, who can say whether the ritual was not African to begin with? Perhaps Europe adopted the celebration from its darker cousins. Whatever its origins, Carnival in Trinidad today is pure inspiration. Full of color, passion, joy, and music, people from all over the world come to absorb its magic.

Tuesday, February 27, 1996, Trinidad

Celebrations   **Foundations**

FEBRUARY 28

In the winter of 1692, young Puritan girls related stories steeped in an African culture so alien that word of it rocked their religious fathers to the core. As a result of their having acquired alien knowledge—or what their elders called "knowledge of the devil"—a hysterical torrent of piety spewed forth. "Witchcraft!" the men charged. And when their volcanic societal eruption was done, 150 had been accused and imprisoned, 2 had died in prison, and 20 had been executed, 14 of whom were women.

This morality tale of religious zeal run wild has fueled centuries of stories. But the story most often overlooked is that of Tituba, the African-Caribbean slave woman. Soon to be charged a "witch," she and her alleged cauldron of heathen tales stirred rumors of sorcery to the boiling point and led to the first warrants of the Salem witch trials, which were drawn on this day, February 28, 1692.

Tituba was brought to New England from the West Indies to cook and tend a family with energetic young daughters. Remembering stories passed down from her African roots, Tituba kept the girls enthralled (and well behaved) with tales of ghostly gods and supernatural powers. Thus she innocently ignited what can now be seen for what it was—a clash between cultures with vastly different philosophical views. For Puritan church fathers in seventeenth-century colonial America, the real issue was power, and strict religious adherence was the battleground.

Interestingly, while societal outsiders were those most often charged as witches, Tituba, as a potential property loss to her slave owner and a wise enough "witch" to confess possession, was spared burning at the stake.

Thursday, February 28, 1692, Massachusetts, U.S.A.
Social History   **Pragmatism**

FEBRUARY 29

February 29, 1940, was Oscar night in Hollywood. Among those nominated was Hattie McDaniel for her role in *Gone With the Wind*.

Not only had McDaniel paid her professional dues rising from vaudeville to on-screen stardom, she had paid an even higher price off camera to those who criticized her for accepting roles that often demeaned Black women—the only roles she was offered in those overtly racist days. Accepting the actor's maxim, "there are no small parts, only small actors," she proudly played her historic part in the film industry's obviously scornful depictions of Black womanhood.

McDaniel was not only "Mammy" in *Gone With the Wind*, she was the mammy in almost every film she ever made. The more successful she became at it, the more fire she endured for accepting those roles. Ironically, her options for work off screen were no better than those on. In her inimitable style, she once quipped, "I'd rather get paid $1500 a week to play a maid, than $15 a week to be one." As she was equally fond of saying, "I portray the type of Negro woman who has worked honestly and proudly to give our nation the Marian Andersons, Roland Hayeses, and Ralph Bunches"—two opera virtuosi and a Nobel Peace Prize laureate.

When the envelope was opened for the best actress in a supporting role, Hattie McDaniel became the first African-American Oscar winner in the history of American film and the only African-American woman to win until Whoopi Goldberg won in the same category in 1990 for her role in *Ghost*. With the thrill and the honor of the Oscar award forever hers, Hattie McDaniel, soon after the ceremony, donated her Oscar statuette to Howard University for all to see and share.

Thursday, February 29, 1940, California, U.S.A.

Film   **Ambition**

MARCH

Never Too Late. Etching from the drawing by Thomas Hovenden. Published by *Harper's Weekly* (June 20, 1882). Author's collection. Reprinted courtesy of the author.

MARCH 1

For Olaudah Equiano, a young African boy kidnapped and sold into slavery in 1756 at the age of eleven, a book was a curious thing. "I had often seen my master. . . employed in reading," he said. "I had a great curiosity to talk to the books as I thought [he] did, and so to learn how all things had a beginning; for that purpose I have often taken up a book and have talked to it and then put my ears to it, when in hopes it would answer me; and I have been very much concerned when I found it remained silent."

Discovering the key to reading, Equiano turned the silence of books into a roar that can be heard to this day. On March 1, 1789, his two-volume book was published in England: *The Interesting Narrative of the Life of Olaudah Equiano, or Gustavus Vassa, the African.* His book spoke to the rape of Africa and slavery, broke ground for "autobiography" as a literary genre, and revealed life in mid-eighteenth-century Africa as seen through the eyes of a child.

Born in Benin, a nation dating to ancient Africa, Equiano was the son of an *enbrenche,* or Ibo chief, in Essaka (eastern Nigeria). "We are almost a nation of dancers, musicians and poets," he wrote. "Every great event such as a triumphant return from battle or other cause of public rejoicing is celebrated in public dances"—that is, there would be a public procession of different groups depicting great battles, "domestic employment, a pathetic story, or some rural sport [with] a spirit and variety which I have scarcely seen elsewhere."

Sadly, this charmed life ended abruptly when he was captured and sold into slavery. But the experiences of his boyhood shaped his manhood. "I was trained up from my earliest years in the art of war: my daily exercise was shooting and throwing javelins; and my mother adorned me with emblems, after the manner of our greatest warriors." With his book, he waged war on slavery until his death in 1797.

Sunday, March 1, 1789, England

Social History   **Dignity**

MARCH 2

By March 2, 1863, Frederick Douglass's strategy for the liberation of the slaves was beginning to show signs of success. His counsel to President Lincoln that freeing the slaves would undermine the South had led to the Emancipation Proclamation (see September 22). Now, although Black men had participated in every war since the nation's founding, this was the first chance for them to take up arms in their own behalf. The year 1863 was the year of "Jubilee," when, as the spiritual phrased it, "the Lord had set his people free." Now it was time to make that freedom last.

In his stirring editorial that provided the text for a Civil War enlistment poster, he declared, "Men of Color! To Arms! Action! is the plain duty of this hour. There is no time to delay. The tide is at its flood that leads on to fortune. From East to West, from North to South, the sky is written all over, 'Now or Never.' 'Liberty won by white men would lose half its luster.' 'Better even die free, than to live slaves.' This is the sentiment of every brave colored man amongst us. . . . We can get at the throat of treason and slavery through the State of Massachusetts. She was first in the War of Independence; first to break the chains of her slaves; first to make the black man equal before the law; first to admit colored children to her common schools, and she was first to answer with her blood the alarm cry of the nation, when its capital was menaced by rebels." As Douglass made clear, a century of struggle had reaped benefits worth fighting to uphold and extend.

While Douglass was helping to swell the ranks nationwide, his own sons answered the call, joining the legendary Fifty-fourth Massachusetts Colored Regiment. By war's end the number of Black Union troops neared two hundred thousand (see January 26, July 18, December 15). Demeaned by Rebel and Union leaders, denied the respect and rights due them as soldiers, they distinguished themselves with their record of greatness, and by their own acts, they seized their rights as men.

Monday, March 2, 1863, Massachusetts, U.S.A.

Journalism   **Respect for Use of Power**

MARCH 3

As Jim Crow custom became entrenched in the law, business traffic on March 3, 1895, marked a milestone in African-American history.

In the early 1890s, each day brought a new outrage. Wire fences went up in public railroad accommodations behind which Blacks were penned like animals. Alternatives were sought, but as we know, they were not always achievable. Segregation was a contemptible way of life that institutionalized humiliation at every level of day-to-day commerce. A Black-owned railroad project was launched, for example, but could not long sustain itself against increasingly insurmountable roadblocks to its operation. But no matter the obstacle, Black entrepreneurs and investment groups continued to mount major efforts to turn a lemon of a situation into the lemonade of business advantage.

One case in point: the National Steamship Company was incorporated in January 1895. By March 3, 1895, its excursion steamboat, the *George Leary*, was launched. And what a steamship it was. Completely state-of-the-art, this side-wheeler was 272 feet long, with three decks, sixty-four staterooms, one hundred berths, and a dining room. And at a time when electricity meant luxury even in the wealthiest of homes, the *George Leary* was completely electrified. Most important, it provided a capacity crowd of 1,500 passengers with peaceful, respectful service on its regular route between Washington, D.C., and Norfolk, Virginia.

When questions are raised on the quality of Black business leadership, the answer is that regardless of the odds against us, African-American business has been and remains a major source of achievement and innovation.

Sunday, March 3, 1895, Washington, D.C., U.S.A.

Business   **Initiative**

MARCH 4

On March 4, 1809, as Thomas Jefferson closed the door on his last day as president, he could count his March 1807 abolition of the slave trade among his greatest achievements. Thanks to the sheer volume of his correspondence, in Jefferson we can watch a man (and through him a nation of men) ridding himself of his dependence upon something he knows to be fundamentally and morally wrong.

Jefferson, a deeply conflicted man, had been both friend and foe to slavery. He openly opposed the institution of slavery, but was a slave owner. He denounced slavery in the Declaration of Independence (see June 29), but ducked responsibility for being a slaveholder, blaming the king for imposing it on the colonies. He fathered children with his slave-lover, Sally Hemings, whom he openly adored in Paris but publicly denied at home. He contracted Benjamin Banneker, the noted African-American inventor and engineer, to lay out the city of Washington, but patronized Blacks in his own household. In a final flip-flop, he questioned "the grade of understanding allotted [Blacks] by nature," yet in one of his last letters as president, he thanked France's Henri Grégoire for the book *Literature of Negroes* with these lines: "Whatever be their degree of talent it is no measure of their rights. . . . I pray you . . . accept my thanks for the many instances you have enabled me to observe of respectable intelligence in that race of men, which cannot fail to have effect in hastening the day of their relief."

Clearly, Jefferson was a man wrestling with his own conflicted feelings. And because he was such a prolific writer, his letters provide a window to debates on the conscience of the times. His note on the *Literature of Negroes* documents the existence of a sufficient body of Black literature to have been compiled into book form by the year 1809. Just think of all the other treasures awaiting modern eyes!

Saturday, March 4, 1809, Washington, D.C.–Virginia, U.S.A.–France

Literature/Letters   **Roots of Rediscovery**

MARCH 5

One of the events that greatly influenced northern anti-slavery sentiment occurred in Boston, Massachusetts, on March 5, 1770. On that day, Crispus Attucks, an escaped slave, became the first man killed in the cause of America's freedom in an event known through the ages as the "Boston Massacre." Because he was the first martyr of the Revolutionary War, it is said that "the blood of Attucks nourished the tree of liberty" from which sprang the American Revolution of 1775–81.

Attucks's heroism in the Boston Massacre not only impassioned soldiers, Black and white, to take up arms for the war five years later but it also had the immediate effect of spurring Massachusetts's slaves to petition the legislature for freedom. In the words of historian Sidney Kaplan, Attucks's example inspired slaves "to fling the shame of slavery into the faces of those who cried 'Liberty or Death.'"

Crispus Attucks had struck his first blow for freedom twenty years earlier, as a newspaper notice dated October 2, 1750, confirms. "Ran away from his Master, a molatto fellow, about 27 years of Age, named Crispas, 6 Feet two inches high, short curl'd Hair, his Knees nearer together than common. Whoever shall take up said Run-away, and convey him to his abovesaid Master, shall have ten Pounds, old Tenor Reward and all necessary Charges paid."

Little is known of Attucks's life, but the freedom fight was thought to be long in his blood. Of indigenous American and African parentage, he was thought to be a descendant of John Attucks, an indigenous Natick executed in 1676 for fighting on behalf of his people during King Philip's War. Seventy years later, John Attucks's great-grandson was still leading the way to freedom.

Monday, March 5, 1770, Massachusetts, U.S.A.

Freedom   **Zest for Life**

MARCH 6

For months, the images beamed from Ethiopia of people dying from hunger had been horrifying beyond words. In the mid-1980s, with all the world's technology and with planes able to span the globe in two days, there was no excuse for this tragedy. On March 6, 1985, nearly fifty of contemporary music's top singers gathered in concert and conscience following the Grammy Awards in Los Angeles for an all-night session to record "We Are the World."

The brainchild of Quincy Jones and Michael Jackson, the project had one goal: aiding famine-stricken Ethiopia. As much as possible, all services were donated to the project—the song itself was written and donated by Jackson and Lionel Richie, the record was produced and conducted by Quincy Jones, all of the singers and musicians donated their work as did the album designers, promoters, production staff, even the caterers.

"USA for AFRICA" (United Support of Artists for Africa) was a nonprofit corporation pledged, as it said on the album jacket, "to use these funds to address immediate emergency needs in the U.S.A. and Africa, including food and medicine and to help the African people become self-sufficient. By buying this record, you are playing an important part in the fight to end an ongoing tragedy that affects all of us—because 'We Are the World.'"

At a "We Are the World" reunion celebration ten years later, the song and the movement it represented were acknowledged for their unprecedented achievements. The record had raised in excess of fifty million dollars to relieve world suffering. It had also generated a lasting legacy: "We Are the World" changed the way people the world over thought about themselves, their responsibility to others, and the ways in which they could turn what they felt into action

Wednesday, March 6, 1985, California, U.S.A.–Ethiopia

Music   **Conscience**

Richard Wright was not supposed to be a great writer, he was supposed to be nothing. But "accidentally," he said, "I came across H. L. Mencken's *Book of Prefaces,* which served as a literary Bible for me. . . . Because I was not prepared to be anything else, I decided to become a writer."

With *Native Son,* and the character of Bigger Thomas, Wright achieved immense success. But Wright didn't invent Bigger — time, circumstance, and Jim Crow had done that. Wright told Bigger's story with such excruciating authenticity that it was an instant best-seller. Within weeks of its publication, a swarm of controversy greeted its success. In an essay entitled "How Bigger Was Born," signed and dated March 7, 1940, Wright wrote that he had known and lived with five different Biggers all his life — Bigger, the childhood bully; Bigger, the hardened, angry teenager; Bigger, the dangerous, uncaring young man; Bigger, the "crazy nigga"; and Bigger, the volcano with nothing to lose. In *Native Son,* with its rats and rage, he wrote what he knew, determined that others should know it and feel it, too.

"I feel lucky to be alive to write novels," Wright wrote of his self-defined mission in a time when, as he said, "if [Edgar Allan] Poe were alive, he would not have to invent horror; horror would invent him." For the horrifying lives of the five Biggers, which Wright knew intimately, demanded a voice — and that was Wright's role as he saw it. Of the space and need he saw for his talent, he wrote that he had made "an awfully naive mistake" with his first book, *Uncle Tom's Children,* "which even bankers' daughters could weep over and feel good about. I swore to myself that if I ever wrote another book, no one would weep over it; that it would be so hard and deep that they would have to face it without the consolation of tears." It was. But what a pity for today's young that Bigger's life was not seen as a warning instead of the icon it has since become; what a pity for those who are offered a bullet when a book is infinitely more powerful as a weapon against the pain.

Thursday, March 7, 1940, Mississippi, U.S.A.

Literature   **Voice**

MARCH 8

If necessity is the mother of invention, what necessities did these mothers of invention confront? On March 8, International Women's Day, we salute "Mothers of Invention"—women and their industrial creativity.

In order truly to acknowledge women as inventors, we must first understand the magnitude of their suppression. While slavery and racial politics swindled all African-Americans out of their rightful claims to their inventions, women dealt with the added burden of sexual politics. There is little doubt that a good number of the patents due women have been subsumed under the names of men well into the twentieth century. In addition, with the number of inventors who have patented their work using their first initials rather than their full names, one can only speculate at the number of women who have concealed their sexual identity in order to stake a claim to their work. By listing the following four women and their inventions, we also honor those women who have been denied the right to their claims:

Miriam E. Benjamin—Patent number 386,286 for a gong-and-signal chair in 1888. Her design was adapted by the U.S. House of Representatives so that members of Congress could call their pages while in session.

Sarah Boone—Patent number 473,653 for the ironing board in 1892. Before her invention with its padded cover and collapsible legs, wooden boards were stretched across the backs of two chairs to make an ironing table.

Sarah Goode—Patent number 322,177 for the folding cabinet bed in 1885. Her invention provided the original concept for the hideaway bed.

Sarah Breedlove Walker, also known as Madame C. J. Walker—Patent number unknown. Her hot straightening comb and conditioning compound made her African-America's first self-made woman millionaire.

Friday, March 8, 1996, U.S.A.

Invention   **Experience**

MARCH 9

If one were to open a nine-hundred-year-old African time capsule, the pictures would reveal an ancient Ghanaian glory so magnificent that there is little doubt why Europeans later referred to this nation as the "Gold Coast." As the main supplier of gold for northern Africa and Europe, Ghana flourished as the height of civilization between A.D. 800 and 1100. Caravans arrived daily bearing treasures for trade and commerce, while rulers maintained elaborate palaces from which they negotiated the affairs of state.

In 1067, an Arab geographer, Al-Bakri, watched and recorded as Tenkamenin, the Ghanaian king, held audience with his people. In Al-Bakri's vivid accounts of Tenkamenin's palace, he writes of a gold nugget so large that the king's horse could be hitched to it. "When he gives audience to his people . . . to listen to their complaints, he sits in a pavilion around which stand his horses caparisoned in cloth of gold; behind him stand ten pages holding shields and gold-mounted swords; and on his right hand are the sons of the princes of his empire, splendidly clad and with gold plaited into their hair. The governor of the city is seated on the ground in front of the king, and all around him are his viziers in the same position. The gate of the chamber is guarded by dogs of an excellent breed, who never leave the king's seat, they wear collars of gold and silver."

The key to ancient Ghana's amazing wealth was control of its own resources with a thriving land-based economy strong in agriculture, in the manufacture of products derived from its mineral wealth, in goldsmithing, and in international trade. Europe did not "bring civilization" to Africa; rather, it sought to dominate and profit from Africans' existing success. When a question is raised on the ability of Africans to govern ourselves, let us first consider the source and the interests motivating the question.

A.D. 1067, Ghana

Government   **Tradition**

MARCH 10

What made the groundbreaking Black action film, *Sweet Sweetback's Baadasssss Song,* so baaad was Melvin Van Peebles's skill as a businessperson. On March 10, 1971, he had so carefully planned and executed his production strategy that he was able to pay off his first financial backers three weeks before the film's opening and widen the crack in the door through which later Black films would gain Hollywood access. From script development through shooting, editing, first print, soundtrack, distribution, and bouts with the Hollywood ratings board, the early triumph of *Sweet Sweetback* was a sweet victory.

Not since the days of pioneer filmmaker Oscar Micheaux in the 1930s had a Black filmmaker achieved success in independent film—and none had yet been welcomed in Hollywood. Produced on the upswing of the 1960s resurgence in Black filmmaking, *Sweetback* was unique in targeting a predominantly African-American audience. In fact, Van Peebles's early payback of investors helped to secure new sources of confidence in and funding for Black film—the Deltas (see January 13), for example, invested in Ossie Davis's *Kongi's Harvest.*

Van Peebles's ongoing achievements as a businessman in film and theater is a valuable reminder to us all as concern grows over today's escalation of negative images of Blacks in the national media. The freedom to disseminate our own images throughout the African diaspora can only be gained by financing our own projects from production through promotion and distribution. As the industry will attest, entrepreneurial skill is the first, foremost, and most persistent hurdle on the way to filmmaking success.

Artists like Van Peebles may model the skill of paying back the investment community. But financially securing a Black film industry is the job of the Black community. Only then can we ensure that "out of vogue" on the Hollywood scene does not mean "out of business" for Black film.

Wednesday, March 10, 1971, California, U.S.A.

Film   **Mutual Responsibility**

MARCH 11

However the story of March 11, 1959, is written — from the vantage point of what preceded it or the vision it inspired — the date marks a milestone in American theater history. On that day, Lorraine Hansberry's *A Raisin in the Sun* opened on Broadway. The play's title came from a Langston Hughes poem. "What happens to a dream deferred? Does it dry up like a raisin in the sun?" he asked. "Maybe it sags like a heavy load. Or does it explode?" And when the curtain rose, the first Broadway play by a Black woman playwright did indeed explode myths about the theater, success, and the family.

In almost forty years of theater history, only a dozen Black dramas had preceded *Raisin* on the "Great White Way," as Broadway is aptly named for its lights — and too often, its racial perspective. Mythmakers said Black plays were "box-office poison," and the number of producers willing to take on this added risk in an already speculative and superstitious industry was kept low. Belying such fears, *Raisin* became Broadway's longest-running drama by an African-American playwright to feature an African-American cast. The play has been admired for the quality of its dramatic writing, and to this day, drama schools use it as the epitome of the "well-made play" for its structure, plot, characters, and dramatic realization.

As a Black family drama on Broadway, *A Raisin in the Sun* broke new ground with its portrayal of an intact, multigenerational, working-class family with its own problems and loves. The characters breathed deep lives of their own, regardless of racism. Poverty shaped their immediate reality; it didn't restrict their image of who they were or what they wanted to be.

Most important for its Black audience, *A Raisin in the Sun* did what good dramas should do. It held up an aspect of our lives for our scrutiny, and we found that the reflected image shone brightly before our eyes.

Wednesday, March 11, 1959, New York, U.S.A.

Theater   **Legacies**

MARCH 12

On March 12, 1790, a satirical article appeared in the *Federal Gazette* using the often-heard rationalizations of slave owners to justify the enslavement of whites. Written under the pseudonym "Historicus," the article was clearly no laughing matter—especially when the author's real identity was revealed. Historicus was, in fact, the internationally revered publisher, philosopher, scientist, and cosigner of the Declaration of Independence, Benjamin Franklin.

Historicus's article was a retelling of the century-old Quaker "Germantown Protest," which had concluded that slavery was violence. As a Quaker, Franklin was well aware of the antiviolence and antislavery roots of his faith. He had violated them both. As a Founding Father, he had encouraged the Revolutionary War. But although his days as a slave owner were over and he had promised to oppose slavery firmly as inconsistent with the goals of freedom, he broke this promise when he signed the Declaration of Independence, sacrificing the freedom of Africans in the pursuit of his own.

Franklin worked hard to rectify this wrong. In 1775, he cofounded the nation's first antislavery society. In 1785, he became president of the Pennsylvania Society for Promoting the Abolition of Slavery and the Relief of Free Negroes Unlawfully Held in Bondage. And as if tying up loose ends, as an eighty-four-year-old in his last two months of life, not only did he publish Historicus's article but he also joined with the Quakers in petitioning Congress to end slavery. In his will, he bequeathed funds to establish a school for Blacks that he named for his friend, the African-American educator Anthony Benezet.

As the old folks used to say, what is in the root is in the branches. Franklin's Quaker roots eventually bore fruit for years to come.

Friday, March 12, 1790, Pennsylvania, U.S.A.

Humor   **Brotherhood**

MARCH 13

"Yet do I marvel at this curious thing," wrote Countee Cullen, "to make a poet black, and bid him sing." The poet could well have been writing of another young poet who would follow him to prominence, Sonia Sanchez. Anyone who has ever read one of her two dozen books knows how tragic a loss it would have been for us all had she never been bidden to sing. But anyone blessed to hear Sonia Sanchez "sing" knows how amazing it is that a voice of such power and range had first to struggle its way free of crippling stutters. As a teenage high school poet living in Harlem in the spring of 1948, as she later told the *Philadelphia Daily News,* she unlocked her voice in this way:

> I'm not so sure you cure a thing as much as it becomes cured. I remember having to give a talk in class and . . . I said to myself, "Maybe I can control this via pain." Maybe this sounds peculiar, but I stuck my fingernails into the palms of my hands as I talked, and at the onset of the slightest stutter that I felt emanating from any place in my body, I'd dig my nails into my hand a little bit more. When I finished my speech, I was really bleeding. But from that point on, I never, never stuttered again. The fascinating thing, though, is that I still heard stutters in my mind. And it took me years to feel good about talking out loud and not hearing those stutters inside my head. One day, I woke up and they were finally gone.

We never know what inhibits a child. Sanchez was raised by a loving father, but one sure inhibitor was the loss of her mother, who died in childbirth when Sonia was a year old. For today's young voices struggling to free themselves from a myriad of obstacles, Sonia Sanchez reminds us, "Many [people] assume the very quiet student is very dull, or not bright, which is a big lie. People never know why you don't speak out in class. It's really tragic."

Spring, 1950, New York, U.S.A.

Philosophy   **Beliefs**

MARCH 14

On March 14, 1794, Eli Whitney was awarded a patent for his invention, the cotton gin. As historians have noted, this one invention so revolutionized agribusiness that it turned southern fields "white with cotton, and dark with slaves." With the cotton gin's ability to do the work of fifty slaves, it reduced the price of cotton and increased demand for it worldwide. It lessened the need for labor in processing but increased the demand for slaves to clear larger tracts of land and plant and sow larger fields of cotton.

By 1855, cotton accounted for half of the nation's exports. By 1865, it was up to two-thirds. As historian William Loren Katz has commented, "masters and overseers treated both slave and land as something to be 'worn out, not improved.' The life span of the field slave fell as cotton production rose." As demand grew, no obstacle was too great to stop the insatiable appetite for cotton and its profits in states north and south. What the South sowed, the North milled. What the South needed industrially, the North supplied—including a blind eye toward the cost of cotton in African lives and indigenous American lands. And what the North lost in revenue at the end of the slave trade, it picked up manufacturing the whips, guns, ropes, chains, and other instruments of torture needed to keep slavery going and growing.

On this day marked by invention, we could find inspiration in the courage of those who escaped to freedom. Instead, today we honor the inventive souls left behind as slaves and later as sharecroppers. We honor those who worked the fields, designed the ball gowns, built the mansions, wove the baskets and textiles, and worked the iron, all without credit or compensation. We honor those who made the music, refashioned the banjos, replaced the drums, retold the tales, and found new ways to laugh—life's greatest invention, by far.

Friday, March 14, 1794, Georgia, U.S.A.

Invention   **Transcendence**

MARCH 15

On March 15, 1933, the NAACP launched its first coordinated attack to end segregation via court challenges to "separate but equal" public education.

Charles Houston (see October 26), the NAACP's special counsel to its Legal Defense Fund (LDF), conceived the plan. His strategy was this: to go for what he called the "soft underbelly of Jim Crow"—segregated graduate and professional school public education, where the "separate but equal" codes denied Blacks access to advanced degrees such as those required for law and medicine. Under the "Houston Plan," wherever Black students were excluded from tax-supported state colleges and universities, the LDF would institute suit after suit until it bankrupted the system of legal segregation.

Under Jim Crow laws, states legally had to provide two "separate but equal" schools, but these schools were hardly "equal" and certainly did not exist at the graduate level. Houston concluded that the issue was twofold—finding a student willing to risk the intimidation and personal safety; and pushing the state to provide two graduate institutions for every field or admit Blacks to the one existing institution. As a test case, Houston chose Thomas Hocutt, a graduate of Amherst College. Hocutt was clearly qualified to continue his studies at the University of North Carolina's School of Pharmacy. But in order to comply with the "separate but equal" Jim Crow law, North Carolina would have to create a new college of pharmacy for one Black student.

As perfect as the Hocutt case seemed, it was rejected on a legal technicality. But within a year the LDF had launched a series of cases that led to the Supreme Court's landmark *Brown v. Board of Education* (see May 17) decision outlawing discrimination in public education at all levels, as the Court mandated, "with all deliberate speed."

Wednesday, March 15, 1933, North Carolina, U.S.A.

Law   **Creative Thinking**

MARCH 16

"We wish to plead our own cause," wrote the editors in the premier issue of the first Black-owned newspaper, *Freedom's Journal.* On March 16, 1827, Samuel Cornish (a minister) and John B. Russwurm (the first Black man to earn a master's degree) founded African-American journalism.

Freedom's Journal heralded a new self-assertiveness and self-affirmation among Blacks. Founded in New York City four months before slavery was abolished in the state, it was a consciousness-raiser for Blacks, publishing the names of Black spies who betrayed their own people for the proslavery cause. For this and other reasons the newspaper's very existence was seen as subversive by some whites. Citing those "who make it their business to enlarge upon the least trifle . . . to the discredit of any person of colour," the journal was an alternative to slanderous attacks in the white press.

Targeting "five hundred thousand free persons of colour, one half of whom might peruse, and the whole be benefitted by the publication of the Journal," the publishers engaged agents in Canada, England, Haiti, and the United States. The journal's mandate was to be both a voice and a chronicle for free Blacks. "We form a spoke in the human wheel, and it is necessary that we should understand our pendence on the different parts, and theirs on us . . . to perform our part with propriety," the editors wrote. Outlining their goals, they cited economic news as essential to their readers' financial independence. Also included would be book reviews of educational materials, freelance articles solicited to encourage the development of new writers, and an exchange of letters to the editor. To meet the unique needs of their community, the editors vowed "to vindicate our [free] brethren, when oppressed," and "not be unmindful of our brethren who are still in the iron fetters of bondage."

With that, the founders of African-American journalism wrote a mission statement for the Black press that is widely applauded—and needed—to this day.

Friday, March 16, 1827, New York, U.S.A.

Journalism   **Foundations**

MARCH 17

Being hot is nothing new to a South Carolina peach farmer—unless you're a fifty-five-year-old debut author with a book that's setting folks abuzz. And on March 17, 1990, that was the delightful predicament in which Dori Sanders found herself as rave reviews poured in for her debut novel *Clover*—not to mention for the lady herself.

Some people had only to skim the velvet texture of her lines to feel enchanted. Others were captivated by the unabashed joy she expressed in television interviews. Few would forget the wonderful jacket photo of Sanders with "that hat," laughing ever so fine. Others were harder to charm until the words and story swept them up in the whoosh of wisdom coming from Sanders's ten-year-old heroine. Sanders was new, different, and just a bit eccentric. She made people smile over luscious memories of wildflowers, stories of selling peaches roadside and of coaxing life's best plans her way. Her pride in father and family stood out amid a rarely dramatized African-American rural middle-class landscape. Hers was a soft, loving, poignant, yet incisive view of Black life—a view that rarely reaches the page.

At Sanders's core was a strength as vital as rain. For years, writing sketches had been her hobby. Somewhere around 1985, she decided to link the stories into a novel and forward them to a publisher. The manuscript was rejected. But book editor Louis Rubin was so impressed with her writing that he wrote her a letter stating the reason for his rejection and making concrete suggestions for improving her work.

For all those who have known the pain of being unknown and snubbed, told they would never be published, that their first novel was hopeless, that few if any readers would identify with a story they wanted and needed to tell, or that they were too old to pursue their dream, Dori Sanders is a hero.

Saturday, March 17, 1990, South Carolina, U.S.A.

Literature   **Family**

MARCH 18

For the Ibos of Nigeria, New Year's Day, Onwa Izizi, comes not on January 1 but just before the vernal equinox. It is the day of the Ibu Afo Festival and marks the start of the spring rains and the planting season.

It must be wonderful for children to know that Ibu Afo is one time when they can make as much noise as they like. And for good reason: this is the day to chase the old year's grief away. Early in the day, people break into a cacophony of strange noises, filling the air with the sounds of the old-year griefs taking their symbolic flight. At the appointed time, they go home and shut their doors on grief. And as they do so, they make as much noise as they can. But one must be at home, or inside, at this time. If caught outside, grief might take you up in its swirl as it flies off with the old year. Then as the sounds wane and grief is spent, it is time for the celebration of a new year of hope and happiness.

Adding the perspective of others to our own heightens life's options. Whatever the time of year, there is always a new (and better) day to come if we take the time to welcome it. Sharing the Ibu Afo Festival with our Ibo cousins today, we, too, can take this moment to renew ourselves and start a new year with new thoughts, unburdened by the past. On this day we can find special pleasure in the duality of our lives as Africans and Americans. How wonderful it is to know that the traditional ways are there for us to rediscover, even in the face of new rites and rituals.

Friday, March 18, 1996, Nigeria

Celebrations   **Perspective**

MARCH 19

An incident that happened in 1911, when Adam Clayton Powell, Jr., was only three, not only provided the lesson of a lifetime for him but also a legacy of political and social achievement that still serves us a quarter century after his death. In his autobiography, *Adam by Adam,* he tells this story:

> "Adam, where art thou?" With this cry as ancient as man himself, my father would humorously call me all through the earliest years of my life. "Adam, where art thou?" The door opened and into the room he came . . . and then a deep laugh came from his groin. He reached down, pried the bars apart, picked me up and said, "Never let anyone keep you contained and never let anyone keep your voice silent." This is my earliest recollection in life. My head had been caught in the iron crib as I pushed it through the bars trying to find out what was on the other side of the world.

Elected in 1944 as Harlem's freshman member of Congress and the Northeast's first Black congressman, Powell took his father's counsel quite seriously. One day he looked up and saw the House press gallery in a way he'd never noticed it before: it was totally white. "Where are the reporters of the Negro press—the daily papers from Atlanta, the weeklies from Chicago, the magazines—where are they?" he remembered thinking. Under the pretense of reserving space for daily newspapers, the press had segregated the gallery with a rule that barred the mostly weekly Black press reporters while providing loopholes to admit whites who worked for weeklies.

Powell took the challenge to the Speaker of the House. He had been elected by the same process that elects every representative. His district and the extended community had as much right as any to know what Congress and its congressman were doing. He was right. On March 19, 1947, the *Afro-American*'s Louis Lautier became the first Black reporter to cover Congress from within its chamber.

Wednesday, March 19, 1947, Washington, D.C.–New York, U.S.A.

Government/Journalism   **Possibility**

MARCH 20

Rarely, if ever, has a book had the impact of Harriet Beecher Stowe's *Uncle Tom's Cabin*, published on March 20, 1852. At first, the odds against its success seemed great, as a Boston congressman and friend told her, "being as it is on an unpopular subject—and by a woman at that!" Stowe accepted just $300 to have it published as a newspaper serial, but there it began to build an audience. Her book sold out its first five-thousand-copy printing in forty-eight hours and became one of the highest-grossing books in publishing history, a record it held well into the twentieth century.

Six months after its publication in book form, it was adapted for the stage and was performed continually worldwide from 1853 through 1930. Proslavery forces despised it, banning it wherever they could. Reams of hate mail were sent, including one package that contained a Black human ear. Despite its detractors, by 1860 the book had been reprinted in thirty British editions and translated into twenty-five languages. Stereotypically sentimental statuettes called "Tomitudes" were a hit worldwide. A duchess sent Stowe a solid gold bracelet cast as a slave shackle. A petition in Stowe's honor was signed by 562,000 British women. Queen Victoria sent praise. And President Lincoln greeted the diminutive Mrs. Stowe at the White House with, "So this is the little lady who wrote the book that made this great war!"

Uncle Tom's Cabin was not a great novel, but it was a powerful book. It was the first American novel to portray Blacks as characters, not jokes or stereotypes. Stowe had brought authenticity to the scenes of slave children being ripped from their mothers by recalling her own feelings on the deaths of her young children. Not only did the book launch a war and is still listed as recommended reading in schools everywhere, but Stowe's version of slavery remains one of the most widely read and influential of views.

Saturday, March 20, 1852, Ohio–Connecticut, U.S.A.

Business   **Values**

MARCH 21

On March 21, 1960, one of the most tragic and unifying events in modern history took place in Sharpeville, South Africa.

The issue was the "pass law," a long-standing point of contention requiring nonwhites to produce on demand a passbook designed to control one's whereabouts. A violation of the law—such as leaving the book at home—was punishable by fine, imprisonment, banishment, or forced labor. A nonviolent protest of the pass law was planned for this March day.

An unarmed crowd in excess of ten thousand peacefully gathered at the local police station without their passbooks to protest the law and present themselves for mass arrest. At 1:40 P.M., as they awaited announcement of a change in the law, the police stormed them, firing over seven hundred shots directly into the unarmed crowd of men, women, and children. When it was over, 69 people had been killed and 180 wounded in the infamous Sharpeville Massacre.

The massacre had incontrovertibly demonstrated the barbarism of which South Africa's white minority government was capable and the extent to which other nations were willing to accept that brutality in the name of respecting another country's "internal, domestic affairs." From the flames of this tragedy rose the quest throughout the African continent and diaspora for what the Kenyans called *Uhuru Sasa:* "Freedom Now!" There was no turning back. By year's end, eleven African states would be resurrected as independent modern-day nations—Zaire, Somalia, Dahomey, Upper Volta, Ivory Coast, Chad, Congo, Gabon, Senegal, Mali, and Nigeria—and in the United States, the civil rights movement renewed its sit-ins, boycotts, and other protests north and south with seasoned eyes and newly committed masses.

Monday, March 21, 1960, Union of South Africa
Pan-African World   **Sacrifice**

MARCH 22

Working in Rome in the spring of 1869, Edmonia Lewis carved an image of herself in stone. Ever since she'd heard the biblical story of Hagar, the Egyptian maiden, Lewis had identified with her story. Like Hagar, she had performed well in every challenge presented her, and she, too, had been driven away, forced to wander alone in the wilderness. She, too, had suffered the pain of being wrongfully accused and abused. That and her extraordinary talent took her to Rome, where she began to make her way as an artist.

As a sculptor and African-America's first great woman artist, Lewis struggled to surmount the prevailing biases against everything she was by birth and nature. She was a woman in the male-dominated art world. She was born of African-American and Chippewa parents. Orphaned at nine, she was "different" from the other young women of her day, with a manner that was born of isolation. A racial incident that took place when she was in college at Oberlin had led to a brutal beating, after which she'd been left for dead. Emotionally and fundamentally, Edmonia Lewis was alone.

In the winter of 1868, she had begun her sculpture of Hagar. Emboldened by her evolving spiritual growth, she returned to the United States with the finished sculpture, *Hagar in Her Despair in the Wilderness*. With her connections among the network of people previously active in the abolitionist movement, in particular one very successful African-American businessman, she eventually earned more for *Hagar* than any other single piece before *Hagar*: $6,000.

During her lifetime, her struggle was so great that all record of her later life has been lost. Yet she left her mark with her art, now in museums and library art collections worldwide, achieving recognition a century later through the Black and women's liberation movements of the 1960s.

Monday, March 22, 1869, U.S.A.–Italy

Art   **Courage**

MARCH 23

In late March 1834, 150 young black men—most of whom were under twenty—gathered at a New York City public school to launch their antislavery youth movement, "The Garrison Literary and Benevolent Association." But when an official found that their organization had been named in honor of the noted abolitionist William Lloyd Garrison, they were told to change their name or leave the school's free facilities. Keeping the name, they rented space elsewhere.

So moved was Garrison that their constitution's preamble was published in the April 19, 1834, issue of his newspaper, *The Liberator:* "If acting conformably to the will of our Creator,—if promoting the welfare of our fellow creatures around us,—and if securing our own happiness, are objects of the highest moment . . . we think it our duty to begin, in early life, to assist each other to alleviate the afflicted. . . . And whereas faithful philanthropists have engaged in our cause, . . . we think it would encourage them with persevering energy to vindicate our cause, to see the youth of color distinguish themselves by their good conduct and intellectual attainments."

These youths demonstrated a level of integrity and sophistication that foretold the type of men they were to become. Heading the group were a very young William H. Day, Henry Highland Garnet, and David Ruggles—three luminaries in the making. Day, age ten, would later become Oberlin College's only Black graduate in the class of 1847 and distinguish himself shortly after graduation as founder of the movement to repeal Ohio's "Black Laws." Garnet, nineteen, would later become a clergyman and ambassador to Liberia and was among the first to address the link between slavery and political and economic exploitation. And Ruggles, twenty-four (see September 24), would excel in business and as an abolitionist newspaper editor.

Sunday, March 23, 1834, New York, U.S.A.

Children   **Conscience**

MARCH 24

On March 24, 1924, Harry Pace's dream of operating his own record company may have seemed a failure, but Black Swan Records had succeeded in launching the African-American music recording industry, which continues to power the music business to this day.

In 1921, Harry Pace founded Black Swan Records, a company named in honor of the "Black Swan," America's first Black classical concert singer, Elizabeth Taylor-Greenfield. Pace's venture was also a first, the first Black-owned recording company. As a former partner of the "Father of the Blues," W. C. Handy, Pace capitalized on his experience as a music publisher with Handy to launch a diversified company. Pace Phonograph Corporation manufactured the records. The Black Swan record label produced and distributed them.

"LOOK—At the finish of this Record . . . made by experienced craftsmen, Masters in the art of making records. . . . The only records made entirely by colored people," Pace's record jackets exclaimed. "LISTEN—To the tone quality of this Record. . . . The only records using exclusively Negro voices."

Black Swan only survived three years before white-owned companies spied a viable new market in Black music and overwhelmed Pace with their competition. On March 24, 1924, Pace pragmatically sold Black Swan to Paramount Records. But because of the short-term success of Black Swan, white companies began to recognize that Black performers had their own audiences and that Blacks could be a major self-sustaining market. Following Pace's lead, companies built their inventory of "race music," as Black music was then called. Because of the need to target marketing campaigns to Black communities, advertising dollars were invested in Black-owned newspapers. And the trails blazed by Black Swan eventually opened the way for the megasuccess of Motown Records in 1959 (see December 29).

Monday, March 24, 1924, New York, U.S.A.

Business   **Music**

MARCH 25

On March 21, 1965, what had begun weeks before as a routine voter registration drive by Dr. Martin Luther King, Jr., in Selma, Alabama, became the historic five-day Selma-to-Montgomery March, one of the most significant events of America's civil rights era. With the eyes of the world focused on the treatment of its newest Nobel Peace Prize laureate, Dr. King, Alabama proved that its race hatred and violence were no respecter of persons.

Into those three gruesome weeks in March poured the legacy of hundreds of violent years. In Selma on March 7, Alabama state troopers and sheriff's deputies attacked civil rights marchers, beating them and then spraying them with tear gas. Also on March 7, three white ministers identified as "nigger lovers" for their support of human rights were attacked on the streets of Selma and beaten so brutally that one, the Reverend James Reeb, died as a result of his wounds. Around the nation, people outraged by these tragedies headed to Alabama, bringing the force of their numbers and their bodies to bear on the nation's shame. On March 21, thousands of demonstrators, led by Dr. King, completed the first leg of his planned march from Selma to Montgomery. Under the protection of the federalized Alabama National Guard and U.S. Army troops, the march continued for four days until it arrived in Montgomery—a ribbon of strength twenty-five thousand people long.

On March 25, the five-day, fifty-mile crusade by foot soldiers of all possible descriptions ended with a mass rally on the state capitol steps in Montgomery. It was the last great march of the civil rights era. President Johnson's civil rights legislation began to be passed by Congress, and by August, the voting rights bill had been signed into law—a bill that was renewed in 1990 only over stiff political opposition and through a major coalition campaign for support.

Thursday, March 25, 1965, Alabama, U.S.A.

Civil Rights   **Endurance**

MARCH 26

The most significant thing about the milestone event that took place on this day is how little is really known about it and how poorly news of it was preserved. But photo documentation does confirm that on March 26, 1964, Martin Luther King, Jr., and Malcolm X had what is thought to be their only face-to-face meeting. For years they played their roles as distant good-cop/bad-cop foils for each other, with King as the saint and Malcolm as the sinner. But their well-honed public personae fooled neither Blacks nor the FBI.

Blacks recognized that both men were on the same team. Martin spoke of integration. Malcolm spoke of liberation. Both had committed their every moment to ending oppression and building Black self-empowerment. Both knew—and Blacks feared equally for them—that they would each very likely pay installments on the price of African-American freedom by sacrificing their lives.

FBI chief J. Edgar Hoover was also convinced that both men were on the same team—a team that threatened white supremacy, a team that he knew all Blacks would join given the slightest opportunity. In Hoover's lexicon—and that of those who kept him in a position of power—all Blacks were threats. As documents released under the Freedom of Information Act would later confirm (see April 11), the Justice Department and Hoover had a good-cop/bad-cop scheme of their own. While the Justice Department officially operated to protect civil rights demonstrators, Hoover (a Justice Department employee as FBI chief) officially persecuted King, Malcolm, and the entire movement.

In the photo taken on March 26, 1964, both Dr. King and Malcolm X are smiling, cordially shaking hands. This picture may have sounded the death knell for both. Certainly it is a testament to each man's courage and conscience despite the pressures he endured. With this photo they declared themselves free men—free to honor themselves, each other, and us.

Thursday, March 26, 1964, New York, U.S.A.

Heroes   **Leadership/Purpose**

MARCH 27

In 1904, the American Academy of Arts and Letters was founded by the National Institute of Arts and Letters to honor the nation's most distinguished artists. At any given time, their number was never to exceed fifty, and new members were only inducted to fill the vacancy left by a deceased member. By 1969, no African-Americans had ever been inducted.

On March 27, 1969, a similarly distinguished group, in recognition of the academy's lack of candor and credibility about the achievements of African-American artists, founded the Black Academy of Arts and Letters. Among the founders were artists and scholars ranging from symphonic conductor Henry Lewis to sociologist Dr. C. Eric Lincoln. Under their learned tutelage, the Black Academy of Arts and Letters was formed to honor distinguished African-American artists, to nurture young talent, and to acknowledge scholarly excellence in the preservation and protection of Black culture.

In 1975, the National Academy of Artists and Letters honored its first African-American, author Ralph Ellison, whose singular novel, *Invisible Man,* truly elevated him to the stature of a dean among modern novelists. Ellison's accession to the academy was followed by the induction of artist Jacob Lawrence in 1983. Lawrence had come to prominence during the Depression with his *Migration Series* and World War II chronicles of Black military life.

During this same period—from 1970 when its first honors were awarded through 1983—the Black Academy of Arts and Letters recognized a few hundred notable African-Americans too long ignored—a role it continues to fill to this day.

Thursday, March 27, 1969, California–Massachusetts, U.S.A.
Arts/Culture   **Self-Determination**

MARCH 28

Dedicated to the thousands of slaves whose suffering and labor built Barbados as an island nation, the statue *Emancipation* was unveiled on March 28, 1985. It was erected by the government and the people of Barbados to commemorate the 150th anniversary of the abolition of slavery throughout the Caribbean and the emancipation of Barbadians.

A passionate sculpture, *Emancipation* was the work of the island's master artist, Karl Broodhagen, African-Caribbean painter, sculptor, and teacher of international acclaim. Dedicated to and inspired by legions of unknown slaves, the statue quickly came to be known and loved by its nickname "Bussa," for the leader of Barbados's most famous uprising in 1816. It is the defiant spirit of a people that the statue captures in its towering bronze slave, from whose shackled wrists the broken chains of slavery still hang.

Symbolizing pride in both the nation's formal achievements and its humble roots, two inscriptions appear on its marble base. On one side is a poem by the esteemed poet K. Braithwaite: "Let my children rise in the path of the morning / Up and go forth on the road of the morning / Run through the field in the sun of the morning / See the rainbow of heaven; God's curved mourning calling."

On the other side is etched the heart of a slavery-era folk song: "De ting come from England / To set we free / Now lick and lock-up done wid / Hurrah fuh jin-jin!"

And hurrah for Karl Broodhagen's powerful work, about which art historian David Gill has written, "[In art] what was, and is still desperately needed, was a reevaluation of our humanity, in fact, a return to humanity and a perception of the innate dignity and divinity of humanity. Broodi did precisely that. He returned to us our dignity as human beings."

Thursday, March 28, 1985, Barbados

Art
Respect for One's Power

MARCH 29

On March 29, 1539, Estavanico, an African explorer with Spain's conquistadors, led an expedition of three hundred in the Spanish quest for the Seven Cities of Gold of Cibola.

In the early sixteenth century, Europe sent frequent expeditions to North and South America. With each of these expeditions came African explorers, seamen, scouts, and slaves. Among them the most famous was Estavanico of Azamov, Morocco, who left Spain for the Americas in 1527 with the Narvaez expedition, just thirty-five years after Columbus's voyage (see October 12). Estavanico had left Spain a Moorish slave, but after twelve years in the Americas, the sheer force of his personality placed him in a leading role in the explorations.

As the historian Monroe W. Work confirms in this eyewitness account from the history of the Zunis who still live in Arizona and New Mexico, "It is believed that a long time ago when the roofs lay over the walls of Kya-ki-me, when the smoke hung over the house-tops, and the ladder-rounds were still unbroken, then the Black Mexicans [the Narvaez exploration team] came from their abodes in Ever-lasting Summerland. . . . Then [came] one of the Black Mexicans, a large man with chili lips [thick, African lips that they assumed to be swollen from eating chili peppers]. . . .Then the rest ran away, chased by our grandfathers and went back towards their country in the land of Ever-lasting Summer."

Period documents by Europeans and indigenous Americans relate Estavanico's color and culture as factors of his success as an intermediary between the conquering whites and indigenous peoples. Estavanico, however, was not the first African in the Americas: an African pilot was part of Columbus's crew, the African mariner prince of Mali sailed to the Americas on a trade mission in 1311, and ancient South American sculptures with African facial features are seen as proof of a still earlier presence. Clearly Africans have been players in the American saga for nearly seven hundred years!

March 29, 1539, Arizona–New Mexico, U.S.A.

Exploration   **Worldliness**

MARCH 30

When we speak of voting rights, we usually think of the twentieth-century push to regain the ballot—a right first granted Black men nationwide with the passage of the Fifteenth Amendment to the Constitution on March 30, 1870.

Some states like Massachusetts had granted Black property holders the right to vote in local elections as early as 1783 (see February 10). But it was not until the end of the Civil War that even free Black men were granted the right to vote throughout the United States and not until 1922 that those same rights were extended to women. But from the period shortly after Reconstruction through the 1960s, Blacks regardless of sex continued to be barred in many states by statute, by custom, and by intimidation as generations of Blacks fought to renew their hard-won protection under the Constitution.

What the Fifteenth Amendment says is this: "The right of citizens of the United States to vote shall not be denied or abridged by the United States or by any State on account of race, color, or previous conditions of servitude. The Congress shall have power to enforce this article by appropriate legislation."

But what the amendment means in human terms was best exemplified on March 31, 1870, as the town of Perth Amboy, New Jersey, gathered to celebrate its passage. On that day, Thomas Mundy Peterson became the nation's first freedman to cast a vote. Two months later, Perth Amboy's citizens presented him a medal in a ceremony at which this commemorative poem was read:

> And so we meet to decorate
> By token on the Freedman's coat
> The man who was in any State
> The first to cast a Freedman's vote.

Today, Peterson's Perth Amboy medal is in the Xavier University archives in New Orleans, Louisiana.

Wednesday, March 30, 1870, Washington, D.C., U.S.A.
Government   **Respect for Use of Power**

MARCH 31

As wife of one president and mother to another, Abigail Adams could have spent her life behind the protective shield of privilege. Unlike those who masked their support of slavery under the cloak of "economic necessity" or "civilizing heathens," this parson's daughter acted as a woman of conscience. In a letter dated March 31, 1776, she chided her husband, John Adams, for turning a blind eye to slavery and women's rights, for being willing to deny others the liberty he held so dear for himself. She wrote to him of slavery:

> I have sometimes been ready to think that the passion for Liberty cannot be Eaquelly Strong in the Breasts of those who have been accustomed to deprive their fellow Creatures of theirs. Of this I am certain that it is not founded upon that generous and christian principal of doing to others as we would that others should do unto us.

She continued on the subject of the rights of women:

> Remember the Ladies, and be more generous and favourable to them than your ancestors. If perticuliar care and attention is not paid to the Ladies we are determined to foment a Rebellion, and will not hold ourselves bound by any Laws in which we have no . . . Representation. That your Sex are Naturally Tyrannical is a Truth so thoroughly established as to admit of no dispute, but such of you as wish to be happy willingly give up the harsh title of Master for the more tender and endearing one of Friend.

It is interesting to note that out of the most prolific writers of her day, Abigail Adams is unique in recognizing the twin evils of racism and sexism that haunted America's Founding Fathers — and founding principles. Not only was she instrumental in refining her husband's views but true to her teachings, her son John Quincy Adams, in 1839, successfully defended the right of the *Amistad* mutineers to resist enslavement (see August 24).

Sunday, March 31, 1776, Massachusetts, U.S.A.
Human Rights   Principles

APRIL

I got a robe

APRIL 1

On April 1, 1966, people of African birth and descent gathered in Dakar, Senegal, for the First World Festival of Negro Arts, which featured a scholarly dialogue on the arts of the diaspora. After more than three hundred years of slavery and colonial oppression, this was the first time Africans had come together under their own sky. Sponsored by the United Nations Educational, Scientific, and Cultural Organization (UNESCO), the event coincided with the emergence of Africa's first modern-day nations.

The lead speaker, Engelbert Mveng, set the stage for the ten-day colloquium: "Africa knows that you speak of her; but she finds it hard to hear even her name through the thick forest of strange vocables. Today, she turns toward you; she asks you: 'What are you saying about me?' She asks you: 'Show me my own face, analyzed by snapshots, by sketches, by pictures. Let me find myself in the mirror of your eyes; for how can I speak of my own beauty when I have never seen myself from a distance?'"

And they did, arriving for the homecoming bearing global riches. Katherine Dunham, the choreographer and anthropologist (see December 4), spoke of the performing arts; author Langston Hughes (see January 19) bore news of "Black Writers in a Troubled World"; and artist-educator James A. Porter (see February 7) surveyed the contemporary arts. Other contributions ranged from the funeral draperies of Dahomey, to two-thousand-year-old Iron Age artifacts from the Nok people, to Uganda's musical stringed harps—together accounting for five thousand years of written and oral tradition. Responding to Mveng's call, forty mirrors in all reflected Africa's lasting image in the diaspora.

Harris Memel-Foté, from the University of the Ivory Coast, summed up the event in words that were both an assessment and a call to action: "The African perception of beauty . . . is liberating, . . . an act of justice and equity. Justice rendered to African art has been useful to humanity."

Friday, April 1, 1966, Senegal

Arts   **Literature**

APRIL 2

In 1830, with the "offer" of Liberian emigration that was rejected by Blacks, whites had begun a campaign to force their exit. In some cases, outright terrorism was used: people would be dragged from their homes in the middle of the night and given thirty lashes until they agreed to emigrate. In other states like Ohio, "legal" remedies were applied, such as enforcing outdated laws that called for Blacks to register their residence and post a prohibitive bond of $500 to remain in the state. As thousands of Cincinnati Blacks prepared to comply with the expulsion order, a terrorist white mob rioted through the Black quarter of town to "help" the Blacks move out faster.

In Baltimore, on April 2, 1830, in response to the trauma and isolation felt by Blacks on a local level, Hezekiah Grice had a great idea—to hold the first annual National Convention of African-Americans. He sent letters to well-known Blacks in each of the free states, requesting their opinions on the need for and feasibility of his plan. Five months later he received a letter from Philadelphia's Bishop Richard Allen, cofounder of the AME Church (see November 26) and one of the greatest men of the day. Grice immediately set out from Baltimore to Philadelphia to meet with Allen. The bishop handed Grice a petition from New York in support of the convention. "My dear child," he told Grice, who was just twenty-nine at the time, "we must take some action immediately, or else these New Yorkers will get ahead of us!" And with that the national convention movement was born; the first of them would be held in Philadelphia on September 20, 1830.

Over the course of American history, it is easy to overlook these steps to our political maturity, easy to discount them because complete freedom is not yet ours. But even if our ideas and actions have yet to move mountains, they have certainly moved us as a people, uniting us to accomplish a shared agenda.

Friday, April 2, 1830, Pennsylvania, U.S.A.

Social History   **Foundations**

APRIL 3

In Memphis on the night of April 3, 1968, Dr. Martin Luther King, Jr., seemed oddly weary and preoccupied as he spoke in support of striking garbage workers and then said good-bye.

It is hard to believe how brief his tenure really was and how young he was when destiny called his name. He was twenty-seven years old and tackling his first pastoral assignment when Rosa Parks's refusal to take a backseat to racism fueled the Montgomery bus boycott of 1955 (see December 1, December 20). His skillful strategizing of the boycott helped to make him our leader over a rough stretch of the road to human rights. For twelve years with Dr. King, we stoked our hopes and put out our fears, redefining ourselves as African-Americans and helping to civilize our reluctant nation.

And so it was that he had now come to Memphis to support the sanitation workers. No one knows for sure how he knew that his end was near. When he rose that evening, Martin Luther King's voice set the room ablaze, speaking to us for posterity and for the last time. "Only when it is dark enough can you see the stars," he said. "I see God working in this period of the twentieth century in a way that men . . . are responding. The masses of people are rising up. And wherever they are assembled, . . . South Africa, Kenya, New York City, Atlanta, Memphis, the cry is always the same. 'We want to be free.' We don't have to live like we are forced to live." With that he stepped down, and within twenty-four hours he was assassinated on the balcony of the Lorraine Motel.

Dr. King was only thirty-nine when he was killed in the cause of freedom. Yet under the horrible conditions of those times—when Black people were regularly beaten, killed, and humiliated—carrying the torch of freedom may have been just what saved his life as long as it did. Because he carried that torch so well, because he loved life and people so much, he inspires us anew on this day.

Wednesday, April 3, 1968, Tennessee, U.S.A.

Speech/Oration   **Life's Work**

APRIL 4

In 1963, Blacks in Mississippi's Leflore County were 65 percent of the population but accounted for only 2 percent of all registered voters—the result of a century of systematic intimidation. Something had to be done. A century after the end of the Civil War and the passage of constitutional guarantees for the civil rights of former slaves, Southerners had devised ways to circumvent the law under the cloak of "states' rights." These were the days when African-Americans who registered to vote could lose their jobs and even their lives for exercising their God-given and constitutional rights. Brutal beatings, torture, murders, and bombings all took place under the steady eye and helpful hands of the "law" and the lawless. A century after slavery's end, Black people still had no rights that these whites felt bound to respect.

Against this backdrop, civil rights workers planned a voter registration drive for Greenwood, Mississippi, on April 2 and 3, 1963. For two days, press observers descended on the town to record the proceedings as supporters arrived en masse to drive, baby-sit, cook, and do whatever else was needed to ensure that the Black population was able to register. By April 4, wave upon wave of demonstrators had filled the jails to overcrowding. Among the demonstrators arrested was the world-renowned activist-comedian Dick Gregory, who later recounted the scene inside the jail: "I was brought downstairs and put in a cell built for twenty-five people. There must have been five hundred of us. There was a little boy, maybe four years old, standing in the corner of the cell sucking his thumb. I felt sorry for him. He didn't even have someone his age to play with. I kind of rubbed his head and asked him how he was. 'All right,' he said. 'What are you here for?' 'Teedom,' he said. Couldn't even say freedom, but he was in jail for it."

Gregory's words remind us of the kinship of that era; perhaps what made the movement so strong was the participation of people of all ages. Freedom was a family affair.

Thursday, April 4, 1963, Mississippi, U.S.A.

Social History   **Shared Bonds**

APRIL 5

Boston, Massachusetts: the site of so many historic American events—and contradictions. Here, the first colonial legislature legalized slavery in 1641. Here, a self-emancipated slave, Crispus Attucks (see March 5), sacrificed his life as the first Revolutionary War martyr in 1770. And here in 1976, the bicentennial celebration year, Theodore Landsmark became the victim of racist hatred and antibusing fever run riot.

A Yale Law School graduate with a degree in architecture, Landsmark represented Black construction firms seeking their fair share of city contracts. On April 5, 1976, while crossing Boston City Hall plaza en route to a meeting with the mayor, Landsmark was unaware of a demonstration brewing on the steps. Supporters of antibusing proponent Louise Day Hicks yelled, "Get the nigger! Kill him!" and lunged after him. Landsmark, a polio victim, couldn't run. He was grabbed from behind, his arms were pinned, and he was speared with the brass eagle atop the American flag to which the crowd had just pledged its allegiance. In a flash, a photo of the assault on Landsmark sparked shame and disgust in millions the world over—all except the district attorney and judge in the case. For the racist demonstrators who shattered a man's nose and all semblance of civility, there was little in the way of prosecution or punishment. Landsmark's attackers were charged with simple assault and sentenced to write a letter of apology.

Said Landsmark of the attack, "I mean I was just on my way to work. Nothing that bad had happened to me in my activist days in Selma [Alabama]." In court, Landsmark certainly lost the battle, but he went on to win the war, later becoming Boston's deputy mayor and a trustee of Boston's Museum of Fine Arts. The candid photo capturing this modern-day Boston Massacre later won a Pulitzer Prize for its photographer, Stanley Forman of the *Boston Herald American* newspaper.

Monday, April 5, 1976, Massachusetts, U.S.A.

Events   **Images**

APRIL 6

On April 6, 1909, Matthew Henson reached the North Pole with Admiral Robert Peary's expedition. It was a triumph that had taken eighteen years, seven Arctic trips, and one aborted attempt when dwindling food and hazardous weather had forced a retreat just 175 miles from their goal. Standing on top of the world at last, Henson said to an Inuit (Eskimo) colleague, "We have found what we hunt." Replied his colleague, "There is nothing here. Just ice." His words had an existential ring to them, but whether the Inuit man was alluding to physical or emotional ice, he did not say. There was little time to savor the victory or decode Peary's temperament. With the days getting longer, the danger of being stranded hundreds of miles from land by melting ice grew by the hour.

By protocol and by race, Peary, as head of the expedition, was the "discoverer" of the pole. But as Peary himself was among the first to admit, Henson's skills as an explorer were extraordinary. Still, Peary was not anxious to share credit. Henson was recognized with a congressional medal along with Peary's five white associates who had been unsuccessful in completing the trek. The four Inuits who finished the trek with Peary and Henson were not cited at all. With his expertise, Henson should have been celebrated in his own right, but Peary demanded Henson's promise that he would not lecture on the trip—a promise Henson kept until twelve years of total obscurity and poverty changed his mind. Fifty-two years passed before Henson was posthumously named codiscoverer of the North Pole with Peary. The truth was that Henson had charted the final route, arriving forty-five minutes before Peary did.

In a racially distorted world, it is easy to get caught up in racism's pecking order. The truth is, of course, that while Henson reached the pole before Peary, four Inuit men—Seegloo, Ootah, Ooqueah, and Egingwah—made both their victories possible.

Tuesday, April 6, 1909, North Pole

Adventure   **Fairness**

APRIL 7

In 1989, as Rockford, Illinois, faced state budget cutbacks, the school board cut costs by closing schools. Even though there were fewer schools in which Blacks were in the majority, Black school closings outnumbered closings of predominantly white ones two to one. Ed Wells, a businessman and longtime resident, decided to get involved. At first, he tried to reason with the board, asking it to reconsider its decision. When the board ignored him, he went to teachers and local leaders. When those people agreed with him but refused to get involved in an issue they thought "too political," he went to a local civil rights attorney. And when the attorney's request for an injunction to stop the closings and force a review was rejected, Wells filed a lawsuit against the schools designed to ensure equal access to education and equal treatment of minority students by the public school system. After a four-year wait, his suit went to trial on April 7, 1993.

The cost of filing suit had been high for Wells. As he told *USA Today*, "I had death threats. . . . I lost most of my friends, most of my landscape business, and developed health problems." But Wells's troublemaking case had greatly benefited the children. Because of the lawsuit, the school board reopened more Black neighborhood schools, improved staff development programs, and increased spending for salaries, books, and equipment.

Why would a man without children go to all this trouble? As a Rockford alumnus, Wells had been bused for integration. "I even had to pay to ride the bus," said Wells. He knew the inequities; he also knew that neighborhood kids needed an advocate. "You have to do more than just move kids around to improve education. . . .[Our goal should be to make minority schools] so good white parents would want their kids in those schools. We can't keep hoping someone else will do it," he said. "Eventually, you find the someone else has to be you."

Wednesday, April 7, 1993, Illinois, U.S.A.

Education   **Politics**

APRIL 8

At the close of the 1973 baseball season, the Atlanta Braves' Hank Aaron was within reach of surpassing all-time home-run great Babe Ruth's record of 714. His children were threatened with kidnapping. He received regular death threats. At parks across the country, he was kept under guard. Then the mail began to pour in from all over the country:

Dear Nigger:

You black animal, I hope you never live long enough to hit more home runs than the great Babe Ruth.

Dear Nigger Henry:

I will be going to the rest of your games and if you hit one more home run it will be your last. My gun will be watching your every black move.

Hank Aaron—
With all that fortune, and all that fame,
You're a stinkin nigger, just the same.

Through it all, Aaron stayed silent about the hate mail and kept hitting home runs. By the end of the 1973 season, he had tied Ruth's record. In Atlanta for the season opener on April 8, 1974, Hank Aaron hit home run number 715, breaking Babe Ruth's all-time major league baseball record. That season he hit numbers 716, 717, 718, 719. . . . Aaron was speaking out against his detractors by letting his unimpeachable record do all the talking—loud and clear.

Through all the terror and intimidation, Aaron never stopped swinging and slammin' 'em out of the park. In 1975, the NAACP awarded him their highest honor, the Spingarn Medal, for courage on and off the field. And when he retired from baseball in 1976, he had reached home run number 755.

Monday, April 8, 1974, Georgia, U.S.A.

Sports   **Courage/Concentration**

APRIL 9

In 1939, a routinely scheduled concert by a world-renowned contralto became an event of international significance. On April 9, 1939, Marian Anderson gave her legendary Easter Sunday concert on the steps of the Lincoln Memorial.

It began with Howard University's desire to host an Anderson concert, as it had done several times before. This time, however, her reputation had outgrown their on-campus hall. Constitution Hall was chosen as the ideal location. That it was owned by the Daughters of the American Revolution (DAR) was incidental. When the DAR spent weeks dodging the request, Anderson's management demanded a direct answer. The DAR obliged: a recital by the Negro singer would violate their policy of segregation. Anderson's manager, the noted impresario Sol Hurok, was outraged. Never one to avoid controversy, he joined Howard in launching a storm of protest and publicity that made headlines around the world. Through it all, Anderson was quiet, even as the press tracked her every move. The more reticent she was, the more inflamed the protest became. The DAR, globally embarrassed but only mildly repentant, offered to book Anderson if it was not seen as setting a precedent. Howard and Hurok rejected the terms, further escalating the debate. When First Lady Eleanor Roosevelt finally spoke out, she resigned her DAR membership; she did not want her membership to be mistaken for support of the DAR. With that, Hurok announced that Anderson would give an open-air concert. The Lincoln Memorial was secured immediately.

"I could see that my significance as an individual was small in this affair," Anderson later recalled. "I had become, whether I liked it or not, a symbol representing my people. I had to appear." The next day she sang to an audience of seventy-five thousand people assembled for the glory of music and of human dignity.

Sunday, April 9, 1939, Washington, D.C., U.S.A.

Music   **Human Rights**

APRIL 10

When the story is told of Jackie Robinson desegregating major league baseball in 1947, it is easy to forget, in the PR of racial politics, that Robinson's real contribution was as a person of principle. Joining the Brooklyn Dodgers on April 10, 1947, he had already achieved a solid public reputation.

Jackie Robinson was UCLA's first four-letter athlete in baseball, track, football, and basketball. He then made a name for himself in the Negro Leagues with the Kansas City Monarchs. While on the road with the Monarchs, he established the precedent of asking to use the rest rooms before buying gas—no access, no gas bought. As his wife, Rachel, said of her first impressions of him, "Jack walked straight. He held his head up and he was proud of not just his color, but his people." For these reasons, the painful compromise he agreed to as a condition for joining the Dodgers is all the more extraordinary—and understandable. It was this: if provoked, he could not fight back; he would have to be "better" than his foes. Team owner Branch Rickey warned him, "They'll taunt you and goad you. They'll do anything to make you react. They'll try to provoke a race riot in the ballpark. This is the way to prove to the public that a Negro should not be allowed in the major league. This is the way to frighten fans and make them afraid to attend the games."

Jack Robinson was an extraordinary man whom history had chosen to score points on the unlevel playing field of baseball. True to his later life in business and civil rights, he used his turn at bat in baseball to increase opportunities for people of color—regardless of the league in which we might choose to play.

Thursday, April 10, 1947, New York, U.S.A.

Sports   **Social History**

APRIL 11

Civil rights activists had long been aware of suspicious members more intent on subverting their organizations than on liberating African-Americans. From Dr. King's Southern Christian Leadership Conference (SCLC) to Elijah Muhammad's Nation of Islam, leaders cautioned against spies and advocates of violence. But the movement could not confirm that there had been an official government plot to destroy it completely until April 11, 1976, when documents acquired in response to a Freedom of Information Act suit began to circulate.

FBI documents revealed FBI chief J. Edgar Hoover's desire to prevent the rise of a "Black messiah." Letters in which associates in the movement defamed each other had been forged. Lies had flooded the press. Dr. King was sent a letter advising suicide: "You are done. There is but one way out for you. You better take it before your filthy fraudulent self is bared to the Nation." An anti-Semitic comic book published by the FBI was sent to Jewish leaders under a forged Black Panther imprint. Years of investigation into the murders of two Chicago Black Panthers confirmed FBI complicity. At the root was the Counter-Intelligence Program, "COINTELPRO"—the term used in an FBI letter dated August 25, 1967, for its campaign to "expose, disrupt, misdirect, discredit or otherwise neutralize the activities of black nationalists . . . and supporters."

In his essay "A Nation of Law?," Gerald Gill writes that FBI actions ostensibly meant "to preserve 'law and order' contributed to the growing loss of trust . . . in the honesty and efficacy of government." By the time it cited the leading advocate of the doctrine of nonviolence—Nobel Peace Prize laureate the Reverend Dr. Martin Luther King, Jr.—for a "propensity for violence," the FBI had lost all credibility and retained only its destructive power.

Sunday, April 11, 1976, Washington, D.C., U.S.A.

Government   **Human Rights**

APRIL 12

Historian Lerone Bennett has written, "The day was Thursday, April 12, 1787. On that day—one month before the first session of the Constitutional Convention and two years before the election of George Washington—eight men sat down in a room in Philadelphia and created a Black social compact. The compact, called the Free African Society, was a prophetic step that marked a turning in the road that is critical to the history of Black America."

Led by Richard Allen (see July 17, November 26) and Absalom Jones (see January 1, July 17, December 30), the Free African Society marked the first time that Blacks had united in a secular body to speak for their rights as free men and women—not solely as agitators for abolition and emancipation. At its root, the Free African Society was a sign of growing Black political sophistication, a model organization whose features would be replicated throughout the nation. Its pioneering insurance plan prophesied the founding of African-American insurance companies a century later. "For the benefit of each other," they agreed to "advance one shilling in silver, Pennsylvania currency, monthly," which they used to provide weekly allowances to members in need. A widow could inherit the benefits entitled to her deceased husband until she remarried. The society would pay for the education of a deceased member's children if no free school was available. For older children, society members would act as mentors to help them secure apprenticeships.

The founding of the Free African Society was a beacon to burgeoning movements in other northern cities—Boston (see May 6), New York, and Newport. Within months, each of those cities had started its own society, and these new groups maintained communication with the others, forming the first Black political and economic network for the betterment of free men and women.

Thursday, April 12, 1787, Pennsylvania, U.S.A.

Social History   **Freedom**

APRIL 13

On April 13, 1964, one month after his very public split with the Honorable Elijah Muhammad, Malcolm X left the United States on a pilgrimage to Mecca. For Malcolm, that holy journey was a spiritual awakening at the font of his religion and a pilgrimage to all he had become.

But Malcolm had no idea of his world stature until he left home. At the time, a letter of approval from the head of the Federation of Islamic Associations in the United States was required of all Americans traveling to Saudi Arabia. Dr. Shawarbi, an admirer of Malcolm, provided him with the required letter, along with the gift of a scholarly book on Islam by an advisor to King Faisal and the telephone number of the author's son in Saudi Arabia. Upon Malcolm's arrival abroad, he telephoned the son while on a layover. From that call, quite unexpectedly, the world opened up before him like the parting of the Red Sea. That call became an invitation to be the guest of King Faisal, and a welcome by leaders in Lebanon, Egypt, Nigeria, and Ghana. Malcolm was a leader completely unaware of the deep appreciation and respect for his work the world over.

With his pilgrimage, or hajj, to Mecca, Malcolm was fulfilling his vow to Islam—and his own potential. Born Malcolm Little (see June 8), he became a disillusioned street-slick known as "Detroit Red," went to prison, resurrected his life as Malcolm X, provided direction and hope for others, achieved national recognition, went to Mecca, discovered himself an international symbol, and returned home with a fuller realization of himself as El Hajj Malik El-Shabazz, his newly given Islamic name.

When we think of Malcolm X, we know the power of the mind to heal itself. By going outside the country—and outside of himself, so to speak—he saw himself at one with all the world's peoples. As a humble "student" of his faith, he found his truth as an African-American ambassador, a major player on a vast world stage..

Monday, April 13, 1964, U.S.A.–Saudi Arabia

Heroes   **Transformations**

APRIL 14

On April 14, 1834, one of the town founders of Oberlin, Ohio, John J. Shipherd, said, "Our Institute and colony are peculiar in that which is good." As a town founded on the principle of racial justice, Oberlin was indeed "peculiar," for those were the days when an escaped slave was guilty of the "theft" of himself as his master's property, and a "slave stealer" was anyone who aided that runaway "fugitive" slave.

A visit to Oberlin today reveals an antislavery heritage nearly 170 years old. It is said that the town's founders, Shipherd and Philo P. Stewart, dreamed of an exemplary utopian community. They found their ideal spot in Oberlin. When the town's Lane Seminary was going bankrupt, a donation from the devoutly abolitionist Tappan brothers, Lewis and Arthur, saved the school and created Oberlin College, America's first school with antidiscrimination clauses in its charter. A public sculpture in the town center depicts an immense railroad track leading underground. Hidden cellars and trapdoors preserved to this day document the trail of runaways. In the old days, a decoy wagon waited just outside the town to distract would-be captors while runaways were carried off to safe haven. The Oberlin-Wellington rescuers (see September 13) hailed from this area, and as people are proud to reveal, two rescuers joined John Brown's historic raid on Harper's Ferry (see October 16).

In 1984, Oberlin's senior citizens preserved these stories and more in their town sesquicentennial Underground Railroad Quilt project, an ongoing legacy with squares representing each moment. As one citizen said, "the quilt is a celebration of the women who are creating living history being bonded by the past." And in Oberlin that past has many faces. Among Oberlin's "many faces" are those bearing living proof of the town's slavery-era utopian spirit and the heritage of openly biracial families that survive to this day.

Monday, April 14, 1834, Ohio, U.S.A.

Freedom   **Legacies**

APRIL 15

"HO FOR KANSAS! April 15, 1878!" a poster called to those "in pursuit of homes . . . at Transportation Rates cheaper than ever was known before."

Less than five years after the Civil War officially ended slavery and just as the last constitutional amendments were ratified guaranteeing African-American citizenship, the demand for cotton was higher than ever. A reign of terror swept the South, openly fueled by once-wealthy planters who were eager to resurrect forced labor, using ex-overseers and the KKK as recruiters. For desperate Blacks, survival meant escape. Wagon trains setting out for territory outside the South were at times circled by southern raiders who killed those who refused to return. Hundreds of attacks were documented in petitions to Congress and the president for relief from the violence. Groups sent appropriation requests to the Freedmen's Bureau for ships in which they could sail to Africa. All to no avail. "We lost all hopes," said ex-slave and Civil War veteran Henry Adams. "The whole South . . . had got into the hands of the very men that held us as slaves . . . and they were holding the reins of government over our heads."

For these desperate people, a savior emerged in 1869 in the person of Benjamin "Pap" Singleton, an ex-slave who had escaped to Canada on the Underground Railroad. For the next ten years, his Nashville Real Estate and Homestead Association helped seven thousand leave the Deep South for Kansas settlements. When drought and crop loss brought new waves of brutality, the ingenuity of Singleton and other developers led to the Great Exodus of 1879. In January and February alone, spurred on by posters like the one just quoted, fifty thousand Blacks left for Kansas by mule, by raft, or on foot. As in the days of the Underground Railroad, Blacks were on the move. But this time they were moving to all-Black towns to live on land that they could work and call their own.

Monday, April 15, 1878, Kansas, U.S.A.

Towns and Cities   Freedom

APRIL 16

In April 1963, Dr. Martin Luther King, Jr., led a protest march in Birmingham, Alabama, that culminated in his arrest on the highest of holy days, Good Friday. He had deliberately chosen this date for its symbolic value, in order to help focus attention on the daily crucifixions and sacrifices of Blacks. While in jail, King read an open letter to the *Birmingham News* written by eight white Birmingham clergymen—self-defined liberal Christians and Jews; the letter criticized his act as "unwise and untimely." Alone in his jail cell, King used the newspaper margins to write a response nearly ten pages long. This handwritten epistle dated April 16, 1963, was smuggled out of jail and circulated. Even today, it remains one of the greatest testaments of faith and conscience for all time: "Letter from Birmingham City Jail."

"My Dear Fellow Clergymen," he began. To their suggestion in favor of negotiation, he reiterated the four steps of his nonviolent campaign: fact-finding, negotiation, self-purification (survival training for demonstrators), and direct action (marches and demonstrations). Citing Birmingham's record as one of the South's most violent segregationist cities and noting its refusal to negotiate with Black citizens in good faith, King said that direct action was mandatory. "History is the long and tragic story of the fact that privileged groups seldom give up their privileges voluntarily." He confessed that he was most disappointed not with the segregationists but with the "white moderate" who "paternalistically feels that he can set the timetable for another man's freedom," preferring peace to justice.

But he was most eloquent and poignant on "why we can't wait," a phrase that would become the title of his autobiography. With history on his side, he answered why in one sentence that included eleven passionate reasons, the most heart-wrenching of which came to him as a father trying to explain the deep of hurts of racism to his own five- and six-year-old children.

Tuesday, April 16, 1963, Alabama, U.S.A.

Human Rights   **Leadership**

APRIL 17

On April 17, 1992, MTV veejay Fab 5 Freddy (Fred Braithwaite) opened the window on the words and phrases of the Hip-Hop generation with the publication of his book, *Fresh Fly Flavor*. Giving the culture of young people their due respect, here's a sampling of their inspired rap, decoded by Fab from A to Z:

Afrolistic—aka (also known as)
Bid—a jail sentence
Clean—well dressed
Deep-six—murder
Ends—money
Flavor—the tone or vibe of a person, place, or situation
Get played—embarrassingly deceived
Hip-Hop—state of mind as established by the originators of the culture
Iced—killed
Jimmy Hat—condom
Kangol—a brand of "hat" popular with Hip-Hop fans
Large—doing well
Max out—relax
New Jack—a person new to a situation making an attempt at being the best
Out box—from the beginning
Poot-but—a lackadaisical, unmotivated, dumb person
Q.T.—quiet
Rock—a basketball
Seven digits—a phone number
Tapped out—penniless, broke
Under wraps—keeping a secret
Vapors—distance from those who want a friendship because of your fame
Word to the mother—"my word is my bond"
You all that—you look good
Zero—a nobody

Get down!

Friday, April 17, 1992, New York, U.S.A.

Hip-Hop   **Respect for Youth**

APRIL 18

Bill Russell was a skillful leader on and off the basketball court. And on April 18, 1966, the owners and managers of the Boston Celtics formally recognized that fact in naming him coach. As the first African-American to coach a professional (that is, predominantly white) team in any sport, his appointment was a milestone in American sports history.

Coming to pro basketball in the 1950s, Russell was named the NBA's "Most Valuable Player" in 1958. To say the least, Russell was known for dominating the court. As he himself recognized, "no one had ever played basketball the way I played it, or as well. They had never seen anyone block shots before. . . . I like to think I originated a whole new style of play."

No one ever called the game the way he did, either: "In America, the practice is to put two Black athletes in the basketball game at home, put three on the road, and put five in when you get behind." To his credit, Russell became the coach when the Boston Celtics were on a high, following eight successive championship seasons. With a bold style and the skill to match—and backed by his newly earned management clout as coach—Russell was able to move the once-acceptable racial politics of "fair game" a lot closer to fair play. This was definitely a winning strategy for the Celtics as a whole and for Russell personally. In 1969, after his tenth victorious season in eleven years, Bill Russell decided to leave the sport on a high, announcing his retirement while the ball of future options was firmly in his court.

Through his career, he paved the way for Black players to enter the ranks of management at last after seventy-five years of American basketball history.

Monday, April 18, 1966, Massachusetts, U.S.A.

Sports   **Zest for Life**

APRIL 19

In the second week of April 1862, Major General David Hunter of the Union Army reached a decision that would change thousands of lives. Within months President Lincoln would notify commanders of his intention to free the slaves. But after capturing South Carolina's Fort Pulaski for the Union, Hunter faced groups of slaves fleeing to the protection of his command. Eight months before the Emancipation Proclamation, Major General Hunter took the initiative and freed all slaves in the vicinity of the fort.

A week later, on April 19, 1862, fourteen-year-old Susie King, accompanied by her uncle and his family, boarded a gunboat and sailed from Saint Catherine's Island to freedom behind Union lines. Becoming free relatively early in the war, the men in Susie's family were among the first Black enlistees. Susie, meanwhile, who had learned to read and write while still enslaved in Savannah, remained with the soldiers head-quartered under Major General Hunter on Port Royal Island off the South Carolina coast. There she became a laundress and, more important, their teacher, nurse, and confidante.

Because she had the good fortune to escape so early in the war with skills she could use to aid in the effort, she had an opportunity to witness some of the more "liberating" moments in the war for Blacks. When vastly outnumbered former slave owners fled the Port Royal area with its 83 percent Black majority population, Susie was part of the South's first paid-labor community of ex-slaves. Years later, she documented her experiences in book form. In 1902, Susie King Taylor's memoir was published, *A Black Woman's Civil War Memoirs: Reminiscences of My Life in Camp with the 33rd U.S. Colored Troops, late 1st South Carolina Volunteers.* This is the only known written account of the war through the eyes of what the military coldly termed "contrabands of war"—the newly liberated African-Americans.

Saturday, April 19, 1862, Georgia–South Carolina, U.S.A.
Civil War/Women   **Perspective**

APRIL 20

On April 20, 1855, Jeremiah Burke "J. B." Sanderson, a free Massachusetts-born abolitionist and educator who had migrated to California, made this entry in his diary:

> Today I opened a school for colored children. The necessity for this step is evident. There are thirty or more children in Sacramento of proper age and no school provided for them by the Board of Education. They must no longer be neglected, left to grow up in ignorance, exposed to all manner of evil influences, with the danger of contracting idle and vicious habits. A school they must have. I am induced to undertake this enterprise by the advice of friends and the solicitation of parents. I can do but little, but with God's blessing I will do what I can.

In the booming 1850s, California's Gold Rush of 1849 and status as a free territory lured Black families. As a community, these Black families were among the nation's most affluent. With their relative privilege, they were able to demand some of the rights due them in such areas as education. And Sanderson's school—the first of several he would start for the children of freeborn Blacks and former slaves—was among those early Black community achievements.

As Sanderson launched each of his schools, he would first act as head teacher until a permanent instructor could be found, all the while lobbying the state for the funds to support the school. His work was a major part of the evolution of a statewide public education system for all of California's students.

Friday, April 20, 1855, California, U.S.A.

Education

Foundations

APRIL 21

On April 21, 1966, Ethiopian emperor Haile Selassie's visit to Jamaica, West Indies, was a moment of unparalleled significance for the Rastafarian movement.

The story of this day actually begins in 1916, when Marcus Garvey (see August 2) left Jamaica for the United States with these parting words to his followers: "Look to Africa for the crowning of a Black King; he shall be the Redeemer." After his departure and under the stress of the island's dire poverty, Garvey's followers fell into disarray. But in November 1930, the group was rejuvenated by news of the coronation of young Ras Tafari as Haile Selassie (meaning "might of the Trinity") in Ethiopia. Garvey's disciples, who now called themselves "Rastafarians," knew their day had come. Ethiopia was the land from which the slave trade had ripped their ancestors and the land to which they would ultimately repatriate. With Ethiopia as their root and Selassie as god and king, is it any wonder that Selassie's arrival in Jamaica on April 21, 1966, was directly translated as "the messiah has come"? A witness at the scene, Dr. M. B. Douglas, related this scene to Rastafarian historian Leonard Barrett:

> There were no less than 100,000 people at the airport to meet him. The morning was rainy and many people were soaking wet. Before the arrival of the plane the Rastafarians said that "as soon as our God comes, the rain will stop." This turned out somewhat like a miracle, because the rain stopped as soon as the plane landed. The Rastafarians responded with a roar of joy and surged out on the tarmac, pushing to get a touch of the plane. When the Emperor saw the people, the Rastafarian flags, [heard] the cheering and singing, he wept.

From the rain at the start of the day to this moment, each of the gods in turn had anointed the event with tears of joy.

Thursday, April 21, 1966, Jamaica, W.I.–Ethiopia

Religion   **Faith/Providence**

APRIL 22

Some of the world's best tall tales (and outright lies) hail from Texas—and some of the most famous are inspired by the Alamo and the year 1836. But few people realize that the story of "the sweetest little rosebud" described in the Texas state anthem, "The Yellow Rose of Texas," was inspired by the story of Emily, a Black woman and slave who changed the history of Texas.

The story begins in March 1836 when Texas declared itself independent of Mexico—in large measure, to preserve slavery—and a republic in its own right (see April 27). Within days of that declaration, a century-old Spanish mission, the Alamo, became the proving ground where the armies of Mexico and Texas battled for control of Texas. In March, Mexico won the first round with three thousand troops led by General Antonio López de Santa Anna. But in April, Texas struck back in the Battle of San Jacinto. With their leader "otherwise engaged," Santa Anna's men were caught off guard. In less than twenty minutes, Santa Anna's 1,500-man army had been decimated. But the general was nowhere to be found until the next day, April 22, 1836, when it was revealed that he had been with Emily.

"She's the sweetest little rosebud that Texas ever knew," people began to sing. In keeping the general occupied, Emily had done Texas history a big favor. But whether her favor was planned or coincidental, no one can be sure. And whether the song and the story are true is also anyone's guess. Several versions of Emily's tale have been told over the years, identifying her as a Black woman. Several more give no clue to her heritage at all. But this is the story we tell for now. And as they sing in the song, "the Yellow Rose of Texas is the only girl for me!" If it's a good enough story for Texas, that's all we need to know.

Friday, April 22, 1836, Texas, U.S.A.

Military   **Folklore**

APRIL 23

In Prince Edward County, Virginia, conditions at the segregated R. R. Moton High School had become intolerable. If parents and teachers weren't willing to do anything about it, the students themselves would have to. On the morning of April 23, 1951, a high school junior, Barbara Johns, set in motion a chain of events that led to a historic Supreme Court decision.

Johns's plan began with an urgent Monday morning phone call to the principal, whom she lured from the high school with "news" that two students were about to be arrested. In his absence a note was delivered to each classroom announcing a special schoolwide assembly. When the student body assembled, the stage curtains parted and there stood sixteen-year-old Barbara Johns, reading an indictment of the school's inhumane conditions. Among other inequities, the school board had built unheated shacks for classrooms, and a history teacher was doubling as the driver of a hand-me-down school bus that had been deemed unfit for use by white students. It was time to act.

As the teachers realized what had happened, they rushed the stage to retake control. Using her shoe as a gavel, Johns pounded firmly and shouted, "I want you all out of here!" On cue, her student supporters removed the teachers. After the reading of the indictment and before the principal returned, all 450 students walked out on strike. A protest notice was then sent to the NAACP, and within one month of the students' action, the NAACP had filed a desegregation suit that was later consolidated under the Supreme Court's landmark decision that desegregated the nation's public schools, *Brown v. Board of Education of Topeka, Kansas, et al.* (see May 17).

Barbara Johns had been well trained in productive rebellion by her infamous uncle, the Reverend Vernon Johns (see June 11). She was truly a chip off her uncle's old block. People said they were both crazy—*purposefully* crazy.

Monday, April 23, 1951, Virginia, U.S.A.

Education   **Respect for Use of Power**

APRIL 24

For more than a century, Spelman College had educated young Black women to believe they could be anything they wanted to be. On April 24, 1987, for the first time in its 106-year history, the school put into practice what it had been preaching. The board of trustees of Spelman College named Johnnetta B. Cole, Ph.D., its seventh president, the first African-American woman so named.

Dr. Cole defined her unique role as that of "sister-president"—administrator by job description; mentor, advisor, and friend by mission. She wrote, "I have consciously lived and studied, taught and written as a Black woman. The issues of race and gender have been central in my life, in my work as an anthropologist, and in my community activities. There is a fundamental question at the base of the anthropology I do: how can people of color, poor people, and women become full, productive, and equal members of the society in which they live?" Under her leadership, that answer would be found in the expanded role she was redefining for Spelman itself.

Founded by two white New England missionaries in 1881, Spelman was originally named the Atlanta Baptist Female Seminary. Classes were held in the basement of a church, and the first students were eleven women, all former slaves. Within a year, the school had two hundred students ages fifteen to fifty-two. John D. Rockefeller, the financier and philanthropist, provided early funding, and in tribute to his wife's family, the school was renamed Spelman College. As it grew, it raised young Black women to triumph in an American society rife with bigotry. A century later, as envisioned by its sister-president, Spelman was to become a center for scholarship on Black women with their rich and diverse histories, and society itself would be the beneficiary of that wisdom.

Friday, April 24, 1987, Georgia, U.S.A.
Women's Education   **Vision**

APRIL 25

At last the world's peoples would recognize themselves as inhabitants of one world with common rights of peace and security. This was the premise that brought hundreds of delegates representing countries the world over to San Francisco, California, on April 25, 1945. There, they were at least united in their mission to draft the charter of the United Nations.

For Africans everywhere, most of whom were oppressed under colonial rule or segregation, the U.N. represented hope for redress of their grievances in the court of world opinion. Among the African-American representatives to that first convocation were Mary McLeod Bethune, the educator and women's rights leader; the scholar Ralph Bunche, who would win a Nobel Peace Prize for negotiating the Israel settlement as undersecretary to the U.N.; the "Father of Pan-Africanism," Dr. W. E. B. Du Bois; and the NAACP's Walter White.

Because the U.N. saw its role as helping to resolve disputes between independent nations, the organization turned an official deaf ear to the world's colonized and disenfranchised peoples. And while the Pan-African world may have been denied its rightful place at the U.N. table, the fact of that denial opened the floodgates on a raging tide—the quest for sovereignty and freedom. As a direct result of Black post–San Francisco activism and the span of a single decade: within a month, Afro-Caribbeans filed their grievances against colonial rule; Du Bois revived the Pan-African congresses, the sixth of which was held in England that fall; Ralph Bunche accepted the U.N. post that ultimately yielded his Nobel Peace Prize; African-Americans documented the atrocities against them in two historic petitions—the NAACP's "Appeal to the World," filed in 1947, and William L. Patterson's "We Charge Genocide," filed in 1951; America's civil rights era was launched in 1954; and by 1956 the Sudan became the first African nation to regain independence.

Wednesday, April 25, 1945, California, U.S.A.
International Relations   **Focus**

APRIL 26

When word of James Beckwourth's newly published autobiography reached his fellow adventurers and Mountain Men in 1856, it is said by historian Bernard De Voto that the regulars of a certain campfire sent a representative into a nearby town to buy the book. Picking up an appropriate-looking book without realizing that it was actually a copy of the Bible, the scout returned to camp with his treasure; there one of his campfire companions jumped right into reading it for the group. As the reader got to the part where Samson was tying torches to the tails of foxes and burning the crops of the Philistines, one of the listeners exclaimed, "There, I'd know one of Jim Beckwourth's lies anywhere!"

In the best tradition of the Mountain Men of the old West, Jim Beckwourth was a great liar, for sure. But as an explorer, trapper, and scout, his reputation is secure. Between 1844 and 1850—some sources cite April 26, 1844, as the exact date—Beckwourth "discovered" a route to the ocean through the mountains of the Sierra Nevada in California, a route that bears his name to this day: Beckwourth Pass. Even the town of Beckwourth was named in his honor. There is also general agreement that Beckwourth, a Black man, founded the Gantt-Blackwell Fort, a re-creation of which is housed at the El Pueblo Museum in Pueblo, Colorado.

Even more impressive is a fact that Beckwourth himself didn't live long enough to find out. In 1868, two years after his death, the route over which he used to lead wagon trains west, which is now named "Jim Beckwourth's Trail," was selected by the railroad as the trail on which they would lay their tracks through the Nevada Territory. When a site was needed for a railroad company town, Reno was created. For that reason, some people still say it's Jim Beckwourth who put Reno on the map!

Friday, April 26, 1844, California–Colorado–Nevada, U.S.A.
Adventure   **Legacies**

APRIL 27

In the annals of Underground Railroad history, an often overlooked point is that the routes of escape did not only lead north to Canada; some routes led southwest to Mexico. One of the most enduring reasons for this was the courageous presence of one man—Vicente Guerrero, an ex-slave of mixed indigenous, Black, and white parentage, who became president of Mexico in April 1825. As president, Guerrero reworked the constitution, outlawed capital punishment and slavery, opened schools and libraries for the poor, and declared all people eligible to vote and hold office. In short, as historian J. A. Rogers has said, Guerrero was the "George Washington and Abraham Lincoln of Mexico."

When Mexico's war for independence from Spain began in 1810, Guerrero was among the first to volunteer. He fought so well that he was soon made captain. As other leaders were imprisoned or killed, Guerrero gained respect and military prominence for his skill, bravery, and unflagging resistance to Spanish rule. When all seemed lost, Guerrero continued the fight in the guerrilla warfare tradition of the Maroons (see August 13). So successful were his warriors in destabilizing slavery and the system of white privilege that the government tried to corrupt Guerrero through his father, who met him with an offer of land and wealth. Despite his desperate situation, Guerrero fought on to victory with a fellow commander who was then named president. But the new president declared himself allied with those eager to exploit the peasantry. Backed by the masses, Guerrero led a successful coup; then, when the popular but undereducated and unpolished Guerrero was passed over for the presidency again, the masses staged a second revolt, the government surrendered, and Vicente Guerrero, the ex-slave and muleteer, became president in 1825.

Nearly 170 years later, the legacies of President Guerrero—abolition and a liberalized constitution—are still major factors in the sizable Afro-Mexican American population that thrives there to this day.

April 1825, Mexico

Heroes **Leadership**

APRIL 28

"I wonder why it is that I have this strange feeling of not living out myself," a young Charlotte Forten writes in her diary, a rare glimpse into a singular mid-nineteenth-century life. The feelings she related so long ago are familiar to centuries of girls on the threshold of womanhood, but as the teenage daughter of a prominent African-American family during the era of slavery, Charlotte Forten's perspective was unique indeed.

"My existence seems not full, not expansive enough. . . . What means this constant restlessness, this longing for—something—I know not what?" As a child born to an abolitionist family that was successful in business, Charlotte was forbidden to attend a segregated school. Instead she was tutored at home and was sent to live in the "elegant country home" of another prominent family outside Philadelphia. Later, she stayed with family friends in Massachusetts in order to attend an integrated school. Living in the two most liberal cities for Blacks of the time, she knew the most renowned abolitionists and intellectuals of her day, and they kept her active mind challenged. If, as it is said, "we read to know we are not alone," then perhaps it was through reading that the impressionable sixteen-year-old found her greatest companion and the courage to meet her future.

On Friday, April 28, 1854, she wrote, "This evening read 'Poems of Phillis Wheatley,' an African slave, who lived in Boston at the time of the Revolution. Her character and genius afford a striking proof of the falseness of the assertion made by some that hers is an inferior race." A few years later, when Forten had become an educator to the children of slaves, the same was being widely said of her gifts as a poet and diarist. As she matured, her published accounts of life with her students survive as some of our keenest portraits of former slaves savoring their first morsels of freedom in the Civil War era.

Friday, April 28, 1854, Pennsylvania–Massachusetts–South Carolina, U.S.A.

Literature　　　　　　　　　　　　　　　　**Coming of Age**

APRIL 29

Before the Civil War, freeborn Blacks found the law to be a perilous thing. Like slaves, they, too, had few rights that a white person was bound to respect, as the Supreme Court would decide in such noted cases as the Dred Scott Affair of 1847–57. But the process of eventually overturning those rulings began in April 1845 when Macon B. Allen became the first African-American licensed to practice law in the United States.

Allen was already a successful businessman in Portland, Maine, when his quest to gain admittance to the bar began in 1844. Aided by friends in the white liberal community, he was nominated for admittance by General Samuel Fessenden but rejected on the grounds that he was not a citizen. Indeed, even free Blacks were not considered U.S. citizens at the time. The following year Allen tried again. This time he was given an "impossible" exam designed to guarantee his failure, which he nevertheless passed, and on April 29, 1845, he was admitted to the Maine state bar.

With few Blacks in Maine, however, Allen knew his potential list of clients would be slim. But with the strong abolitionist movement in Boston nurturing a vibrant and growing community of free and self-emancipated Blacks, he applied to the Massachusetts bar and was admitted on May 3, 1845. At a time when most states denied Blacks the right to testify in court at all, Allen's achievement was an important step on the road to legal self-defense.

Tuesday, April 29, 1845, Maine, U.S.A.

APRIL 30

On April 30, 1992, the highly publicized final episode of TV's *Cosby Show* aired just as so much that it had achieved in improving the racial landscape on television literally went up in smoke.

In its unprecedented eight-year TV success, *Cosby* was big business—enriching sponsors, network TV, and syndicators, while empowering Black talent on camera and behind the scenes. It revived the family sitcom, family viewing, and in many confessed cases, family togetherness itself. *Cosby* featured shows on critical thinking and conflict resolution, a tribute to the March on Washington, and a plot on learning disabilities that boosted Special Education budgets nationwide.

Few shows had ever been as successful—especially not with a healthy, nonstereotyped Black family at its center. Economically, this was a major distinction, since the number of Black households measured under the Nielsen rating system is statistically insignificant. Therefore, its achievement as a Black show was determined by its number of white viewers—even if sponsors chose to target Black viewers. And *Cosby* even succeeded at that. When *Cosby* was on, the most influential living room guest in America was an African-American man. And for a little while, a meeting of the minds across race and class actually seemed possible. Ironically, on April 30, 1992, the day of the final episode, the verdict unjustly exonerating white police officers in the video-documented beating of Rodney King was announced.

As Los Angeles erupted in flames and illusions were shattered, *Cosby*'s TV family graciously exited through the fire door. A stunned nation paused to wonder when the day would come again for conscience and profit to waltz into our lives with such skill and ease.

MAY

"MUSTERED OUT" COLORED VOLUNTEERS AT LITTLE ROCK, ARKANSAS.—[SEE PAGE 315.]

Mustered Out. Etching from the drawing by A. R. Waud. Etching published by *Harper's Weekly* (May 19, 1866). Reprinted courtesy of the author. For more information, see May 13.

MAY 1

On May 1, 1950, Gwendolyn Brooks was awarded the Pulitzer Prize for her book of poetry, *Annie Allen*. In the over thirty years during which these prizes had been awarded in numerous categories, she was the first African-American to be so honored, breaking the color ban on celebrating literary achievement in America.

"Conduct your blooming in the noise and whip of the whirlwind," she said years later, as she received one of her more than twenty-five honorary degrees. As poet laureate of Chicago, the Windy City, what else could she do? Her first book, *A Street in Bronzeville,* was notable for its carefully detailed and truthful portraits of everyday poor people living on her Chicago turf. Brooks was in love with what she called "the wonders language can achieve." And with that love, she created what critic Jeanne-Marie A. Miller called "city-folk poetry"—the poetry inherent in the voices of the "unheroic Black people who fled the land for the city—only to discover that there is little difference between the world of the North and the world of the South. One learns from them." In *Annie Allen,* her second, prize-winning book, those voices turned inward to reveal truths about herself—and us.

There is always something a little suspicious about being called the "first Black" to do anything—the appellation seems to give credence to the very racism that had denied all the others who could have been "firsts" long before, if only the world had seen otherwise. But for Gwendolyn Brooks to be that "first," as a writer of "city-folk poetry," was special to us as a people. It was as though she were the honored guest at the most exclusive party—and got to take her entire neighborhood along. With this "first," it seemed a tribute to the full spectrum of African-American life.

Monday, May 1, 1950, Illinois, U.S.A.

Poetry   **Publishing**

MAY 2

The first game of the National Negro Leagues was played on May 2, 1920, in Indianapolis. It was a rather uneventful game in which the hometown ABC's beat the Chicago Giants 4–2. But it was made memorable by the size of the crowd that came out to see it: eight thousand. The game was most notable perhaps for what it foretold about African-Americans and the future of baseball. In 1923, attendance reached four hundred thousand for that season alone. The *Chicago Defender* described that 1923 season opener in Chicago this way:

> The opening ceremonies consisted of a parade of automobiles, some 300 in number, led by a squad of motorcycle police, . . . a truck filled with . . . jazz hounds. One of their favorite pieces was ["Toot, Toot, Tootsie Good-Bye"]. They played nothing else but, and if Tootsie isn't gone she'll never get away because the band played her good-bye all through town, in and out and around and up and down the hills, stopping the . . . street cars en route. It was a great day for the opening: warm weather and the folks coming out like a lot of bees hidden away all winter and getting active when the sun shines.

The Negro Leagues were such a success that they challenged the all-white major leagues' claim to be the only "organized" baseball. As the Kansas City Monarchs' Sammie Haynes would later recall, with "two leagues, a 140-game schedule, an annual all-star game, and a World Series," they had it all.

Today, the Negro Leagues are history—a history well preserved and undergoing a resurgence thanks to former Monarchs' player Buck O'Neil, founder of the Negro Leagues Baseball Museum in Kansas City, Missouri.

Sunday, May 2, 1920, Indiana, U.S.A.

Sports   **Self-Determination**

MAY 3

When one looks at the gross national product of the United States, the truly gross part has too often been the manufacture and export of racism. And few events have made the point more clearly than the moment when, in 1987, Prime Minister Yasuhiro Nakasone of Japan gave a speech on Japanese-American trade that was filled with racist slurs, misconceptions, and outright inaccuracies. The Japanese prime minister was not the only one responsible for his speech. Much of his misinformation on African-Americans had come directly from the pages of America's newspapers, with their tendency to accentuate the negative, and from the type of "scholarly research" that regularly surfaces to question the "innate" intelligence of Blacks—it is the same "scholarship," one might add, that is only slightly more generous to Asians and less so to other peoples of color.

Nakasone's diplomatic gaff illustrated how systematic misinformation and prejudice has constricted the ability of African-Americans to compete globally. It also underscored how powerful racism can be in shaping the way one people of color perceives another. The lessons were there: it is the responsibility of each group to tell its own story; each member of a group is an ambassador for the whole; and Blacks must build our own bridges via our designated ambassadors, our elected officials.

On May 3, 1987, Prime Minister Nakasone met with the Congressional Black Caucus to discuss the speech that had so angered Blacks. After a frank exchange of perspectives, Nakasone agreed to help secure Japanese investments in minority-owned American banks, to develop exchange programs between Japanese colleges and America's historically Black colleges, and to encourage Japanese companies to locate offices in predominantly Black areas. With that clearing, the next task was to widen and strenghten the bridge.

Sunday, May 3, 1987, Japan–U.S.A.

Government/Business   **Self-Assertion**

MAY 4

In the early sixties, the Congress of Racial Equality (CORE) resurrected its "Journey of Reconciliation" of 1947 as the "Freedom Rides." Despite the 1950s' Supreme Court orders and federal guidelines on desegregated interstate bus travel, Blacks were still being beaten and harassed throughout the South whenever they dared to sit in the front of buses. Using "whites only" rest rooms in bus terminals resulted in being forcefully ejected, jailed, or beaten. To bring attention to this ongoing crisis, CORE director James Farmer, on May 4, 1961, led an integrated group of thirteen Freedom Riders on a bus trip across the South with these results:

May 4: Thirteen Freedom Riders begin bus trip through South.

May 14: Their bus is bombed and burned near Anniston, Alabama, and demonstrators are beaten; additional Riders join the trip.

May 20: A Montgomery mob attacks the Riders, and the attorney general sends in four hundred U.S. marshals for their protection.

May 21: Governor Patterson of Alabama declares martial law in Montgomery and calls out the National Guard.

May 22: Kennedy orders two hundred marshals to Montgomery.

May 24: Mississippi sheriffs arrest twenty-seven Freedom Riders.

May 26: The Freedom Ride Coordinating Committee is established in Atlanta.

June 12: Mississippi arrests more than one hundred Riders.

September 22: The Federal Interstate Commerce Commission desegregates all buses.

November 29 to December 2: Riders are attacked in McComb, Mississippi, by mobs in the bus station.

December 12: Freedom Rides spread as a city-by-city strategy.

Two years later in 1964, President Johnson signed a federal civil rights bill desegregating all public accommodations.

Thursday, May 4, 1961, Regional (South) U.S.A.

Desegregation   **Endurance**

MAY 5

In 1935, the only African nation to fight off European domination successfully was again under attack when Italy invaded Ethiopia in a colonial siege. Emperor Haile Selassie (see April 21) had been forced to flee his country. His address to the League of Nations, pleading Ethiopia's cause, was totally ignored. With their alliances and "gentlemen's agreements," each nation turned an official blind eye on the imperialistic aggressions of the other. Ignored but not outdone, Selassie began to recruit a liberation army from all over the world.

In America, stalwart supporters of Marcus Garvey's badly hobbled Universal Negro Improvement Association (see August 2) once again sang their "Universal Ethiopian Anthem" so popular in the 1920s: "Ethiopia, thou land of our fathers/Thou land where the Gods love to be/As the storm cloud at night suddenly gathers/Our armies come rushing to thee."

Even African-Americans who knew nothing about Garveyism, as well as those who did not see themselves as "Black" or "African" when those words still seemed so distasteful to so many people—even they identified with the plight of the Ethiopians. Although the U.S. government discouraged Black volunteers to the Ethiopian cause, African-Americans sent funds to aid Selassie, who had liquidated most of his personal assets in silver and crown jewels to provide relief for Ethiopia's refugees. In 1940, Selassie met with his chiefs to strategize the expulsion of Italy, and he returned to fight with his people. On May 5, 1941, he made a triumphant return to his capital city of Addis Ababa at the head of a liberating army, and there he reassumed his throne.

Guided by the principle of "Africa for the Africans," Emperor Haile Selassie rebuilt Addis Ababa as the symbol of a reemerging continent. Within a decade, the Organization of African Unity and the United Nations Economic Commission for Africa would have their headquarters in Addis Ababa.

Monday, May 5, 1941, Ethiopia

Pan-African World   **Commitment**

MAY 6

The year 1787 marked a turning point in the way African-Americans viewed themselves as free people in America. In Philadelphia, the Free African Society was founded (see April 12), becoming the first secular Black organization in the country, and in Boston on May 6, 1787, Prince Hall founded the world's first Black Masonic lodge.

Unusual for his time, Hall was neither a preacher nor an educator; rather, he was an organizer, African-America's first. In 1777 he worked on the historic petition to abolish slavery as anathema to the notion of freedom, an action that led to Massachusetts's abolition of slavery in 1783. Hall's mission was to nurture Black social, political, and economic vitality. Like other Blacks in the Northeast's metropolitan areas, Hall first tried to participate in the existing organizations of his day. On March 6, 1775, he was one of fifteen Blacks inducted into a British Masonic lodge, but the new members were denied access to the lodge's full privileges. They formed their own African Lodge No. 1 that July, which met for nine years before Prince Hall, in 1784, wrote to England for official recognition of the group as a Masonic lodge. Although the authorization was issued that September, it took over three years for the letter to reach Boston, where it finally arrived on April 29, 1787. One week later, African Masonic Lodge No. 459 was founded—a "regular Lodge of Free and accepted Masons, under the . . . denomination of the African Lodge."

Prince Hall's lodge launched a movement. In 1797, Providence, Rhode Island, chartered an African Lodge, followed by Philadelphia in 1798. These three lodges were known as "the Prince Hall Solidarity." As a network, they were active in the Underground Railroad movements, where, interestingly enough, some of the codes used came from the African Masonic lodges. Two hundred years after their founding, the Prince Hall lodges are still going strong as African-America's oldest fraternal organization.

Sunday, May 6, 1787, Massachusetts, U.S.A.

Organizations   **Foundations**

MAY 7

By the mid 1960s, Fannie Lou Hamer had become a visible and vocal force for the rights of the most disfranchised of African-Americans. A sharecropper's daughter born in Mississippi to a family of twenty children, she went to the cotton fields at age six and stayed there for forty years until 1962, when she lost her job for registering to vote. She was jailed in her hometown of Ruleville, Mississippi, in 1963 and brutally beaten for her participation in a lunch-counter desegregation demonstration. In 1964, Mrs. Hamer seized the national conscience as a member of the Mississippi Freedom Democratic Party at the 1964 Democratic Convention (see August 26).

On May 7, 1971, Hamer, who had earned the right to be called one of the world's most powerful women, addressed the NAACP Legal Defense Fund Institute in New York City with this message on her proudest achievement, the Freedom Farm:

> Sunflower County, the county where I'm from, is Senator Eastland's county, which owns 5,800 acres of some of the richest black fertile soil in Mississippi and where kids suffer from malnutrition. In 1969 I founded the Freedom Farm Co-op. We started off with forty acres of land. In 1970 in Sunflower County, we fed 1,500 people from this forty acres of land. On the fourteenth of January 1971, we put $85,400 on 640 acres of land, giving us a total of 680 acres of land. We also have sixty-eight houses. We hope sometime in '71 we will build another hundred houses. . . . We have a job as Black women to support whatever is right and to bring in justice where we've had so much injustice.

Well after many thought the need for the civil rights movement had ended, Hamer knew it had only begun. For her work on the Freedom Farm, she was shot at, and in 1971 her house was firebombed. But she kept on, building a strong and lasting legacy. Fannie Lou Hamer was indeed a powerful woman.

Friday, May 7, 1971, New York, U.S.A.

Heroes   **Courage/Stature**

MAY 8

It was real. In 1963, after a century of colonization and eleven years of war, Kenya would soon be independent.

Kenyans had gone through a brutal struggle to rid themselves of colonial rule. In an attempt to repress the population and terrorize them into giving up their fight for independence, British colonizers had invented the perfect evil enemy: a vicious group of Blacks they named the "Mau Maus." Though this group did not, of course, exist, the British used it as an excuse to torture, imprison, and even kill Kenyans. Yet despite all this terror, on May 8, 1963, Kenyans held their first election. And when it was done, Jomo Kenyatta waved the traditional fly whisk in victory as Kenya's first president.

Convicted by the British as the alleged "manager" of the so-called Mau Mau movement, Jomo Kenyatta had spent seven years in prison. Kenyatta, leader of the Kenya National Union (KANU), was the revolutionary hero of the Kenyan people. Throughout the independence struggle, Kenyans had rallied behind the war cry, *Uhuru Sasa!* Freedom Now! Now with the election won, it was time to move on. By June 1, internal self-rule would begin, and the full transfer to independence was scheduled for December 31, 1963. A new rallying cry was in order. They found one in a word regularly used by boating and fishing crews, a Ki-Swahili word meaning "Let's all pull together": *Harambee!*

With Kenya's story as inspiration, the word became a rallying cry for African-Americans as well. The following years saw the establishment of Harambee schools, Harambee community organizations, a Harambee businessperson's networking club, and Harambee, the first national book club devoted to African-American literature.

Wednesday, May 8, 1963, Kenya

Independence   **Transformations**

MAY 9

In 1918, when Europe's imperialist skirmishes had escalated into a full-blown world war, the controversy over the sacrificing of African-American lives for American aims resurfaced. Dr. W. E. B. Du Bois argued for the enlistment of Blacks, convinced that their efforts in this war would garner respect and clout for them in the real war that awaited them at home—the war against Jim Crow. He was wrong. And as a historian, he should have known better.

For centuries, African-American men had cast their lot with American causes only to be betrayed. Despite their Revolutionary War sacrifice, Blacks had been legally designated "three-fifths of a man." Despite their Civil War gains, KKK night riders, Jim Crow laws, and northern denial were the rule. And as soon as Black men enlisted for World War I, it became clear that they'd been tricked again. Even at the battlefront, the U.S. high command undermined Black soldiers, humiliating and intimidating them and even executing one soldier after falsely accusing him of rape. Was this the future for which Du Bois had argued?

As NAACP board chair Joel Spingarn said, Du Bois's credibility was in need of "resuscitation." DuBois could not undo the betrayal of Black soldiers, but he could document it. Armed with the NAACP's blessings, he joined a press junket following President Wilson to the Versailles peace conference (see February 19) with the goal of researching a "Negro history of the war." Upon his arrival in Europe, Du Bois launched an investigation so thorough that it gave the Black soldiers a voice at last.

Du Bois's extensive report was published by *The Crisis* in May 1919. So powerful (and truthful) was his work that the postmaster general tried to suppress it. The May issue sold 106,000 copies—double its regular circulation. And Du Bois's study became useful in the push to desegregate the military, which culminated in President Truman's executive order of 1948.

Friday, May 9, 1919, New York, U.S.A.
Journalism/Leadership   **Responsibility**

MAY 10

In 1800, the South's jockeys were mostly slaves who had spent their lives tending horses. The first professional jockey was "Monkey" Simon, a compact man four feet six inches tall and so good at racing that in 1806 he (or, more often, his slave master) was earning in excess of $100 per ride. He got the nickname "Monkey" from an encounter with General Andrew Jackson. As recounted by Charles Parmer in his book *For Gold and Glory*, in May 1806 the general, who was recuperating from wounds he'd acquired in a duel, was spending much of his time at the Clover Bottom Race Course near Nashville, Tennessee. There he met Simon:

> "Monkey!" Jackson bellowed to Simon at some distance as a crowd gathered around sensing something dramatic. Slowly, Monkey Simon turned around. Flecking his boots with his whip, he looked up insolently: "You speakin' to me, white man?" "Yes, to you! Now listen: None of your monkeyshines today. When my horse starts to pass you, don't you dare spit tobacco juice in his eyes—or in the eyes of my jockey. Understand?" Simon glared. Turning his head, he spat against a post, then said: "General, I've rid ag'in many of yo nags, but none ever got close enough to catch my spit."

As things turned out, Monkey Simon was the leader in a long line of African-American jockeys. The first winning jockey at the opening race of the Kentucky Derby at Churchill Downs on May 10, 1875, was also a Black jockey, Oliver Lewis.

There is an interesting and provocative sidebar on the history of Black jockeys: in the countryside during the pre–Civil War era, the statue of a Black jockey holding a lantern was the Underground Railroad signal for a safe house. Perhaps Monkey Simon's independent streak derived from a legacy that went far deeper than one might think.

Monday, May 10, 1875, Kentucky, U.S.A.

Sports   **Spirit**

MAY 11

Three weeks after Dr. King's assassination in Memphis, the members of the civil rights movement were depressed and in mourning, but they were not defeated. Dr. King had traveled to Memphis to raise support for striking garbage workers (see April 3). The situation in Memphis symbolized the plight of poor Americans of every color and hue—the effects of low-paying jobs or of the lack of any paying job at all. Before his murder, Dr. King and the leaders of the Southern Christian Leadership Conference had conceived of a multiracial assembly of poor people in Washington, D.C., to be called the Poor People's Campaign of 1968.

Determined to keep the work going, a delegation of leaders representing poor communities of every race and hue met with congressional leaders and cabinet officials in late April. They came to address their demands for jobs, a minimum guaranteed income, welfare reform, and an end to the slaughter of poor people in Asia due to the rapidly escalating war in Vietnam.

In May, nine caravans of poor people made their way to Washington, gathering supporters along the way and dramatizing the plight of this nation-within-a-nation. Arriving in the capital on May 11, 1968, the demonstrators erected a shantytown of plywood shacks and tents on a sixteen-acre campsite within walking distance of the White House and Capitol Hill. They called it "Resurrection City." There they stayed for the next month—2,500 strong—living in the mud, shuttling back and forth to Capitol Hill, and gaining the support of 50,000 demonstrators, including Rosa Parks (see June's lead illustration), who joined them for the Solidarity Day March in mid June.

When the campaign was originally conceived, supporters had been promised the presence of Dr. King. In the wake of his murder, their demonstration became a memorial tribute.

Saturday, May 11, 1968, U.S.A.

Human Rights   **Self-Affirmation**

MAY 12

On May 12, 1828, the Holy Spirit came to Nat Turner with a vision of his destiny: to fight the serpent of slavery. When the time was right, Turner would see a sign in the sky, the vision told him. Until then, he should watch and pray.

Nat Turner was thought to be a "born mystic," the man other slaves called "Prophet." As one of the few slaves able to read, Turner studied the one history book available to him, the Bible, all the time. The revelations that came to him in signs from nature confirmed what he had learned from the biblical texts. This knowledge gave him strength and provided him with a strategy. For revolt was in Nat Turner's blood. His mother had been so opposed to delivering a child into slavery that she had had to be tied down in order to prevent her from killing her baby at birth. His father had been kidnapped in Africa, brought to America, escaped, and as rumor had it, returned to Africa. Nat Turner, too, tried to escape, but he was caught and brutally lashed.

Because of Turner's spirituality and his reliance on natural signs and signals for the timing of his actions, it is interesting to note that of the best-known nineteenth-century slave rebellions, his was the only one to be fully realized without being betrayed (see August 21). Whatever the forces that guided Turner, the blow he struck for freedom was the most profound that slave owners would feel until John Brown's raid of 1859 (see October 16).

Monday, May 12, 1828, Virginia, U.S.A.

Religion   **Better Worlds**

MAY 13

On May 13, 1862, Robert Smalls was a man in the right place at the right time who knew what to do with his good fortune.

Enslaved from birth, Smalls was hired out from the age of twelve for odd jobs around the sea town of Charleston, South Carolina. At some point, he was freed. By his early twenties, he had become a skilled sailor and an expert pilot. These were the days when in many parts of the South, whether by law or custom, Blacks were often prohibited from learning to swim, much less to sail and pilot, in order to eliminate the possibility of their escape by water. And Smalls's story illustrates why.

In the early years of the Civil War, Smalls was employed on the Confederate transport steamship, the *Planter*. On May 13, 1862, with his wife, children, and five other passengers aboard, Smalls stole the *Planter* from its moorings, sailed through Confederate lines and a Union blockade, and delivered the *Planter* as war booty to the Union forces. It was an act of such heroism that the *Planter* was immediately appropriated by the Union Army and Smalls was appointed its pilot. In December of the following year, with the *Planter* now refitted as a gunboat, Smalls successfully navigated the ship while under Confederate attack. For his bravery, he was named captain. If there was any one event that was pivotal in Secretary of War Edwin Stanton's decision to allow Blacks in the Union Army, it was this one. One month after Smalls had appropriated the *Planter*, Stanton authorized the recruitment of Black volunteers.

When the Union took Fort Sumter in 1865, Smalls made history again by bringing two thousand slaves to freedom. On May 13, 1865, the Civil War's last battle was fought at White's Ranch, Texas.

Tuesday, May 13, 1862, South Carolina, U.S.A.

Maritime   **Opportunity**

MAY 14

Sometime around 1773 Jean-Baptiste Pointe Du Sable, a French Afri-Caribbean fur trader, arrived in the land the Potawatomis called "Eschikagou," where he started a trading post and thus founded Chicago.

Du Sable was an interesting man. Born in Haiti to a French mariner father and an enslaved African mother, he was educated in Paris and later worked as a seaman for his father. Shipwrecked in New Orleans and fearful of being enslaved, he left the South, skirting the slave states as best he could and heading to the free Native American lands to the north and west. With a growing reputation as a fur trapper, he built a modest cabin in Eschikagou to which he brought an interesting collection of assets—twenty-three works of European fine art. He married, raised two children, and increased his wealth, expanding his home and lands into a major settlement that included a bake house, dairy, smokehouse, poultry house, workshop, stable, barn, and mill. He even acquired an additional eight hundred acres in Peoria.

Then suddenly, in 1800, he decided to leave the area he had so meticulously built up over the past twenty-seven years. On or about May 14, 1800, Du Sable sold all his Chicago holdings to a white trader for $1,200 and left to live with his son on property they co-owned in Saint Charles. No one knows for certain why, but he vacated just when his land was becoming more valuable and desirable as the "westward expansion" began. During the Revolutionary War, he had been imprisoned by the British for no other reason than the fact that he was a free, bilingual, self-employed Black man considered equally suspicious by the French, British, and Americans. Perhaps he left Chicago because he had had his fill of controversy.

Whatever the reason for his hasty departure, he left behind this historical fact, captured in a Native American saying: "The first white man to settle in Chicago was a Black man."

Wednesday, May 14, 1800, Illinois, U.S.A.

Towns and Cities   **Enterprise**

MAY 15

Perhaps the greatest single development in bringing Black singers to the opera stage—outside of their own obvious stellar gifts—was the appointment of Hungarian-born Laszlo Halasz to head the New York City Opera company in the 1940s. As director, Halasz built his season around the operas themselves and focused on consistently high production values—not on selecting a roster of high-profile opera stars. Thus, he could use his position at the opera to launch new careers, and he went in search of talent without regard to race. As a result, the New York City Opera became the first major company in the United States to introduce talented African-American singers to American audiences. In 1945, baritone Todd Duncan became the first guest performer in *Carmen,* and in 1948, baritone Lawrence Winters made his debut in *Aïda.*

On May 15, 1946, soprano Camilla Williams made history performing the title role in *Madama Butterfly.* It was a debut so well performed and received that the *New York Times* proclaimed her "an instant and pronounced success in the title role." As the first Black diva signed to a full contract with a major United States opera company, she broke the color bar in American opera for all who followed her.

But the benefits of her success at the New York City Opera did not stop at singers. As of 1980, that company was still the only American company to have produced an opera by a Black composer—the dean of Black "classicists," William Grant Still, whose opera about Haiti, *Troubled Island,* was staged in 1949.

Wednesday, May 15, 1946, New York, U.S.A.

Music   **Firsts**

MAY 16

◇ "I lent Isaac's life to a neighbour here & some one was so smitten with it as to carry it off 'unbeknown.'" Historian Charles Campbell was truly in possession of a most unusual "life," or biography. And while he may have intended a meaning other than the one implied when he penned that line on May 16, 1845, there is little doubt that the statement was accurate. Isaac's entire life had been lent about and carried off for seventy-plus years as the slave of Thomas Jefferson and his heirs.

The very contents of *Memoirs of a Monticello Slave* (Isaac's autobiography as dictated to Charles Campbell) provide a unique insight into what it meant to be owned in body and mind. For Isaac's "life" is hardly about Isaac. It is billed as a "faithful account of Monticello & the Family there, with notices of many of the distinguished Characters that visited there, his Revolutionary experience & travels, adventures, observations & opinions"; Isaac's "life," in other words, was Jefferson's life. Only in Jefferson's farm book, where his "property" was recorded, does Isaac's life have distinct value. There it tells us that Isaac was born the son of Great George and Ursula in December 1775. When Isaac was sixteen, British captors seized "Jefferson's property" and took him to Yorktown. After the war, Isaac was returned with Jefferson's other assets.

Significantly, there are two versions of Isaac's biography— with and without the paragraph on Jefferson's slave and mistress, Sally Hemings. The uncensored edition confirms that eleven-year-old Sally was brought to Paris by Jefferson. After that mention, Isaac abruptly shifts the focus to Sally's children (whom historic accounts identify as Jefferson's). As for poor Isaac, a daguerreotype portrait dating from the mid-1840s depicts him, in his loose linen shirt and blacksmith's apron, as a stoic man of strong African features. What a life.

Friday, May 16, 1845, Virginia, U.S.A.

Slavery

Self-Worth

MAY 17

On May 17, 1954, the U.S. Supreme Court handed down its landmark decision declaring Jim Crow laws governing racial segregation in public schools unconstitutional. In the interest of children nationwide, the NAACP legal team argued that "slavery is perpetuated in these statutes. In the field of public education the doctrine of 'separate but equal' has no place." With a single ruling in four state cases collectively titled *Brown v. Board of Education of Topeka, Kansas, et al.*, the Court agreed. A year later, the Court further ordered school desegregation to proceed "with all deliberate speed," effectively ending the era of American apartheid.

For most Blacks, and particularly for the young students involved in those early challenges, the process of school desegregation was quite painful—and often humiliating. But the *Brown* case offered hope and an opportunity to pass on the baton of African-American courage.

Historically, every positive turn for Blacks has improved this nation as a whole. For example, the push to educate the children of ex-slaves and freeborn Blacks in the eighteenth century nurtured the creation of the public school system for children of all races. The achievement of voting rights for Black men reduced the property requisites for whites and paved the way for women's suffrage. Amid the unchecked lynchings of the 1950s—both the actual physical lynchings and the political rampage of the McCarthy era that labeled civil rights crusaders "Communists" in order to undermine the movement—the *Brown* decision gave the nation a conscience. It was a platform from which to claim human rights too long denied.

In what may be its most lasting legacy, the *Brown* decision made its lead attorney the symbol of justice. Thurgood Marshall later became the first African-American member of the Supreme Court. His decisions and dissents of supreme conscience have provided precedents and guidance that will last for centuries to come.

Monday, May 17, 1954, Kansas–Washington, D.C., U.S.A.
Law   **Legacies**

MAY 18

On this day in 1896, the Supreme Court handed down its *Plessy v. Ferguson* decision (see June 7), which institutionalized racism, made "separate but equal" segregation a way of life, contaminated with hatred the lives of Americans regardless of color, and disrupted—or worse, destroyed—millions of African-American lives just as slavery had done for centuries. Today, as we unravel the damage still being done to ourselves and our children, it is important to know that in our historic roots lie traditions designed to celebrate our children, to tell them how special they are in every way.

Among the Yoruba of Nigeria, for example, traditions have evolved that are now woven into the fabric of the culture. Throughout the world, the birth of twins is considered the sign of a special blessing; Yoruba culture honors this blessing with two unique rituals. First, special names are given the twin spirits at birth. Taiwo and Kehinde designate the older and the younger twin, respectively. And then some families perform the special Yoruba *ibeji* ceremony for their twins as often as once a month.

In Yoruba, the word *ibeji* refers to twins who are believed to have divine powers. Family and friends gather for special dinners to celebrate this special gift of the twin spirits. If one of the twins dies, parents have an *ibeji* doll made to represent the departed child. In many African societies, an empty plate is set for the ancestors. This concept is reflected in the *ibeji* suppers where the doll is dressed like the living twin and seated at the table. Sometimes a mother will even offer a tiny bit of food to the *ibeji* doll. And when dinner is done, she will sing lullabies to honor both of her children.

In our world, where so many have suffered the loss of a child or a sibling and where our children seem so threatened, we can reach deep within our multilayered culture for time-tested ways to help us cope and grow. Honoring our moments in the eternal chain with a special ritual begun today can become our gift of tradition as the ancestors of tomorrow.

May 18, 1896, Nigeria

Family   **Responsibility to Youth**

MAY 19

When Claude McKay penned "If We Must Die," one of the most famous poems of the Harlem Renaissance, it was a call to Black people to fight back against the mob violence and lynchings of the American South—a call raised when appeals for justice were falling on officially deaf government ears. So it was ironic that when the American government finally acknowledged McKay's words on May 19, 1943, Prime Minister Winston Churchill of Great Britain was the one who issued the call.

The United States Congress was gathered in joint session for Churchill's historic visit. Riveting the high-level audience with his speechmaking, Churchill pleaded for continued American support for his country's cause and pledged imminent victory over Germany. As he concluded, he rallied the assembly to a final crescendo with his rendition of "If We Must Die": "If we must die, let it not be like hogs / Hunted and penned in an inglorious spot. . . / Like men we'll face the murderous, cowardly pack, / Pressed to the wall, dying, but fighting back!"

His choice was ironic not only because the poem sprang out of McKay's anguish over American policy but also because McKay was born and raised in Jamaica (West Indies), a British colony. Just as the poem had rallied African-Americans after the white mobs had terrorized Blacks in that awful "Red Summer" of 1919, over the next decades it became the rallying cry throughout the diaspora to throw off the yoke of European and American domination. When his voice rang out with McKay's immortal words, we witnessed the spectacle of one oppressor rallying another with the words of their mutual victim—a Caribbean-American Black man.

But there is no substitute for a good idea. With the end of the war, colonized (and segregated) people everywhere pushed toward the goal of freedom and independence as never before.

Wednesday, May 19, 1943, Washington, D.C.,
U.S.A.–England

International Affairs   **Philosophy**

MAY 20

We know so little about the life of the man who has ranked among the world's greatest thinkers for the past 2,500 years, since the sixth century before Christ. But this we do know: his name Aesop (Esop, Ethiop, and Aethiop are among its alternate spellings) means "African," and contemporary descriptions of his facial features and skin coloring support this designation. His dates of birth and death are unknown, but this inspired moment, as related by historian J. A. Rogers, is thought to have taken place around 520 B.C.:

> Aesop's first master was Xanthus, who saw him in a market where he was for sale with two other slaves, a musician and an orator. Xanthus asked the musician what he could do. He replied, "Anything." The orator, to the same question, replied, "Everything." Turning next to Aesop, Xanthus asked, "And what can you do?" "Nothing" was the reply. "Nothing!" repeated Xanthus, at which Aesop replied, "One of my companions says he can do anything and the other asserts that he can do everything. That leaves me nothing."
>
> Struck by the reply, Xanthus said, "If I buy you, will you promise to be good and honest?" "I'll be that whether you buy me or not," retorted Aesop. "Will you promise not to run away?" "Did you ever hear a bird in a cage tell his master he intended making his escape?" demanded Aesop. Xanthus, pleased at Aesop's wit, was strongly tempted to buy him, but hesitated because of [his color and look]. He said, "[You] will set people hooting and gaping at us wherever we go." "A philosopher," replied Aesop calmly, "should value a man for his mind and not for his body." The purchase was made.

Despite his early slave status, Aesop became one of his day's most venerated men. He was unequaled as a teacher whose examples, drawn from his life and nature, continue to provide perspective on our own complex times.

520 B.C., Phrygia (Africa/Asia)

Philosophy/Folklore   **Assets**

MAY 21

It's been said, "Nothing is more powerful than an idea whose time has come." And in civil rights movement lore, few stories provide greater testament to this truth than that of Jo Ann Robinson, an English professor at the historically Black Alabama State College.

In 1949, she got on a bus, her arms full of packages. It was Christmas. She was not thinking about "her place" on the segregated bus or about taking a backseat to racism. The driver was, however, and barked out a degrading command to give up her seat. Humiliated, she fled the bus. After the holidays, she urged fellow members of the Women's Political Council (WPC), a community organization of Black women, to join her in protest. But her story fell on weary ears. With no support, she backed down—but she never forgot.

Five years later, on May 21, 1954, Robinson (who now headed the WPC) wrote to Montgomery's mayor. "Three-fourths of the riders [on the buses] . . . are Negroes," she challenged. "If Negroes did not patronize them, they could not possibly operate. People are already arranging . . . to [carpool] to keep from being insulted . . . by drivers." This was a bold move for the woman who remembered years of humiliating bus rides. But the times were changing. People were stirring. Not only were others beginning to see things her way, they were now willing to act on what they saw.

Eighteen months later, when Rosa Parks was arrested for refusing her seat to a white passenger, the time for Robinson's idea had undeniably come. She stayed up all night mimeographing thirty-five thousand flyers for her students to distribute the next morning. On Monday morning, as Mrs. Parks went to court, empty buses rolled the routes. The Montgomery bus boycott was born (see December 1), a milestone in civil rights history and a personal victory for Jo Ann Robinson.

Friday, May 21, 1954, Alabama, U.S.A.

Civil Rights   **Productive Patience**

MAY 22

On May 22, 1974, representatives from every part of the African diaspora were gathered in Dar es Salaam, Tanzania. Of all the Pan-African congresses since the notion had first been formed in 1899 and realized in 1900 (see July 23), this was the first congress to convene without its founding member, Dr. W. E. B. Du Bois; it was also the first to take place since the defeat of colonial rule had given birth to independent nation-states, and the first to take place on the mother continent, Africa.

Since the founding congress in London, there had been five others—in Paris in 1919; in London, Brussels, and Paris in 1921; in London and Lisbon in 1923; in New York in 1927; and in Manchester, England, in 1945. At the first event, the goal was "home rule" (self-rule) for colonized peoples. The newly coined term, "Pan-Africanism," while rooted in a desire to find common relief from the terrible weight of discrimination, was also born of a need to heal the still-open wounds left by the slave trade. As people severed from their African roots, few attendees of the congresses had personal knowledge of the continent. Du Bois himself, for example, initially held a rather paternalistic view of Africa as incapable of self-government. Over the years, the bonds made and the isolation dispelled at the congresses have led to the forging of a Pan-African or "Afrocentric" worldview—a concept that grew out of necessity, out of the shared colonial experience.

Three-quarters of a century later, as the congress came home at last, Africans by birth and descent met for eight days from May 19 to 27, 1974, with one common goal: "Africa for the Africans."

MAY 23

When you think about it, *Shuffle Along*, the first all-Black Broadway musical play, had no right to be as successful as it was when it opened on May 23, 1921. First, it was so poorly funded before it opened that the only location the producers could afford to rent was the dilapidated Sixty-third Street Theater. Second, the casting director had rejected the soon-to-be-legendary Ethel Waters as a "cheap honky-tonk singer." But to the show's credit, in the cast were three superstars-in-the-making: Florence Mills, Paul Robeson, and Noble Sissle, and the unbelievably rich orchestra featured vaudeville's Eubie Blake on piano, future choral director Hall Johnson on viola, and seminal composer William Grant Still on oboe. Within weeks of its opening, the show was so successful that the city's Traffic Department had to turn the block in front of the theater into a one-way street.

Shuffle Along made history. With lyrics and music by the team of Sissle and Blake and a book by Flournoy Miller and Aubrey Lyles, *Shuffle Along* transcended its roots in minstrel revue to bring a Black folk drama to life. Because Broadway was supported by a predominantly white audience and by an all-white theater establishment, the nature of Black theater was still constrained by what whites were willing to accept. But in *Shuffle Along*, a story, albeit trite, was being told to music, and for the first time the aesthetic was all-Black. The Austrian theater great Max Reinhardt saw the production as, "[the] most modern, most American, most expressionistic. . . . To me they reveal new possibilities of technique in drama."

Shuffle Along played a milestone 504 performances before launching a road company the following year; the legendary Josephine Baker began her career as a chorus girl in the touring cast. Not only was the show a hit in the 1920s but with its return to Broadway in 1952 it became a bona fide classic!

Monday, May 23, 1921, New York, U.S.A.

Theater **Re-visioning**

MAY 24

On May 24, 1961, after weeks of brutality, twenty-seven Freedom Riders arrived in Jackson, Mississippi (see May 4), to find themselves arrested as perpetrators of the disturbance rather than as victims of the violence that had been hurled against them. Yet as soon as they were bailed out of jail, they continued their historic mission to desegregate public transportation.

In today's world, it is difficult for some to understand how African-Americans of the 1950s and 1960s became a nonviolent multigenerational army of foot soldiers, all in the name of freedom. If you want to understand it or to remind yourself of a similarly historic day that you lived in civil rights history, if you want to feel the power of that time, then the National Civil Rights Museum in Memphis, Tennessee, is the place to go.

Taking the pain and turning it into a testament of triumph, the museum is an interactive see-hear-and-touch time capsule built on the grounds of the historic Lorraine Motel where Dr. King was assassinated on April 4, 1968 (see April 3). The room in which he stayed and the balcony on which he was shot are preserved, while the rest of the entire motel has been gutted and remodeled for the museum.

In another display, Rosa Parks's life-sized look-alike sits on a bus, which visitors enter only to be told to move to the back, with a jarring effect. A full-sized lunch counter brings back the sit-ins. And a burned-out shell of a Greyhound bus leaves little question about the heroism of the Freedom Riders and all those who participated in the civil rights era.

One of the most beautiful aspects of the movement was its ability to bring together everyday people in everyday acts of courage and rebellion that cumulatively brought about the desegregation of America. All these qualities are memorialized here.

Wednesday, May 24, 1961, Mississippi–Tennessee, U.S.A.
Civil Rights   **Memory**

MAY 25

◆ On May 25, 1857, the final round of one of the most shameful Supreme Court decisions in history was at last brought to a satisfactory resolution when Harriet and Dred Scott were freed in Missouri by the estate of their "owner."

The *Dred Scott* case in fact consisted of two cases dating to Scott's 1846 attempt to buy his family's freedom as residents of a territory that prohibited slavery. The owner refused, and Scott filed suit. When Scott's wife was slapped by his owner, Harriet Scott charged trespass, assault, and false imprisonment in a second suit. But an 1847 court backlog threatened what was thought to be their "impending" freedom. The Scotts were advised that whatever happened in Dred's case should determine Harriet's. The linking of the two separate cases reflected the legal status at that time of all women as secondary to their husbands. As a result, Harriet Scott was twice victimized, by race and by gender.

For ten years, the Scotts fought for their freedom and for ten years they were denied. In its infamous *Dred Scott* decision, the majority opinion of the Supreme Court reasoned that Blacks "had for more than a century before been regarded as beings of an inferior order . . . and so far inferior, that they had no rights which the white man was bound to respect." Finally, in 1857, shortly after the owner's death, the Scotts' attorney received title to Dred Scott without explanation and manumitted the family within days.

While the middle of the twentieth century saw a Supreme Court–backed end to segregation (see May 17, December 20), recent decisions have wavered in protecting those gains. Based on the full history of Supreme Court decisions, one may reasonably conclude that it has served less as a blind arbiter of right and wrong than as a barometer of the prevailing political winds.

Monday, May 25, 1857, Missouri, U.S.A.

Law   **Truths**

MAY 26

When Liberian President Edwin Barclay arrived at the White House on May 26, 1943, to pay an official state visit to President Franklin Delano Roosevelt, it was the first time the United States had welcomed an African head of state.

The dynamics of the event were certainly complex and interesting. There was America's historic involvement with the African continent as the enslaver of its people. There was the dubious legacy of the African Colonization Society (ACS), which had established American colonies in Liberia and Sierra Leone. The ACS had taken advantage of Back-to-Africa yearnings by helping, and sometimes forcing, free Blacks to emigrate. ACS's controversial "aid" was later revealed to be prompted by its real goal: to shield the institution of slavery from constant agitation by the free Black abolitionist movement (see January 24, February 6, February 24). With the ACS's duplicitous plan revealed, there could be little doubt about American attitudes toward Liberia itself. When Liberians claimed their independence in 1847, it should have been a reminder to Americans that for one former colony to colonize another was hypocrisy and tyranny of the highest order; so, too, for one formerly oppressed group to similarly oppress another. It did not.

Thus, as the century-old Liberia, in the person of President Barclay, called upon its former colonial power, it was the first U.S. diplomatic corps recognition of African sovereignty. And it was the first recognizable breeze in what British prime minister Harold Macmillan would later call the "winds of change"—a change in the willingness of the world's people to submit to the impositions of colonial rule. As President Barclay's presence and welcome made clear, the "winds of change," in the wake of World War II, were purifying the air over Africa with the spirit of freedom and nationalism.

Wednesday, May 26, 1943, U.S.A.–Liberia
Politics/Pan-African World   **Self-Determination**

MAY 27

On May 27, 1958, Ernie Green became the first Black student to graduate from Central High School in Little Rock, Arkansas. That day marked the end of a year-long school desegregation ordeal that he and eight others had suffered as the "Little Rock Nine." Ever since the 101st Airborne Division troops had escorted them past an angry segregationist mob thousands strong on September 25, 1957, the Nine had formed an inseparable bond (see October 22). But now, as the only senior, Green was the lone Black graduate in a class of six hundred whites.

On graduation day, the troops were still there, along with the press, the FBI, every city police officer, and a violence-prone audience of 4,500. The only people not allowed to attend were Green's supporters—the other eight, their families, and the Black press—as authorities allegedly opted to limit the number of Black people that they would have to guard. Each honoree crossed the platform to a round of cheers. Then it was Green's turn to accept his diploma. Listening to their radios at home, the other eight prayed for Ernie. As he stepped onto the platform, the cheers became a pin-drop silence. "Who cares if they applaud, they didn't shoot him," said the grandmother of Melba Pattillo, one of the Nine.

After a year at Central High, what had been learned? Blacks learned that their human rights cause carried power in the world arena. Whites learned that terrorization would no longer force Blacks to continue to validate notions of white privilege. And school boards learned the effects of pouring salt on the wounds of caste and class: bypassing the upper-class "lily-white" high school, the board had assigned less privileged whites to bear the brunt of desegregation. Ultimately, the antidesegregation debacle cost taxpayers an estimated $5,000,000, 10 percent of which was spent on graduation day alone—and that was just the dollar amount. The total charge will be assessed by those who reap its benefits in the next century and beyond.

Tuesday, May 27, 1958, Arkansas, U.S.A.

Desegregation   **Courage**

MAY 28

To visit the borough of Brooklyn in New York City with its annual "West Indian Day Parade" and other reminders of the Caribbean and Africa is to get the distinct impression that Blacks have always lived in this section of New York. We have.

No one knows when the first people of African descent actually saw North America for the first time, but the earliest documentation of Blacks in New York during the colonial era dates back to 1626. After working for the Dutch East India Company for eighteen years, four were manumitted. Their names survive to give us a sense of their native lands: Simon Congo, Paul D'Angola, John Francisco, and Anthony Portuguese.

On May 28, 1643, the first property holder in the Gravesend section of Brooklyn to walk land he could call his own was a descendant of northern Africa, Antonie Jansen Van Salee. Like his white colonial counterparts, he was not able to read and write and could only put his X on the first land patent, called a ground-brief, issued by Dutch Governor Kieft for the Dutch East India Company. Van Salee's parcel of one hundred morgen, or approximately two hundred acres, was to be divided into two sections: "Old Bowery" and "Twelve Morgen." His land stretched so far that the "Old Bowery" portion is now considered part of Unionville, Long Island. His "Twelve Morgen" section is what we now call Little Neck.

Interestingly enough, although the land was assigned to him in 1643, its title was retroactively dated back to August 1, 1639, exactly thirty years after the arrival in America of the first so-called African indentures. Clearly, even with the moral affront of kidnapping people into "indenture" and slavery (see August 1), there were established options to redress the terrible wrongs done to Africans.

Thursday, May 28, 1643, New Netherlands

Social History   **Foundations**

MAY 29

On this date in 1912, a mother brought home a belated birthday gift from her employers to her thirteen-year-old son. This was the birthday gift that told Aaron Douglas he would become an artist (see October 30).

Douglas's artistic ability had manifested itself while he was quite young, and his mother regularly hung his drawings and paintings in their home. It was her encouragement, which was supported in turn by his father, that nurtured his youthful confidence. "I guess [my mother] is responsible for my becoming an artist. One of the families she worked for was the Malvane family [who] established what is now the Malvane Museum of Art at Washburn University in Topeka. I guess my mother must have talked to them about me because one day she came home with a magazine that they had given her. It had in it a reproduction of a painting by Henry Ossawa Tanner [see September 25]. It was his painting of Christ and Nicodemus meeting in the moonlight on a rooftop. I remember the painting very well. I spent hours poring over it, and that helped to lead me to deciding to become an artist."

Using the gift his mother had nurtured in him, Douglas became the preeminent painter of the Harlem Renaissance. As he once decreed boldly, "I refuse to compromise and see Blacks as anything less than a proud and majestic people." He was the first African-American artist to derive his primary inspiration from the wealth of African art.

His *Building More Stately Mansions* (1944) appears on the cover and as January's lead illustration. Of this masterwork Romare Bearden and Harry Henderson have praised Douglas in *A History of African-American Artists* for "identifying his people—not machines—as a constructive force in American life." For Douglas, knowledge of our past was a powerful tool to build our "stately mansions" and implement our future.

Wednesday, May 29, 1912, Kansas, U.S.A.

Art   **Building Dreams**

MAY 30

On May 30, 1974, the oldest surviving African-American church in the United States, Boston's African Meeting House, was officially named a national historic landmark.

The first Blacks were brought to Boston as slaves in 1638, and while Massachusetts was the first colony to legalize slavery, in 1783 it became one of the first states to abolish it. After gaining the freedom of their persons, these African-Americans next set out to attain religious freedom. In 1805, Thomas Paul, an African-American preacher from New Hampshire, formed the First African Baptist Church, with services held at Faneuil Hall, Boston's social, political, and cultural hub. From that base, the congregation launched plans to build a church of their own. One of the members, the African-born Cato Gardner, personally raised more than $1,500 of the total $7,700 cost. Black hands did almost all of the construction work on the building. And on December 6, 1806, the African Meeting House was dedicated, with a full house of multiracial supporters in attendance.

In this building, most of Boston's Black religious, educational, social, and political activities took place. And with its obvious abolitionist mandate, it even served as a haven for fugitive slaves. Nevertheless, despite its position at the center of all Black life for over a century, the African Meeting House was sold in the late 1800s, having been abandoned as the Black community migrated to the outlying neighborhoods. Not until 1972, when it was acquired by the Museum of African-American History, was it restored to its place of respect in our cultural life.

It is worthwhile to remember on this day that all around the country, other treasures of our history are fast fading away. If we don't protect our past for the glory of our future, who will?

Thursday, May 30, 1974, Massachusetts, U.S.A.

Social History   **Preservation**

MAY 31

 In Virginia there is a mighty oak tree whose roots grow deep in the spiritual soil of Africans; this tree is Hampton's Emancipation Oak.

On this and many other days in the spring of 1861, Mrs. Mary Peak, a freedwoman, could be found teaching the children of former slaves with only this tree for shelter. Her open-air classroom was the first such organized form of education in Virginia, a state where it had been illegal to teach Blacks the rudiments of education—reading and writing. From this humble start, an adjacent site was selected for the first free school for Black children in 1863, the Butler School.

Also beneath this tree people first learned of their freedom from slavery. Although President Lincoln's Emancipation Proclamation took effect on January 1, 1863, it would be two more years before Union victory and the end of the Civil War would make its words a reality for Virginia's slaves. In the spring of 1865, the decree was read underneath this tree, forever consecrating the spot as hallowed ground and designating the tree as the "Emancipation Oak."

Seeking land for a missionary school for Blacks, General Samuel Chapman Armstrong chose the present site of Hampton Institute because it was the ground on which the beloved oak had kept its covenant with nature and faith. And when the Hampton Normal and Agricultural Institute officially opened in 1868, its founder still sought inspiration from the oak under which he planted acorns of knowledge in his earliest students.

Today, the Emancipation Oak has been officially recognized by the state of Virginia for its significance in the history of education. Known worldwide for the beauty of its bearing and meaning, the National Geographic Society has named it one of the ten greatest trees in the world.

Friday, May 31, 1861, Virginia, U.S.A.

Education   **Potential**

JUNE

Rosa Parks at the Poor People's Solidarity March (June 19, 1968). Photographer unknown. Reprinted courtesy of the author. For more information, see May 11, December 1.

JUNE 1

On June 1, 1835, thirty-five freeborn and manumitted Blacks from six states and the nation's capital gathered in Philadelphia for the annual National Convention (see April 2). Following an emotional debate, they sought refuge from the continued abuses of racism by placing their very identity as "African" Americans on the auction block: "Resolved, . . . that we recommend . . . to our people to abandon the use of the word 'colored' . . . concerning themselves; and especially to remove the title of 'African' from their institutions, the marbles of churches, and etc."

Surely, these were trying, desperate times. Just the summer before, England had officially abolished slavery throughout its colonies. But in the United States, the terror continued unabated. In New Hampshire, an otherwise dormant state, a mob and one hundred head of oxen dragged a Black school from its moorings into a swamp. In the face of such hatred, Blacks were sacrificing all not to offend. Yet although they were well aware that freemen and freewomen ran the risk of being enslaved for aiding runaway slaves, they would compromise on everything but this:

> Resolved, That our duty to God, and to the principles of human rights, so far exceeds our allegiance to those laws that return the slave again to his master, that we recommend our people to peaceably bear the punishment those inflict, rather than aid in returning their brethen again to slavery.

Sadly, though, in their attempts at not "offending" the very people who had more than "offended" them and their forebears, they had sacrificed more than a name; they had sacrificed themselves. With the denial of their shared identity and plight as Africans in the Americas came the inevitable loss of the reason undergirding their bond. With that, the annual National Convention movement died—not to be revived for a century until the national Negro Congress of 1936.

Monday, June 1, 1835, Pennsylvania, U.S.A.
Social History   **Identity**

JUNE 2

On June 2, 1863, Harriet Tubman was the first and, for the next two hundred years, the only woman to lead American troops in battle. Her expertise was honed as the most famous Underground Railroad conductor of all. As "Moses," she had led nineteen rescue missions through enemy territory in states north and south.

Moses couldn't read or write. But she could read the stars, the sun, and the character of those she met. From nature, she knew the time of day, the patterns of the seasons, and how to chart her routes. Using her legendary survival skills, she made all of her missions during the winter, when the nights are longer than the days. She regularly wore several layers of clothing for warmth and disguise, often traveling as a man. But it was as a woman that she served the Union Army as scout and leader, as the *Boston Commonwealth* reported:

> Col. Montgomery and his gallant band of 300 black soldiers, under the guidance of a black woman, dashed into the enemy's country, struck a bold and effective blow, destroying millions of dollars' worth of [supplies], striking terror into the heart of rebeldom, brought off near 800 slaves . . . without losing a man or receiving a scratch. . . . They were addressed [by] the black woman who led the raid and under whose inspiration it was organized and conducted. . . . Many times she has penetrated the enemy's lines and discovered their situation and condition, and escaped without injury, but not without extreme hazard.

Hazard was nothing new to Harriet Tubman. In the mid 1800s, rewards for her capture had reached $40,000, the equivalent of a few million today. But, she said, "there were two things I had a right to, liberty [and] death. If I could not have one, I would have the other. No man would take me alive. . . . And when the time came for me to go, the Lord would let them take me." Her Lord let her live to be ninety-two.

Tuesday, June 2, 1863, South Carolina, U.S.A.

Military/Civil War   **Possibility**

JUNE 3

On June 3, 1941, Dr. Charles Drew, the inventor of blood banks, said no to "blood money."

With a fellowship to Columbia University's College of Physicians and Surgeons, Dr. Drew was appointed to a surgical residency where he became interested in the concept of blood transfusion. Although the procedure was widely practiced, the means of preserving blood for later use had not been developed. Researching this critical need at the college's Presbyterian Hospital, Dr. Drew developed his doctoral dissertation, "Banked Blood," in 1940. His Ph.D. in medicine was the first ever awarded to an African-American. The timing of his work coincided with the beginning of the war in Europe. When Great Britain requested immediate access to his discovery, Drew became famous overnight. Within two weeks of being appointed the medical supervisor of the Blood for Britain program, Drew had instituted the process that would save thousands of lives. Now he was both famous and in demand.

As the war escalated, the United States planned a national Red Cross blood drive that prohibited the use of "black blood." Every scientist knew there was no such thing as "black blood" or "white blood." Yet the program's doctors remained silent. Adding insult to injury, a "solution" was reached, allowing Blacks to donate blood but segregating their plasma.

Outraged, the founder of blood-banking himself resigned from the program on June 3, 1941. His devotion to saving lives extended far beyond science. Dr. Charles Drew said no to the implications of the restrictions on his work and no to the insanity of those who would compromise the benefits of his work—even in battle. In refusing the Red Cross's "blood money," he was refusing to pursue blood research that was tainted by bigotry. For Dr. Drew, the issue was not "white blood" or "black blood"; it was bad blood. As an African-American and as founder of the life-saving blood-bank concept, he could not expose his work to contamination.

Tuesday, June 3, 1941, New York, U.S.A.

Medicine   **Dignity**

JUNE 4

In 1969, as California governor Ronald Reagan's administration sought a cause around which to build its political agenda, the image of a twenty-five-year-old Black professor of philosophy provided just the ticket. When Angela Davis refused to sign an anti-Communist "loyalty oath," she became Reagan's public enemy number one. Fighting for her job and her constitutional freedom of speech, her message of conscience resonated deeply with a generation committed to Black Studies, women's liberation, and the antiwar movement. For Davis's personal philosophy went far deeper than that of her elite education in Europe. The four girls killed in the Birmingham, Alabama, church bombing of 1963 (see September 15) had been her childhood friends; she was committed to justice for life.

Then, in August 1970, the infamous Marin County courthouse shoot-out took place, killing four people—among them a judge and one of the alleged perpetrators, a Black prisoner and friend of Davis. The permit for one of the weapons used had been legally issued to Davis. A warrant was issued for her arrest, Davis went underground, a national dragnet ensued, and her name was listed among the FBI's "Ten Most Wanted" felons. All this for a woman the FBI said had not been present or fired a shot during the incident.

In October 1970, Davis was captured in a New York hotel and extradited to California, where she was charged with murder, kidnapping, and criminal conspiracy. Imprisoned and periodically held in solitary confinement, Davis became a national cause célèbre complete with defense-fund rallies and "Free Angela!" vigils. The case of the *People of the State of California v. Davis* began on February 28, 1972. On Sunday, June 4, 1972, after two days of deliberation, the jury confirmed what everyone had always known: Angela Davis was not guilty.

Sunday, June 4, 1972, California, U.S.A.

Law   **Justice**

JUNE 5

Few have acquired as broad a range of knowledge as Alain Locke. Of his many achievements—first and only African-American Rhodes Scholar during his lifetime, philosopher, educator—it was the critic in him who served us best. Unable to "let things be," he nurtured the gifts of others and built our appreciation for their work.

When Jesse Moorland donated his papers to Howard University in 1914 for what would become the noted Moorland-Spingarn Research Collection, Locke proposed a course on race and race relations based on the papers. But this was the era when the board, the president, and a large proportion of the faculty were white, so the course was denied on the grounds that despite Howard's acknowledged role in educating Blacks, it was a "nonracial" institution. Undaunted, Locke got the local NAACP chapter and the Social Science Club to sponsor a two-year "Extension Course of Lectures" instead. This led to his work as a pioneer in adult education at the college level.

Throughout his forty-one-year affiliation with the university, Locke improved Howard—often in spite of itself. When he retired, Howard offered its unprecedented thanks. In a rare move, on June 5, 1953, Howard University awarded its highest honor to one of its own with this citation:

> [Your] intellectual interests have been as broad as life itself. You have been a valuable critic of dogmatic ideology, a creator of free-moving ideas, an appreciator of the great cultural diversity in American life, and a gentle, but persuasive apostle, of that unity of America and the world which thrives upon the coexistence and cooperation of individual and cultural differences.

It was a worthy tribute, both for the author of seminal works in art, culture, and criticism and for the school that had recognized his contributions.

Friday, June 5, 1953, Washington, D.C., U.S.A.

Education   **Culture**

JUNE 6

In 1962, via television, thousands escorted James Meredith up the steps of the University of Mississippi under military guard as he became the first Black student to register for school, integrating "Ole Miss" (see September 30). Four years later, and one year after the passage of the federal Voting Rights Act, Meredith was championing a new crusade. Of the one million eligible Blacks, less than twelve thousand had registered to vote. Meredith was leveraging his national reputation to tackle the real issue head-on: fear. With unbelievable courage and faith, he began a 220-mile solo homecoming trek from Memphis, Tennessee, to Jackson, Mississippi, his "March Against Fear." Starting out, he anticipated the walk would take a few weeks. But on June 6, 1966, one day into his solo march, an assassin pumped a round of bullets into Meredith and elevated a lonely ripple of the civil rights movement into a full-blown tidal wave.

A candid photo of the fallen Meredith's agonized scream was seen on televisions and in newspapers nationwide. It struck deep wounds as thousands of people around the country stopped whatever they were doing and headed for Mississippi. The next day, June 7, Meredith's crusade moved on, thousands of marchers strong. In the lead were Martin Luther King, Jr., activist-comic Dick Gregory, Floyd McKissick (head of the Congress of Racial Equality), and Stokely Carmichael of SNCC (the Student Nonviolent Coordinating Committee). Enraged by the shooting down of Meredith's peaceful intention, Carmichael armed himself with a forceful new battle cry. "Black Power!" he exclaimed. "Black Power!"—the marchers took up his impassioned cry, uttered for the first time on this eventful journey.

On June 26, Meredith rejoined the march for its rallying climax at Mississippi's state capitol; thirty thousand marchers bore the standard of his courage to a finish line that Meredith, himself, could never have anticipated.

Monday, June 6, 1966, Mississippi, U.S.A.

Social History   **Mutual Aid**

JUNE 7

On June 7, 1892, the coachman of a Louisiana train ordered a passenger to vacate his first-class seat and move to the segregated "colored" car. Homer Plessy refused, was arrested under the Louisiana Separate Car Act of the 1890s, and maintained his innocence up to the Supreme Court in the infamous test known as *Plessy v. Ferguson*. This is the case that on May 18, 1896, made "separate but equal" segregation an American way of life.

According to trial records, Plessy was "a passenger of the colored race," "one-eighth black," whose "mixture of colored blood [was] not discernible." *Plessy* challenged political extremism bent on guaranteeing one thing—white male supremacy no matter the injustice or cost. Segregation was profitable—especially in the former slave states where Blacks often outnumbered whites. Blacks were overcharged and undercompensated; on every level, they paid full price for sub-standard returns. With the Supreme Court's *Plessy v. Ferguson* decision of 1896, the "separate but equal" doctrine legalized segregation, legitimized the violence required to sustain it, and institutionalized the blight of Jim Crow.

In his written dissent, Justice John Marshall Harlan called the majority opinion as "pernicious as the *Dred Scott* case" (see May 25)—the Court's 1857 decision that "under law, blacks had no rights a white man is bound to respect." Harlan's voice of conscience raised on May 18, 1896, went ignored for sixty years until *Brown v. Board of Education* (see May 17). In 1954, the Court overturned the doctrine of "separate but equal" public schools, signaling the end of legal segregation. With the back-to-back anniversaries of *Brown* and *Plessy* on May 17 and May 18, we witness the terrible teeter-totter of American justice. And we remember Homer Plessy, who acted with courage and sanity at a time when both weighed little in the balance.

Tuesday, June 7, 1892, Louisiana, U.S.A.

Law   **Pride**

JUNE 8

Malcolm X (né Malcolm Little) definitely suffered a tragic childhood. When Malcolm was six, his father was killed in a streetcar accident that was very likely a racially motivated murder. With the death of his father came the destruction of his family and the loss of his childhood. When Malcolm was thirteen, his distraught mother, who had to stand helpless while social workers took away her children "for their own good," was committed to an insane asylum. With his family in shambles, Malcolm traded his top grades and his ambitions to become a lawyer for street smarts and six years in prison.

How did he reclaim his life and find his life's mission? His parents, Earl and Louise Little, had blazed quite a trail for him to follow. The Littles were active in Marcus Garvey's Pan-Africanist Universal Negro Improvement Association (see August 2). Mrs. Little wrote for the Omaha chapter's newspaper. Mr. Little was widely respected for his teachings on African heritage. But in spite of Klan threats and the torching of their home, they held to their beliefs and nurtured their children.

On June 8, 1927, with Garvey jailed as a political prisoner, Earl Little petitioned President Coolidge "that by the power vested in you, you release Marcus Garvey from the 5-year sentence . . . which shall be your priceless gift to the Negro people of the world thus causing your name to be honored with generations yet unborn." More than forty years later, when documents in Malcolm X's FBI file were released under the Freedom of Information Act, the Coolidge letter emerged. After its receipt at the White House in 1927, it was sent to the Department of Justice and intercepted by the FBI's J. Edgar Hoover, a longtime opponent of the movement for African-American rights.

Elders say, "What's in the root is in the branches." Malcolm X's convictions sprouted from strong family roots with their well-grounded determination to work for better days.

JUNE 9

For two years William Pinkney sailed the seas on *Commitment*, his forty-seven-foot sailboat. Ending his thirty-two-thousand-mile solo voyage around the world on June 9, 1992, he had a message he wanted to share with young people: "I did this to disprove the message I was given. . . . As a young Black male I was told that I'd end up in jail, on drugs, or dead. The thing is, I didn't believe that."

Pinkney was only physically alone as he set sail from Boston harbor. Raised by a single mother on welfare, he was a man out to prove a point, and a lot rode on his shoulders. The lucrative marketing career he had so carefully nurtured could be jeopardized by his failure. But Pinkney's marketing savvy was just what made his mission both possible and useful for hundreds of lives. And his mission also gave him a good deal of company and extra pleasure. En route, he produced a newsletter, video, curriculum guide, and maintained constant communication with schools via modem. Down the coast of North America, he sailed past the Caribbean islands, the South American coast, across the Atlantic Ocean to Cape Town, South Africa. Then, crossing through the South Seas to Tasmania and around Cape Horn, he came back up the South American coast and headed home. Through letters, model boats, hands-on lessons in math, science, navigation, and geography, the children shared his trip.

As he returned to Boston harbor on June 9, 1992, a victorious Pinkney was met by hundreds of schoolchildren. Together they had shared the joy of *"Commitment"* and the proof that a person can do what he or she sets out to do. Through his national lecture tour and the book about his journey, Pinkney continues to share his profoundly empowering view. "No matter who you are, where you are, or what people say, your dreams are important. If you get a sound basic education, if you are willing to work and never, never quit, you can make your dreams come true."

Tuesday, June 9, 1992, Massachusetts, U.S.A.

Adventure   **Commitment**

JUNE 10

As the will of a wealthy white Georgian, David Dickson, was read in 1886, his whole family came down with a case of the vapors. But they recovered their composure quickly in order to challenge the will in state court. The bachelor Dickson had willed seven-eighths of his estate to his biracial daughter and her Black mother. The remaining eighth was willed to his already comfortable family. Foul! cried the white side of his family as they went to court. "Disgusted as well as disappointed" is how the *New York Times* characterized their feelings. The Dicksons charged that the disposition of an estate by a white man to his "colored illegitimate child" was a violation of public policy.

If Dickson had been considered well off before the Civil War, after it he was wealthier still. As a member of one of Georgia's staunchest slaveholding families, with three hundred slaves on his ledger, he turned his agricultural holdings into a fortune after the war—even with the new social order. At the time of his death, David Dickson was worth $600,000 in nineteenth-century currency.

Taking their fight to the state supreme court, the Dickson family was told that a new social order did indeed exist. Under law, Blacks had the same civil rights as whites. The court ruled that David Dickson's will would stand. Amanda Eubanks inherited her father's estate, becoming the wealthiest African-American of her day.

Even in 1886 as the country was turning back the hands of history's clock to the "good ole days" of open slavery, Blacks stood their ground wherever and whenever possible, demanding enforcement of the few rights we had.

Thursday, June 10, 1886, Georgia, U.S.A.

Social History   **Principle**

JUNE 11

In a moment all too characteristic of the old warrior, on June 11, 1964, Vernon Johns, the notorious ex-pastor of the historic Dexter Avenue Baptist Church in Montgomery, Alabama, died with his boots on. Said civil rights era historian Taylor Branch, "After delivering one of his most famous lectures, 'The Romance of Death,' at Howard University, Johns himself dropped dead, in a sequence his admirers swore Johns had prearranged with God."

Self-educated in Virginia, Johns spent his days reciting poetry behind the plow and his nights reading every book he could find. He ran away from home to enter Oberlin College. Upon arrival, the dean reminded Johns that he'd been rejected because of insufficient credits. "I got your letter," Johns shot back. "But I want to know whether you want students with credits or students with brains." When Johns proved his exceptional knowledge of both German and Latin, the dean agreed to enroll him.

Years later in Montgomery, Johns was tough on his congregation—not for what they did but for what they didn't do. "It's Safe to Murder Negroes," he preached when a lynching went unchallenged. He saw his congregants throw out the baby of agri-business with the bathwater of slavery, by avoiding contact with the land. And, he mocked false pride, wore overalls to church, and sold fish and melons from the front steps.

In 1950, one of his frequent resignations was finally accepted. Retreating from confrontation, the war-weary church recruited a new young minister, fresh from divinity school, the Reverend Dr. Martin Luther King, Jr. It seemed that no matter how hard the church tried, there was no escaping its destiny and the times. It was only a short time until Rosa Parks's courage led to the Montgomery bus boycott (see December 1), goading the young minister and his congregation into action, and international acclaim.

Thursday, June 11, 1964, Washington, D.C.–Alabama, U.S.A.
Religion   **Purpose**

JUNE 12

On June 12, 1956, at the height of the McCarthy era and the anti-Communist scare, the consummate actor and singer Paul Robeson appeared before Congress. As a successful artist, Robeson experienced a rare type of personal freedom. Yet with doors open to him worldwide, he consistently refused to go anywhere as a celebrity that he could not go as a Black man.

In 1950, the State Department revoked his passport "in view of [his] frank admission that he has been for years extremely active politically in behalf of independence of the colonial peoples of Africa." His work for freedom worldwide netted him a subpoena to appear before the infamous House Un-American Activities Committee (HUAC) on June 12, 1956. Branding him a "Communist sympathizer," HUAC's chairman demanded to know why Robeson had visited Russia and not stayed. Robeson responded, "Because my father was a slave and my people died to build this country, and I am going to stay here and have a part of it just like you. And no Fascist-minded people will drive me from it. Is that clear?"

The chairman asked how Robeson, as a college graduate, could speak of prejudice. With his rich bass voice, Robeson replied, "The success of a few Negroes . . . can[not] make up for [the exploitation of] thousands of Negro families in the South. . . . I have cousins who are sharecroppers, and I do not see my success in terms of myself. That is the reason my own success has not meant what it should mean: I have sacrificed literally hundreds of thousands, if not millions, of dollars for what I believe in."

Prevented from reading his prepared statement before HUAC, the caliber of Robeson's spontaneous remarks proved the committee no match for the legal mind, the actor's command, and the unshakable belief in law and justice of the man who sacrificed everything for the cause of human rights (see October 19, November 28).

Tuesday, June 12, 1956, Washington, D.C., U.S.A.
Heroes   **Sacrifice**

JUNE 13

On June 13, 1994, the John D. and Catharine T. MacArthur Foundation officially acknowledged the genius of Arthur Mitchell with a life achievement award for his work as founder of the Dance Theatre of Harlem. In its quest to reward those individuals whose contributions enrich us all, the foundation had been providing its five-year fellowships, the so-called genius awards, since 1980 with the express purpose of freeing the individual from financial constraints.

The first African-American male dancer contracted as a permanent member of an American dance company, Mitchell joined the New York City Ballet in 1955. Within short order, he rose to prominence as a principal dancer. He started the Dance Theatre of Harlem in 1968 to satisfy a promise made to himself. Upon learning of the assassination of Dr. Martin Luther King, Jr., he vowed to establish a memorial to Dr. King by providing others with access to the opportunities that Mitchell himself had been given. That summer of 1968, he went home to the Harlem neighborhood that had nurtured him. Within months of the assassination, he had used his own savings to open a studio in a remodeled garage. And within a year, with the help of his mentor and teacher, Karel Shook, and a grant from the Ford Foundation, the Dance Theatre of Harlem had been formally incorporated as a school and professional dance company.

In 1994, he could look back over almost twenty-six years of achievement. With a company of thirty-six dancers, a repertoire of over seventy-five works, a school with 1,300 students, and thousands of alumni, Mitchell would now do what he had always done—just what he had promised: he would continue to build new opportunities for African-Americans in the world of dance and to provide audiences with new levels of artistic achievement and lasting images of rare beauty and insight. With the help of the MacArthur award, there was little doubt that Mitchell would make—and keep—a few more promises that would further benefit us all.

Monday, June 13, 1994, New York, U.S.A.

Dance   **Commitment**

JUNE 14

The year 1937 was rough everywhere. It was the era of the Great Depression. And, while Blacks and other people of color were the ones least responsible for the financial crisis, they were the ones worst hit by it. "How's things going in town?" folks would ask. "White folks in the lead" was the standard reply.

If there were few jobs for Black women, there were virtually none for Black men. One employment agency's books showed in a full year it managed to place 475 women and 3 men. And the job offers to Black women were these: full-time work plus two nights a week, salary $3 a week; full-time combined cook and typist, $35 a month. Jobs were in such great demand that the menial jobs that had long been held predominantly by Blacks were now being filled by whites. And on the street made famous the world over by Blacks, Harlem's 125th Street, African-Americans couldn't even get jobs in the stores they patronized.

Seeking to provide some relief, the Reverend John H. Johnson of Harlem's Saint Martin's Church launched his "Buy-Where-You-Can-Work" campaign. The *New York Age* newspaper backed his call, targeting 125th Street's own department store, Blumstein's, where 75 percent of the store's clientele was Black but all of its clerks and cashiers were white. And Abyssinian Baptist's the Reverend Adam Clayton Powell, Jr., lent his support by delivering a rallying sermon on economic empowerment to his congregation of two thousand.

On June 14, 1937, a ring of pickets surrounded Blumstein's and stayed in place for six weeks until sales dropped to a trickle and William Blumstein ended the boycott by agreeing to hire thirty-five Blacks for clerical and sales positions. As the *Christian Century* prophetically editorialized, "here is a weapon which the Negro is only beginning to realize he holds in his hands. . . . What would happen in the average southern city if its Negro population should determine not to patronize stores which discriminate against the Negro?"

Monday, June 14, 1937, New York, U.S.A.

Labor   **Collective Responsibility**

JUNE 15

June 15, a day of firsts in African-American military history. On June 15, 1877, West Point Military Academy graduated its first Black cadet, Henry O. Flipper of Georgia. And on June 15, 1917, the fortieth anniversary of Flipper's graduation, the army opened its first Black officers' training academy, Fort Des Moines, Iowa, or as it was called, the "Black West Point."

Flipper was not the first Black cadet admitted to West Point. That distinction belonged to James W. Smith of South Carolina in 1870. Ironically, as a Southerner from a slaveholding state appointed to West Point just five years after the Civil War, Smith was forced to withdraw by the mistreatment he received at the hands of the northern West Point establishment. The violence perpetrated against him during hazing was so bad that his life was in constant jeopardy. Flipper, on the other hand, had the benefit of Smith's years as the "first," and although his years at West Point were hardly smooth, he was able to complete his degree.

As the Black West Point, Fort Des Moines took in its first candidates during the nation's moral downturn, the era of Jim Crow. It was founded in response to lobbying efforts for the training of African-American officers by such leaders as Dr. W. E. B. Du Bois and backed by the NAACP. It was also a "payback" of sorts for the recruitment of Blacks during World War I.

Taken in the context of their times, each June 15 was its own special "high" on the teeter-totter of Black involvement in the military. Blacks had fought in every American conflict since the Revolutionary War. With each, Black soldiers and nurses received a host of promises, only to be denied their due credit afterward. Each June 15 in its own way, therefore, marked an important step toward the goal of desegregating the military and according African-Americans in uniform their due respect.

Friday, June 15, 1877, Iowa–New York, U.S.A.

Military   **Ambition**

JUNE 16

This is what we know of Denmark Vesey. In the late 1700s, he spent twenty years of his life as the slave of a slave trader. In 1800, he won a lottery and purchased his freedom. For the next twenty years, as a free Black man in Charleston, South Carolina, he plied his trade as a carpenter. In 1822, he refused an offer to emigrate to Africa because, as he said, "he wanted to stay and see what he could do for his fellow creatures." By June of that year, he had recruited what some historians estimate to be as many as nine thousand men for his planned revolt against slavery. What makes June 16, 1822, special is the response of his men to the fact that their revolt had been betrayed by a slave.

Vesey's chief of staff was Peter Poyas, a strategic genius. It was Poyas who pinpointed the greatest danger to a slave revolt: house slaves—slaves trained to personally identify with their slavemasters. He was right. One of their soldiers had disobeyed orders and recruited a house slave, who soon grew fearful, and within five days, the plan had been betrayed to authorities. Word reached Vesey's organization that Poyas and another leader, Mingo Harth, were under suspicion. And in an amazing test of wits between the rebels and the authorities, the town became a virtual chessboard of tactical activity.

Instead of fleeing, Poyas and Harth went directly to the mayor's office and indignantly demanded to clear their names of such terrible accusations. With this head-on confrontation, they were released by officials convinced that guilty slaves would not behave that way. It bought the Vesey group time, but the damage to the plot was too great to overcome completely. Within weeks, Vesey and his five closest comrades had been tried and hanged. But they had remained true to the group's code, and whatever other secrets they knew had died with them. As the officials had accomplished their mission—suppression—so had the Vesey group. They put Charleston on notice that true people do not stand complacently by to watch others suffer as slaves.

Sunday, June 16, 1822, South Carolina, U.S.A.

Freeman's Revolt!   **Principles**

JUNE 17

On June 17, 1972, a Black security guard, Frank Wills, detected a break-in at a Washington, D.C., office building and, out of his devotion to his job and the truth, apprehended the five burglars, brought in the police, and brought down the president of the United States. The burglars were the so-called Plumbers, engaged in political espionage for the Republican party, and the target of the burglary was the Democratic National Party headquarters in the Watergate office building and apartment complex.

As the facts of the case unraveled in the two years after Frank Wills uncovered the Watergate break-in, the trail of deceit led to the Oval Office and to the seat reserved for President Richard Nixon.

Wills should have been a hero. As the man whose on-the-job performance led to disclosure of a serious breach of executive power and one of the nation's most historic events, Wills should have been lauded as a symbol of the quintessential "common man." Instead, he suffered the fate of all too many whistle-blowers, a fate compounded in his case by racism. Instead of being given a hero's reward, he went from being considered untrustworthy to being shunned, being blamed for the national shame, and sometimes being the victim of outright harassment. Unable to cope, he bounced from job to job, which only increased allegations of his "unreliable" and "unstable" nature.

Finally, in 1974, Wills was officially honored in a ceremony led by Dr. Ralph Abernathy, head of the Southern Christian Leadership Conference. Were it not for Wills's work, Nixon's "Plumbers," "secret police," "enemies' list," and other direct attempts to subvert the democratic process might never have come to light.

Saturday, June 17, 1972, Washington, D.C., U.S.A.

Politics   **Honor**

JUNE 18

In the first northern mass student demonstration, the public school students of Boston, Massachusetts, held a one-day school boycott on June 18, 1963.

Inspired by the civil rights activism of young people throughout the South, the parent-supported protest was staged by three thousand African-American students from kindergarten through twelfth grade. Nine years had passed since the Supreme Court's historic *Brown v. Board of Education* decision had outlawed "separate but equal" education. The Court had mandated an end to segregation "with all deliberate speed." But the process had become quite deliberate and the remedy quite slow in coming. The South's de jure (by law) segregation and the North's de facto (by custom) segregation were both in place, and if there was any change taking place at all, it was most likely to be found in the South. Too many northern school districts had been allowed to remain in denial while the glare of violent racism plagued the South. The North talked equality but was no more inclined to put those words into practice than the South had been. With the Boston boycott, African-Americans forced the spotlight to be placed on the North's persistent and hypocritical de facto school segregation.

Often, people forget that school districts receive their allotments from the state based on the number of students in attendance each day. The boycott of three thousand students on one day got the attention of the Boston schools in a meaningful way. It also got the attention of parents who began to seek alternatives for their children in a network of private, independent schools. Soon, the battle was being fought over obtaining state accreditation for these schools, since each student who transferred meant money lost to the public schools. A new battle was on. But the days of denial were officially over.

Tuesday, June 18, 1963, Massachusetts, U.S.A.

Children   **Alternatives**

JUNE 19

It was a day for the history books. For many, it was the first real "glory day" of the many they hoped would follow: June 19, 1865 — "Juneteenth," as it would be remembered and celebrated annually afterward. On that day, a Union soldier rode into Galveston, Texas, declared all Confederate legislative acts of the previous four years void, and announced to slaves that their freedom day, centuries overdue, had arrived at last.

Nearly three years had passed since President Lincoln had signed the Emancipation Proclamation. Now the war was over and his life had been sacrificed just two months before. Within months, the Thirteenth Amendment forever outlawing slavery would be ratified by a majority of state governments and added to the Constitution. But for the majority of the three million known slaves throughout the United States, news of their emancipation was dependent on the word of former slave masters embittered not only by the loss of the Civil War but also by the loss of their "property," the slaves themselves. For months — and in some cases, years — after the proclamation became law, slaves remained ignorant of their freedom. And so in the most remote areas, it was left to Union soldiers to travel to the plantations spreading the news.

With the last battle of the Civil War fought at White's Ranch, Texas, on May 13, Major General Granger reached Galveston on June 19, 1865. What a day for rejoicing that was! And what a day of celebration it has remained ever since as Juneteenth, an annual Texas state holiday with an ever-increasing number of observances nationwide.

Monday, June 19, 1865, Texas, U.S.A.

Celebrations   **Joy**

JUNE 20

On June 20, 1939, the noted sculptor August a Savage presented the First Annual Exhibition Salon of Contemporary Negro Art at her own New York studio. One of the pivotal sculptures in her career—and the one that best represented her personal philosophy—was a bust of the Black nationalist leader, Marcus Garvey (circa 1930). Garvey would sit for Savage on Sunday mornings whenever he was available. With this work Savage began the process of adapting Garvey's motto, "Do for Self," into an ethic that led to the formation of her own salon for the promotion of a range of African-American talent. Her salon was the beginning of a movement toward Black aesthetic and promotional control over African-American art.

Savage's opportunities as a sculptor were unquestionably constricted by the bias against her as a Black woman. But, ironically, this very discrimination catapulted her to international notoriety in 1923. Savage had been named for a merit scholarship to a summer art school sponsored by the French government and located in Fontainebleau. But when Americans involved in the selection process discovered that she was Black, the scholarship was rescinded. Her response, as reported in the *New York World*, testified to the character of the woman. "I don't care much for myself . . . but other and better colored students might wish to apply sometime," said Savage. "This is the first year the school is open and . . . I don't like to see them establish a precedent."

With the experience gained from this publicity, Augusta Savage became a leader in the struggles of Black artists. The fight cost her dearly in terms of time lost and backlash suffered from critics, gallery owners, and patrons. But it contributed much to the opportunities given other African-American artists. Thus, through her efforts, we have all been greatly enriched.

Tuesday, June 20, 1939, New York, U.S.A.

Art/Business   **Generosity**

JUNE 21

Black women have played a unique role historically in rejecting the arguments of those who would pit the interests of "Blacks" against those of "women"—as though racism and sexism were not both human rights issues. Among the women who have challenged this dichotomy was a slave named Isabella. Inventing a new name to match her self-emancipated life, she vowed to be a traveler, Sojourner, in the name of Truth. By the time she arrived at the Women's Rights Convention in Akron, Ohio, on June 21, 1851, she was every bit her name.

At first, the predominantly white audience denied her the platform, protesting that the gathering was not an abolitionist convention. But when she rose to address the conference, she put the meeting in perspective. As Margaret Washington has said in her introduction to Truth's nineteenth-century narrative, Truth "saved the day for the women's cause." In part, this is what she said, as reported by the *Anti-Slavery Bugle:*

> The poor men seem to be all in confusion, and don't know what to do. Why children, if you have a woman's rights, give it to her and you will feel better. I can't read, but I can hear. I have heard the Bible and have learned that Eve caused man to sin. Well, if woman upset the world, do give her a chance to set it right side up again. . . . And how came Jesus into the world? Through God who created him and a woman who bore him. Man, where is your part? But the women are coming up, blessed be God, and a few of the men are coming up with them. But man is in a tight place, the poor slave is on him, woman is coming on him, he is surely between a hawk and a buzzard.

Sojourner Truth, Harriet Tubman, and Frederick Douglass—each of whom bore the scars of slavery—understood the historic parallels between the oppression of women and that of people of color. How interesting it is that what they saw so clearly then has been made to appear so cloudy today!

Saturday, June 21, 1851, Ohio, U.S.A.

Women   **Worldliness**

JUNE 22

On June 22, 1937, in the midst of the Great Depression, when African-American manhood was taking one of its worst whippings since the days of slavery, Joe Louis defeated James J. Braddock for the heavyweight boxing championship of the world. For Blacks who had stayed glued to their radios cheering him on, this was the moment the ancestors had told them would come. In the ring at Chicago's Comiskey Park, Louis had won more than a boxing match—Joe Louis had won the fight!

At the news, grandfathers swooped up armloads of children and raced into the night. This was one for their grandchildren's grandchildren to know about. "History!" they screamed, their voices forming a triumphant arch across the blocks and alleyways and boulevards and rivers from Chicago to Detroit, Memphis, New York, Dallas, and every city in the land. Real history was made the night Joe Louis won! This was a moment that surpassed all hope and expanded the realm of possibility, that filled the heart and eyes to overflowing with tears of anguish turned to joy. With his hammerin' hands of pride, Joe Louis had come through for the folks—just when we needed him most!

The story of Joe Louis's victory only improved with age—the age of the storyteller, and the number of times the story was told. The stakes in prizefighting had long been high in matches between Blacks and whites. Before the last Black champ, Jack Johnson, had won in 1910, a *Chicago Tribune* sportswriter reported, "If Johnson gains the victory, it will increase the confidence [Blacks] feel in themselves and, some persons fear, cause them to be less respectful of the power of the whites." After Johnson's victory, white rioters attacked Blacks nationwide. Johnson was vilified and victimized for his win, his temper, his bravado, and for having a white mistress in America. Still, as Talladega College's Professor William Pickens wrote of Johnson's victory in the *Chicago Defender,* what Johnson did for Blacks was "missionary work." With Joe Louis, religion was in again.

Tuesday, June 22, 1937, Illinois, U.S.A.

Sports   **Storytelling**

JUNE 23

The year 1926 was a productive one for African-American intellectuals. Two achievements set the standard for Harlem Renaissance writers and readers.

On June 23, 1926, Langston Hughes published his now-classic essay, "The Negro Artist and the Racial Mountain," in *The Nation:* "We younger Negro artists who create now intend to express our individual dark-skinned selves without fear or shame. If white people are pleased we are glad. If they are not, it doesn't matter. We know we are beautiful. And ugly too. The tom-tom cries and the tom-tom laughs. If colored people are pleased we are glad. If they are not, their displeasure doesn't matter either."

And then there was *Fire!*, a magazine inspired and edited by dramatist, journalist, and novelist Wallace Thurman. In 1926 the first and only issue of *Fire!* brilliantly captured the Harlem Renaissance literary movement. With its keen attention to quality and detail, it was simply too expensive to produce. Included in this first issue were plays by Zora Neale Hurston and Thurman; poems by Arna Bontemps, Countee Cullen, and Hughes; a story by Gwendolyn Bennett; and art by Aaron Douglas. Each was a Renaissance luminary in his or her own right. It opened with this rather stylish foreword:

> FIRE . . . weaving vivid, hot designs upon an ebony bordered loom and satisfying pagan thirst for beauty unadorned . . . /The flesh is sweet and real . . . /the soul an inward flush of fire . . . . Beauty?. . . / Flesh on fire—on fire in the furnace of life blazing. . . /Fy-ah, Fy-ah, Lawd, Fy-ah gonna burn ma soul!

As Hughes had said in his essay, "We build our temples for tomorrow, strong as we know how, and we stand on top of the mountain, free within ourselves." His essay and the temple of *Fire!* marked important cultural milestones and gave African-American arts and letters two lasting collector's items.

Wednesday, June 23, 1926, New York, U.S.A.
Literature/Harlem Renaissance   Energy

JUNE 24

On June 24, 1932, as thousands gathered in Washington, D.C., to fight for veterans' rights, they won an important victory over racial divisiveness.

In the summer of 1932, long after World War I had ended, a new battle was just beginning for impoverished veterans—the battle they would fight with their own government for the bonuses due them as vets. Three years into the Great Depression, men who had lent a hand when the country needed it most were left in desperate and dehumanizing poverty.

Twenty-five thousand "Bonuseers"—as the vets, Black and white, were called—headed to Washington, D.C., with their families. Setting up shacks and tents for their sit-in, they demanded immediate payment of the $50 to $100 bonuses that would be due to them in 1945, as provided by legislation. But this was the era of the Great Depression; they were desperate now. For months they lived in squalor, their plight ignored by callous members of Congress, which adjourned on July 17 without even acknowledging them. On July 28 an attack by the D.C. police left two veterans dead. President Hoover then ordered the army to attack the Bonuseers' defenseless and demoralized camps and drive them out of the city. In the process, scores of vets and their families were injured. Amazingly, despite their desperate circumstances, the Bonuseers never resorted to the all-too-frequent American problem solver: racial scapegoating.

As NAACP observer Roy Wilkins noted, "one of the many significant aspects of the Bonuseers banishment of Jim Crow is the lie it gives to United States Army officials who have been diligently spreading the doctrine that whites and blacks could not function together in the army." The "divide and conquer" tactic had been used on every American battlefront, whether military or societal, at home or abroad. The fact that it did not work with the Bonuseers was one more precedent leading to the eventual desegregation of the military in 1948.

Friday, June 24, 1932, Washington, D.C., U.S.A.

Veterans' Rights   **Honor**

JUNE 25

On June 25, 1941, President Franklin D. Roosevelt issued Executive Order No. 8802 banning racial and religious discrimination in all war-related industries and government programs. But this move did not occur without a fight.

In 1940, when World War II had seized Europe but America had not yet entered the conflict, the first major boost in jobs since the start of the Depression twelve years earlier was taking place in war-related industries. As companies vied for federal contracts, Blacks would have to make an early bid for fair employment.

If there are too few African-Americans in Congress to state our case today, there were none in 1940. The most revered Black labor leader, A. Philip Randolph, took the lead. Just four years earlier his leadership had successfully founded the first Black labor union, the Brotherhood of Sleeping Car Porters (see October 1). He and other Black leaders formed the Committee on the Participation of Negroes in the National Defense Program, which met with President Roosevelt in October of 1940. Six months later, that meeting had generated little more than empty promises. Finally, on May 1, Randolph called for a hundred thousand Blacks to march on Washington to protest the military-industrial complex's discriminatory policies. On June 18 under threat of the march, Roosevelt met with Black leaders and requested that the march be called off. Randolph refused and plans went forward. One week later, on June 25, President Roosevelt asserted his executive power to ban discrimination in the war industries. With the order issued, Randolph called off the march.

Randolph had long before conquered any fear of intimidation. Having built up a shield of African-American support, he cautiously moved forward with his strongest weapon in hand—a healthy regard for the use of his own power.

Wednesday, June 25, 1941, Washington, D.C., U.S.A.

Labor   **Strategy**

JUNE 26

Dr. W. E. B. Du Bois was nearing ninety when he decided to write his "Last Message to the World" on June 26, 1957. Fortunately, we would benefit from his wisdom for another six years before he died in Ghana on the eve of the historic March on Washington in 1963.

He and his wife, the author Shirley Graham Du Bois, moved to Ghana in 1961 when they found that even at his advanced age of ninety-three he was targeted for his Pan-Africanist views and efforts at African-American liberation and labeled a "Communist." In 1961, news came that the Supreme Court would soon issue a ruling that could result in the cancellation of his passport, making it impossible for him to travel. In response, he left the States on six weeks' notice, determined never to return. In truth, he had never joined the Communist party, but now he made a point of doing so in protest as he exited his native land. Accepting a standing invitation from Ghana's president Kwame Nkrumah, he sent word that he would come; there he would develop the long-awaited *Encyclopedia Africana*, a history of Africa and its peoples.

In 1957, Ghana was the third African nation to win its independence. Du Bois had been instrumental in creating a climate receptive to African independence since the first Pan-African Congress met in London in 1900. Two years into his exile, the Father of Pan-Africanism (see February 19, May 22, and July 23) was at last enjoying the fruits of his labors. So revered was he in his new homeland that when he died, Nkrumah ordered a full state funeral, and Du Bois was buried on the grounds of the presidential palace. There, Du Bois's "Last Message" was read to the thousands assembled in his honor:

> One thing alone I charge you. As you live, believe in life! Always human beings will live and progress to greater, broader, and fuller life. The only possible death is to lose belief in this truth simply because the great end comes slowly, because time is long. Good-bye.

Wednesday, June 26, 1957, Ghana

JUNE 27

Throughout the Depression-afflicted America of 1932, there was poverty, there was hopelessness, and for hundreds of thousands in cities across the country, there was a miracle—Father Divine. As a prophet, Father Divine had led his "angels" (followers) from the depths of despair to financial security with the cooperative economic philosophy of his Harlem-based Peace Mission. As the African-American leader of a Black and white following, he was controversial and uncompromising. His formula for the "good life" defied joblessness, built cooperative businesses, and outwitted de facto segregation as he engaged white "fronts" to buy homes in which his followers could live.

For lifting them from the fate of Depression-era despair, Father Divine's angels called him "God." Among the "proofs" that supported their conviction was this incident that culminated on June 27, 1932:

Originally based in predominantly white Sayville, Long Island, just outside of New York, Father Divine was arrested for maintaining a public nuisance—his home, which was open to all those in need of food or shelter. At one of the many protest vigils held while he was jailed, one of his followers told the group not to despair: if the judge sentenced Father Divine to prison, Father would "sentence" the judge. The judge nevertheless risked jailing Divine and three days later the judge suddenly died of a heart attack.

The replacement judge quickly reassessed the case and freed Divine. Leaving jail, Divine was asked to comment on the sudden demise of the judge who had sentenced him. Never one to miss an opportunity, Father Divine responded that the judge's demise was regrettable; indeed, "I hated to do it." With that, the angels swooped him off with barely a ripple of dissent from the government or the press.

Monday, June 27, 1932, New York, U.S.A.
Religion/Humor   **Bravado**

JUNE 28

Boxing's "greatest," Muhammad Ali (born Cassius Clay), was idolized for his quick jab, quicker wit, and world heavyweight boxing championship title. How could he be a pacifist opposed to the idea of war? That was the question before the Supreme Court in the case known as *Clay v. United States* on June 28, 1970.

Technically, the case was that of a man refusing military induction during wartime on religious grounds. But with a professional boxer of Ali's stature, nothing was simple. Nor did he make things easy for himself with this political barb:

> *Keep asking me, no matter how long*
> *On the war in Vietnam, I sing this song*
> *I ain't got no quarrel with the Viet Cong.*

Or as he would say in a more somber moment, "I am not going ten thousand miles from here to help murder and kill and burn poor people simply to help continue the domination of white slave masters over the darker people." For Ali, the issue was racism. For the powers-that-be, the issue was maintaining control in the face of mounting antiwar protest and the growing Black Power movement. His title bouts were canceled. His access to the press was censored.

Whether Ali's draft reclassification as "1A" was a political move from the outset was not an issue the Court would consider. Nor was it interested in the politically charged rebuke of a Black man who had renounced Christianity to adopt Islam (see February 26). But the fact that the FBI had, at the height of its COINTELPRO era (see April 11), tapped his phone was an issue for review. On that technical ground, the Court overturned his lower-court conviction, five-year prison sentence, and $10,000 fine. Ali's personal victory was a symbolic high for those who saw in his struggle the history of African-Americans and the awful weight of the Vietnam War. For some, a pariah at home—he was a hero the world over.

Sunday, June 28, 1970, Washington, D.C., U.S.A.

Heroes   **Conscience**

JUNE 29

For two historic days, June 29 and 30, 1776, the fundamental premise upon which the nation was founded — the Declaration of Independence — confirmed the wrongs of slavery. In Thomas Jefferson's original draft, an indictment against England's king for the African slave trade read, "He has waged cruel war against human nature itself, violating its most sacred rights of life and liberty in the persons of a distant people who never offended him, captivating & carrying them into slavery in another hemisphere, or to incur miserable death in their transportation thither." But while the king was charged, his accusers never saw the wrong of their own acts as slaveholders.

Through a skillful twist of revolutionary logic, the colonists could fight for their freedom, but slaves were wrong to fight for theirs. Thus, the king was also guilty of "exciting those very people to rise in arms among us, and to purchase that liberty of which he has deprived them."

Ultimately these paragraphs were excised from the Declaration as those who owned slaves and those who did not reached a compromise. Men with nothing more than "property" at stake used, as bargaining chips, the lives of a whole race of people.

It is instructive to read these founding documents in which the root cause of our national racial disease is so clearly exposed.

In a recent conversation on the reluctance of some people to accept multicultural studies, a white educator admitted sadly, "The teachers and parents are afraid that if we tell the children the truth, they will think their ancestors were bad." How many Black children's lives are being sacrificed daily in the compromise called curriculum? How many white children's futures will be wasted defending the indefensible? When we are afraid to tell them our awful truths, can the worlds we invent do them any good?

Saturday, June 29, 1776, Pennsylvania, U.S.A.

Enslavement   **Knowledge**

JUNE 30

Sometimes you just have to fight for what you believe in—no matter what the cost. The story of June 30, 1958, provides just one example of the steely determination of our oldest continuously operating civil rights organization.

In June 1956, the state of Alabama outlawed the NAACP, charging that its activities were injurious to peace in the state. It was an order meant to harass all Blacks, whether or not they belonged to the organization. The action reflected the climate of the times. Less than a year earlier, fourteen-year-old Emmett Till had been beaten, shot, and mutilated in nearby Mississippi, charged by his murderers with "disrespecting a white woman." With each day of the Montgomery, Alabama, bus boycott (see December 1) came new threats for Blacks of being fired from work, beaten, or worse. Martin Luther King, Jr.'s home was firebombed in retaliation for his leadership of the boycott. Lynchings continued to go unprosecuted; when charges were filed, witnesses would not risk their lives to confront the guilty. All-white male juries freed confessed murderers.

In the midst of this unchecked terror, the state of Alabama ordered the NAACP to present its membership list to local "authorities," many of whom were known to be active members of the Klan. When the NAACP refused, a state appellate court issued a contempt-of-court ruling and fined the NAACP a hefty $100,000 dollars—a sum that would be the equivalent of at least $1,000,000 today. With its strong legal defense team, the NAACP came to its own aid, carrying the case to the Supreme Court, which overturned the ruling on June 30, 1958. The Court upheld the NAACP's right not to help marauding whites terrorize Blacks. It was just one more example of the critical role the Supreme Court has played—for better and, at times, for worse—in articulating the nation's racial and moral posture.

Monday, June 30, 1958, Alabama, U.S.A.

Law   **Human Dignity**

JULY

The Flying Ace. Marquee poster and production stills, Norman Studios (1926). Reprinted courtesy of the author. For more information, see July 7.

JULY 1

On July 1, 1829, an African family, ravaged by slavery, moved one step closer to reunion in what is now Guinea, West Africa. There, Ibrahim, a Futa monarch's son, was born in 1762 and educated at Timbuktu. In 1788, as a soldier in his father's army, Ibrahim was captured, sold into slavery, and shipped to Mississippi where a series of uncanny events revived his link to home.

First, a fellow Futa recognized him on the streets of Natchez. As word spread of his royalty, people mocked him, calling him Prince. In 1807, a newly emigrated British doctor recognized Prince as Ibrahim of Timbuktu, whose family had saved the young doctor when they found him dying of starvation near Futa land. Grateful, Cox tried to free Ibrahim, but the owner refused. Later, a Natchez printer convinced the now-legendary Ibrahim/Prince to write a verse of the Koran in Arabic and sent the writing to a contact in Morocco. There, news of it reached the king, who then wrote U.S. Secretary of State Henry Clay, offering to pay for Prince's freedom and his "return" to Morocco. With this inducement, the owner finally freed Prince after forty years of slavery.

Upon his arrival in Washington, D.C., with his wife, who was also freed, Ibrahim revealed that he was not Moroccan but that the rest of the story was true. There, he met President John Quincy Adams, began a speaking tour to raise funds to free the rest of his family, and then sailed for Africa. On his arrival in Liberia, Ibrahim's story reached his Futa homeland. On July 1, 1829, a caravan was en route to meet him. Sent by his long-lost family, it bore gold that would deliver his American-based family to freedom. Sadly, before the caravan could reach him, Prince died on July 6, and his family's emissaries returned home, having missed him by days. But through the contacts and monies Prince and his wife generated on tour, two of their sons, with their families, returned to Africa in 1830. The quest for home had been achieved at last.

Wednesday, July 1, 1829, Mississippi, U.S.A.–Guinea/Mali
Family   **Endurance**

JULY 2

In the 1820s, discrimination against freewomen of color was a given in Baltimore, Maryland. The extraordinary thing was what happened when four women dedicated their lives to helping children. Émigrés who leaped from the frying pan of the Haitian revolution into the flames of life in an American slave state, Marie Magdalene Balas, Rosine Boegue, Almaide Duchemin, and Elizabeth Lange became the first African-American nuns on July 2, 1829.

In an era when Catholics were estranged from the dominant Protestant community, the Black Catholic stronghold in Baltimore offered a supportive environment for Haitian émigrés. Arriving in the early 1820s, Lange opened her home as a school for free children of color. Aided by Balas, the school became a respected part of the community, and they were soon joined by two other émigrés, Boegue and Duchemin. In 1827, Father Nicholas Joubert, the French-born cleric assigned to the Black community, approached the teachers with an interesting dilemma: Black Catholic children were unable to understand their faith fully because they could not read.

With Joubert's support, the four women decided to address this larger problem by founding a religious community. But while the Catholic Church was willing to have Black parishioners, it was unwilling to have Blacks take its sacred vows. Finally, in 1829, after two years of controversy, the bishop approved the order. The women decided to make a spiritual offering to the greater good. In the language of their Catholic faith, their act was called an oblation; thus, they called themselves the Oblate Sisters of Providence. On July 2, with Lange as their first mother superior, Sister Mary, the Oblate Sisters were founded. That year, they opened Saint Francis Academy, and the school's chapel served as the parish church for the wider Black community.

Today, there are three hundred Oblate Sisters in the United States and Costa Rica. Building on that base, three other orders of Black nuns have since been formed.

Thursday, July 2, 1829, Maryland, U.S.A.

Religion   **Life's Work**

JULY 3

Nat Love was a cowboy of heroic proportions made even more legendary by the publication of his book in 1907: *The Life and Adventures of Nat Love, better known in the cattle country as "Deadwood Dick," by Himself—A True History of Slavery Days, Life on the Great Cattle Ranges, and on the Plains of the "Wild and Woolly" West, Based on Facts and Personal Experiences of the Author.* Some say Nat Love's imagination was even better than his roping.

By his own account, this is how Nat Love got the name "Deadwood Dick": On July 3, 1876, Nat Love and a group of fellow cowboys drove three thousand head of cattle to Deadwood, South Dakota. For four years, he'd been a cowboy in love with the life of risk and adventure that typified the "wild sons of the plains whose home was in the saddle and their couch, mother earth, with the sky for a covering." But what made Nat Love atypical was his attitude. The need to be excellent at each of the tasks of his trade—roping, shooting, bronco breaking—became a personal contest he had to win with himself. This "fever" gained him such respect among his peers that he was the subject of many a bragging contest, too. As plans for the July 4 centennial celebration in Deadwood got under way, the cowboys took up a purse of $200. The excitement and the challenge mounted.

The next day, Love cut a romantic figure, as later photos attest. All done up in his "fighting clothes"—chaps, spurs, neckerchief, holster heavy with bullets—and posing with his rifle and a saddle piled with ropes, he was a handsome cowboy, his shoulder-length hair flowing out from under a flapped-back hat. By the end of the day he had roped, bridled, saddled, and mounted an untamed bronco in record time. After he won each of the shooting contests as well, the town proclaimed him "Deadwood Dick," as all the world would soon find out. And so, no matter what folks say to the contrary, this is the truth—just as he wanted it known!

Monday, July 3, 1876, South Dakota, U.S.A.

Adventure   **Aspirations**

JULY 4

In 1852, citizens of Rochester, New York, asked their neighbor, Frederick Douglass, to deliver a Fourth of July address. He was repulsed by the thought of a national celebration of freedom while some Americans held others prisoners of slavery. Mindful of his responsibility to maximize the opportunity by asking the question, "What to the Slave Is the Fourth of July?," he took center stage for human rights:

> Fellow Citizens: Pardon me, and allow me to ask, why am I called upon to speak here today? What have I or those I represent to do with your national independence? Are the great principles of political freedom and natural justice, embodied in that Declaration of Independence, extended to us? Would to God, both for your sakes and ours, that an affirmative answer could be truthfully returned to these questions. But such is not the state of the case.
>
> What to the American slave is your Fourth of July? I answer, a day that reveals to him more than all other days of the year, the gross injustice and cruelty to which he is the constant victim. To him your celebration is a sham; your national greatness, swelling vanity; your sounds of rejoicing empty and heartless; your sermons and thanksgivings, a thin veil to cover up crimes which would disgrace a nation of savages.

Even today, how many people feel secure enough to be this forthright? The fact that Douglass had the courage publicly to challenge a system still willing to enslave him in punishment, to publish his "subversive" abolitionist newspaper, and to act as an Underground Railroad stationmaster speaks to the character of the man. He also reminds us of the care with which he regarded each opportunity en route to his ultimate goal.

Sunday, July 4, 1852, New York, U.S.A.

Speech/Oration   **Character**

JULY 5

Following in the footsteps of Althea Gibson as the first African-American to break the color line in tennis with her victory in the women's singles championship at Wimbledon in 1957, on July 5, 1975, Arthur Ashe made sports history as the first to win the men's singles title at the same tournament.

Ashe's perspective on his stellar tennis career was always interesting. It's easy to attribute his change of heart on tennis as the driving force in his life to the heart attack that ended his career and ultimately led to his death from an AIDS-tainted blood transfusion during heart surgery. But Ashe himself said otherwise. Ashe was truly a citizen of the world who used the bargaining chip of his fame to leverage a better life for others.

In citing his legacies, he pointed to his work for human rights worldwide, his participation in the crusade to liberate South Africa, his advocacy for AIDS patients and AIDS research, and his family. But in his work, he took special pride as a scholar. His unprecedented history of the African-American in sports from 1619 to 1989, *A Hard Road to Glory*, explored the legacy passed down to him as an athlete and a man. A stunning saga, the three-volume work compiled the social and cultural history of African-Americans as told in the language of sports. In charting a 270-year continuum of excellence, Ashe provided a unique perspective on the determined strivings of African-American people when sports was one of the only arenas in which we could fulfill and gain recognition for our genius.

When Ashe cited his trophies, *A Hard Road to Glory* headed his list. Arthur Ashe was a champion for whom sports was a means to a truly inspirational end.

Saturday, July 5, 1975, England

Sports   **Perspective**

JULY 6

Choices. We all have the power to choose whether our actions will count for good or evil. On July 6, 1906, a group of white union workers chose the good, avoided the pit of "divide and conquer," and did themselves proud.

The Cecelia Asphalt Paving Company in New York City had been replacing African-American union workers with nonunion newly emigrated Irish and German workers. The Black agent reported these occurrences to the officers of the International Union of Pavers and Rammersmen, noting that Black unionists were not getting a "square deal." "Then we'll call out all of our union members," the officers said, and in short order all the white workers laid down their tools for an immediate and decisive wildcat strike. The asphalt company supervisor tried to persuade the white unionists to stay on the job, using every ploy in the book. But the workers held out, demanding a written guarantee of the recognition of all their members. "I'll give you the letter tomorrow morning at ten o'clock," the supervisor finally conceded. "Then we'll go back to work tomorrow at ten o'clock," said the union men. Clearly, the unionists knew about what West Indians call "today for you, tomorrow for me" logic. A victory for an unscrupulous contractor on the grounds of race that day would have been a victory for an unscrupulous contractor on any grounds the next.

This story is worth retelling not only for what it says but how it was said and who was responsible for first saying it. This story of labor solidarity was reported in the *New York Age* on July 12, 1906, in a newspaper account that totally refrained from using words like "Negro" and "colored." Typical of the standards of its African-American publisher, T. Thomas Fortune, even in 1906 the workers were referred to as "Afro-Americans." That sign of respect was a refreshing choice for African-American readers in an era when Fortune's publishing contemporaries made a point of referring to Blacks in the most derogatory and inflammatory terms.

Friday, July 6, 1906, New York, U.S.A.

Labor   **Standards**

JULY 7

In July 1926, the must-see movie of the summer was *The Flying Ace* with its story of a daring and dapper Black aviator who rescues the Black romantic female lead in midair (see July's lead illustration from the film poster). Just one of many "race movies" featuring all-Black casts, it was produced by the Norman Studios of Arlington, Florida, and boasted that it had "situations in it which HAVEN'T BEEN SHOWN IN A WHITE PICTURE." That was for sure.

While Hollywood produced films that consistently degraded African-Americans, independent Black- and white-owned film studios popularized alternative "race movies" as early as 1916. These films specifically targeted the Black community with rich plots and characters who could be anything they wanted to be. Race films represented the range and reality of African-American lives. There were all-Black Westerns, mysteries, steamy romances, and drawing room dramas, and they included characters who were professionals in every field from medicine to law. As film historian Donald Bogle has written, "in such films as . . . *The Flying Ace,* Black America saw itself incorporated into the national popular mythology, and a new set of archetypes emerged: heroic Black men of action, who were walking representatives of Black assertion and aggression, who, of course, gave the lie to America's notions of the Negro's place."

Among African-American filmmakers, the legendary Oscar Micheaux was dean. Despite the hardships of financing and distributing his films, between 1919 and 1948, he wrote, produced, and directed almost thirty films, including *Within Our Gates* (1920), with its consciousness-raising lynching sequence, and *God's Step Children* (1937), with its independent-minded heroine.

Well into the 1950s, audiences for race pictures kept the Black film industry growing in theaters north and south. And while the term "race movie" is now gone, the tradition of independent Black filmmaking is very much alive in the work of Julie Dash (see January 15), Spike Lee, and Melvin Van Peebles (see March 10).

Wednesday, July 7, 1926, Florida, U.S.A.

Film   **Self-Assertion**

JULY 8

"I am a very loyal American," said the small chunky woman in proper hat and modest veil, with classic understatement. Indeed she was. Who else with talents and opportunities to match those of Eslanda Cardozo Goode would suffer the excesses of American politics? Few, to be sure, other than her husband, Paul Robeson, the world-renowned performer. Together, the Robesons sacrificed comfort and wealth in their unflappable commitment to human rights the world over—including in America.

On July 8, 1953, when she was seated before Senator Joseph McCarthy's publicity-seeking "Red scare" committee in an era of stereotypically minor roles for Blacks and women, her subpoena was rare confirmation of just how notable Mrs. Robeson was. Since her marriage in 1921, she had been lit by her husband's spotlight, but she was a major force in her own right.

As granddaughter of the founder of South Carolina's first school for Blacks, she knew the value of education. She obtained her bachelor of science degree in chemistry at Columbia University with such distinction that Columbia Presbyterian Hospital broke its color ban to hire her as a surgical pathology chemist. In Europe with her husband, she gained an anthropology degree at the London School of Economics. As an accomplished photographer, she published photographic essays in the cause of world freedom. As a delegate to Ghana's All-African People's Conference in 1959, she campaigned for women's rights. As she once said, "I have never been aggressive. . . . But I have never been meek. I am convinced that meekness invites pushing around, and brings out the worst in people." As a "very loyal American," she worked tirelessly to leave a better world than the one she had found.

Wednesday, July 8, 1953, Washington, D.C., U.S.A.
Politics   **Confidence**

JULY 9

Late on the night of July 9, 1893, James Cornish was rushed to the hospital with a stab wound to his heart. The next day he made history.

As Cornish lay wounded, two factors combined to make the twenty-four-year-old's death a near certainty—racial prejudice and his grave condition. But two even stronger factors combined to bring about his recovery—he had been taken to the emergency room of Provident Hospital, Chicago's first hospital open to people of all races; and Provident's founder, Dr. Daniel Hale Williams, was available and willing to try a radical procedure that might save Cornish's life. On July 10, 1893, Dr. Williams and a team of six staff surgeons made an incision in Cornish's chest. Suturing the artery, they closed the wound in the heart and successfully completed the world's first open-heart surgery.

Frustrated with the treatment of Black physicians, nurses, and patients, Dr. Williams had founded Provident Hospital in 1891 so that doctors could intern and medical staffs would receive proper training. For Cornish and medical history, Williams's founding of the hospital was quite provident indeed.

Sunday, July 9, 1893, Illinois, U.S.A.

Medicine   **Enterprise**

JULY 10

Both the sun and the speech-making were generous over Lincoln Park on July 10, 1974, as the first national monument on capital grounds honoring an African-American—Mary McLeod Bethune—was unveiled. It was a posthumous birthday present and celebration on what would have been her ninety-ninth birthday, and the bronze sculpture of two children playfully circling her life-size likeness was a fitting tribute to the youth advocate, college founder, civil rights leader, and presidential adviser. Fitting, too, was a question a young celebrant was heard to ask: "How come?" As in life, Mrs. Bethune's own words serve as the best answer:

> [As school founder] I have learned already that one of my important jobs was to be a good beggar; I rang doorbells and tackled cold prospects without a lead. I wrote articles for whoever would print them, distributed leaflets, rode interminable miles of dusty roads on my old bicycle, invaded churches, clubs, lodges, chambers of commerce. If a prospect refused to make a contribution I would say, "Thank you for your time." No matter how deep my hurt, I always smiled. I refused to be discouraged, for neither God nor man could use a discouraged soul.

After Mrs. Bethune tilled the fields of service to her fellow human beings for fifty years, her successor as head of the National Council of Negro Women, Dr. Dorothy I. Height, has thankfully carried on the tradition well. By erecting the monument to her mentor, it stands in tribute to both of them—and to all those with whom they served over the years.

JULY 11

In July 1913, the historian and bibliophile Arturo A. Schomburg (see November 20) addressed a session of Black teachers at the nation's oldest historically Black college, Cheyney Institute in Pennsylvania. Entitled "Racial Integrity: A Plea for the Establishment of a Chair of Negro History in Our Schools, Colleges, etc.," the paper was an important forerunner of a movement that would take sixty years to catch up with him—the Black Studies movement of the late 1960s and early 1970s.

Indeed, despite today's talk of "multiculturalism," most school districts have yet to substantively address the need outlined by Schomburg over eighty years ago when he said, "I am here with a sincere desire to awaken [your] sensibilities, . . . to fire [your] racial patriotism by the study of Negro books." While he asked teachers to "amend" rather than "revolutionize" the curriculum, eighty years later it is clear that the slightest amendment is revolutionary indeed. What we see in the name of multicultural education today is what was asked for in the name of integration forty years ago. While people of color are included in the picture, our truths are rarely part of the story.

Sadly for us all, Black Studies—e.g., the study of the effect of American history on Blacks and other peoples of color, and the history of the world's peoples regardless of continent of origin—has yet to find its way into the general American curriculum. This lack cripples all Americans intellectually, socially, and politically. For without the formalized study of African-American civilization, how can there be accredited scholars to shape the general curriculum from kindergarten through twelfth grade? Without an across-the-board course of study for all students, regardless of race and area of concentration, how can the most learned among us make well-informed, nonbiased decisions in matters of public policy? Clearly, it is up to each of us to pull in the gaps for ourselves and share the wealth.

July 1913, Pennsylvania, U.S.A.

Historiography   **Knowledge**

JULY 12

"The real McCoy"—an accolade meaning the real deal, the genuine article—originated with the work of African-American inventor Elijah McCoy. On July 12, 1872, he patented his first self-lubricating engine. It was a manufacturing breakthrough, yet the Patent Office designated it simply an "improvement," determining that his device was a mere enhancement of the one more widely used—"elbow grease." For this first generation of Blacks allowed to file patents in their own names, a major element of the patent application process would have to include reeducating the Patent Office—and patience. Undaunted, McCoy secured three more patents under his name in the next three years. Soon his mechanical lubricators were so prized that customers insisted on getting no less than the genuine article—the real McCoy!

Elijah McCoy was born in Ontario, Canada, in 1843 to parents who had escaped slavery via the Underground Railroad. He studied mechanical engineering in Scotland, yet soon found his ambitions thwarted by racism back home in Canada and the United States. Discouraged but still hopeful, he took a menial job oiling railroad cars by hand, and this led to his earliest lubricator patents and the more than seventy-five other patents later registered in his name.

Yet even with inventions like the lawn sprinkler to his credit and millions of his lubricators in use, Elijah McCoy died penniless in 1929. Just as the names and rights of the nineteenth century's enslaved and freeborn Black inventors had been swallowed up under their slave owner's or sponsor's imprints, now by law and by custom even the most prolific Black inventors rarely profited from their successful inventions. Even today's Black inventors are rarely able to negotiate the same licensing agreements as their white counterparts, and thus their ability to profit from their own inventions is still limited. This, too, is the real McCoy!

Friday, July 12, 1872, Michigan, U.S.A.–Canada–Scotland
Invention   **Authenticity**

JULY 13

When the history of the quest for political parity in the United States is written, it is often stated that Jesse Jackson was the first Black presidential candidate. That twentieth-century distinction, however, actually belongs to Shirley Chisholm, the nation's first African-American woman in the House of Representatives. On July 13, 1972, at the Democratic National Convention in Miami Beach, Florida, Shirley Chisholm was nominated for the presidency on the first ballot and actually won 151 votes from the delegates polled.

Elected to the House from Brooklyn, New York, in 1968, the Barbados-born Caribbean-American congresswoman had made quite a name for herself since her arrival there. In 1969, determined to put American money to use "for people and peace, not for profits and war," Chisholm announced she would vote NO! on every appropriations bill in the House.

In January 1972, she had the temerity to announce her candidacy for the presidency. While dramatic, it was hardly a popular decision with either the Black or white political establishments. But as the title of her autobiography proclaimed, Shirley Chisholm was a woman *Unbossed and Unbought.* As a presidential candidate, her foreign policy platform put her against the Vietnam War and against white-dominated European and American governments thwarting the liberation of African and Asian peoples. She wanted to end European colonial rule and overthrow the minority white governments of Rhodesia and South Africa. And she was for the self-determination and human rights of all people.

Said the renowned renegade representative known for her no-nonsense approach to politics and her willingness to take the hard knocks as they came, "Service is the rent you pay for room on this earth."

Thursday, July 13, 1972, Florida, U.S.A.

Politics   **Sincerity**

JULY 14

An ad in the *Daily Houston Telegraph* of July 14, 1868, tells a special story of African-Americans and baseball: "Black Ballers—There is a Baseball club in this city, composed of colored boys bearing the aggressive title of 'Six Shooter Jims.' They wish us to state that they will play a match game with any other colored club in the state."

Long before Jackie Robinson desegregated modern baseball in 1947, before the Negro Leagues were founded in 1920, before Moses Fleetwood Walker became the first Black player with the majors in the pre–Jim Crow 1880s, the national pastime reflected a unique picture of America and race. Even free Blacks were restricted in their ability to play and enjoy the sport openly before the Civil War. After the war, when Blacks got their turn at bat, they came out swinging.

White teams of the Reconstruction era were riddled with gambling and corruption. Disparagingly, the *New York Times* referred to professional white players as "dissipated gladiators." Not so the African-Americans. Black baseball players were heroes; hailing from relatively affluent families, able to afford the time spent away from family businesses and farms, the added cost of travel, and the speculative nature of a baseball income. In 1867, the *Brooklyn Daily Union* ran this article on an upcoming game between the Philadelphia Excelsiors and the Brooklyn Uniques: "These organizations are composed of very respectable colored people, well-to-do in the world . . . and include many first class players. . . . We trust, for the good of the fraternity, that none of the 'white trash' who disgrace white clubs, by following and brawling for them, will be allowed to mar the pleasure of these social colored gatherings."

Black baseball scored high on good, clean, family fun. For a people conscious of shaping a new era, baseball was a perfect metaphor, with its rules for playing and scoring, its strategy and skill, and its notion that each player should have his turn at bat—regardless of his position on the playing field.

Tuesday, July 14, 1868, Texas, U.S.A.

Sports   **Aspirations**

JULY 15

In the summer of 1954, the long arm of the *Brown v. Board of Education* decision prohibiting segregation in education began reeducating the public in other areas of American life. On July 15, 1954, music lovers of all backgrounds gathered under the stars for the inaugural concerts of the Newport Jazz Festival.

At last people could feel free to give Black music its long-overdue respect—one part of which was to recognize that body of work for what it was: a landmark contribution celebrated everywhere in the world but in the land of its birth. While the term *jazz* only refers to part of the spectrum of twentieth-century secular and largely instrumental African-American music, with the Newport Jazz Festival the masters of the art could perform for the full spectrum of its audience. To this day, jazz is too often forced to flourish in the most negative of situations—bars, brothels, and backstreets. This singular fact has made it extremely difficult for Black children to grow up with live access to their own great forebears of classical African-American music.

Now celebrated as a New York City music festival each summer, the Newport Jazz Festival has made a major contribution to the growth and dissemination of African-America's most treasured classical music.

Thursday, July 15, 1954, Rhode Island, U.S.A.

Music   **Preservation**

JULY 16

On July 16, 1963, singer Miriam Makeba addressed the United Nations on behalf of the South African people. With African National Congress (ANC) leaders Nelson Mandela and Walter Sisulu in prison and banned, carrying their message had become a criminal offense. Makeba herself had been exiled for her outspoken views, her international reputation, and her strategic position in New York, but she had carefully honed a powerful presence in her own right. The advice of her mentor and friend, Harry Belafonte, as she began her U.S. career just four years earlier, had served her well. "You must always be careful how you conduct yourself onstage and off," he told her. "Someday you will have a chance to speak on behalf of your people." Now that day had come.

"My country has been turned by the government into a huge prison," she told the United Nations Special Committee. "Most of the world's big powers have only paid lip service to the appeals of my people for help. I must urge the U.N. to impose a complete boycott on South Africa. The first priority must be to stop the shipments of arms. I have not the slightest doubt that these arms will be used against African women and children." Her words bore the weight of personal experience. Among the 249 men, women, and children killed or wounded in the 1960 Sharpeville Massacre (see March 21) were two of her uncles.

After an exuberant response from the world's ambassadors, the press awaited her. "I am not a politician or a diplomat. I am a singer," she told them. And it was Makeba, the singer, against whom the South African government retaliated by banning her records. However, her recordings were smuggled into Africa in secret shipments. She later recalled, "Once again, a totalitarian state tries to drive a wedge between an oppressed people, and it only brings us closer together." Her appearances also brought her people closer to the sanctions that helped end apartheid and release its first modern-era African president, Nelson Mandela, from prison.

Tuesday, July 16, 1963, United Nations – South Africa
Pan-African World   **Conscience**

JULY 17

It had taken seven years to arrive at the historic events of July 17, 1794. The trail had begun with the fateful 1787 exit of free Blacks from the predominantly white Philadelphia church in which they had long worshiped (see November 26). Adamant in their need for unity for the survival of their community against the enemy of racism wherever it appeared, they founded the following year the Free African Society, the first general institution organized and managed by African-Americans (see April 12). But as Philadelphia's freemen and freewomen of color flowered into an independent community, their need for a church of their own remained. As ministers and leaders, both Absalom Jones and Richard Allen preferred to remain affiliated with the known rituals of the Methodist Church. But most of their followers did not—especially after the way they had been treated by the Methodist Church, which had forced their exit in 1787. Some followers wanted to temper their familiar Christian worship with African-inspired traditions. Others wanted a more African-oriented religion all their own. Thus, in 1794, out of the roots of freedom sprang two new congregations.

On July 17, 1794, Absalom Jones and his followers left the Methodists for Episcopalianism, dedicating the African Church of Saint Thomas. A month later, those who wanted a denomination all their own started the African Methodist Episcopal (AME) congregation. On August 12, 1794, Richard Allen and his followers formally established the first AME church under the name Mother Bethel AME.

Worshiping separately, the groups maintained a solid survival-oriented secular unity. Two hundred years later, Mother Bethel AME still stands—the oldest property in America continuously owned by Blacks.

Thursday, July 17, 1794, Pennsylvania, U.S.A.

Religion   **Freedom**

JULY 18

On July 18, 1863, the Fifty-fourth Massachusetts Colored Regiment launched its now-legendary assault on Fort Wagner, South Carolina, which later inspired the movie *Glory* (see January 26). Not only was it one of the war's most famous battles, it was also a symbolic victory for the 200,000 African-American volunteers nationwide.

From 1862 on, when the first Black troops joined the Union Army, this had been "their" war—the war for Black liberation. And while a man should not have to battle his own nation's ridicule in order to join the army, that was exactly the plight of Black soldiers in the Civil War, despite the great personal sacrifices they made. Upon threat of death, some fled slavery to join the Union side. Others risked their free status in the event of capture. Some left the safe haven on Native American lands, and in Mexico and Canada, to which they had fled aboard the Underground Railroad. Among their regiments were the Third U.S. Colored of Maryland, with its motto "Rather Die Freemen than Live to Be Slaves!"; the Second U.S. Colored Light Artillery of Illinois; the soldiers of the First Louisiana Native Guard; the Thirteenth Colored Infantry of Tennessee; and the first recipients of the Congressional Medal of Honor, the Fifty-fourth (see January 26, March 2).

This eyewitness account of the assault on Fort Wagner by Nathaniel Paige appeared in the *New York Tribune*: "The First Brigade assaulted at dusk, the Fifty-fourth Massachusetts in the front. . . . Notwithstanding the loss of their colonel, the regiment pushed forward, and more than one-half succeeded in reaching the inside of the fort. . . . the evident purpose of putting the Negroes in advance was to dispose of the ideas that the Negroes could fight. . . and get rid of them. Many officers spoke of them unfavorably before and favorably since."

When the toll was taken at Fort Wagner, and at battlefields nationwide, African-American soldiers had suffered heavy casualties and earned the respect of their enemies on both sides of the war.

Saturday, July 18, 1863, South Carolina, U.S.A.

Military   **Sacrifice**

JULY 19

He had been one of Dr. King's young lieutenants, had become a minister, founded Operation PUSH, and registered more Black voters nationwide than anyone in recent memory. He had overcome death threats, media ambush, and hideous adversity in his 1984 presidential bid. His second bid in 1988 successfully elevated politics-as-usual to a serious national debate. On July 19, 1988, when Jesse L. Jackson stepped up to the podium of the Democratic National Convention in Atlanta as first runner-up among six contenders for his party's nomination, America could no longer overlook him. It was late when his turn to speak finally came, but millions stayed up until nearly 2:00 A.M. to cheer him on:

All of us who are here think we are seated. But we're really standing on someone's shoulders. My right and my privilege to stand here before you has been won—won in my lifetime—by the blood and the sweat of the innocent. . . . When I was a child growing up in Greenville, South Carolina, and Grandmomma could not afford a blanket, she didn't complain and we did not freeze. Instead she took pieces of old cloth, . . . only patches good enough to wipe your shoes. With sturdy hands and a strong cord, she sewed them together into a quilt, a thing of beauty and power and culture. Now, Democrats, we must build such a quilt. Farmers, you seek fair prices, and you are right, but your patch is not big enough. Blacks and Hispanics, when we fight for civil rights, we are right, but our patch is not big enough. Gays and lesbians, when you fight discrimination and [for] a cure for AIDS, you are right, but your patch is not big enough. But don't despair. Be as wise as my grandma. Pull the patches and the pieces together, bound by a common thread. . . . We the people can win.

Tuesday, July 19, 1988, Georgia, U.S.A.

Politics   **Understanding**

JULY 20

As Margaret Walker has said of the Civil War, "white Southerners claimed they fought a war between the states for independence; white Northerners claimed it was a rebellion of the Southerners against the Union, and Negroes said it was a war of liberation."

In the grand scheme of such Civil War ideals as "freedom," we often overlook the most intimate freedoms denied both enslaved and freeborn African-Americans during the slavery era—such as the freedom to love and be loved, the freedom to enjoy and maintain the loving bonds of family that are such an essential part of life. In this letter dated July 20, 1863, Anna and Frederick Douglass's son, Lewis, wrote his fiancée:

My dear Amelia:

I have been in two fights, and am unhurt. I escaped from amidst that perfect hail of shot and shell. It was terrible. . . . My thoughts are with you often, you are as dear as ever, be good to remember it as I no doubt you will. I must necessarily be brief. . . .

This regiment has established its reputation as a fighting regiment, not a man flinched, though it was a trying time. Men fell all around me. A shell would explode and clear a space of twenty feet, our men would close up again, but it was no use, we had to retreat, which was a very hazardous undertaking. How I got out of that fight alive I cannot tell, but I am here. My Dear girl I hope again to see you. I must bid you farewell should I be killed. Remember if I die I die in a good cause. I wish we had a hundred thousand colored troops, we would put an end to this war.

Good Bye to all. Your own loving— Write soon— Lewis

The significance of this letter is heightened when we think of how "fortunate" Lewis and Amelia were in comparison with their Black contemporaries. They could read and write, send and receive mail, plan a marriage, retain family ties, fight on their own behalf—all aspects of normal life that were denied their enslaved brethren. No wonder they were so in love.

Monday, July 20, 1863, South Carolina, U.S.A.

Family   **Love**

JULY 21

Throughout history, it is interesting to see the way we have bartered and forged our identity as people of African descent and to note the issues around which African-American women have formed their own distinctive unity.

On July 21, 1896, in a meeting at the Nineteenth Street Baptist Church in Washington, D.C., two women's groups merged, demonstrating an important sign of the times and consolidating the strength of Black women behind a unified leadership. On this date, the National Federation of Afro-American Women and the Colored Women's League joined together to form the National Association of Colored Women (NACW) with the noted educator Mary Church Terrell as its newly elected president.

The two groups grounded their unity on journalist Ida B. Wells-Barnett's leadership of the national antilynching campaign. Among those at this historic founding meeting were Ellen Craft, whose daring escape from slavery had brought her international acclaim (see January 5); Frances Ellen Watkins Harper, author of the first known novel by an African-American woman; Rosetta Douglass Sprague, daughter of Frederick Douglass, the leading male abolitionist and feminist of his day; and Harriet Tubman (see June 2), the most famous of all Underground Railroad conductors, who entered the meeting to a standing ovation.

With their alliance based on a critical human rights issue, lynching, the founding of the NACW was a major step in the evolution of the modern civil rights movement.

Tuesday, July 21, 1896, Washington, D.C., U.S.A.

Women   **Unity**

JULY 22

On July 22, 1918, a young immigrant arrived in New Bedford harbor aboard a whaling ship. He was just one of thousands of Blacks from the Caribbean emigrating to the United States. He married and raised three daughters, working as a laborer in a variety of jobs. But Wilhelm Alfredt Landsmark's special gift was his ability to relate history through stories. Years later, his daughter Muriel Helena Landsmark told this story about him:

> I remember my father considered the *New York Times* the best newspaper and he insisted that we read it, too. But we were too young. On Sundays, therefore, we had a ritual. After Sunday School he would buy peanuts and roast [them]. He would place a big cup in front of him, and when they were all shelled into the cup, we would sit down, eat peanuts, and Daddy would read us the *New York Times*. . . . He would read a passage and tell us, "Now, this is what they said, but the politicians really mean this. . . ." He would read another part and say, "Now you have to read between the lines. What do you think about this part?" My mother would get dinner, and we would all sit down together. . . . We'd listen to him tell us what was going on all over the world. I think that's why my sisters and I still love to read and interpret. We're still fascinated by what we read.

In 1988, seventy years after Landsmark's unheralded immigrant arrival in the United States, his daughter's account, "Peanuts and the Sunday Times," was published in a children's book. It went on to be included in a reader and later translated into other languages where its tale of a poor man's quest to read, and to share his love of reading with his children, continues to inspire youngsters worldwide. (For a photograph of William Landsmark's mother, Jane Ver Ter Pool, see February's lead illustration.)

Monday, July 22, 1918, New York, U.S.A.–Saint Eustatius
Family   **Continuity**

JULY 23

Over the past century, the concept of Pan-Africanism has represented a variety of needs, from "Africa for the Africans" to the common experiences by people of African descent of white domination via colonialism, slavery, apartheid, and segregation.

However the philosophy is defined, the term was first coined by Henry Sylvester Williams, a Trinidadian-born London barrister, in a letter to an associate in 1899. As a founder of the African Association, an organization of West Indian expatriates in London, Williams used the term to express "a feeling of unity and to facilitate friendly intercourse among Africans in general; to promote and protect the interests of all [British] subjects claiming African descent, wholly or in part, in British colonies and other places." The next year, the term became more widely known when a three-day meeting took place from July 23 to July 25, 1900. The man who would come to be known as the "Father of Pan-Africanism," Dr. W. E. B. Du Bois, delivered the final address at the conference.

To this day, wherever and whenever the struggle for human rights by people of color the world over is raised, Du Bois's prophetic closing statement at that meeting is repeated: "The problem of the twentieth century is the problem of the color line."

Monday, July 23, 1900, England

Pan-African World   **Prophecy**

JULY 24

History does not document the lives of the first twenty African "indentures" (see August 1) whose arrival paved the way for slavery in 1619. But the record of Anthony Johnson sheds light on an early African-American family.

In 1621, Johnson arrived in Virginia as an indenture from England. Uncharacteristically for the period, he worked off his indenture and began to accumulate property. Thirty years later, in 1651, he paid for five indentures, and on July 24, 1651, Anthony Johnson and his family acquired 250 acres in Northampton County, Virginia. The family came into its land by the "head-right" system: for each person planters imported into the colonies, fifty acres of land was granted. With their land on the banks of the Pungoteague River, the Johnsons founded one of the earliest African-American communities. The following year, 1652, Johnson's son John was granted 550 acres after importing eleven Europeans into the colonies.

Some historians speculate that someone in the Johnson family of 1651 may have been among the first twenty Africans captured into indenture/slavery. But there is no evidence to support or deny the claim. Nor is there any evidence that the Johnsons' Black indentures later became slaves. What is known is that a third-generation Johnson named the homestead Angola—insight, perhaps, into the family's African origins. While the Johnsons were successful as an individual family, that does not negate the fact that the 1650s were perilous times for most Africans—indentured, enslaved, or free. Ten years earlier, in 1641, Massachusetts had become the first colony to legalize forced slavery, followed by Connecticut in 1650 and Virginia in 1661. Significantly, while slavery has been most often associated with the South in the eighteenth and nineteenth centuries, it actually first took root in the North in the seventeenth century. The last of the colonies to legalize slavery was one of its most brutal and ardent advocates—Georgia in 1750.

Monday, July 24, 1651, Virginia, U.S.A.

Social History   **Expectations**

JULY 25

On July 25, 1992, General Colin Powell, chairman of the joint chiefs of staff and the nation's highest-ranking military officer, dedicated the Buffalo Soldier Monument at Fort Leavenworth, Kansas. It was fitting that he head the group assembled for the dedication, because it was he who had raised the issue of commemorating his African-American ancestors in the military.

In 1982, as a brigadier general, Colin Powell discovered two graveled walkways at Fort Leavenworth. These were all that remained of the site that had been home to the Ninth and Tenth Cavalries, the famed "Buffalo Soldiers." There was no other recognition of the men or the credits they had amassed in the years between the Civil War and the desegregation of the military in 1952, during which time they had patrolled the West and fought in two wars—the Spanish-American War and World War II.

Ten years after Powell's rediscovery, an African-American navy commander, Carlton G. Philpot, had raised $850,000 for a monument to be created by African-American sculptor Eddie Dixon.

Embedded in our history are deep contradictions that must not be overlooked. As "patrollers" of the West, the Buffalo Soldiers participated in the seizure of Native American lands. Blacks participated, therefore, in the equivalent on American soil of the seizure of African lands, the colonization of a continent, and the herding of Africans onto reservations such as those the white-minority South African government called *Bantustans.* Relatively more Africans survived their holocaust, fewer Native Americans survived theirs. During slavery and in later years when Blacks fled the post-Reconstruction terror of the KKK and its sympathizers (see April 15), Native Americans consistently provided Blacks with escape routes. This is a very complicated and conflicted story that must never be allowed either to tarnish the honor due the Buffalo Soldiers or to diminish the debt owed Native Americans.

Saturday, July 25, 1992, Kansas, U.S.A.

Military   **Perspective**

JULY 26

As a soldier, Charles Young had distinguished himself long before World War I, when all bets were riding on him—the son of ex-slaves—to become the first African-American general. As a West Point graduate, he had commanded a Spanish-American War regiment, acted as military attaché to Haiti and Liberia, and was squadron commander in the war to oust Mexico's legendary Pancho Villa. But in 1917, with the United States gearing up for its entrance into World War I, the battle in which Lieutenant Colonel Young would earn his highest stripes was the one he fought with the U.S. Army.

By merit and tenure, Young was the logical candidate for a field command or to head the new Fort Des Moines Black officers' training academy (see June 15). But that hope was dashed when a routine examination yielded this comment about Young: "a very intelligent colored officer, hampered with characteristic racial trait of losing his head in sudden emergencies." Then a junior-ranking white Mississippian wrote his senator that if forced to be subordinate to Young, he might be brought to the point of committing homicide. The race war was on. By July 26, 1917, a dubious finding of high blood pressure became the army's excuse for blocking Young's promotion and for retiring him as an active officer. Hardly one to go down without a fight, Young decided to demonstrate his fitness publicly with a five-hundred-mile, sixteen-day ride on horseback from Ohio to Washington, D.C., an event that was cheered throughout the Black press. Nevertheless, the army held to its decision to retire Young. A year later, however, still feeling pangs of guilt over Young, the army suddenly recalled him to active duty and promoted him to full colonel just five days before the armistice, when they knew he would never achieve command.

Exactly thirty-one years later, on July 26, 1948, President Harry S Truman issued Executive Order No. 9981 on "equality of treatment and opportunity," thereby desegregating the military.

Thursday, July 26, 1917, Iowa–Ohio–Washington, D.C., U.S.A.
Military   **Conviction**

JULY 27

In the depths of the Great Depression, President Franklin D. Roosevelt put forth his New Deal legislation to ease the massive unemployment and get Americans back to work. In 1935, the Works Progress Administration (WPA) was funded, the single most important and influential social program introduced as part of that master plan—a program of work for people in the arts designed to inspire projects for the greater social good. In theater, the Federal Theater was established with nine African-American production companies from New York to Seattle providing experience in every phase of theater operation. In art, Richmond Barthé produced marble reliefs for the Harlem River Houses, and Charles Alston painted his *Magic and Medicine* mural for Harlem Hospital, while similar projects were realized in public buildings all across the country. But among the WPA's most successful efforts was the Federal Writers Project (FWP). Founded on July 27, 1935, it subsidized writers and made a lasting investment in preserving the nation's past and enriching its future.

Because of the dedicated leadership of its director, Harry Hopkins, the WPA did what private industry and the pre-Depression government had refused to do. Hopkins issued a directive prohibiting discrimination and put pressure on local cities to force compliance. Because of his actions, some of the people who would become the twentieth century's major artists—novelists such as Richard Wright and Margaret Walker—received subsidies and steady work that enabled them to shape their talents and literary identities. Throughout the 1930s, the Writers Project subsidized an oral history project that resulted in the collection of the largest available cache of narratives by the last living slaves. Because of the WPA's oral historians, those last surviving slaves—many of whom spent their lives unable to read and write—can speak to us in their own voices to this day.

Saturday, July 27, 1935, Washington, D.C., U.S.A.
Cultural History   **Legacies**

JULY 28

At noon on Saturday, July 28, 1917, ten thousand African-American men, women, and children filed down Manhattan's Fifth Avenue in the historic Negro Silent Protest Parade. Days before the protest march, leaflets were passed out that read, "We march because we want to make impossible a repetition of Waco, Memphis, and East Saint Louis by rousing the conscience of the country and to bring the murderers of our brothers, sisters, and innocent children to justice." The fact that three cities were listed was a tragic commentary on the escalation of anti-Black violence. The march had originally been planned to focus on a particularly gruesome lynching fever that had swept Memphis.

On July 28, 1917, few could fail to acknowledge the cause of the marchers who bore their pain with such dignity and passion, carrying banners inscribed with, as they said in their preparatory meetings, "our loyalty through our whole history in this country and calling attention to the acts of discrimination, 'Jim Crowism,' segregation, disfranchisement, and of brutal and heathenish lynchings and burnings which have been practiced in return." As the silent parade filled the streets in protest, among the leaders in support was America's first self-made African-American woman millionaire, Madame C. J. Walker (see March 8, September 19), who used major sums of her extraordinary wealth to fund antilynching campaigns.

Three months into America's involvement in World War I, the sponsors and marchers knew that only with this kind of protest would they attract world attention through the national and international press. In so doing, the march was an important forerunner of the campaigns of conscience that formed the strategic base of "nonviolent protest" during the civil rights era.

Saturday, July 28, 1917, New York, U.S.A.

Events   **Racial Dignity**

JULY 29

In 1928, nineteen-year-old Chester Himes was the son of a professor and a teacher, a student at Ohio State University, and a convicted felon sentenced to twenty years in prison for armed robbery. It would have been more accurate if he had been found guilty of desperation—an inability to cope with the pain and perversions of racism as a boy coming of age in the Jim Crow 1920s. The immense brutality he witnessed before and during his incarceration inspired his first stories, written while in prison and published in *Esquire* magazine signed with his name and prison number. As a jailhouse writer, he achieved acclaim for his fiction and thrillers. But whatever the plot in his dozens of works, the subtext was always the same: the ritual murder of the human spirit by lethal doses of racism.

A lifetime later, on July 29, 1954, with nearly eight years of prison and eighteen free years behind him, he would assess himself as a man enjoying his forty-fifth birthday in the south of France: "I looked ten years younger and had the physique of a prizefighter. I was the color of new bronze in the sun. I had a nice smile, showing two faint dimples, and tiny laugh wrinkles from the corners of my long-lashed brown eyes. I had wide shoulders and narrow hips, and Alva always said she envied my legs. I had an almost unlimited vitality. All in all, I was an attractive man."

It was an amazing transformation—momentary perhaps, but for a Black man who had once been so corrupted by pain, it had a special poignancy. "I have almost completely forgotten prison, what it was like and what I was like while there," he wrote in his autobiography, *The Quality of Hurt*. "The only impression it left absolutely and irrevocably is that human beings—all human beings—will do anything and everything. And I think it has partly convinced me . . . I can never again be hurt as much as I have already been hurt, even though I should live one hundred thousand years."

Confronting his demons, Himes had grown to know both transformation and reclamation of the spirit. It suited him well.

Thursday, July 29, 1954, U.S.A.–France

Literature   **Self-Concept**

JULY 30

On July 30, 1987, Aretha Franklin went against all manner of music industry "conventional wisdom" to return to her roots in church music with what would be called "the most challenging and fulfilling album project of her career." Her third inspirational and fifty-fifth album to date, *One Lord, One Faith, One Baptism*, was Aretha Franklin's first solo venture as a producer.

During three sweltering days in Detroit, Aretha's classic revival meeting was recorded at the New Bethel Baptist Church with an all-star pastoral and musical cast that included the Reverend Jesse Jackson, singer Mavis Staples, and the music of the legendary Clara Ward. The live audience had obtained free tickets through churches and promotional radio giveaways. And in keeping with the traditions of the service, a collection plate was passed, raising thousands of dollars to aid the Detroit Children's Hospital and to feed the hungry.

When it was done, "conventional wisdom" claimed victory for what it had "always known"—or at least, for what it had long benefited from and indeed supported—the fact that Aretha Franklin was a winner! With *One Lord, One Faith, One Baptism*, she won her fifteenth Grammy for "Best Soul Gospel Performance, Female," and in a rare move, the Grammies gave a special notice to the track on the album titled "Speech by the Reverend Jesse Jackson." This record-within-a-record received a Grammy for the "Best Spoken Word" recording.

Thursday, July 30, 1987, Michigan, U.S.A.

Music   **Faith**

JULY 31

Since its founding in 1870, the Metropolitan Museum of Art was meant to be the most comprehensive museum in the United States and among the world's greatest collections. But the growth of its collection of works by African-American artists had been marred and stunted by racial politics. In 1976, all that changed with an exhibit honoring the nation's bicentennial and called "Selections of Nineteenth-Century Afro-American Art." In range of subject and style, it offered a long-overdue hallelujah!

From its first revealing images, the show demanded attention and got it. *Ashur Moses Nathan and Son,* Jules Lion's 1845 painting of a white father in fond Victorian embrace with his clearly biracial son, graced the cover of the catalog and set the theme for the entire show—the untold stories of America in art. To get to the founders of African-American art, the show dated the earliest known Black artists from a Boston newspaper notice of a British-trained portraitist in 1773; it quoted the admiration of famed portraitist to presidents Gilbert Stuart for slave artist Neptune Thursten in the eighteenth century. The show resurrected the nineteenth-century artistry of African-American "face vessels" and "voodoo pots." It exhibited stylistic comparisons "too close to be coincidental" in artifacts from Georgia, the Carolinas, and northern Underground Railroad trails with the West African wooden and pottery vessels of Zaire.

In the introduction to the catalog, art historian Regenia A. Perry wrote, with classic understatement, "One of the most remarkable facts about Afro-American art is that it exists at all." When the show ended its two-month run on July 31, 1976, a record number of museum visitors had been stunned by the breadth, artistry, and sheer fact of that remarkable existence.

Saturday, July 31, 1976, New York, U.S.A.

Art   **Better Worlds**

AUGUST

A Brown Study. Etching from the drawing by William Hunt. Published by *Harper's Weekly* (March 5, 1870). Reprinted courtesy of the author.

AUGUST 1

On an August day in 1619, a Dutch ship sailed into colonial Jamestown, Virginia, traded its human cargo for food, and launched an industry so successful that nearly four hundred years later, vast stretches of Africa remain underpopulated. A letter written by John Rolfe is the earliest known documentation of what was to become a regular occurrence for the next two hundred years: "About the latter end of August, a Dutch man-of-warre [ship]. . . arrived at Point Comfort. He brought not any thing but 20 and odd negars which the Governor . . . bought for victualle [food]."

No one knows who the twenty were, how they came to be captured, or where they originated. All we know is this: The captain's name was Iope. The pilot was Marmaduke, an Englishman. Among the twenty were Antoney, Isabella, and Pedro. Because they had been given Spanish names but arrived in Jamestown on a Dutch vessel, the British colonists assumed they had been stolen from a Spanish ship by pirates. While the history of Europeans enslaving Africans dated to 1444, slavery had not yet become a colonial way of life. The African captives were designated "Indentures," because white indentured servitude was an established practice. Beyond that we know that Antoney and Isabella found love together. Isabella gave birth to the first African-American, William, in 1623 or 1624. Colonial governments north and south soon legalized slavery and granted white business lasting relief in the form of low-cost, self-renewing labor for the next two hundred years. All tolled, the American slave trade consumed what Dr. W. E. B. Du Bois estimated to be no less than one hundred million African lives.

The Jamestown site is now a national historic landmark — an empty point on the river. Because the actual landing date is unknown, no anniversary is observed. Perhaps inspiration can be derived from our own thoughts until the collective consciousness swells into an annual Day of Remembrance for our "20 and odd" Jamestown forebears..

Thursday, August 1, 1619, Virginia, U.S.A.

Events   **Collective Self-Determination**

AUGUST 2

On August 2, 1920, one of the largest gatherings of African-Americans ever to assemble rallied at New York City's Madison Square Garden to hear the stirring message of Marcus Garvey. "Up, you mighty race, you can accomplish what you will," said Garvey, challenging and boosting the twenty-five thousand followers and sympathizers gathered in support of his Universal Negro Improvement Association (UNIA). "Africa for the Africans at home and abroad!" From his newspaper, the *Negro World*, to his shipping company, the Black Star Line, Garvey quite simply gave people great hope and greater plans.

The NAACP's James Weldon Johnson noted that in two years the UNIA collected "more than any other Negro organization had ever dreamed of"—ten million uninflated 1920s dollars! Among Garvey's most lasting achievements were his effect on a young Kwame Nkrumah, who would become Ghana's first president after the country gained its independence in 1957, and the design of the Black nationalist flag still in use today. In 1921, Garvey announced the formation of an African republic with himself as its provisional president—a bold move in the age of Jim Crow America and the colonization of the African continent. That year Garvey unfurled the flag of the oncoming age: black (for race), red (for its blood), green (for our hope).

Monday, August 2, 1920, New York, U.S.A.

Pan-Africanism   **Vision**

AUGUST 3

Shortly before Mary McLeod Bethune (see April 25, July 10, October 5, December 5) died at age eighty on May 18, 1955, she dictated her "Last Will and Testament" to *Ebony* magazine. Treasured for its literary and inspirational merit, the full text (excerpted here) was published in *Ebony*'s August 1955 issue and later in book form.

My worldly possessions are few. Yet my experiences have been rich. From them I have distilled principles and policies in which I believe firmly, for they represent the meaning of my life's work. They are the products of much sweat and sorrow. Perhaps, in them there is something of value. So, as my life draws to a close, I will pass them on . . . in the hope that an old woman's philosophy may give them inspiration. Here, then, is my legacy.

I leave you hope. . . .

I leave you a thirst for education. . . .

I leave you the challenge of developing confidence in one another. . . .

I leave you a respect for the use of power. . . .

I leave you faith. . . .

I leave you racial dignity. . . .

I leave you, finally, a responsibility to our young people. . . .

Faith, courage, brotherhood, dignity, ambition, responsibility—these are needed today as never before. The Freedom Gates are half ajar. We must pry them fully open. As I face tomorrow, I am content, for I think I have spent my life well. I pray now that my philosophy may be helpful to those who share my vision of a world of peace

These were the values Mrs. Bethune prized in order to make a people whole. To these she added a range of life-tested strategies to help maintain her legacy as a renewable resource.

Wednesday, August 3, 1955, Florida, U.S.A.

Heroes   **Passion**

AUGUST 4

In Mississippi, the summer of 1964 was "Freedom Summer," when students from the North were invited to the South as volunteers in a campaign to educate and register Black voters. What was to be just one more in the series became historically significant on August 4, 1964, when the disappearance of three civil rights workers came to a tragic conclusion. On this day, a tip led to the discovery of the bodies of James Chaney, Andrew Goodman, and Michael Schwerner in an earthen dam on a farm near Philadelphia, Mississippi. All three had been shot in the head. Chaney, the one Black victim, had also been brutally beaten and his skull fractured.

All that is known about the events leading up to their murder was that the three had been stopped in their car by a deputy sheriff who had then jailed the "mixed-race" occupants for "speeding." Late that night they were released. When they were first reported missing, the local sheriff said, "If they're missing, they're just hid somewhere trying to get a lot of publicity out of it, I figure." Ironically, the "mixed-race" status of the three, which contributed to their murder, also increased public pressure and interest in finding them. During the search for these two whites and one Black, several other long-missing Black bodies were found—and ignored. Meanwhile, the FBI offered a $30,000 reward for information on the "mixed-race" case. Typical of other cases, however, when the FBI's work brought indictments for murder against twenty-one whites, including several police officers, local authorities and customs insured that all charges were dropped.

In what might be called "good news" in the face of what is so terribly bad, there was an element that the sheriff didn't "figure" on, and that was the recent civil rights legislation. When charges against the twenty-one were dropped, the federal government stepped in. Six of the twenty-one were tried, convicted, and sentenced for violating federal civil rights law.

Tuesday, August 4, 1964, Mississippi, U.S.A.

Human Rights **Milestones**

AUGUST 5

In the aftermath of the assassination of Dr. Martin Luther King, Jr., in April 1968, rioters flooded the streets of major cities nationwide. *Esquire* magazine interviewed James Baldwin, the author who had warned America of "the fire next time" five years earlier (see January 27). In the August 1968 issue of *Esquire*, Baldwin reflected on the civil rights movement and the loss of Dr. King.

The interviewer asked what could be done to "cool things off" in this immensely tragic year. Baldwin responded, "It is already very, very late."

EM: What about the role of some of the Black institutions? Does the church have some meaning still in the Black community . . . ?

JB: . . . The fact that we have a Black church [or white church] is an indictment of a Christian nation. Martin Luther King used [the church] most brilliantly. That was his forum. It's always been our only forum. But it doesn't exist anywhere in the North anymore. . . . It exists in the South, because the Black community in the South is a different community. There's still a Negro family in the South, or there was. There is no Negro family essentially in the North, and once you have no family you have no church. And that means you have no forum.

EM: Then the Black church is dead in the North?

JB: Let me rephrase it. It does not attract the young. Once that has happened to any organization, its social usefulness is . . . debatable. Now that's one of the great understatements of the century.

Rereading Baldwin's thirty-year-old comments in the light of contemporary developments, some will say that he was pessimistic; some will call him prophetic. Others will say that he was simply telling the truth. And as Baldwin himself—a teenage preacher turned author—would remind us, "the truth shall make us free!"

Monday, August 5, 1968, New York, U.S.A.

Journalism   **Expression**

AUGUST 6

Arriving in Denver, Colorado, or Cheyenne, Wyoming, on this day in 1863, if you wanted to leave Civil War cares behind for a while, you might have treated a friend to "the squarest meal between two oceans." For a good night's rest at a hotel that catered to the horse-and-carriage trade of prospectors and presidents alike, one of the InterOcean hotels would have been the place. You would be graciously welcomed to the saloon "stocked with the very finest liquors and cigars that gold or greenbacks can control of first hands in the eastern markets." In the restaurant you would have "game of all kinds, trout &c., constantly on hand for regular and transient customers, and served in a style second to no other restaurant in the West." And the barbers didn't conduct business in an ordinary shop, theirs was "a shaving and hairdressing saloon" in first-class style.

For despite repeated suspicious fires and a score of equally suspicious business woes, and despite the fact that his hotels catered to patrons regardless of race—a fact that may have angered many—Barney L. Ford was back in business and advertising that fact with the words just quoted from the *Rocky Mountain News* of August 6, 1863.

In 1895, the definitive *History of the State of Colorado* was published, and the entry on Barney L. Ford exceeded the space devoted to Colorado's most prominent whites, but no mention was made of the fact that Ford was Black. In later editions, Ford's picture was replaced with that of a white man. A century after his insistent and persistent ads in the *Rocky Mountain News* of 1863, the only official reference to Ford as an African-American was at a mound near Breckenridge, Colorado, where legend had it that Ford had once struck gold. That mound was called "Nigger Hill" until 1964, when it was renamed "Barney Ford Hill." Now, when the story of the nineteenth century's African-American entrepreneurs is told, Barney L. Ford's name is high on the list.

Thursday, August 6, 1863, Colorado–Wyoming, U.S.A.
Business   **Enterprise**

AUGUST 7

As the suffrage movement pressed for women's rights, *The Crisis* of August 1915 published "Votes for Women: A Symposium by Leading Thinkers of Colored America." Then as now, divisive forces sought to strenghten their own positions by fomenting dissent between two disfranchised camps: "Blacks" and "women." Among the supporters:

James Weldon Johnson, lyricist of "Lift Ev'ry Voice" and a former consul to Nicaragua, wrote, "There is one thing very annoying about the cause of Woman Suffrage and that is the absurdity of the arguments against it which one is called upon to combat. . . . It takes only a glance to see the striking analogy [to] the old pro-slavery arguments."

In an entry signed "Mrs. Paul Laurence Dunbar," Alice Nelson Dunbar wrote, "It is difficult to love your home and family if you be outcast and despised by them; perplexing to love humanity, if it gives you nothing but blows; impracticable to love your country, if it denies you all the rights and privileges which as citizens you should enjoy."

Nannie Burroughs, secretary of the Women's Auxiliary to the National Baptist Convention, remembered being asked, "What can the Negro woman do with the ballot?" She answered, "What can she do without it? . . . She needs it to ransom her race."

Said educator-activist Mary Church Terrell, honorary president of the National Association of Colored Women, "Even if I believed that women should be denied the right of suffrage, wild horses could not drag such an admission from my pen or my lips. . . . What could be more absurd . . . than that one group of individuals who are trying to throw off the yoke of oppression themselves . . . should favor laws and customs which impede the progress of another unfortunate group and hinder them in every conceivable way."

Amazingly, powerful voices still renew this debate periodically to sidetrack progress; worse still, many who should know better continue to fall into the trap.

Saturday, August 7, 1915, New York, U.S.A.

Human Rights   **Perception**

AUGUST 8

Clement G. Morgan, a first-generation child of emancipation, was a restless soul in search of the opportunities denied his parents. In 1893, as Jim Crow discrimination was tightening its squeeze, Morgan became the first African-American to earn two Harvard degrees—his baccalaureate, and a master's in law. On August 8, 1893, he was admitted to the Massachusetts bar and immediately began his law practice in Cambridge. The charge is too often made that privileged Blacks turn their backs on their less fortunate brethren. It is a charge quickly proved wrong when tested by the lives of people like Morgan. His notion of privilege was the honor of practicing law in service to his people for thirty-six years of his life.

A brilliant student, Morgan won scholarships despite the prejudice of his detractors, worked his way through school as a barber, and lived out his philosophy of patience, sincerity, and unselfishness. Morgan could have been the perfect candidate for Booker T. Washington's cadre of privileged Blacks—a group that publicly denied the misdeeds of racism in order to prosper from the favors of whites (see September 18). Instead, Morgan was among Washington's most conscientious of objectors. In a diplomatically phrased international press release, Morgan said he was "without personal bitterness toward . . . a distinguished American," but questioned Washington's truisms versus his opportunisms. "Large financial responsibilities have made [Washington] dependent on the rich charitable public and . . . for this reason, he has for years been compelled to tell, not the whole truth, but that part of it which certain powerful interests in America wish to appear as the whole truth."

In 1903, Washington's powerful allies leveled criminal charges of causing a riot with his editorial dissent against Monroe Trotter, the Black activist-publisher of *The Guardian*. Morgan put himself in the line of fire to defend Trotter. Equating privilege with working for the common good, Morgan laid new ground in the legal battle for human rights.

Tuesday, August 8, 1893, Virginia–Massachusetts, U.S.A.
Law   **Life's Work**

AUGUST 9

On August 9, 1936, as the Olympics came to a close in Berlin, Germany, Jesse Owens had won four gold medals in track and field events, a feat that was not duplicated until another African-American, Carl Lewis, won four golds at the 1984 Olympics. Of the sixteen new records set in Berlin in 1936, four belonged to Owens:

One hundred meters: Gold medal — 10.3 seconds
Two hundred meters: Gold medal — 20.7 seconds
Long jump: Gold medal — 25'5½"
Four-hundred-meter relay: Gold medal — 39.8 seconds

With the world in the grip of imperialism, fascism, and murderous racism, Owens's victories had special significance. In September 1935, the Nuremberg Laws stripped German Jews of their citizenship rights and equal protection under the law on grounds of Aryan "racial supremacy." Two weeks later Italy invaded Ethiopia. While the official United States response was apathy, the government took an active stance in preventing Black men from volunteering to fight to liberate their Ethiopian cousins. And so, with Germany's supremacist views so widely shared by white Americans, it was particularly ironic that the American press made so much of Hitler's alleged Olympic "snub" of Owens. On the opening day of the Olympics, two Germans won medals. Hitler invited them to his box. He then invited a winning Finn but left the stadium as a Black athlete, Cornelius Johnson, took honors in the next event. It was not until the second day that Owens won his first medal; by then, Hitler had stopped inviting winners. As such, if anyone was snubbed, it was Johnson. But the story was good press, and it swelled into legend.

Stunning as his records are, no statistics can capture the significance of Jesse Owens's victory. He represented the struggle of every oppressed human being to successfully break free of the bonds of caste — just when a world bent on fascism was attempting to prove such a thing couldn't be done.

Sunday, August 9, 1936, Germany

Sports   **Greatness**

AUGUST 10

Despite conscious efforts to destroy our collective knowledge of African history and civilization during the eras of slavery and colonialism, a rich array of material has survived. Today, historians are able to reconstruct a picture of ancient Africa from contemporary accounts preserved in Arabic, the oral histories of the griots, and writings on temple walls. Because of these accounts, we have been introduced to one of the most famous African leaders of the medieval period, Mansa Musa, who rose to power in 1307 and built Mali into one of the medieval world's greatest empires. On this day in 1324, Mansa Musa was at the helm of a historic pilgrimage to Mecca. Historian Lerone Bennett describes the scene:

> He went in regal splendor with an entourage of sixty thousand persons, including twelve thousand servants. Five hundred servants, each of whom carried a staff of pure gold weighing some six pounds, marched on before him. Eighty camels bore twenty thousand pounds of gold, which the black monarch distributed as alms and gifts. Musa returned to his kingdom with an architect who designed imposing buildings in Timbuktu and other cities of the Sudan.

It is tempting to see in this account proof that as a people we've always known where we needed to go; the only question is what we are willing to go through to get there. Upon his return to Mali, Musa was well prepared to direct the building up of Timbuktu as one of the greatest centers of international commerce and scholarship on a site where the world's first university was destined to appear (see September 1).

When ancient civilizations are studied in school, too often our knowledge of Africa begins with ancient Egypt and skips across two thousand years to the coming of European colonization and slavery. The story of Mansa Musa is one small part of a much larger story that can help us reshape our view of the continent and fill in the gaps in our knowledge of its history.

Thursday, August 10, 1324, Mali
Government/Philosophy   **Knowledge**

AUGUST 11

Frederick Douglass felt a long, well-documented bond with the island of Nantucket off the Massachusetts coast. It was there that the man who had escaped slavery just three years earlier made his "maiden" speech as an abolitionist on August 11, 1841. The occasion was the First Antislavery Convention at the Nantucket Atheneum, a gathering conducted in the manner of a Quaker meeting where anyone can rise and openly speak his or her mind.

Two days earlier Douglass had attended an antislavery meeting in his adopted city of New Bedford. There, he and William Lloyd Garrison, the abolitionist and publisher of *The Liberator*, met for the first time. They so impressed each other that Garrison invited Douglass to join the group that would be traveling to Nantucket.

There is no written transcript of Douglass's first speech, but as he recalled the moment four years later, "it was a severe cross, and I took it up reluctantly. The truth was, I felt myself a slave, and the idea of speaking to white people weighed me down. It was with the utmost difficulty that I could stand erect, or that I could . . . articulate two words without hesitation and stammering. [Yet] I spoke but a few moments when I felt a degree of freedom, and said what I desired with considerable ease. The audience sympathized with me at once, and from having been remarkably quiet, became much excited."

Indeed they were. For, as one participant later recalled, "when Douglass told his story to the public, he spoke with unquestionable authority, a late graduate from the peculiar institution with his diploma written on his back." With the mark of authenticity, a feeling of responsibility to those still enslaved, and a loyalty to all those whose voices would never be heard except through his, Douglass rose to the task. He never stopped speaking for the cause of freedom until he died in 1895 (see July 4, September 3, December 3, December 31).

Wednesday, August 11, 1841, Massachusetts, U.S.A.
Speech/Oration   **Conviction**

AUGUST 12

Langston Hughes loved children. As an author, he accepted invitations to speak all across the country. And wherever he went, he regularly donated his time to speak to children and encourage them. But with the children of his beloved P.S. 24, the neighborhood school a block from his Harlem home at 20 East 127th Street, he built a special relationship. This is how their bond took root and grew.

In the 1950s, the yards of Hughes's Harlem brownstone were regularly tended by a gardener appropriately named Mr. Sacred Heart. But no matter what was planted in the small front patch, it was always trampled by the children. It's quite likely that the children, knowing that "someone famous" lived at the house, just wanted to get a look at the famous Hughes up close. Trampling his garden was a mere by-product of their awe. But Hughes didn't know that, then. Nor was he a man who thought of himself as a "celebrity" worthy of the children's curiosity. All he knew was that his garden and Mr. Sacred Heart's work were taking a beating.

Finally, Hughes came up with an ingenious solution. He decided to share the tiny plot with the children as their garden. Together Hughes and Mr. Sacred Heart shepherded the children through choosing and setting their own individual plants, beside which a white picket marker was placed with the child's name. Weeded and watered by the children with help from the two men, the garden flourished—each little sprout spreading as broadly as the smiles planted on the faces of Hughes and his "Garden of Children," their pride captured in a treasured photo taken on or about August 12, 1954.

Writers regularly use their understanding of human nature to build their characters. But for writers, as for any of us, it's rare to witness the characters they build blossom with such beautiful and lasting effect.

Thursday, August 12, 1954, New York, U.S.A.

Life and Art   **Understanding**

AUGUST 13

While the stories of African enslavement and the destruction of Indigenous Americans are often told, stories of both groups' resistance are rare.

Yet, according to British Council documents of August 13, 1670, imperial rule of Jamaica was constantly jeopardized by what the council called "the Insults of those slaves who begin to grow both numerous and powerfull."

These rebel slaves were the Maroons. From their resistance movement a legendary hero emerged sixty years later, Chief Cudjoe. With Cudjoe's leadership and, after his death, with his inspiration, a steady campaign was waged against plantation slavery that gave the island a reputation for being unsafe for whites—a factor still reflected in the demographic mix of Jamaica to this day (90 percent Black and 10 percent white).

Well into the late nineteenth century and throughout the Americas, these Maroons—isolated groups of Blacks and indigenous peoples—eked out a life in the woods and swamps and steadfastly resisted capture, slavery, and extermination. Their "guerrilla" raids were an unrelenting threat to slavery and colonial dominion over the original indigenous nations. To Europeans, these Maroon communities of escaped slaves and indigenous Americans were renegades and outlaws. To conquered peoples, they were a liberating army. Operating from the most remote regions, the Maroons endured excruciating hardship in exchange for their freedom. In the earliest eighteenth-century South American Maroon settlements, the largely African-born population built societies modeled on those in Africa. Later, as they assimilated with their indigenous hosts, they forged a still-thriving "Black Indian" heritage.

With the growth of the plantations throughout North and South America and the Caribbean, the Maroons never ceased their fight for independence. Highlights of the Maroon legacy include the Black president of Mexico, Vicente Guerrero (see April 27) and such extant Maroon communities as that of the former Dutch colony of Suriname.

Wednesday, August 13, 1670, Jamaica

Liberation   **Self-Determination**

AUGUST 14

On August 14, 1966, playwright-actor Douglas Turner Ward's article "American Theatre: For Whites Only?" was published in the *New York Times*. In it, Ward called for a fully autonomous Black theater company where upcoming Black artists could have control over their own creative destinies. The article had been commissioned by the *Times* as a commentary on a production of Ward's pair of one-act plays, *Happy Ending/Day of Absence*.

These were both the right idea and the right article, published at the right time. The article came to the attention of Ford Foundation executives, who contacted Ward with a question: would he be interested in putting his words into action? Encouraged by their interest, Ward brought in his current partners, producer Gerald Krone and actor Robert Hooks. Together, they turned the premise of Ward's article into a proposal for a new theater company. When the Ford Foundation responded positively, the Negro Ensemble Company was born—New York's premier Black repertory theater company, which has toured throughout the United States and brought contemporary African-American theater to audiences worldwide (see January 2).

Sunday, August 14, 1966, New York, U.S.A.

Theater/Journalism   **Vision**

AUGUST 15

In August 1974, Joanne Little was the victim of an attempted rape while in jail pending the appeal of her burglary conviction. The perpetrator was her white male prison guard. Little fought back, stabbing the guard with an ice pick, and upon the guard's death, Little was indicted for first-degree murder.

For a solid year the case raged through the courts and the national press, challenging two liberation movements, the prison system, and the credibility of the courts. The African-American liberation movement had traditionally cast the needs of all Blacks in decidedly male terms, making issues of special relevance to Black women secondary to those of significance to Black men. Similarly, the women's liberation movement had traditionally viewed itself as the province of white women with only a secondary emphasis on the special needs of women of color. The rights of Black women fell in the chasm that existed between these two uncompromising camps. But the case of Joanne Little was one on which all could agree. Whether prisoner or not, a woman had a right to the sanctity of her own body, and an incarcerated individual, whatever his or her sex, had the right to personal security even behind bars. The question thus became whether the legal system—which traditionally subverted the rights of women and people of color to those of white men—would support a finding of self-defense in the attempted rape of a Black woman.

On August 15, 1975, Joanne Little was exonerated by a hard-fought acquittal. With her case, the historic clash between the African-American rights and women's liberation movements found rare common ground.

Friday, August 15, 1975, North Carolina, U.S.A.

Women   **Sanctity**

AUGUST 16

Among the greatest tragedies in literary history is this: Zora Neale Hurston, author of a dozen books—from such seminal works of African-American anthropology as *Tell My Horse* to such vibrant works of fiction as *Their Eyes Were Watching God*—died a pauper in 1960. Living her last years in the Saint Lucie County, Florida, welfare home, she was buried in an unmarked grave in a segregated cemetery. Among the greatest triumphs of that history is this: on August 16, 1973, one of Hurston's "literary daughters," Alice Walker, the Pulitzer Prize–winning author of *The Color Purple,* set out to research and resurrect Hurston's memory and legacy.

Moved by the injustice and the terrible irony of Hurston's demise, Alice Walker went to Eatonville, Florida, in search of Zora's grave. Unable to find it, she nevertheless erected a headstone for her, engraved with a line from another Harlem Renaissance luminary, Jean Toomer:

Zora Neale Hurston—
"A Genius of the South"—Novelist Folklorist—Anthropologist—
1901–1960

Why did things turn out so badly for Hurston, this friend of Langston Hughes, peer of Dorothy West, and beacon of the Harlem Renaissance? How could the woman who said, "I love myself when I am laughing and then again when I am looking mean and impressive" die in obscurity? Who can know? But Alice Walker captured the experience of attempting to retrieve her in her own essay, "Looking for Zora":

> There are times—and finding Zora Hurston's grave was one of them—when normal responses of grief, horror, and so on do not make sense because they bear no real relation to the depth of the emotion one feels. It was impossible for me to cry when I saw the field full of weeds where Zora is. Partly this is because I have come to know Zora through her books and she was not a teary sort of person herself; but partly, too, it is because there is a point at which even grief feels absurd. And at this point, laughter gushes up to retrieve sanity.

Thursday, August 16, 1973, Florida, U.S.A.

Literature   **Life**

AUGUST 17

A visit to Harper's Ferry, West Virginia, is filled with ghosts. But in a town made infamous by John Brown's historic raid, a glance up at the crest of the mountain reveals now-empty buildings that recall the glory days of what was once the historically Black campus of Storer College. It was here that Frederick Douglass established a professorship as a tribute to John Brown's infamous antislavery raid. Douglass donated his lecture fees to help fund an academic chair. Here, generations of Black families made a pilgrimage to their history. And here, the Niagara Movement was housed for a conference that led to the founding of the NAACP three years later. On August 17, 1906, Dr. W. E. B. Du Bois and the founding members of the Niagara Movement conducted their historic Barefoot March down the hillside to the site of the old firehouse that was turned into a fort during John Brown's raid on the arsenal in downtown Harper's Ferry (see October 16, December 2). On this site, Du Bois's group commemorated the sacrifices that led to emancipation.

A casualty of the 1954 Supreme Court desegregation order, Storer College was closed because the state could not see that a historically Black college was more than just a "duplication of services" available at a predominantly white school. Today, high on the hill overlooking Harper's Ferry, Storer College is gone but not forgotten, for it has been designated a national historic landmark site, preserving a legacy and providing inspiration for generations to come.

Friday, August 17, 1906, West Virginia, U.S.A.
Education/Social History   **Priorities**

AUGUST 18

When assumptions are made about the theater as a middle- and upper-class urban diversion in America, it's great to know about the work begun in the early 1960s that dramatized and paralleled the rise of the civil rights movement. Throughout the rural South, the Free Southern Theater (FST) brought out poor Black communities for plays grounded in their own experiences, plays that melded the talents of local and professional performers.

On a sweltering August 18, 1965, night, as a crowd overflowed Union Hall in Bogalusa, Louisiana, the Free Southern Theater put on a show about Bogalusa itself and the height of segregationist paranoia and intimidation. As one contemporary account recalled, "outside across the dirt road, the police chief leans against his automobile talking with several of his deputies. The chief is not sure what a play is, but he is present in case any 'trouble' develops. . . . The Deacons for Defense of Equality and Justice are also present. They had escorted the FST without incident from McComb, Mississippi, Monday, and will provide a protective caravan of cars tomorrow morning when the company leaves for New Orleans."

No, theater is neither safe nor elite. Theater is the voice of people.

Wednesday, August 18, 1965, Louisiana, U.S.A.
Theater   **Voices**

AUGUST 19

As mathematician, inventor, and astronomer, Benjamin Banneker was eager to promote his newly published work, *Benjamin Banneker's Pennsylvania, Delaware, Maryland, and Virginia Almanac and Ephemeris, for the Year of our Lord 1792.* Banneker was also eager to put his work to use in making a special point about the capabilities of Black people. Fifteen years after the Declaration of Independence had proclaimed that "all men are equal" and four years after the Constitution had categorized Blacks as "three-fifths a man," Banneker sent Thomas Jefferson a preview copy of his new almanac with this letter dated August 19, 1791:

> Sir, I suppose that your knowledge of the situation of my brethren is too extensive to need a recital here; neither shall I presume to prescribe methods by which they may be relieved, otherwise than by recommending to you, and all others to wean yourselves from those narrow prejudices which you have imbibed with respect to them, and as Job proposed to his friends 'Put your Souls in their Souls' stead.'"

On August 30, 1791, Jefferson responded:

> . . . No body wishes more than I do to see such proofs as you exhibit, that nature has given to our black brethren, talents equal to those of the other colors of men, and that the appearance of a want of them is owing merely to the degraded condition of their existence, both in Africa and America.

Throughout American history, we have taken racism to heart precisely because, as its target, it has penetrated our lives so deeply. Because it hurts us to the core, we do not see racism for what it is—not a bearer of truth but a strategy. Thankfully, exchanges like the Banneker-Jefferson correspondence remain to remind us that when the achievement of someone as brilliant as Banneker isn't answer enough, there is something wrong with the question.

Friday, August 19, 1791, Maryland, U.S.A.

Invention/Astronomy   **Self-Affirmation**

AUGUST 20

In August 1987, venture capitalist Reginald Lewis structured the $985 million leveraged buyout of Beatrice Foods by his own Wall Street investment firm, the TLC Group. With that, TLC became the largest Black-owned business ever! It also ushered in a new era in which Black entrepreneurs would succeed in a global marketplace. With this deal, Lewis had leveraged his abilities as an attorney into the front lines of mergers, acquisitions, and high finance.

His firm had begun by specializing in venture capital development for small- and medium-sized businesses. This led to the acquisition of the McCall's Pattern Company in 1984, in which he invested $1 million of his own earnings to acquire the $25 million company. With skillful management, three years later he sold McCall's for a handsome profit ninety times his original investment. With the profits from that deal, he strategized the acquisition of Beatrice.

In an interview with *Black Enterprise* magazine, Lewis was clear about how he viewed business and himself as a businessperson: "To carry around the notion that if I fail it's going to mean that no other Black person will ever have a similar opportunity, or if I succeed that it's going to somehow open a floodgate of opportunity for other Black Americans misses the point. . . . I don't want to pay 5 percent more on a deal because we're going to be the first Americans of African descent to do it. If our work is perceived as an indication that Americans of African descent can function in a global competitive situation, that's nice. But I've always believed that anyway!"

Thursday, August 20, 1987, U.S.A.

Business   **Confidence**

AUGUST 21

As a student of the Bible, Nat Turner must surely have read this passage: "From that time began Jesus to show unto his disciples, that he must go unto Jerusalem, and suffer many things of the elders and chief priests, and scribes and be killed." As a prophet, Nat Turner knew his life's mission was to live out the meaning of the Scriptures, to strike a blow to the head of the serpent of slavery. In 1821 in Jerusalem, Virginia, leading his disciples, Turner fulfilled a mission for which he had been groomed since childhood (see May 12).

Nat Turner had waited for the heavenly sign that would set his date with destiny. With the solar eclipse of February 1831, he began to gather his troops. On August 21, 1831, Nat Turner's men launched the most successful slave revolt in U.S. history. The insurrection consisted of seven men, one hatchet, a broadax, and the scars of slavery. As the revolt progressed, their number would swell to seventy. The first killed were Turner's owners. After that followed the slaughter of fifty-seven of slavery's perpetrators and beneficiaries. As historian Lerone Bennett notes, "it is not true that Nat Turner initiated a wave of violence. . . . The violence was already there. Slavery was violence, and Nat Turner's acts . . . were responses to that violence. [But] none of this was apparent or even relevant to the white citizens of Southampton [County, Virginia]." In the aftermath, innocent slaves were tortured and massacred in retaliation, and Turner's army was executed. But Turner himself eluded capture for over two months.

At his trial he pleaded "not guilty" because he said he did not feel guilty. On the day he was hanged, November 11, the sky grew dark and it rained in the midst of a dry spell, just as he had prophesied—a fact of great moment to both Blacks and whites. As author W. S. Drewry has commented, Nat Turner's revolt "was a landmark in the history of slavery . . . , and was, indirectly, most instrumental in bringing about [its abolition]."

Sunday, August 21, 1831, Virginia, U.S.A.

Slave Revolt!   **Knowledge/Faith**

AUGUST 22

At midnight on August 22, 1791, one hundred thousand enslaved people of African descent rose up in a revolution that changed history and years of European assumptions about the meaning of leadership. One enslaved man, Toussaint-L'Ouverture, achieved the confidence of his fellow slaves, raised an army, and led the revolt of his people; together they established the first independent nation of people of African descent in the Western Hemisphere.

On that August night, 1,400 coffee and sugar plantations were set on fire. Over the next three weeks, the army of slaves revolted against a century of French oppression. One French planter who survived the revolution said, "Picture to yourself the whole horizon a wall of fire, from which continually rose thick vortices of smoke, whose huge black volumes could be likened only to those frightful storm clouds which roll onward charged with thunder and lightning. The rift in these clouds disclosed flames as great in volume, which rose darting and flashing to the very sky. Such was their voracity that for nearly three weeks we could barely distinguish between day and night, for so long as the rebels found anything to feed the flames, they never ceased to burn."

And in their burning passion, the rebels burned the buildings, the machines, the houses, and the assumption that Blacks would forever consent, even under duress, to live as slaves.

Since its revolution, Haiti has never been free to develop the fruits of its sovereignty. As was the case over two hundred years ago, tiny Haiti has always been seen as a threat to European and American domination. But Haiti's failures also challenge our assumptions about the nature and character of the enemy. The greatest enemy may arise from within. Freedom can only be sustained with the most dedicated vigilance.

Monday, August 22, 1791, Haiti

Liberation   **Racial Dignity**

AUGUST 23

For all that has been said about Booker T. Washington's turn-of-the-century accommodationism, his philosophy provided a protective mask behind which he could exercise an unusual degree of autonomy in the midst of extreme oppression. What some would call accommodationism, others might call pragmatism. But whatever the label, no one disputes the fact that his singular focus powered the growth of Tuskegee Institute as one of the nation's finest colleges. With his constricted freedom, he nurtured others from apprenticeship to professionalism. And among professionals, he sought those who would undergird his prominence and, through him, achieve their own—and he took credit as publicly as possible for what he was able to achieve. True to the spirit of a school that had begun as an agricultural college, what Washington had built was a solid root system.

One example of this skillful leveraging of his reputation was his work as cofounder and first president of an alliance of Black businesses. The year 1900 saw 106 reported lynchings and several Black communities stormed by white mobs. Among the most frequent causes of this terror was a fear that one group of poor people would lose their jobs and place in the world to another. Adopting a posture of active self-defense for Black economic development, over two hundred men and women from Florida to California gathered in Boston for a two-day convention on August 23 and 24, 1900. There they founded the National Negro Business League and elected Booker T. Washington its first president. Among their primary goals, to encourage entrepreneurism and to educate young people for business careers.

Thursday, August 23, 1900, Massachusetts, U.S.A.

Business   **Cooperative Economics**

AUGUST 24

In Farmington, Connecticut, the marker on a grave and a small bedroom and privy on the second floor of a privately owned barn put a human face on the tragedy and triumph that began in the spring of 1839. Early that year, the slave ship *Amistad* loaded its cargo of Mendi families that had been captured into slavery and left the coast of Africa for Havana, Cuba. Sailing eight weeks en route from Havana to the midcoastal states, the slaver zigzagged its way through Atlantic waters in an approach-avoidance conflict with the American shoreline. As captor and captive pitted their navigational wits against the common enemy of the sea, what happened aboard that ship made its way into history as the Amistad Mutiny—the only successful revolt by captured slaves in American history.

On August 24, 1839, as the *Amistad* anchored at Culloden Point off Long Island, the Africans were taken into custody and put on trial for overthrowing their captors. Championing their right to resist capture and slavery, their case was defended up to the Supreme Court by John Quincy Adams, America's sixth president. Imprisoned for two years while on trial for mutiny, they finally won their case in 1841. From prison they were taken to Farmington, the crossroads of Connecticut's Underground Railroad, where they lived in private homes until the funds could be raised for their return trip home to Africa (see November 27).

One among them, Foone, decided to walk home instead of remaining one more day in America. His grave marker is proof that he did, indeed, make his way to freedom. The bedroom in the barn belonged to Joseph Cinque, the man who had led his fellow captives in mutiny and guided their determined crusade to return to their Mendi home. Foone's and Cinque's lives are a testament to their people and to us that nothing is impossible for those who truly believe.

Saturday, August 24, 1839, Connecticut–New York, U.S.A.
Freedom   **Echoes**

AUGUST 25

The one hundred guests assembled in Amherst, Massachusetts, on August 25, 1974, had come to celebrate the gift of a new life—a three-week-old baby boy—with a traditional naming ceremony.

In welcoming the firstborn child of Godwin and Saundra Oyewole, the guests were transported across the centuries via the legacy of a ritual as old as the Yoruba themselves. On this day, the ancestors would speak through the person of Nigerian artist and drummer Bayo Oduwole. As he poured libation on the ground to give thanks for the ancestors' presence and sprayed the sacred wine into the air to clear the space of unwanted spirits, the ritual began. The ancestors called the name of the new son: Ayodeji Babatunde Olusegun (in English, "our second joy" and "father has returned"). Dressed in his traditionally patterned and embroidered Yoruba robe, young Ayodeji was cradled in his mother's arms for his introduction to the world. One by one, tiny bits of honey, pepper, salt, lettuce, sugar, fish, and oil were placed on his tongue—the varied flavors that would be offered him on his journey through life. Predictably, he was not yet ready for the spice of life and rejected each pungent sample with a healthy, discerning protest.

For many of the guests, the ceremony was as joyous as it was melancholy. At last, the predominantly African-American clan had a chance to know what had been lost to them for so many years. For Tunde, as his family and friends now called him, the ceremony said, "Welcome to our world." And for the African-American friends gathered in his honor, the meaning was just about the same. It was indeed a fine welcome to the ancestral home of which they had so little knowledge. For them, it was the calling of many of their names, as well. Inspired by what they had heard and seen, almost all, within a few years, would answer the call with their first visit to the African continent.

Sunday, August 25, 1974, Massachusetts, U.S.A.–Nigeria
Family   **Experience**

AUGUST 26

It was "Freedom Summer," when the road to the Democratic National Convention had been paved with the blood of civil rights workers, Black and white, throughout the South (see August 4). And no one had a better right to be at that convention than those who bore the scars of proof.

On August 26, 1964, Fannie Lou Hamer, Robert Moses, and their Mississippi Freedom Democratic Party (MFDP) marched onto the convention floor with borrowed passes as the television cameras rolled, capturing this moment in history. For four days their way had been blocked by the leading political triumvirate of Lyndon Johnson, Walter Mondale, and Hubert Humphrey.

On August 22, when Mrs. Hamer had appeared before the Credentials Committee, the Mississippi delegation tried to silence her by calling her "Communist!"

On August 23, Johnson, Mondale, and Humphrey tried to reach a compromise that would seat two white and two Black delegates.

On August 24, both delegations rejected the compromise proposal.

On August 25, the MFDP stepped onto the convention floor with borrowed credentials from other state delegations, only to be removed by guards.

On August 25, Lyndon Johnson was officially nominated for reelection, and MFDP returned to the floor as the cameras carried their message to the world.

Said Mrs. Hamer, "If the MFDP is not seated now, I question America." The MFDP was not seated, and Mrs. Hamer's question remains unanswered to this day. Fannie Lou Hamer never missed an opportunity to respond to unanswered questions with the truth, and her unbowed determination continues to motivate us today as her spirit joins with the ancestors in guiding our way.

Wednesday, August 26, 1964, Mississippi–New Jersey, U.S.A.
Politics   **Inheritance**

AUGUST 27

In the summer of 1967, the Artists Workshop of the Organization of Black American Culture of Chicago (OBACC) painted a mural on a wall at Forty-third and Langley to recognize contemporary African-American achievers. And when their "Wall of Respect" was dedicated on August 27, 1967, they had contributed a major achievement all their own.

With their art, they wanted to make a statement that would energize and serve their community, offering them heroes of their own making as opposed to those the national media might have selected for them. In words and pictures, they painted their struggle for unity, solidarity, and self-determination. Accompanying the words of the poem "SOS," by Imamu Amiri Baraka (né LeRoi Jones), were the faces of their heroes. And behind the selection of these heroes were the community's cultural roots and values.

Among those portrayed were James Baldwin (author), Lerone Bennett (historian), Gwendolyn Brooks (poet), H. Rap Brown (organizer), Stokely Carmichael (organizer), Wilt Chamberlain (athlete), Ornette Coleman (musician), John Coltrane (musician), W. E. B. Du Bois (Pan-Africanist), John Oliver Killens (author), Martin Luther King, Jr. (human rights activist), Malcolm X (nationalist), and Thelonius Monk, Max Roach, Nina Simone, and Sarah Vaughn (musicians).

As stated by OBACC (pronounced oh-bah-see), the goal of the wall was to achieve a free context in which artists could explore the African-American experience. The "Wall of Respect" was painted by several artists guided by Jeff Donaldson, who would later be named head of Howard University's Art Department. There he would bring the message of the wall to new generations of artists.

Sunday, August 27, 1967, Illinois, U.S.A.

Arts   **Reclamation**

AUGUST 28

It was 1963, the centennial anniversary of the Emancipation Proclamation and one of the most brutal, violent years in the domestic street war to realize its promise. Ten men issued a call for Americans to march on Washington to demand of the government the full birthrights and guarantees of citizenship due African-Americans. Among them were the six top national civil rights leaders: James Farmer (CORE), Martin Luther King, Jr. (SCLC), John Lewis (SNCC), A. Philip Randolph (Negro American Labor Council), Roy Wilkins (NAACP), Whitney M. Young (National Urban League), and a white labor leader, Walter Reuther, head of the nation's largest union, the AFL-CIO.

Answering that call on Wednesday, August 28, 1963, over 250,000 people of all descriptions descended on Washington by every means possible. But the man who said, "By any means necessary," was absent—or so it seemed. The truth is, however, that Malcolm X had come, too. March strategist Bayard Rustin spotted Malcolm holding an impromptu press conference outside the headquarters the night before the march: "'This is nothing but a circus, it's nothing but a picnic!' I said, 'Now, Malcolm, be careful—there are going to be a half million people here tomorrow, and you don't want to tell them this is nothing but a picnic.' He looked at me, and there was a twinkle in his eye. He said, 'What I tell them is one thing. What I tell the press is something else.' Later on, I saw him talking to some of the marchers. I said, 'Why don't you tell them this is just a picnic?' He was being affable. He just smiled, and again there was a twinkle."

The march was a very special demonstration of unity. Whatever you could do, the civil rights movement had a place for you. And perhaps that was the movement's greatest threat. It was dangerous because it was so inclusive; it destroyed the fundamental principle of exclusion upon which so much history had been grounded.

Wednesday, August 28, 1963, Washington, D.C., U.S.A.

Events   **Empowerment**

AUGUST 29

On August 29, 1833, the Reverend Nathaniel Paul, a British abolitionist of African descent, wrote a scathing letter to a Canterbury, Connecticut, magistrate announcing his intention to publish far and wide the news of the strange case of a Quaker educator.

In the popular discourse on slavery, it is often conveniently forgotten that one of the largest slaveholding states was Connecticut. Its northern nineteenth-century anti-Black proslavery stand was so vehement that when Prudence Crandall admitted one Black girl to her school, white parents boycotted her. When she responded by admitting Black girls only, a mob attacked her school, traumatized her students, and severely damaged school property. When it was time for justice, Crandall herself was imprisoned for creating the disturbance with her "terrible" deed—educating Black girls!

"I have seen your name . . . and have read your noble and praiseworthy deeds, in regard to the establishment of a school in your town, conducted by one Miss Prudence Crandall, for the instruction of young ladies of color!" wrote Paul to the magistrate who jailed Crandall. "As I have been for some months past and still am engaged in travelling and delivering lectures upon the state of slavery as it exists in the United States . . . Britons shall know that there are men in America, and whole towns of them, too, who are not so destitute of true heroism but that they can assail a helpless woman, surround her house by night, break her windows, and drag her to prison, for the treasonable act of teaching females of color to read!!!"

Over 160 years after the Crandall affair, when the naysayers catalog those young people who have given up on the society that has given up on them, let us also take time to praise those students who, despite terrible obstacles and inhumane assumptions put in their way, are intent on plodding the rough road to their ultimate success.

Thursday, August 29, 1833, Connecticut, U.S.A.

Education   **Integrity**

AUGUST 30

In 1975, Dorothy Redford Spruill was so moved by television's most successful miniseries, *Roots*, that she spent the next eleven years researching her family history. Her hard work led to an unprecedented family reunion. On August 30, 1986, the family gathered on the site of the plantation where their ancestors had been slaves, at the invitation of the descendants of the family that had enslaved them. In their honor, North Carolina governor James B. Martin attended the event and presented a special proclamation that read:

> Two hundred years ago this summer, eighty Africans arrived at Edenton aboard the brig *Camden* bound for slavery at Somerset plantation in Washington County, North Carolina. There they joined other slaves in carving out a prosperous plantation from a swampland, enduring the inhumane hardships of grueling, hazardous work as well as a life of bondage in a foreign land with an unfamiliar language.
>
> These slaves and their descendants are recognized as having made significant contributions to . . . the United States. They persevered in the new land under harsh conditions, developing a unique culture that remains a part of the American fabric. With the long-awaited abolition of slavery, the Somerset plantation slaves dispersed throughout this nation, in many cases losing ties with family members. . . . Now, more than 120 years after receiving their freedom, . . . thousands of Somerset slave descendants will rekindle family bonds.

And what a time they had, as the family gathered for its historic celebration of life and legacy. As Dorothy Redford Spruill later wrote, "I have crossed many waters—some deep, some stagnant, some muddy—but strong, supportive bridges were always there for me" as she moved toward this day. One of her relatives expressed the feeling well when, as she walked the fields that had so consumed her ancestors of four generations ago, she exclaimed, "We are found!"

Saturday, August 30, 1986, North Carolina, U.S.A.
Family/Genealogy   **Roots**

AUGUST 31

The history of recorded African slave revolts in the Americas dates back to November 1526 when slaves fled the Spanish captors with whom they had sailed to the Americas and escaped to Native American lands where they were allowed to remain. But the first great U.S. slave revolt of lasting impact was led by Gabriel Prosser on August 31, 1800.

Less than a month from the planned date, several thousand slaves were pledged to the revolt. Given the period, the size of such an army is hardly surprising. Blacks were not cut off from the news and fervor of the times. Nineteen years after the American rebellion in which Blacks had fought and by which they had been betrayed, nine years after the greatest slave revolt of all had liberated Haiti, seven years after enactment of the first fugitive slave law, and six months after the new year's antislavery petition to Congress (see December 30), a revolt had become inevitable.

But Prosser's revolt was not destined to be the one. It was thwarted within hours of the planned strike when two slaves informed their owner. As the lead army of one thousand gathered outside Richmond, a thunderstorm washed out the bridge into town, leading slave masters to comment that God was indeed on their side. Thirty-four men were charged and hanged, but not before one of them made this speech: "I have nothing more to offer than what General George Washington would have had to offer had he been taken by the British and put to trial by them. I have adventured my life in endeavoring to obtain the liberty of my countrymen, and am a willing sacrifice in their cause; and I beg, as a favour that I may be immediately led to execution."

Whether the speaker was Prosser or one of his men is unrecorded. But as history would reveal, it could have been made by any one of thousands of African-Americans in whom the seed of possibility had been nurtured. Their daily acts and rebellions kept the long march toward freedom on course.

Sunday, August 31, 1800, Virginia, U.S.A.

Slave Revolt!   **Principles**

SEPTEMBER

Cyril Carlisle, circa 1925. Photographer unknown. Reprinted courtesy of the author.

SEPTEMBER 1

As students return to school, we gratefully honor the unique heritage of the historically Black colleges. When we think of them, Spelman, Tuskegee, Cheyney (America's oldest), and nearly a hundred others come to mind. We think of the contributions of such graduates as the noted neurosurgeon Dr. Ben Carson, Dr. Martin Luther King, Jr., author Alice Walker, and former Virginia governor Doug Wilder. We also recall that the earliest historically Black college is actually the world's first university—the University of Sankore of ancient Timbuktu in Mali, West Africa.

Arriving in Timbuktu on September 1 in 1340, we would have found ourselves in the intellectual Mecca of the world, noted for its singular gathering of scholars. This was a bustling city of one hundred thousand people living among the stone and lime buildings created by Mansa Musa's architects (see August 10). Here, Africa's Muslim world studied law, history, literature, and medicine under the tutelage of scholars from northern Africa, Europe, and the sub-Saharan south. Here gathered scholars whose knowledge of the oceans and stars guided Mali's famed Mariner Prince to the Americas 180 years before Columbus.

As our students of every age enjoy the privilege of school on this day, they stand on a centuries-old tradition of educational excellence, achievement, and leadership throughout the African diaspora.

Thursday, September 1, 1340, Songhay (Mali/Ghana)
Education   **Knowledge**

SEPTEMBER 2

On September 2, 1960, Wilma Rudolph did the impossible—she ran. From a young girl plagued by polio, she had become an Olympic athlete.

As a child, Rudolph thought her greatest moment had come in 1950 when she walked into church without the help of her leg braces, under the grateful eyes of the congregation who had prayed her through the years. But in 1952, an even greater moment had surely arrived when her mother mailed her braces back to the Nashville, Tennessee, hospital from which they had first come so long ago. Once she began to walk, she wanted to run to rebuild the muscles in her legs. In 1956, she ran fast enough to become the bronze medalist at the Olympics in Melbourne, Australia. But in 1960, in the greatest of great moments for Wilma Rudolph, the entire world shared her triumph via television as she won three Olympic gold medals—a true glory day for a runner who doctors once thought would never be able to walk.

To those who may never walk, to those with life-threatening ailments, those with deeply dispirited hearts, those whose life may never grant their deepest wish, it would be cruel to say that all things are possible. But this we can say: with Wilma Rudolph as proof, miracles do happen!

Friday, September 2, 1960, Tennessee, U.S.A.
Children/Sports   **Courage**

SEPTEMBER 3

Escaping from slavery on September 3, 1838, Frederick Douglass was determined never to look back. But ten years later, he did. On the tenth anniversary of his self-emancipation, Douglass wrote this letter, his own special "freedom paper," to Thomas Auld, the man who had once considered himself Douglass's owner:

When a child about six years old, I imbibed the determination to run away. The very first mental effort that I now remember on my part, was an attempt to solve the mystery, Why am I a slave? I had, through some medium, . . . got some idea of God, the Creator of all mankind . . . and that he had made the blacks to serve the whites as slaves. How could he do this and be good, I could not tell. . . . One night while sitting in the kitchen, I heard some of the old slaves talking of their parents having been stolen from Africa by white men, and [having been] sold here as slaves. The whole mystery was solved at once. Very soon after this my aunt Jinny and uncle Noah ran away, and the great noise made about it by your father-in-law, made me for the first time acquainted with the fact, that there were free States as well as slave States. I resolved I would some day run away.

The morality of the act, I dispose as follows: I am myself; you are yourself; we are two distinct persons, equal persons. God created both, and made us separate beings. I am not by nature bound to you, or you to me. Nature does not make your existence depend upon me, or mine to depend upon yours. I cannot walk upon your legs, or you upon mine. I cannot breathe for you, or you for me; I must breathe for myself, and you for yourself. We are distinct persons, and are each equally provided with faculties necessary to our individual existence. In leaving you, I took nothing but what belonged to me, and in no way lessened your means for obtaining an honest living. Your faculties remained yours, and mine became useful to their rightful owner.

Sunday, September 3, 1848, New York–Maryland, U.S.A.
Freedom   **Inner Peace**

SEPTEMBER 4

On September 4, 1781, forty-four settlers put down grateful roots upon their safe arrival in the "city of the angels," founding Los Angeles, California. Of these forty-four second-wave settlers, at least twenty-eight were people of African descent.

As cited by H. H. Bancroft in *The History of California,* these founders were:

Joseph Moreno, Mulatto, 22 years old, his wife a Mulattress, and five children;

Manuel Cameron, Mulatto, 30 years old, and his wife a Mulattress;

Antonio Mesa, Negro, 38 years old, his wife a Mulattress, and six children;

Jose Antonio Navarro, Mestizo, 42 years old, his wife a Mulattress, and three children;

Basil Rosas, Indian, 68 years old, his wife a Mulattress, and six children.

As our contemporaries bemoan the "majority-minority" complexion of California, and of the Los Angeles area in particular, we must remember that it was always that way. Not only were its original residents Native Americans, but even after their expulsion and the seizure of their land, the next wave of "settlers" in the reincarnated Los Angeles of 1781 were a "majority-minority" mix as well. As with its earthquakes and spontaneous canyon fires, California is a region where nature will go to extremes to have its way. In that, Los Angeles seems destined to be what it will be.

Tuesday, September 4, 1781, California, U.S.A.

Cities   **Ancestors**

SEPTEMBER 5

When a neurosurgical team performed the world's first successful operation to separate Siamese twins on September 5, 1987, heading the team was an African-American doctor, Ben Carson, who had seen more than his share of life-threatening situations. Wielding his surgical knowledge in the operating room that night, he was able to do so by virtue of having taken to heart one of the world's oldest counsels years before: "Physician, heal thyself."

As a teenager he had performed his first surgical feat by extracting the poison of hatred from his veins. While understandable, in view of his environment, it was putting severe pressure on his head and heart. He had been raised with lasting lessons in how to be mean. He had physically attacked his family, and one day, as he was literally about to kill another teenager, something within stopped him. Through it all, his mother, whose education had ended at the third grade, fought with him—and for him—every step of the way to change his ways. Together, their determination guided him to medical school and a specialty in one of the most delicate and dangerous fields of medicine, neurosurgery.

Because he had healed himself, he was able to learn how to heal others. And he realized he could help change the prognosis for the lives of others by sharing his story. For the story of Dr. Ben Carson's *Gifted Hands* (as his biography is so aptly titled) has the potential to heal many pre- and post-surgical lives that sorely need him.

Saturday, September 5, 1987, Maryland, U.S.A.

Medicine   **Growth**

SEPTEMBER 6

On September 6, 1922, the African-American journalist-publisher turned industrialist, P. W. Chavers, was issued the official federal certificate of charter for his Chicago-based Douglass National Bank. With his banking experience and his knowledge of a series of ongoing bank failures in the pre–Great Depression days, he developed a piece of landmark legislation requiring banks to fully insure their depositors. Chavers's bill, HR number 8977, was introduced to the House of Representatives by Illinois congressman T. A. Doyle in April 1924 and referred to the Committee on Banking and Currency. There, it was allowed to languish—politically suppressed—until 1931, two years after the stock market crash in 1929 shut down banks and cast the nation into disarray.

Chavers's HR number 8977 was the earliest bill to feature a guarantee for bank depositors. And although Congress never acted on it, Chavers's initiative identified a critical problem, proposed the solution, and led to the creation by the legislature of the Federal Deposit Insurance Corporation in 1933. From the original maximum of $2,500 on all deposit accounts, since 1933 that ceiling of protection has gradually been raised to a high of $100,000.*

*FDIC maximum deposit insurance as of May 1995.

Wednesday, September 6, 1922, Illinois, U.S.A.

Business   **Investments**

SEPTEMBER 7

As Frederick Douglass once said of Dr. Martin Delany, "while I thank God for making me a man, Delany thanks God for making him a Black man." On September 7, 1859, a very grateful Black man found himself at sea en route to Africa. After years spent as a doctor, Underground Railroad agent, author, and publisher, Delany was now fulfilling his lifelong dream to see his ancestral homeland. And the details of the nine-month-long voyage only serve to improve the story.

Seven years before the trip, Delany had published his book *The Condition, Elevation, Emigration, and Destiny of the Colored People of the United States Politically Considered.* In it he explored the thesis that African-Americans were "a nation within a nation," thus making a major contribution to the future of Black nationalism. "Every people should be the originators of their own designs, the projector of their own schemes, and creators of the events that lead to their destiny — the consummation of their desires," he had written. And by 1859, he had laid important ground toward realizing his goal — "a project for an Expedition of Adventure, to the Eastern Coast of Africa." Forming an investment team with three Black merchants, he financed the purchase of a ship for the voyage, the *Mendi,* named for the Mendi people who had fought off their captors, resisted enslavement in the historic Amistad Mutiny, and ultimately sailed back to Africa (see August 24, November 27). Inspired by them, he headed "home" to visit several regions including the Niger Valley. There, in Abeokuta, a city-state of today's Nigeria, he signed a treaty with the *alake,* or king. Under the treaty, Egba chiefs granted Delany land where members of the "African race in America" could establish a self-governing homeland.

With spiritual beliefs firmly rooted in the notion of "by any means necessary," Delany explored all realistic opportunities for the liberation of African peoples.

Wednesday, September 7, 1859, U.S.A.–Niger–England
Pan-African World   **Enterprise**

SEPTEMBER 8

As a Chicago teacher in the early 1970s, Marva Collins was frustrated with the bureaucratic hassles and misplaced priorities that stood between her and the children who needed the knowledge and nurturing she could provide. On September 8, 1975, she put her frustration to work for the greater good by opening the Daniel Hale Williams Westside Preparatory School in a college basement classroom.

"The first thing we are going to do here, children, is an awful lot of believing in ourselves," Marva Collins would say at the beginning of each day of learning. Anyone who has observed Collins at work knows that she is a superb educator. Even those who condemned her for deserting the ranks of public education did so because they respect her so much. Who else would say to reluctant classroom participants, "I could just cry that you have no sounds, for sounds make up words, and words are thoughts. Ideas. And the thoughts and ideas in your heads make you what you are. Well, you will have the sounds. Sounds are like keys, opening the door to words. If you don't have the right key, you can't open the door to your house, can you?" Collins is a special kind of magician spelled T-E-A-C-H-E-R. Collins has not only empowered her students, she has transformed the way we view education. "The strange thing was that if a child didn't learn, no one held the teachers responsible. If an eighth grader didn't know how to read, no one went back to that child's first-, second-, or third-grade teacher to ask what went wrong. No, it was always the child's fault. I couldn't stand all that."

As the school's reputation grew around the country, word reached the producers of TV news magazine *60 Minutes*. The show's feature brought Westside Prep international acclaim and empowered those who had long advocated that the key to the academic success of African-American children could be found in the raised expectations of educators and administrators.

Monday, September 8, 1975, Illinois, U.S.A.

Education   **Zest for Learning**

SEPTEMBER 9

On September 9, 1915, entrepreneurial historian Dr. Carter G. Woodson founded the Association for the Study of Negro Life and History in Chicago in order to disseminate Black history for the benefit of those who needed it most—African-Americans themselves.

To everyone who knew and admired him, Woodson was an impossible man. Seized by the magnitude of his vision and the critical need of millions to get the job done, he was irritable and intolerant. Woodson knew that whenever others had attempted to tell the true history of the African diaspora, the effort had been easily sabotaged by the withdrawal or denial of funding by those who controlled the academic and scholarly purse strings. He knew what had to be done, and he knew how to do it.

Born into a family too poor to send him to school, he was a self-taught child who worked his way through borrowed texts and correspondence study to earn a Ph.D. in history from Harvard at age thirty-seven. As a trained historian, he extended his definition of history beyond political and military tomes to include the economic and social involvement of Blacks in building the United States. But his greatest contribution was in understanding the need for an independent financial base from which to conduct and disseminate research on the African diaspora. Thus, Woodson cofounded the Association for the Study of Negro Life and History.

The association was designed to be a self-sustaining organization that would finance its work with the publication of journals, newsletters, and books, free from the economic pressure of those who would like to continue to manipulate the American future through a misinformed history. Today, eighty years later, the association continues its work, true to Woodson's founding principles.

Thursday, September 9, 1915, Illinois, U.S.A.

Education   **History**

SEPTEMBER 10

The "Dope Jam" rap concert tour was scheduled for the Nassau Coliseum on September 10, 1987. Ticket holders were heading to the coliseum from all parts of the tristate New York metropolitan area, excited about hearing some of rap's finest: Kool Moe Dee, Boogie Down Productions, and Doug E. Fresh. But unknown to promoters, performers, and the eager audience, two groups of ticket holders—rival gangs—were also en route to the coliseum, intent on destruction. Their tickets had been purchased for a show of their own—an evening of mayhem during which they planned to terrorize and rob the audience. When the two gangs were done, the coliseum was in shambles. In the melee, one teen was murdered, many had been stabbed, hundreds injured, and as many robbed.

Throughout the weekend, the national press headlined stories on "rap violence," as though the two words were synonymous. On Monday morning, phones started ringing throughout the industry. The artists, producers, record companies, and promoters decided to take back control of their shared art form. From the start, some of rap's biggest talents were ready to sign on: Boogie Down Productions, Chuck D, D-Nice, KRS-One, Ms. Melodie. And their efforts produced an unprecedented collaboration among the music, concert, publishing, and video industries in cooperation with the National Urban League.

Their goals were clear: (1) to raise public awareness of in-group violence—its causes, costs, and possible solutions; (2) to raise funds for groups actively involved in preventing crime and ending illiteracy; and (3) to present the image of rap as a partner in the positive encouragement of inner-city youth. United in their mission, they launched the "Stop the Violence Movement." From this movement came concerts, a video, and a book all focused on the theme: "Stop the Violence—Overcoming Self-Destruction." But what it really celebrated was an underplayed truth: the initiative and integrity of African-American youth.

Thursday, September 10, 1987, New York, U.S.A.

Music   **Images**

SEPTEMBER 11

In the fall of 1991 as construction workers excavated the lower-Manhattan site of a planned thirty-four-story office tower, the ancestors literally rose in protest, demanding their place in history. On September 11, 1991, archaeologists designated the site the most significant find since King Tut's tomb (see November 29)—the long-lost African Burial Ground bearing the skeletal remains of America's earliest Black community.

In the 1600s, free and enslaved Blacks were not only discouraged from following their African religions but were also refused access to New York's white churches and churchyard cemeteries. Instead, city elders located the "Negroes' Burial Ground" in a remote section of Manhattan. As the city grew, the land was seized, its identity covered over and removed from maps.

As the Reverend Thomas F. Pike, rector of Saint George's Episcopal Church, said, "the [landmark] designation cannot undo the fruits of slavery, prejudice, and exploitation that brought the burial ground into existence and later contributed to its convenient disappearance from the city's active memory. Today we are recognizing the lives of thousands of men, women, and children who were African-Americans. Their struggles against incredible odds, their capacity to experience joy, hope, and love in a hostile environment have consecrated the soil in which they were buried." And with that the city's Landmarks Preservation Commission designated the site the "African Burial Ground and the Commons Historic District" in February 1993 and temporarily relocated the remains at Howard University for analysis.

Using modern scientific techniques, scholars can now study the daily lives of Africans for whom no written records exist. Some were buried with coins in hand. A shell was next to one head; one man's clothing had decomposed, but his British marine officer's uniform buttons had not. Now, researchers may learn how first African-American lived and died, their diet, customs, and degree of assimilation in America.

Wednesday, September 11, 1991, New York, U.S.A.

Archaeology   **Messages**

SEPTEMBER 12

After a twelve-year civil war that began with one of the bloodiest coups in modern history, Nigeria lifted its state of emergency on September 12, 1978. Nigeria was a wealthy country enriched by three main heritages and a host of natural resources—oil, rubber, gas, coal, and cocoa among them. Yet Nigeria was impoverished by a terrible soul sickness.

Nigeria was actually three nations in one—Biafra, Ibo, and Yoruba. It had been carved out, to the detriment of its people, according to Europe's economic interests. And when Biafra decided to secede from Nigeria's tripartite union, civil war broke out just six years after the country had achieved independence. Nigeria's military ruler, General Gowon, who had seized power in a coup, led a brutal suppression of the Biafrans. Among the voices raised against the violence was that of the man who would become the 1986 Nobel laureate for literature, Wole Soyinka. From 1967 to 1969, Soyinka was imprisoned, spending much of his time in solitary confinement. During that time, in the margins of the few books smuggled in to him, he wrote poems, essays, bits of plays, a novel, and the prison notes that were published in 1982 as *The Man Died*.

In the final days of his imprisonment, he was transported through "an exhilarating storm" for medical care long denied him. "I gave into it, turning it to the strength of a thousand combative resolves. . . . Soaked to the skin, lashed by the wind . . . I was struck suddenly by the phenomena of these wild, free yet governed motions of the elements and us," wrote Soyinka. "It had to do with liberty but not with the gaining of it. It was a passionate affirmation of the free spirit, a knowledge that because of this love [of freedom], my adversaries had lost the conflict. That it did not matter in the end for how long they maneuvered to keep my body behind walls, they would not, ultimately, escape the fate of the defeated at the hands of all who are allied and committed to the unfettered principle of life." With that he closed the book on his years in prison.

Tuesday, September 12, 1978, Nigeria

SEPTEMBER 13

In the years following the Fugitive Slave Act of 1850, when the forces of slavery and abolition staked opposing philosophical turf, the Oberlin-Wellington rescue of September 13, 1858, marks a turning point in mass civil disobedience.

For weeks rumors of "Negro catchers" on the backroads had haunted Wellington, Ohio, a town populated by freemen of all means—those who'd been freed by their "owners," who had bought their freedom, freed themselves by escape, and the fortunate few who were freeborn. Prepared for danger, families kept children home from school to avoid capture. When marshals seized John Price, a fugitive from "justice," word quickly reached the free-spirited town of Oberlin, Ohio—a town with a reputation for never having yielded a life back to slavery. In a feat of covert cooperation, townspeople Black and white thundered down to their coconspirators in Wellington, resolved to "rescue" Price. Snatching the endangered youth on September 13, they spirited him to Canada along the Underground Railroad. As a thirty-seven-man body, the group proudly answered charges of violating the Fugitive Slave Act. Among them was Charles H. Langston, whose impassioned statement left little doubt from whom his grandson, Langston Hughes, inherited his way with words.

Months after the rescue, when John Brown enlisted antislavery volunteers into his "Army of Liberation," two of the Oberlin-Wellington rescuers were among those who joined the historic raid on the federal arsenal at Harper's Ferry (see October 16).

Monday, September 13, 1858, Ohio, U.S.A.

Events   **Respect for Use of Power**

SEPTEMBER 14

For five days in early September 1971, a rebellion at Attica prison in upstate New York terrified the nation as corrections officers reported each day's gruesome events. Castration. Mutilation. Knife-wielding prisoners slitting their hostage's throats. The governor ordered the National Guard and state troopers to retake the prison. When it was done, the combined hostage-prisoner toll was 38 dead and 110 wounded. Even more astonishing was the discovery that every story of torture had been fabricated by corrections officers.

On September 14, 1971, Dr. John F. Edlund, the county medical examiner, bravely told the truth. The results of his autopsies revealed that every hostage had died of gunshot wounds, killed by guardsmen and state police storming the prison. Under mounting pressure to produce a report that matched the "official version," Edlund resisted. When the titillating sexual mutilation stories were cited as "evidence," Edlund finally snapped. "You don't have to be a medical expert to be able to determine if someone's genital organs have been mutilated!"

The day before the riot, angered by the "dastardly bushwhacking of two prisoners," inmates balked at this last straw. On September 9, inmates seized hostages and control of the prison. "WE are MEN!" they wrote. Their demands called for an observers' committee (including the press, religious and political leaders, and an attorney), a Spanish-speaking Latino doctor, a racially diverse corrections staff, fair wage and labor practices, religious freedom, and educational programs.

Herman Badillo, an official observer and U.S. congressman, summed up the still relevant lessons of the event: "This castration story, and the enthusiasm with which it was repeated . . . tells us perhaps more than we want to know about the psychology of the authorities. What kind of fear and anger and hatred are we dealing with in the breasts of these men who wear uniforms and are our shields against lawlessness?"

Tuesday, September 14, 1971, New York, U.S.A.

Penal System   **Courage**

SEPTEMBER 15

In the killing season of 1963, the depravity of the violence finally struck heart and home on September 15, when the Sunday morning bombing of a Black Birmingham, Alabama, church killed four young girls at prayer. They were Addie Mae Collins, Denise McNair, Carole Robertson, and Cynthia Wesley, all under the age of fourteen. On that day Birmingham police also murdered a Black boy in the street with a shotgun blast to the back. And on that same merciless Birmingham Sunday, a thirteen-year-old Black boy riding a bicycle was killed by a white mob. With no room for pretense or political pandering, President John F. Kennedy appeared on television that night. He called for an end to the violence that had been out of control for centuries but never before so out in the open, available for the instant judgment of television and still cameras. He decried the violence that would, within two months, take his life as well. For once, Kennedy seemed personally involved as he "took sides" in defense of conscience over political expedience. It was a national milestone.

Days later, Dr. Martin Luther King, Jr., delivered this eulogy for the four young girls:

> God has a way of wringing good out of evil. . . . History has proven over and over again that unmerited suffering is redemptive. . . . The holy Scripture says, "A little child shall lead them." The death of these little children may lead our whole southland from the low road of man's inhumanity to man to the high road of peace and brotherhood. These tragic deaths may lead our nation to substitute an aristocracy of character for an aristocracy of color. . . .

> May I now say a word to you, the members of the bereaved families. . . . Your children did not live long, but they lived well. Where they died and what they were doing when death came remain a marvelous tribute to each of you and an eternal epitaph to each of them.

Sunday, September 15, 1963, Alabama, U.S.A.

Social History   **Life's Work**

SEPTEMBER 16

One of the most often overlooked features in the career of Countee Cullen, the noted poet, columnist, editor, novelist, playwright, and children's book writer, is that he was also a teacher. From 1934 until the year of his premature death, 1946, he taught French and English to the young students of Frederick Douglass Junior High School in Harlem. While we often speak of one creative generation's influence upon the next, we do not often witness it in action. In September 1943, Cullen published his essay "The Development of Creative Expression," recently reprinted in *My Soul's High Song*, an anthology of his work. In it he excerpted these revelations, the rarely heard young voices of children and life in the heart of Harlem:

> Spring rings the doorbell of the seasons . . .
> Rain is the flowers' reservoir . . .
> At night the stars make the skies a Broadway of the heavens
> When it rains, it is just the angels crying with joy over the good
>   things we have done (it doesn't rain much, does it?). . .
> Spring is here, and all the earth has turned Irish . . .
> Night is a blue coat God wears every twenty-four hours
> Snow is nature's salt . . .
> The sea is a footless realm which only dead men tread . . .
> Snow is the yarn with which the polar bear spins his coat . . .
> Trees in winter remind me of unfurnished houses . . .
> Winds are violent songs in motion . . .
> Spring is an invitation to summer . . .
> Snow is harmless, friendly bombs . . .

What a pity that in today's school budgets, in the name of "fiscal responsibility," the classes that are among the first to go are those of creative expression.

Thursday, September 16, 1943, New York, U.S.A.

Literature   **Self-Expression**

SEPTEMBER 17

When we think about the ability to attract and develop major-market business resources in the Black community, here's one for the books:

On September 17, 1928, the Rockefeller family, long successful in banking, opened its first Harlem institution, Dunbar National Bank, named in honor of the acclaimed poet, Paul Laurence Dunbar. On this first day of business, five thousand Harlemites visited the bank, the majority of whom opened new accounts. And the bank received this magnanimous Harlem welcome despite its failure to appoint Black directors to the bank's board and offer 50 percent of stock in small lots to potential Black shareholders, as it had promised.

What misdirected wealth we have within our reach!

SEPTEMBER 18

On September 18, 1895, Booker T. Washington raised his hand and spread apart his fingers to show how separate the races could be. "In all things that are purely social we can be as separate as the fingers," he said dramatically, in a statement that effectively supported the enactment of Jim Crow law. And then he balled up his fist. "Yet [we can be] one as the hand in all things essential to mutual progress." That speech, dubbed Washington's "Atlanta Compromise" because it was delivered at the Atlanta Exposition of 1895, has fueled a century of controversy.

For most whites, the speech sounded just the right reassuring note of submission. But as one reporter wrote, "most of the Negroes in the audience were crying, perhaps without knowing just why." For many Blacks, the speech sounded the death knell of the racial dignity for which they had worked for so long. For others, it was the bugler's morning reveille rallying new recruits to action. For Tuskegee Institute, which Washington had built up from scratch, it was a guarantee of much-needed funds to continue the educations of thousands of students with little money for tuition. And for us today, it is the record of a strategy. Faced with lemons, Mr. Washington made lemon juice. No matter what its potential to quench the thirst, it was a bitter thing to swallow indeed. There wasn't much sugar in those early Jim Crow days.

Wednesday, September 18, 1895, Georgia, U.S.A.

Politics   **Perspective**

SEPTEMBER 19

On September 19, 1911, the Madame C. J. Walker Manufacturing Company was incorporated. For Madame Walker, it was a turning point in the way she and almost every other Black woman would view herself. As a businesswoman and the inventor of a hair-straightening process, she had her insights empowered a predominantly Black and female international work force in excess of three thousand who became part of her Indianapolis-based cosmetics empire.

Born dirt-poor in a Delta, Louisiana, log cabin in 1867, Madame Walker—born Sarah Breedlove—knew hard times. Orphaned at six, widowed with a young child at twenty, it's no wonder her hair fell out from stress. She later told the story of how a Black man came to her in a dream, giving her the recipe for hair growth. The miracle potion not only restored her hair, it straightened it. Carrying her inspirational message from parlors to pulpits, she crisscrossed trade routes throughout the United States and the Caribbean, recruiting customers and agents along the way.

As contemporary as her business tactics seem today, they were revolutionary then. Walker Company profit-sharing opportunities promised financial independence unimaginable elsewhere. Employees were organized into a network of Walker-related business and social clubs. Sales and service strategies were shared at national conventions for the Walker-owned retail and mail-order businesses, hairdressing shops, and vocational training beauty colleges. "Perseverance is my motto," Madame Walker said. "I got my start by giving myself a start. I believe in push and we must push ourselves."

Rallying profits with praise, pride, and prophecies of a great life and career to come, her motto was "Look your best for success." Her impeccable credentials of leadership and vision marked a milestone in African-American business history, made her the first self-made Black woman millionaire, and generated profits used to fund antilynching efforts, schools, scholarships, and other critical needs of the day.

Tuesday, September 19, 1911, Indiana, U.S.A.

Business   **Creativity**

SEPTEMBER 20

A report dated September 20, 1823, by Colonel Henry Leavenworth to General Henry Atkinson on the matter of Edward Rose, a Black fur trapper, states: "He appeared to be a brave and enterprising man, and was well acquainted with those Indians. He had resided for about three years with them; understood their language, and they were much attached to him. . . . This was all I knew of the man, I have since heard that he was not of good character. Everything he told us, however, was fully corroborated."

This letter employs a familiar tactic: impugning a person's accomplishments with a character defect that can be neither proved nor, more important, disproved. This was a pattern used consistently to thwart African-American achievement; the more accomplished the achiever, the more scurrilous the attack. As blatant as the paper trail was for the lesser-known Edward Rose, it was worse for James Beckwourth, the legendary Mountain Man and explorer who charted a route through the Sierra Nevadas still known as Beckwourth Pass (see April 26). As frontier scholar Francis Parkman noted: "Much of this narrative is probably false. Beckwourth is a fellow of bad character—a compound of white and black blood." General William Tecumseh Sherman commented, "Jim Beckwourth was . . . one of the best chroniclers of events on the plains that I have encountered, though his reputation for veracity was not good."

Shameful as these ploys are, it is important to have such documented proofs—and reminders. Does being the "first Black" to do something really mean being the "first Black" *capable* of doing it? How many children's lives have been ruined by confidential school records? With such documentation we are aware that being denied recognition does not always mean not having earned recognition. As we celebrate the achievements our family, friends, and we ourselves experience each day, we honor something no one can ever discredit.

Saturday, September 20, 1823, Kansas, U.S.A.

Military   **Truth**

SEPTEMBER 21

On September 21, 1956, hundreds of writers were in attendance as the First International Conference of Black Writers and Artists gathered at the Sorbonne in Paris [September 19–22, 1956]. The presentations and panels were wonderful, the papers and camaraderie still better. But perhaps the most significant thing about the conference was that it had not taken place before, and that when it did, it took place outside the United States, where a climate of McCarthyism still prevailed.

In an effort to provide the "intellectual" grounds on which to deny the Supreme Court's landmark school desegregation decision of two years earlier, opponents of desegregation in 1956 produced a resurgence of "scientific" evidence of inferiority. New reports were rushed into print containing all manner of "proof" that could only lead to one logical conclusion — that Blacks were unfit for everything, unless, of course, it was underpaid, undervalued, and undermined.

Away from the madness, the conference simply took place with people doing what they were supposed to do — work and meet and go on with the enjoyment and fulfillment of their lives without allowing others to distract them from that pursuit. If for nothing else besides its normalcy, the conference participants must have enjoyed a glorious time indeed.

Friday, September 21, 1956, France

Arts/Culture   **Defining Ourselves**

SEPTEMBER 22

"Power never accedes without the demand. It never has and it never will," said Frederick Douglass. And for 243 years African-Americans petitioned, pleaded, ran, fought, killed, died, and unbelievably enough, bought themselves for freedom. Still, millions remained in bondage. Only an act of government could free them all. Douglass approached President Lincoln with a strategy to end the Civil War: to undercut the South's strength, free the slaves!

Lincoln's political wobble on slavery is a matter of record. Neither an abolitionist nor a slaveholder, he favored sending free Blacks to colonize Africa as a compromise. But regardless of the options he considered, in the end Lincoln issued this order on September 22, 1862:

> I, Abraham Lincoln, president of the United States of America, and commander in chief of the army and navy thereof, do hereby proclaim and declare . . . That on the first day of January in the year of our Lord one thousand eight hundred and sixty-three, all persons held as slaves within any state or designated part of a state, the people whereof shall then be in rebellion against the United States, shall be then, thenceforward, and forever free; and the executive government of the United States including the military and naval authority thereof, will recognize and maintain the freedom of such persons, and will do no act or acts to repress such persons, or any of them, in any efforts they may make for their actual freedom.

Two days later, Executive Order No. 139, the Emancipation Proclamation, began its relay from the War Department adjutant general's office to all forces throughout the states north and south.

Monday, September 22, 1862, Southern Slave States, U.S.A.
Abolition/Emancipation   **Sacrifice/Survival**

SEPTEMBER 23

Never has the love affair between a city and one of its adopted citizens achieved such legendary renown. This is how it began: on September 23, 1925, Josephine Baker saw Paris and Paris saw Josephine Baker for the very first time.

Eight years before, Baker had been a child crouched in a doorway as the infamous white mobs of the East Saint Louis riots traumatized her youth. She made a firm determination to flee her hometown. Now, arriving in Paris as a working performer with a Black theater troupe, Josephine Baker was about as far from home as she would ever need to go. As her biographer Phyllis Rose has written, "Paris seemed small to Baker compared with New York, but she knew immediately she would love it and set out to conquer it, like a hero in a Balzac novel. Her strategy from the first was to think of the city as a lover and try to seduce it. The French waiters in New York had told her how: be chic and make them laugh. It took her a few weeks to learn to be chic—the first time she went sightseeing, she wore golf pants—but she certainly knew how to make them laugh."

That talent had brought her acclaim as a chorus girl and understudy in *Shuffle Along*, Broadway's first Black musical. Now it would take her where she wanted to go—and beyond. For Josephine Baker was a woman determined to invent herself and a world of her own imagining.

Wednesday, September 23, 1925, U.S.A.–France
Dance/Theater   **Self-Portraiture**

SEPTEMBER 24

While the 1840s found the majority of Blacks enslaved, there was also a vibrant free community whose hotly debated issues were as passionate as our own. The September 24, 1841, issue of *The Liberator* carried comments by David Ruggles (see March 23), a New York bookseller, abolitionist, Underground Railroad organizer, and publisher of the first Black magazine, *Mirror of Liberty,* founded three years earlier. Reminding his peers that "the truth will set us free," his comments have self-explanatory, contemporary appeal:

> While every man's hand is against us, our every hand is against each other. I speak plainly, because truth will set us free. Are we not guilty of cherishing, to an alarming extent, the sin of sectarian, geographical, and complexional proscription? The spirit abroad is this: Is that brother a Methodist? He is not one of us. A Baptist? He is not one of us. A Presbyterian? He is not one of us. An Episcopalian? He is not one of us. A Roman Catholic? He is not one of us. Does he live above human creeds, and enjoy the religion of the heart? He is of Beelzebub.
>
> Again. Is that brother from the East? He is not one of us. From the West? He is not one of us. From the North? He is not one of us. From the middle States? He is not one of us. Is he a foreigner? He can never be of us. . . . Is that brother of a dark complexion? He is of no worth. Is he of a light complexion? He is of no nation. Such, sir, are the visible lines of distinction, marked by slavery for us to follow. If we hope for redemption from our present condition, we must repent, turn and UNITE in the hallowed cause of reform.

Friday, September 24, 1841, New York, U.S.A.

Freedom   **Unity**

SEPTEMBER 25

What shapes greatness?

Henry Ossawa Tanner was one of the late nine-teenth and early twentieth centuries' greatest artists. Fortunately for us all, he was African-American by birth and passion, and he was one of the earliest artists consistently to commit Black life and tradition to canvas while sustaining himself with his more commercial, paid commissions. To understand Tanner, we must know that his parents were ardent abolitionists. Benjamin Tanner, a bishop in the AME Church, was a freeborn Pittsburgh native and one of the few Blacks to graduate from college before the Civil War. Sarah Miller Tanner was born enslaved but was brought to Pittsburgh as a girl by her manumitted parents. In 1859, Sarah Tanner gave birth to her son, Henry, in an Underground Railroad station house. His middle name, Ossawa, was a sym-bol of his parents' deep admiration for John Brown (see October 16, December 2), who in defending antislavery home-steaders had killed proslavery vigilantes in Osawatomie, Kansas. Given the times and their proximity to proslavery forces, the Tanners gave their son the abbreviated name Ossawa, along with the fire-in-the-belly determination to com-bat prejudice that it represented.

When Henry and Jessie Tanner's son was born in New York City on September 25, 1903, the next-generation Tanners named him Jesse Ossawa Tanner, inducting their baby into a family legacy that combined the fight against oppression with the creation of alternative images of beauty and harmony that would someday, hopefully, improve their world.

Friday, September 25, 1903, New York, U.S.A.

Family   **Legacies**

SEPTEMBER 26

In the long history of cases in the courts, the case of Miss Mary Hamilton stands out for the simplicity of its request, the excesses of its charge, and the extent to which Miss Hamilton was willing to go to demand respect for herself and legal precedent for us all.

On September 26, 1963, Mary Hamilton was on the witness stand in a local Alabama court. The prosecutor insisted on referring to Miss Hamilton by her first name. The witness agreed to answer all questions but only if properly addressed. The questioning never got beyond her name. In the test of wills between the prosecutor and his caged bird, the judge intervened by citing Miss Hamilton for contempt of court, sentencing her to five days in jail and a $50 fine. From the court transcript, it is clear that the prosecutor seized upon the opportunity to continue to provoke the witness, knowing that he could see her found guilty of something—anything. It is equally clear that Miss Hamilton was just as adamant about making her point. She appealed her conviction to the Alabama state appellate court, Alabama state supreme court, and up to the United States Supreme Court where, alas, a judgment was handed down on March 30, 1964. "The petition for writ of certiorari is granted. The judgment is reversed," wrote the Court, vindicating her, in its full twelve-word decision.

Through all the centuries of having one's name taken away, all the centuries of being called "Nigger Mary" and "Auntie" or ". . . (grunt). . . (scowl). . . (grunt). . . ," a Black woman had a right to her name. Mary was legally Miss Hamilton at last.

Thursday, September 26, 1963, Alabama, U.S.A.

Law   **Self-Respect**

SEPTEMBER 27

On September 27, 1912, W. C. Handy published the first blues work, "Memphis Blues," with a combined melody and rhythm so haunting that crowds literally "danced in the streets" when he first played the number in 1909 as a political campaign song.

Handy wasn't the inventor of the blues, but as a composer, band leader, and music publisher, he was its greatest popularizer. When his band played "Memphis Blues," they catapulted to the head of the line of bands in a town known for music. And the popularity of the piece launched what would become Handy's international career, which brought him and his music company, Handy & Pace, to New York in 1918 (see March 24).

No one really knows how the blues began as a musical form. As an influence in the writing of "Memphis Blues," Handy cited a "lean, loose-jointed Negro" in rags with a face that held the "sadness of the ages," who sang and played on his guitar the "weirdest music" Handy had heard since his Alabama boyhood. When Handy brought the blues to phonographs and concert stages the world over, he was bringing with him the story of African-Americans in long, intricate fourteen-bar musical tones.

Friday, September 27, 1912, Tennessee, U.S.A.

Music   **Aural Histories**

SEPTEMBER 28

Throughout slavery, the greatest fear of white Americans north and south was the threat of slave revolt—in other words, of justice. Thirty years after the success of the Haitian revolution and seven years after an aborted revolt by ex-slave Denmark Vesey and his men to free the slaves of Charleston, South Carolina, had successfully poked deep holes into the assumptions surrounding "people as property" (see June 16), David Walker published his historic antislavery and pro-uprising pamphlet, *Walker's Appeal, in four Articles: Together with a Preamble, to the Coloured Citizens of the World, but in particular and very expressly, to those of the United States of America, written in Boston, State of Massachusetts, September 28, 1829.*

"Walker's Appeal" was a forty-fourth-birthday gift from Walker to himself. Born to a free mother in Wilmington, Delaware, on September 28, 1785, he was so sickened by slavery that he moved to Boston where he made a living trading in used clothing, grew active in Boston's vibrant antislavery movement, became a sales agent for *Freedom's Journal* and a leader of Boston's Colored Association. With a first-hand knowledge of slavery and from the systematic lessons obtained through his work, his appeal called to slaves and freemen to join in overthrowing the institution of slavery.

Just as every positive reform for Blacks has benefited the nation as a whole, so, too, has every negative turn of events had a negative effect. While Boston was among the most enlightened early-nineteenth-century cities, slavery in the South raised great profits for the industries of the North. In writing his appeal, Walker knew that he could be jailed or killed for it. And indeed, the pamphlet's 1829 publication was followed by the mysterious disappearance and death of David Walker in 1830. It was also accompanied by that escalation of revolutionary fervor known as the Underground Railroad.

Monday, September 28, 1829, Massachusetts, U.S.A.
Abolition/Emancipation   **Life's Work**

SEPTEMBER 29

The lack of a strong alliance between indigenous people and African-Americans is a sad fact. Stories like that of September 29, 1891, all too often demonstrate the desperation both groups experienced in the 1880s and 1890s.

When the Creeks found oil on their reservation, it was the worst thing that could have happened to them. In February 1889 when whites demanded access to their "share" of the oil-rich land, the U.S. government stepped in, cast the Creeks out, opened those lands up to white "settlers," and unleashed a historic "land grab" at high noon on April 22, 1889. Sadly, and ironically, this tragic loss to Creeks enabled the exodus of terrorized Blacks.

On September 29, 1891, Blacks fleeing KKK terrorism arrived in Oklahoma, founding Langston, the state's first all-Black town. It was named for John Mercer Langston. One of the first African-American lawyers, he successfully defended the Oberlin-Wellington rescuers (see September 13), became the founding dean of Howard University Law School (see January 6), represented Virginia in the House of Representatives, and helped produce a grandnephew named Langston Hughes.

Within two years, Langston was a bustling town of two thousand. Life there was recalled in this account in the *Journal of Negro History*, volume twenty-one (June 1946):

> For some time, every few days the Santa Fe train from Texas would pull in a couple of coaches of some southern railroad loaded to the roof with Negro immigrants, Langston bound. They brought their families and their household goods. It was really something to see. Some even came in wagons and lots on foot. Lots of people who came here were so disappointed that they went back home. It took real enterprising folks to stick it out. There wasn't but one building in town so most of the families lived in tents while houses were being built for them.

Today, most of the Creeks are gone and the town is no longer Black, but their stories survive at the historically Black Langston University.

Tuesday, September 29, 1891, Oklahoma, U.S.A.

SEPTEMBER 30

The courage exemplified by Black students determined to demand their right to an education can never be overstated. On September 30, 1962, as crowds literally demanded his head—which they planned either to pummel to death or put at the end of a rope—James Meredith (see June 6) arrived at the Mississippi State University campus known as "Ole Miss" under helmeted federal escort.

To make the point of his enrollment visible and firm, Meredith, an air force veteran, was flown in from Tennessee, served up for enrollment on a carefully arranged platter of federal marshals as a symbol of the new Black man for a New South. As he walked up the steps to register under the glare of television cameras, a segregationist riot went wild. Two whites were killed and hundreds more wounded in what Meredith would call the battle between the United States and Mississippi. "On August 18, 1963, I drove out of Mississippi with the U.S. marshals to Tennessee, after [receiving my] degree. . . . A serious question kept plaguing my mind: Did this constitute the privilege of attending the school of my choice?" asked Meredith. "We drove at top speed down the four-lane highway that led to Memphis. But this was still not fast enough for my friend and great freedom fighter, Robert L. T. Smith Jr., who rode with me. Everyone was silent. Finally, looking at the marshals' cars in front and in back of us, Robert asked, 'J., was it like this all of the time?' Without waiting for a reply, he continued, 'Man, I don't see how you stood it! I just don't see how you could take it.'"

Today's students need to know that the true cost of their education was overpaid long ago. They also need to know that they are deeply loved and their future is highly prized, for there are those who preceded them who thought their as yet unborn lives well worth the defense.

Sunday, September 30, 1962, Mississippi, U.S.A.
Education   **Trailblazing**

OCTOBER

Cookman Institute boarding students (April 6, 1895). Photographer unknown. Reprinted courtesy of the author. For more information, see October 5.

OCTOBER 1

In the summer of 1937, after a twelve-year struggle for recognition—during which the national labor movement itself sometimes helped to sabotage their infant union—the Brotherhood of Sleeping Car Porters signed a collective-bargaining agreement with the Pullman Company. By October 1, 1937, its implementation guaranteed an added $2,000,000 in income to Black porters and their families.

While the brotherhood was not the first union of Black men—that tradition dates to the founding of a Baltimore caulkers' union in 1838—it was the first Black union to attain an international charter and formal recognition by national labor boards and to sign an exclusive labor agreement with a major corporation. It was a milestone in the history of American labor relations—especially for a people whose labor had historically been taken for granted. Before the union, porters had been required to spend unpaid time on call, had been assigned on the basis of favoritism, and had been paid only for their time on duty. They worked four-hundred-hour months and had no leave, no job protection, no retirement plan. Their pay was so low that many were forced to perform demeaning tasks in order to protect their tips. When patrons commanded a porter to dance the buck-and-wing to entertain them, it was do it or lose his job. Out of their meager wages, porters were required to buy their uniforms, food, and even such job-related supplies as shoe polish for customer use. After the union was established, they had a 240-hour month, guaranteed pay, guaranteed rest hours, and retirement benefits.

The porters had always been among the Black workers' elite. With the brotherhood, their stature was further enhanced. Its prime organizer, A. Philip Randolph, stated, "Traditionally, Negroes have been expected and generally have not failed to beg for what they need and want." The porters had broken that forced tradition by investing in themselves and the future of Black workers for generations to come.

Friday, October 1, 1937, New York, U.S.A.

Labor   **Building Dreams**

OCTOBER 2

In 1850, Congress passed a second Fugitive Slave Act, tougher than the first, which conscripted every American into service as slave catchers for slave owners. Whites who violated the law faced imprisonment and stiff fines. Blacks would be sold into slavery as punishment. In New York City, eight days after the passage of this legislation, the case of James Hamlet tested both the law and the resolve of slavery's staunchest opponents—free Blacks.

While Hamlet was working as a porter at 58 Water Street in lower Manhattan, an enforcement officer arrived with the act's first certified warrant in hand. Hamlet was immediately placed under arrest to be returned to his "owner" in Baltimore, but it was also made known that the woman, Mary Brown, would allow him to be ransomed for $800. At that news the Black community went to work. Up went the posters, and handbills were passed out everywhere:

The Fugitive Slave Bill!
The Panting Slave!
Freemen to be Made Slaves!

Let Every Colored Man and Woman Attend the Great Mass Meeting to be Held in Zion Church on Tuesday Evening!

Shall we Resist the Proposition? Shall we Defend Liberties? Shall we be Freemen or Slaves?

—By order of the Committee of Thirteen

Fifteen hundred people jammed into Zion Church for the "Great Mass Meeting" to free James Hamlet. Eight hundred dollars were raised to the penny, the first $100 of it donated in one lump sum by a Black man, Isaac Hollenbeck. On October 2, 1850, an emissary was dispatched to ransom Hamlet and restore him to freedom, family, and friends. Within days Hamlet came home to New York and a fond hero's welcome..

Wednesday, October 2, 1850, New York, U.S.A.
Social History   Unity

OCTOBER 3

Almost thirty years after the birth of commercial radio in 1920, the pioneer Black-owned radio station WERD took to the air in Atlanta on October 3, 1949. Unfortunately, the station did not survive, and little is known about it. But the story of African-Americans in radio neither began nor ended there.

In the twenties, although radio shows featured Black singing groups, Blacks were not allowed to talk on the radio — a tradition maintained well into the late 1980s when Johnny Carson's *Tonight* show would feature Black musical talent but not invite even the top Black performers over for "couch talk" with Johnny. This tradition was finally broken when Bill Cosby was hired as one of the show's rotating guest hosts. On the radio, the change in this policy began at 5:00 P.M. on November 3, 1929, when "The All-Negro Hour" premiered on Chicago's white-owned WSBC with Cincinnati vaudevillian Jack L. Cooper as host and radio's Black talk pioneer.

Today, there are several Black-owned and -oriented radio networks. And Black broadcasters have staked their place on the rosters of general-market radio stations throughout the country.

Monday, October 3, 1949, Georgia, U.S.A.

Radio/TV   **Firsts**

OCTOBER 4

In Oscar Hunter's short story, "Seven Hundred Calendar Days," which takes place during the Spanish Civil War of the 1930s, a wounded soldier explains why he volunteered for the Abraham Lincoln Brigade, a real-life contingent with African-Americans: "I wanted to go to Ethiopia and fight Mussolini. . . . This ain't Ethiopia, but it'll do."

When Italy invaded Ethiopia in 1935, Europe looked on and winked, but America went even further in its undocumented support of Italy, levying travel restrictions to block potential volunteers from joining the liberation army of deposed Ethiopian emperor Haile Selassie. However, although the government could block African-Americans from joining with Selassie, it could not stop the pro-Ethiopian fervor sweeping Black communities nationwide.

As Langston Hughes wrote in his "Ballad of Ethiopia":

> *All you colored peoples*
> *Be a man at last*
> *Say to Mussolini*
> *No! You shall not pass. . . .*

On October 4, 1935, Blacks across the United States responded to the invasion of Ethiopia with mass protest meetings to raise funds for the Ethiopian cause: the liberation of Abyssinia! (See May 5.) For those still filled with the nationalist zeal of their days as Garveyites (see August 2), for others simply filled with disgust at their ongoing mistreatment as African-Americans, Ethiopia was the first mainland battle of the fight to retake "Africa for the Africans" that would lead to the independence movements of the 1950s, to the establishment of free African nations in the 1960s, and in its most recent incarnation, to the resurrection of South Africa.

Friday, October 4, 1935, Ethiopia–U.S.A.

Pan-African World   **Understanding**

OCTOBER 5

Mary McLeod Bethune had a dream—Florida's first school to educate Black students beyond the elementary grades—and that dream became the Daytona Educational and Industrial Institute. Itemizing her assets on founding day, October 3, 1904, she had "five little girls, $1.50, faith in God," and one tangible item that she and the girls cooked up as a fund-raiser—her recipe for sweet-potato pie:

> *4 pounds (approx. 9 medium) cooked and mashed sweet potatoes or yams*
> *1 cup (2 sticks) butter, softened*
> *½ cup granulated sugar*
> *½ cup firmly packed brown sugar*
> *½ teaspoon salt*
> *¼ teaspoon nutmeg*
> *3 eggs, well beaten*
> *2 cups milk*
> *1 tablespoon vanilla*
> *3 unbaked 9-inch pie crusts*

Boil sweet potatoes until tender. Peel and mash. Preheat oven to 350°F. Combine butter, sugars, salt, and nutmeg in a large bowl, beating until creamy. Beat in sweet potatoes until well mixed, then eggs. Gradually add in milk and vanilla. Spoon about four cups filling into the pie crusts. Bake at 350°F for fifty minutes or until set. Serve at room temperature.

Clearly, a recipe for success. Try it. Loved by the bricklayers and benefactors alike, it made palatable all sorts of requests for help to make her school a reality. Bethune's marketing and fund-raising skills and her educational leadership raised her dream into Bethune-Cookman College, now nearing its centennial. (For a photograph of Cookman Institute's boarding students in 1895, see October's lead illustration.)

Wednesday, October 5, 1904, Florida, U.S.A.

Business   **Aspirations**

OCTOBER 6

The twentieth century had gotten off to a terrible start. Resurrecting the arrogance and legacy of slavery, whites vigorously asserted their power over Blacks for their own financial and psychological gain. Every Black legislator had been manipulated out of Congress through redistricting, trumped-up criminal charges, and an erosion of the spirit and intent of the Thirteenth, Fourteenth, and Fifteenth Amendments enacted during Reconstruction. Blacks were demonized in the press for crimes that had in many cases never been committed. With antislavery groups disbanded and antisegregation forces not yet formed, people sank into despair. But when Dr. W. E. B. Du Bois's "Credo" was published on October 6, 1904, spirits rallied.

> Especially do I believe in the Negro race; in the beauty of its genius, the sweetness of its soul, and its strength in that meekness which shall inherit this turbulent earth. . . . I believe in pride of race and lineage itself; in pride of self so deep as to scorn injustice to other selves; in pride of lineage so great as to despise no man's father; in pride of race so chivalrous as neither to offer bastardy to the weak nor beg wedlock of the strong, knowing that men may be brothers in Christ, even though they be not brothers-in-law. . . .
>
> Finally, I believe in Patience—patience with the weakness of the Weak and the strength of the Strong, the prejudice of the Ignorant and the ignorance of the Blind; patience with the tardy triumph of Joy and the mad chastening of Sorrow—patience with God.

"Credo" touched people so deeply that it was widely reprinted in the Black press and hung on the wall in thousands of homes, literally making Du Bois a "household name." As a milestone in his growing reputation, "Credo" gave Du Bois the clout to launch his Niagara Conference (see August 17), which led to the founding of the NAACP and the Pan-African congresses (see February 19), and this in turn led to Du Bois being honored as the Father of Pan-Africanism.

Thursday, October 6, 1904, Georgia, U.S.A.

Human Rights   Faith

OCTOBER 7

By the early 1960s, years of intimidation, segregationist filibusters in the Senate, and a series of laws expressly designed to circumvent the Constitution had all taken their toll. In Selma, Alabama, only 156 of the 15,000 eligible Blacks were registered voters. Under the leadership of James Forman, the Student Nonviolent Coordinating Committee (SNCC) proclaimed October 7, 1963, "Freedom Day"—the day of their mass voter-registration drive.

In the months leading up to Freedom Day, workshops were held to educate and encourage prospective voters in filling out registration forms and overcoming red tape. Every month the local sheriff's officers targeted prospective voters for harassment by collecting the names of those who attended these workshops.

Over the next two years, a succession of Freedom Days saw hundreds of people courageously line up to register at the courthouse. And each Freedom Day brought out the sheriff; the helmeted, gun-toting deputies, wielding their billy clubs; the photographers to snap a picture of each person in line; and a question: "Does your employer know you are here?" On one such Freedom Day, a man having difficulty writing his address as his hands shook with age was abruptly told to leave the line by the registrar. "I am sixty-five years old," the unnamed man answered. "I own one hundred acres of land that is paid for, I am a taxpayer, and I have six children. All of them is teachin', workin'. . . . If what I done ain't enough to be a registered voter . . . then Lord have mercy on America!"

The wisdom of this elder brought sanity and clarity to the struggle. By the 1968 elections, these heroic voter registration campaigns would return Blacks to Congress, for the first time exceeding the high set a century earlier. The drives also paved the way for the national voter registration movement led by Jesse Jackson in his presidential campaigns of 1984 and 1988.

Monday, October 7, 1963, Alabama, U.S.A.

Voter Registration   **Racial Dignity**

OCTOBER 8

In the fall of 1930, one year into the Great Depression, the Jones Tabernacle AME Church in Philadelphia decided to hold a Negro Authors' Week. By October 8, 1930, eight authors were on the church's roster for the celebration, which would include readings, lectures, and exhibits, scheduled to begin Monday, December 8, 1930. The idea was to feature an author each night, charge nominal admission, and "encourage the young Negro to greater aspiration in the field of literature; to acquaint the citizens of Philadelphia with the achievements of the Negroes in literature; and to increase interest in the same." About 300 people came each night, 1,500 people in all, 1,200 of whom attended at least one lecture. This is how their program went:

Monday: James Weldon Johnson, the lyricist of "Lift Ev'ry Voice" (see January 3), presented "The Negro in Art and Literature."

Tuesday: Howard University's Dr. Kelly Miller delivered a paper, "The Negro Writing in His Own Defense," about the development of Black journalism.

Wednesday: Dr. W. E. B. Du Bois, editor of *The Crisis*, brought the week's largest audience with "Opportunities for the Negro in the Field of Fiction."

Thursday: Dr. Carter G. Woodson, historian and director of the Associated Publishers of Washington, D.C., discussed the researching of Black history.

Friday: While illness forced Langston Hughes to bow out, the audience was "enthusiastic under the spell" of Dr. Leslie P. Hill's introduction to poetry and the noted poet Georgia Douglass Johnson's sketches of her poetic friends.

As the report on the event concluded, "we do not hesitate to say that if such a Negro Authors' Week under efficient management should be held every year in a hundred American cities, the outlook for Negro literature would be entirely revolutionized."

Wednesday, October 8, 1930, Pennsylvania, U.S.A.

Social History   **Sustenance**

OCTOBER 9

In the fall of 1831 on a Virginia plantation, Cyrus McCormick completed development of the mechanical reaper that would revolutionize grain harvests for a century to come. From the moment the patent was issued, McCormick cited the assistance he had received from a slave, Jo Anderson, in the machine's development.

Because of the relationship between Anderson and McCormick, the company built on their joint invention, International Harvester, was founded upon a nondiscriminatory hiring policy that it maintained even in the South. In addition, the company struck a centennial medal honoring Jo Anderson as the reaper's coinventor.

In truth, Jo Anderson was not the only slavery-era inventor. And even if he were, as some suspect, the actual inventor of the machine, Anderson's status as a slave or freeman would have prevented him from obtaining the patent in his own name. Among the perks of slave ownership was the fact that the "owner" owned title to the slave, the slave's labor, creativity, ideas, thoughts—everything. The slave owner, by law, owned credit for work he or she did not do. Free American-born Blacks were also denied credit or protection for their creative work. On the theory that as Blacks, they could not be U.S. citizens, they were, therefore, unable to enter into contracts with white individuals or the government. Hence, they could not patent their work, even as "free" men or women. Of course, the lack of citizenship of foreign-born whites, on the other hand, did not prohibit the protection of their ideas.

When the point is made that the Fourteenth Amendment to the Constitution is superfluous—as it was as recently as 1995 when Mississippi became the last state officially to ratify it— think of the Black inventors whose work has kept America growing and whose names we will never know.

Sunday, October 9, 1831, Virginia, U.S.A.

Invention   **Redefinitions**

OCTOBER 10

A front-page special report in the *New York Times* on October 10, 1990, had a headline guaranteed to draw attention and spread further debate around the country: "Inspirational Black History Draws Academic Fire." The strategic positioning of the piece was a major salvo launched in the backlash against the "multicultural" curriculum. It was also a major lesson in how to write and how to read a newspaper article.

These were the opening lines:

> Reaching for ways to inspire black students, . . . educators are trying to tell them more about their own ancestors, bringing tales of African kings and little-known black inventors, scientists and artists into the classroom. The efforts have drawn praise from educators eager to shift the perspective of black students away from the sense that they are descendants of minor players in the development of civilization. But others, including some prominent historians, argue that these efforts, often called "Afrocentrism," sometimes distort facts and turn history into "ethnic cheerleading."

The article continued in a second section, where this was the header and first line: "History as therapy?. . . Afrocentrism sometimes teaches questionable facts in a way that promotes racial resentment."

Then in a three-column blur of text came this explanation:

> Few educators would dispute that history as taught in American schools, at least until the 1960s, was "Eurocentric." Often it leapt from prehistoric times to Greece and Rome and then shifted west to Europe and made its way to modern America, either ignoring the rich cultures of Africa, Asia, the Near East, India and elsewhere or relegating them to chapters that never quite got assigned.

In short, the article was structured to back up the inflammatory pitch of the title. Facts that discredited the lead were "buried," as newspaperpeople say, where most readers would never see the facts. Black history was "little known"—that is, insignificant—rather than, as the article later stated, untaught. Nature knows best: If we tell the truth, the world is multicultural.

Wednesday, October 10, 1990, New York, U.S.A.

Education/Historiography   **Truths**

OCTOBER 11

In early September 1773, with the help of her "owners" and sponsors, the enslaved poet Phillis Wheatley saw her book of poetry, *Poems on Various Subjects, Religious and Moral*, published in England. Returning to the United States later that month, by October 11, 1773, she had been given her freedom. She had been bought by the family as a child, captured and shipped to slavery in America so young that she was just losing her baby teeth when she arrived. Living in Boston in 1773, she was approximately twenty years old and the first African-American woman author with a book of her own—and the second American woman of any race to publish a book.

The fact that Wheatley was a literary pioneer, both as a woman and a Black person, not only made her unique; it also made it impossible for her to be published in colonial America, where the majority of whites, let alone Blacks, could not read. If her talent threatened the conventional view of women and slaves, it also shielded her from the worst aspects of slavery.

As that curious thing and showpiece, a slave poet, she was welcomed into the homes of wealthy Bostonians, for whom she wrote grateful verses. In England for the publication of her work, she was showered with gifts and given the recognition her talent, imagination, and skillful self-invention clearly deserved.

Monday, October 11, 1773, Massachusetts, U.S.A.–England
Literature   **Liberty**

OCTOBER 12

On October 12, 1492, under the leadership of Christopher Columbus, an international crew landed on the island of Guanahani, changing history, political geography, and the way in which every world culture would define itself for the next five hundred years.

Columbus described the scene in his log: "At dawn we saw naked people, and I went ashore, armed, followed by the captains of the *Pinta* and the *Niña*. After a prayer of thanksgiving I ordered the captains to bear faith and witness that I was taking possession of this island for the King and Queen. To this island I gave the name San Salvador, in honor of our Blessed Lord."

Columbus's mission was conquest. "They are friendly and well-dispositioned people who bear no arms except for small spears, and they have no iron. I showed one my sword, and through ignorance he grabbed it by the blade and cut himself. . . . They ought to make good and skilled servants, for they repeat very quickly whatever we say to them."

Contrary to myth, Columbus did not "discover" anything. Guanahani, where he landed, was a fully inhabited island in a region whose name is translated as "Turtle Island" by some of its indigenous descendants. Later, this region would be renamed "the Americas." Despite the mistake of misnaming people Indians and arrogantly reenforcing the error for 500 years, Columbus was not lost en route to India. He kept two journals of his trip, one of which clearly demonstrates that he knew where he was headed. In 1492, a year after the end of the Moorish Wars, Africans lived throughout Europe, and Columbus's biracial crew included Moors. Identified as a North African Moor, Pietro Alonzo Niño of the *Santa Maria* crew is listed in Columbus's log as a pilot. Because Africans had sailed trade routes to the Americas for over two centuries, it was logical to hire a pilot who knew where he was going.

Wednesday, October 12, 1492, Guanahani (Bahamas) — Spain

Events   **Knowledge**

OCTOBER 13

After three-hundred-plus years of condescension toward Blacks, a new social conscience movement arose in the 1960s to reverse this tradition—and almost immediately hit a blockade. Many who were sympathetic to the basic crusade against segregation weren't willing to confront the deeply rooted hatreds that resurfaced again and again. On October 13, 1968, a *New York Times Magazine* letter to the editor signed "Jacques Preston, New York," addressed the question "What more do Negroes want?" with this parable on race:

An innocent man was once condemned to life imprisonment. He took his case to the highest courts, wrote letters to the authorities, went on hunger strikes and finally became violent. He protested against everything: the prison conditions, the wardens, and of course, his life sentence. After years of disgraceful behavior, the prison authorities gradually and reluctantly made some concessions toward improving prison conditions. The prisoner's cell was heated when the outside temperature dropped below 40 instead of 20 degrees; he was given two solid meals a day instead of one; he was also given a second blanket. You will notice that in each case there was 100 percent improvement in living conditions. Surprisingly enough, the prisoner continued his protests. The prison officials became indignant and threatened him with severe reprisals, and finally exasperated beyond endurance, they asked how many more improvements they would have to make, and at which point would he desist from his extremist behavior. The answer, of course, is simply when the sentence is vacated and he is compensated for the time spent behind bars.

Thirty years into cutbacks in fairness and funding, the thermostat is now set at 30 degrees, ketchup is called a vegetable, the blanket is found to be polyester, "what more do Negroes want" has become "we already gave"—and still we go on with greatness and grace.

Sunday, October 13, 1968, New York, U.S.A.

Social History   **Perspective**

OCTOBER 14

From the day he purchased his brother-in-law's Natchez, Mississippi, barbershop—October 14, 1830—until his death twenty-one years later, William Johnson never stopped working for his success and documenting his journey in meticulous cashbooks and two thousand diary pages. A century after his death, he was still making a name for himself when his diaries were published in 1951. The diary had been found in 1938 in the attic of the three-story brick home he'd built in central Natchez. As a singular literary-historical treasure, the diary portrayed the daily life and times of a free Black man in the heyday of slavery, "King Cotton," and the plantation economy of the antebellum South.

As a barber, Johnson had his pick of the gossip. From politics to pistols, fires to fisticuffs, high-brow entertainment to hanky-panky, he was a man with uniquely "colored" insights on the tangled web of race, class, sex, and society that was the Old South. But he was not just an outsider looking in. On July 19, 1832, Johnson hired two carriages to drive himself and "the Ladys" out to Lake Pontchartrain for dinner, drinks, and dessert. On March 24, 1835, he paid Bon, a tailor, $48.87 to make the wedding coat he would wear to marry a newly freed Ann Battles. Even in the Panic of 1837, when banks shut their doors, the notes he held as a moneylender to customers both Black and white kept him going.

As a gentleman landholder, Johnson was truly a man of his times. In business, he employed whites and Blacks, free and slave. As a slave master he was a deeply conflicted man. On December 31, 1843, he wrote, "[It's] a very Sad Day; many tears was in my Eyes to day On acct. of my Selling poor Steven." January 1, 1844: "I would not have parted with Him if he had Only have Let Liquor alone but he cannot do it." For Steven's life, Johnson accepted payment of $600. What more can one say about a slave owner who was born a slave! (See January 21.)

Thursday, October 14, 1830, Mississippi, U.S.A.
Journalism/Business   **Self-Concept**

OCTOBER 15

On October 15, 1943, as the opening jitters and bustle of movement seemed to go on without end, the Barnett-Aden Gallery was about to make history. Its formal inaugural exhibit, *American Paintings for the Home,* scheduled to open the next day in the small Washington, D.C., row house, would grow to international prominence.

As the actual home of Professor James V. Herring, who founded Howard University's Art Department in 1922, and Alonzo J. Aden, the University Gallery's curator, the Barnett-Aden would also become home to some of the most magnificent works of modern African-American art. It would thus help to relieve the isolation and obscurity that racial prejudice had created for the artists themselves. But the gallery was also unique as an institution because although it emphasized African-American art, its goal was to nurture all artists regardless of heritage, and it would give many their first gallery show.

Thus, from the day of its founding, the objective of the collection was to gather and preserve as much art as possible. In rejecting prejudice as a tool of decision-making, the Barnett-Aden was free to amass one of the best contemporary collections anywhere.

Among the talents represented in its permanent collection are Charles Alston, Edward Bannister, Romare Bearden, Elizabeth Catlett, Aaron Douglas, David Driskell, Lois Mailou Jones, Jacob Lawrence, James A. Porter, Henry Ossawa Tanner, and Charles White. Today, the collection is owned by the Florida Fund, which continues to preserve the works of these geniuses of twentieth-century African-American art.

Friday, October 15, 1943, Washington, D.C., U.S.A.

Art   **Freedom**

OCTOBER 16

The mid 1800s were tense years as the conflict between pro- and anti-slavery forces gripped the country and war loomed. The stockpiling of weapons in the federal arsenal at Harper's Ferry became both a sign of the times and the target of John Brown's historic raid. On October 16, 1859, with his "army of twenty-one men," Brown took over the arsenal and struck a blow against slavery. His purpose was to seize weapons that would be used to enforce slavery and put them to use instead in the cause of abolition.

Brown, a deeply religious man, was known to be honest to a fault. As a white "conductor" on the Underground Railroad, he was friends with such famed former slaves and fellow conductors as Harriet Tubman and Frederick Douglass. The army he amassed included one of his sons, two Oberlin-Wellington rescuers (see September 13), and Dangerfield Newby, in whose pocket this letter was found: "Dear Husband. Please find a way to buy me. For if you do not, I will be sold." Indeed, Harriet Newby was sold downriver when the letter was found on her husband's body.

When the raid was done, those who survived, including Brown, were hung (see December 2 and December's lead illustration). Of the three who escaped, the only Black man, Osborne Anderson, made his way to Canada on foot, arriving nearly dead from exposure and starvation (see October 29). Frederick Douglass, who had actually counseled against the raid, came under intense government scrutiny, and to avoid capture and the punishment of reenslavement, he fled to England. While there, friends raised funds to buy his freedom.

Even today, Brown's historic raid brings sharp condemnation by those still resentful of a white man who would lead a biracial "band of outlaws" (as detractors referred to Brown's army) in an uprising against slavery. But those who honor his achievement concur with historians in citing his ill-fated and heroic act as the "opening shot" of the Civil War.

Sunday, October 16, 1859, West Virginia, U.S.A.

Revolt!   **Conscience**

OCTOBER 17

On October 17, 1968, in front-page newspaper photos, people the world over saw for themselves what they had heard on the news the day before. In a silent demonstration on the victory platform of the 1968 Mexico City Olympics, two of the world's three top athletes in the two-hundred-meter event—Tommie Smith and John Carlos, both African-American—accepted their gold and bronze medals with a raised fist gloved in black leather.

It was 1968, the year when America's greatest emissary of peace, Dr. Martin Luther King Jr., had been shot down and, with him, the faith in America once felt by those he left behind. It was 1968, and a disproportionate number of young men of color were being shipped overseas to oppress an Asian people of color. The two athletes who had worked so hard throughout their entire young lives were unable to savor their victory under such a heavy cloud of racism, and they were protesting that fact.

Said Smith, "I wore a black right-hand glove and Carlos wore the left-hand glove of the same pair. My raised right hand stood for the power in Black America. Carlos's raised left hand stood for the unity of Black America. Together, they formed an arch of unity and power. The black scarf around my neck stood for Black pride. The black socks with no shoes stood for Black poverty in racist America. The totality of our effort was the regaining of Black dignity."

As they raised their fists in the Black Power Salute on October 16, what they may not have realized was that their victory, their pride, their doubts, and their commitment were occurring on the 109th anniversary of John Brown's raid. On that day, too, other men had raised arms for justice in America.

Thursday, October 17, 1968, Mexico

Sports   **Dedication**

OCTOBER 18

With her background as a fashion designer, Ellen Stewart had a unique vision of theater: Just do it! Create a space in which theater artists can work, try new ideas, and grow. On October 18, 1961, she rented a basement at 321 East 9th Street in New York City for $55 per month and began providing that space.

"The people in the building . . . were furious that a colored was living amongst them," Stewart told *I Dream a World* author/photographer Brian Lanker. "Somebody called the Health Department and told them that prostitution was going on in the building and that a Negress had entertained sixteen white men in five hours. Well, many young men were helping me, building, putting the floor in, trying to make this little place into a room.

"An elderly man came with a summons for my arrest. We told him what we were about and he turned out to be a person from vaudeville. So he says, 'Listen, become a restaurant and you can get a license.' He asked what our name was for the place. My nickname has always been 'Mama,' so he wrote that down and, laughing, said, 'Well, if you're gonna call it Mama, call it La Mama.' And that's how we got the name." Café La Mama (now called La Mama Experimental Theatre Club) was born!

Not only was Ellen Stewart's basement theater Off Broadway, as a new wave of theater had been called since the mid 1950s, it was Off-Off Broadway. And with that designation, the avant-garde experimental theater movement took on new life and form. It was so new in form, in fact, that no one knew how to label her theater, because no one knew how to label her as a Black woman. Blacks decided her theater was too white. White foundations thought it was too international. Yet artists not only Black and white but Asian, European, African, and Indigenous have worked and flourished in the over 1,400 productions she has since staged. With characteristic insight, Stewart has defined her vision of theater (and life) in this way: "We do not work to communicate with the audience; theater must communicate with the gods!"

Wednesday, October 18, 1961, New York, U.S.A.

Theater **Purpose**

OCTOBER 19

As the curtain rose on Paul Robeson in the title role of *Othello* on October 19, 1943, the Theatre Guild production marked the start of a 296-performance run, a record for a Shakespearean play on Broadway. With Robeson's success came a new era for Black actors in the "legitimate theater" and a gradual change in the images of Blacks projected from the stage.

In general, the theater of the 1940s accurately reflected the societal bias of the day. As Mabel Roane, secretary of the Negro Actors Guild of America, would report, "apparently two-thought opinion still prevails among critics and theater-minded people as to how the theater should handle Negro actors and roles. In recent years there has been increasing agitation by many Negroes for more dignified roles, and the elimination of the so-called stereotype roles customarily assigned to Negro performers . . . [and] the integration of Negro actors into plays simply as actors—denoting no particular race." But in response to the "better-roles campaign," the stereotypic parts that would have been assigned to Black actors were simply "written out" of plays and film, leaving less work for the actors than before.

But there were some bright spots as well. *Anna Lucasta* was a success on tour with its all-Black cast. Famed actor Canada Lee was featured in *The Duchess of Malfi* on Broadway in whiteface, and Todd Duncan, who opened as Porgy in *Porgy and Bess,* sang the title role of *I Pagliacci* with the New York City Opera company (see May 15). All told, in the postwar years of 1946–48, of the twenty-two productions with Black actors, four had all-Black casts, and the other eighteen had racially mixed casts. But on several levels the hit of the era was *St. Louis Woman.* As the longest-running show of the time, it was coauthored by two giants of African-American literature—Arna Bontemps and Countee Cullen. Based on a short story by Bontemps, *St. Louis Woman* gave the predominantly white theater audience an important view of Blacks in the military, just as President Truman's 1948 executive order to desegregate the military needed support (see July 26).

Tuesday, October 19, 1943, New York, U.S.A.

Theater   **Images**

OCTOBER 20

Two years after the Supreme Court upheld "separate but equal" segregation, Black folks' lives weren't worth a dime to the insurance industry. With the founding of the North Carolina Mutual Insurance Company (NCM) on October 20, 1898, African-Americans demonstrated that they greatly valued their lives by nurturing a Black-owned company that was still operating nearly a century later with $220 million in assets and $9.5 billion of insurance in force.

NCM was the brainchild of John Merrick, an ex-slave and entrepreneur, Aaron McDuffie Moore, Durham's first Black physician, and five investors who funded the company with $50 each. But the engine powering NCM was Moore's nephew, Charles C. Spaulding. How did he do it? Said Spaulding of NCM's early days, "When I came into the office in the morning, I rolled up my sleeves and swept the place as a janitor. Then I rolled down my sleeves and was an agent. And later I put on my coat and became general manager."

Spaulding's sales strategy was this: sell hard, saturate the market with the company's name, and pay out quickly. When the company was just a year old, a recently sold life insurance policy turned into a $40 death claim, more money than the infant company had on hand. With cash from their own pockets, Spaulding, Merrick, and Moore established their credibility by immediately paying the claim.

From these humble one-room, one-man roots, the company's success attracted over 150 Black-owned businesses to its Durham hometown. Together they founded and nurtured each other's growth through the Durham Business and Professional Chain. So stable were area businesses that the National Negro Finance Corporation, capitalized at $1 million in 1924, located its headquarters in Durham. By 1939, NCM was the nation's largest Black-owned business, and by the 1940s, the city's downtown district had built a reputation as America's "Black Wall Street."

Thursday, October 20, 1898, North Carolina, U.S.A.

Business   **Values**

OCTOBER 21

If anyone thought the Birmingham church bombing (see September 15) that killed four girls in 1963 would steer young African-Americans off course, they were wrong. It inspired these young people to new levels of commitment across the country. It had been nine years since the Supreme Court's *Brown v. Board of Education* school desegregation order and six years since the Little Rock Nine had sacrificed their childhood. For young people—especially after the death of the four girls—it was time for their agenda to be met.

In Chicago, 225,000 students staged a one-day "Freedom Day" boycott of the public schools to protest continued school segregation. And on October 21, 1963, one hundred young people staged a lunch counter sit-in at Woolworth's in downtown Atlanta. They filled every available seat and refused to leave until served, which they weren't. True to the tactics of the sit-ins, if they couldn't receive service, no one would. Whites would have to pay the price of segregation with a loss of revenue.

As one of the civil rights movement's most ardent demonstrators and unique griots, comedian Dick Gregory chronicled the day:

> I wanted all those years to be admitted to the Woolworth lunch counter, and now I find I don't like anything on their menu!
> The waitress said to me, "Sorry, we don't serve colored people here." I said to her, "That's all right, I don't want to eat any. Bring me a chicken."

Gregory had been arrested as a demonstrator often enough (see April 4) to know when to make people laugh. He was able to transform the students' message into an anecdote that people would retell for years to come. For these are the stories that remind us of the legacies and ongoing commitment of Black youth, of the courage our young people have always manifested.

Monday, October 21, 1963, Georgia, U.S.A.

Youth/Children   **Courage**

OCTOBER 22

October 22, 1987: thirty years ago the "Little Rock Nine" had been teenagers terrorized by daily violence as they desegregated the now-legendary Little Rock Central High School. In the immediate aftermath of that crisis, they had received numerous honors, including the NAACP's Spingarn Medal. They had toured northern cities as heroes. Then life took them their separate ways. Now, on their first Arkansas reunion in thirty years, they gathered for a historic pajama party in the suite of a hotel in the since-desegregated downtown. Within hours, they would return to Central, but this one night would be spent securely wrapped in their unique bond.

That bond was inextricably sealed on September 25, 1957, as the 101st Airborne Division escorted them into history past an angry segregationist mob (see May 27). Melba Pattillo Beals recalled that day when the mob stormed the school in search of the nine, all of whom had been called together in the principal's office. "Even the school officials were panicked. Someone made a suggestion that if they allowed the mob to hang one kid, then they could get the rest out while they were hanging the one kid." Leading them down to the basement and into two cars, their drivers were told to start driving and not to stop for anything. "So the guy revved the engine and came out of the bowels of this building," Beals continued. "I could see hands reaching across the car. I could hear the yelling. I could see the guns. . . . He dropped me off at home, and I remember saying, 'Thank you for the ride.' I should have said, 'Thank you for my life.'"

Now thirty years later, in the morning they will take another very public walk up Central's steps. Also accompanying them will be their spouses and their own teenage children. They will be greeted by Governor, soon-to-be-President, Bill Clinton, his wife, Hillary Rodham Clinton, and the president of Central High School's student government, Derrick Noble, an African-American student.

Thursday, October 22, 1987, Arkansas, U.S.A.

Desegregation   **Better Worlds**

OCTOBER 23

In the 1820s, Thomas Day was known as an exceptionally fine furniture maker in a state that would achieve wide recognition for its furniture craftsmanship, North Carolina. So highly prized were his carved chairs and tables of imported West Indian mahogany that they are collector's items today. His Milton-based business grew so rapidly that he quickly became a major source of employment and apprenticeship for area craftsmen, Black and white. Starting his business sometime around 1820, by 1823 he was so successful that he bought the old Yellow Tavern (which still stands) for use as his factory and home. But the town's and Day's prosperity—including his marriage, the ability to live and work in North Carolina, the livelihoods of his white (not to mention his Black) employees, and the Milton town economy—were all threatened by an 1826 state law designed to harass free Blacks.

Passed in October 1826, the statute took effect in 1827. Under the law, free Blacks not only had to have white sponsors in order to live in the state but they were required to pay heavy fines and penalties. Day refused to pay the penalties and threatened to leave town, taking his business with him. With jobs and the town economy at stake, the citizens of Milton came up with a solution. A petition was filed to exempt Day and his wife from the law. It was introduced in the state legislature and approved by the General Assembly with a vote of 74 to 40. Day was deemed a person whites could trust. In a decision clearly influenced by the 1822 slave revolt led by Denmark Vesey, a free Black man (see June 16), it was determined that as a slave owner himself, Day would be likely to report to authorities any disturbances afoot among Blacks.

What is a Black person in American society? And what are the penalties still being levied against African-Americans—even our Black employers and business leaders? Clearly, Tom Day's example is worth note. He took exception to, and found exemption from, a hostile society's definition of what it means to be a Black.

Monday, October 23, 1826, North Carolina, U.S.A.
Business   **Self-Worth**

OCTOBER 24

Charles Williams owned several Los Angeles night-clubs in the early 1940s. As a photographer himself, one of the special features of his clubs was the "Camera Girls," Black women photographers who roamed the clubs taking pictures. These were the years of World War II, when film and flashbulbs were all at a premium. Both the silver used to make the film and the enlargement paper were restricted by the war effort. But groups of professionals buying their supplies in bulk could gain access to film.

Interestingly, although the Camera Girls were actually a new twist on the old cigarette-girl idea, the Camera Girls wore their own street clothes instead of the scanty costumes worn by the cigarette girls to entice customer purchases. The Camera Girls were professionals whose job it was to take good pictures and sell lots of them. As the Camera Girls took pictures out front with the customers, Williams had a darkroom set up in the back to process the film immediately so that the customers could go home happily with their pictures in hand. The object was to take the pictures first, then sell them after. With several shots available, people were likely to buy more than one photo at a time. It was a good concession, and the Camera Girls would start out with a fixed guaranteed nightly wage and then earn commissions on each photo sold. Some of the women began as amateurs, but the job launched many of them into professional careers.

Taken on a night like this one, October 24, 1944—with a new wave of recruitment beginning on the day after General MacArthur returned to the Asian theater of operations, and with the Allies taking Germany in house-to-house fighting—many Camera Girls' photos became pictures to last a lifetime. For soldiers and their loved ones in those war years, the Camera Girls captured the good times of their last days together before shipping out. For us, their work provides a wonderful social history of nightlife in the forties.

Tuesday, October 24, 1944, California, U.S.A.
Photography   **Images**

OCTOBER 25

On October 25, 1886, the last rivet was secured on the Statue of Liberty, a vision twenty-one years in the making. While the monument was built to honor shared dreams of liberty and a lasting Franco-American friendship, most African-Americans felt alienated from both the monument and its realization. Little do people know that the statue bears an African-inspired pedigree.

The idea for erecting the monument dates back to an informal conversation at a French dinner party in 1865, hosted by the head of the French Antislavery Society, Edouard-René Laboulaye. Among his guests that evening was a young sculptor, Frédéric-Auguste Bartholdi, whose visit to Egypt in 1856 had left him in awe of such antiquities as the Sphinx, the pyramids, Thebes, and the granite statuary of Abu Simbel. Shortly after the dinner, Bartholdi accepted a commission for a Suez Canal lighthouse monument. Its statuesque draped female figure with northern African facial features, holding a torch aloft, was called *Egypt Bringing the Light to Asia*. Though sponsorship for this project was withdrawn, the torch continued burning in Bartholdi's vision, and he immediately set to work to realize the "dinner project." He called it *Liberty Enlightening the World*—a statuesque draped female with Greco-Roman features, holding a torch aloft, but on her foot was a broken shackle of bondage turned to freedom. To commemorate the independence movements of France and the United States, she held a tablet in her left hand that bore the date of the signing of the Declaration of Independence, July 4, 1776.

In total support of Bartholdi's effort, Laboulaye provided letters of introduction to his American friends—a network built up through his antislavery efforts, which had been instrumental in blocking French support for the South during the Civil War. That network shepherded Bartholdi's vision through the process of raising interest and funds until the international project took its final form on October 25, 1886, as the Statue of Liberty.

Monday, October 25, 1886, New York–New Jersey,
U.S.A.–France

Art   **Images**

OCTOBER 26

On October 26, 1934, focusing on the need to eliminate segregation altogether, the NAACP named Charles H. Houston to head its campaign to destabilize the legal underpinnings of segregation.

This was the Charles Houston: Amherst College undergraduate with a Phi Beta Kappa key, Harvard University Law School graduate and the first Black editor of the *Harvard Law Review*, and former vice dean of Howard University Law School.

Houston once said, "A lawyer's either a social engineer, or he's a parasite on society." As a social engineer with an NAACP mandate, Houston began implementation of his plan to dismantle segregation. He would lead a team of lawyers in an unrelenting series of legal raids designed to make the policy too expensive to maintain. With this strategy, Houston began his "soft-underbelly" attack on Jim Crow (see March 15) by targeting higher education. Houston's team would take cases up to the Supreme Court in a test of the "separate but equal" law that required a state to provide two distinctly separate, and equal, graduate schools in a range of disciplines for the few Black graduate students needing them. He knew a violent rebuff was likely, but that was always a factor regardless of strategy. The only legal alternatives were to (a) develop "separate but equal" graduate schools for Blacks (much too expensive); (b) pay Black students' tuition and living expenses to study out of state (still too expensive); or (c) desegregate the existing colleges.

Unfortunately, Houston died in 1950—too soon to see Thurgood Marshall carry the "NAACP/Houston strategy" to victory in *Brown v. Board of Education*, the official beginning of the end of legal segregation. However, in a fitting tribute to Houston's stature as a constitutional lawyer, five Supreme Court justices were in attendance at his funeral.

Friday, October 26, 1934, Washington, D.C., U.S.A.

Law   Legacies

OCTOBER 27

An advertisement for the "African Company" in the October 27, 1821, issue of the *New York National Advocate* read, "The gentlemen of color announce another play at their pantheon, corner of Bleecker and Mercer Streets on Monday evening. . . . They have graciously made a partition at the back of the house, for the accommodation of the whites."

The earliest known African-American theater troupe, the African Company, began producing plays at the African Grove Theater in 1821. Included in their repertory were productions of Shakespeare's *Othello* and *Richard III*, with comedic interludes between the acts and a full operatic closer that would have done any house proud. So admired were their productions that as the ad suggests, they were attended by whites as well as Blacks. But when too many white rowdies began to storm the theater, it was closed by police officers who feared the disruptions.

The theater did, however, reopen in a new location, "in Bleecker Street, in the rear of the One Mile Stone, Broadway," as a handbill notice for June 20–21, 1823, confirms:

> The Performers of the African Company have kindly
> united their services in order to contribute a Benefit to their
> Manager, Mr. Brown, who, for the first time, throws himself
> on the liberality of a generous public. Mr. Brown trusts that
> his unrelinquished exertions to please, will be justly considered
> by the Gentlemen and Ladies of this City, as on them depends
> his future support, and they can declare whether he is "To be—or
> not to be—That is the question."

That closing remark continues to speak for the generations of theater professionals who have, thankfully, persevered "to be."

Saturday, October 27, 1821, New York, U.S.A.

Theater   **Perception**

OCTOBER 28

When the family of Josiah and Charlotte Henson and their four children reached land on October 28, 1830, they were in heaven — otherwise known as Canada. "When my feet first touched the Canada shore," wrote Josiah Henson, "I gave way to the riotous thrill of my feelings with such antics that a stranger asked what was the matter with me. I jumped up and told him I was free! 'Oh,' said he, with a hearty laugh, 'is that it? I never knew freedom to make a man roll in the sand before.' To me, however, it was little wonder."

For six weeks they had traveled from Kentucky to Canada, most of the way on foot. They had escaped late one Saturday night in mid September, with the help of another slave who rowed them across the river on a dark, moonless night. It was a sudden, desperate act by a slave who had been so loyal that his master promised that Henson's family would never be sold or separated. This master was immortalized many years later as Uncle Tom in Harriet Beecher Stowe's historic novel, *Uncle Tom's Cabin*. When Henson overheard his master's plan to go back on the promise, he prepared his family for an immediate escape.

For two straight weeks they walked by night and rested during the day until their food was gone. Sometimes they doubled back toward the South to escape suspicion as runaways. They were helped with shelter and food by Underground Railroad station-masters and Native Americans whose lands they crossed. A ship's captain warned Henson about nearby slave catchers and then sailed the family from Sandusky across Lake Erie to freedom.

"There was not much time to be lost in frolic — even at this extraordinary moment," Henson recalled. "We were strangers in a strange land, and would now have to make our own way." And make a way they did, for themselves and other refugees. As a "conductor," Henson helped others escape, making a home and a new day for them at his family's Dawn Settlement, a farm in Ontario, which he supported with European speaking tours and the sales from his book.

Thursday, October 28, 1830, Maryland, U.S.A.–Canada

Freedom   **Courage**

OCTOBER 29

The October 29, 1852, edition of Frederick Douglass's newspaper, *The North Star*, reports the activities of the first African-American woman publisher, Mary Ann Shadd. A member of a family active in Philadelphia's Underground Railroad movement, she had exiled herself to Windsor, West Canada, in order to continue her political activities. There, she launched *The Provincial Freeman*, a weekly targeting the rapidly growing community of freemen, freewomen, and former slaves who fled the United States for Canada to escape the terror unleashed by the Fugitive Slave Act of 1850. Shadd established herself as an abolitionist so firm in her commitment that she was voted secretary of the Society of Colored Citizens of Windsor, West Canada. This was the event that inspired Douglass's article, and it was noteworthy because this was a rare position of leadership for a woman.

Among her first acts as secretary was the sponsorship of this resolution:

> Resolved, that we do not regard the Refugees' Home Society as a benevolent institution designed to benefit a formerly downtrodden people. . . [but an institution which by] giving fresh impulse and a specious character to the begging system, will materially compromise our manhood by representing us as objects of charity, injure seriously the character of this country and tend to the pecuniary advantage of its agents and theirs only.

With her determined independence, she practiced what she preached. As a publisher, she was responsible for the memoir of Osborne Anderson, the only Black member of John Brown's army to survive the raid. And as a woman in her mid-forties, she returned to the States after the Civil War to become one of Howard University Law School's first women students. Practicing law in Washington, D.C., Mary Ann Shadd is thought to be the first African-American woman lawyer. The example of her professional life expanded the options of women for generations to come.

Friday, October 29, 1852, U.S.A.

Heroes   **Stature**

OCTOBER 30

October 30, 1949, marked a rare opportunity to understand what thought process underlies works of art and what defines an artist's greatness. In an interview, Aaron Douglas (see May 29) spoke of his four murals collectively titled *Aspects of Negro Life: The Negro in an African Setting, From Slavery Through Reconstruction, An Idyll of the Deep South,* and *Song of the Towers.* He had painted the murals for Harlem's Countee Cullen Library almost twenty years earlier in tribute to the inspiration provided him by Africans the world over.

For two hundred years, being accepted as a Black artist meant excelling at European-oriented images and the "discreet" inclusion of Black faces and themes. A visionary, Douglas sought the roots of his self-expression where no African-American artist before him had dared go: Africa. Dipping into that wellspring of images, he shaped his own distinctive "geometric symbolism" and earned our gratitude as the Father of Black American Art.

Arriving in New York City at the height of the 1920s Harlem Renaissance movement, Douglas entered a world where Blacks were in vogue but things "African" were officially disdained. But "New Negro" writers like Langston Hughes and Wallace Thurman (see June 23) prized his vision and used his works for their book and magazine illustrations. Fisk University's president commissioned murals for the university's library in 1930. And in 1933, Douglas painted the four *Aspects of Negro Life* murals for the Countee Cullen Library.

Telling the story of his murals, Douglas spoke of "the exhilaration, the ecstasy, the rhythmic pulsation of life." Of his work he said, "I refuse to compromise and see blacks as anything less than a proud and majestic people."

Sunday, October 30, 1949, Tennessee, U.S.A.

Art   **Enthusiasm**

OCTOBER 31

Free at last!

On October 31, 1809, George Hicks of Brooklyn offered a $25 reward to anyone who could solve the riddle of his missing slave with this advertisement: "Negro woman named Charity and her female child . . . 25 years of age, five feet high, of a yellowish complexion . . . has lost the use of one of her fingers, occasioned by a felon . . . [she] took with her several suits of clothes."

Before the invention of the "iron rail" provided metaphorical grist for the escape route known as the Underground Railroad, African-American lore recorded news of such departures as proof that our "people could fly." In its own way, Charity's flight was one giant step for a woman, one small leap for humankind, to paraphrase another heroic death-defying act 160 years later. In an overwhelming contest to conquer distance and fear and to flee the bonds of the earthly demands put upon her, Charity was most definitely triumphant.

The fact that a man would value the life of a woman and her child at any price, much less twenty-five dollars, speaks for itself. As for Charity, hers was just one more heroic daily act of rebellion leading to the overthrow of slavery.

Tuesday, October 31, 1809, New York, U.S.A.

Social History   **Self-Determination**

NOVEMBER

Southern Sketches. Etching from the watercolor by T. W. Wood. Published by *Harper's Weekly* (July 31, 1875). Reprinted courtesy of the author.

NOVEMBER 1

Since 1942 when he published the first issue of his first magazine, *Negro Digest*, November 1 has been John H. Johnson's special day. On November 1, 1945, he started *Ebony*. And on November 1, 1951, he started *Jet*. In other Novembers, he launched Fashion Fair Cosmetics and Supreme Beauty Products, and he purchased controlling shares in Supreme Life Insurance, the company whose founder gave him his start. With all this, perhaps November 1 isn't so much Johnson's "good luck" day as it is his "dare to dream" day. His new magazine was officially published that day because his mother had offered her dream—the furniture she had worked for and dreamed about all her adult life—as collateral for the $500 loan that would help yield his dream. He wasn't even sure he could make enough money to publish a second issue. But he was highly motivated: "In 1942, my mother and I were recent graduates of the relief [welfare] rolls. And I decided that I was never going down that road again."

The idea for *Negro Digest* sprang in the grunt work he'd done for his mentor, the owner of Supreme Life—reading Black newspapers and giving his boss a summary, or "digest," of the most important stories each week. With his employer's permission, he had access to a mailing list and a duplicating machine to send out a letter soliciting subscriptions for *Negro Digest*.

In 1942, Johnson was twenty-four years old and waiting to be drafted into World War II, taking the risk of a lifetime. As he tells it, "I'd lived all my life on the edge of poverty and humiliation. People say a lot of foolish things today about poverty. But I know—I've been there. It's not so much pain in the belly; it's pain in the soul. It's the wanting and not having." On November 1, 1942, he was, as he says, "poor, ambitious, and scared to death." On November 1, 1987, the date on which his autobiography begins, he is in the presidential suite of a Los Angeles hotel, in town for the taping of a television show, and he is "rich, ambitious, and scared to death." He is also an inspiration to millions.

Sunday, November 1, 1942, Illinois, U.S.A.

Journalism   **Success**

NOVEMBER 2

On November 2, 1971, the day Ayodele Nailah and Dara Rashida Roach were born, the news reached celebrated New York City disc jockey Eddie O'Jay who was hosting his show on WLIB, and he turned the day's programming into a broadcast marathon in honor of their birth and their father, the noted musician, Max Roach.

These were the first great-grandchildren of two Afri-Caribbean immigrants who had come to the United States to make a better life for themselves. Their great-grandfather died the winter before they were born. But their mother was pregnant with them when she carried his ashes to Africa and delivered them to the departing sea. Their great-grandmother, a twin herself, lived to see them born days before her own eightieth birthday. When they came home, she couldn't stop looking at them. In them she saw herself and her sister in the Caribbean isle of Saint Kitts and remembered that as premature babies, no one had expected them to survive. Ayo and Dara were also premature, and on the day they were born, there was doubt about whether they or their mother would survive. But they did.

There are family stories that each of us needs to share with our children and with each other. These are the stories that belong to my daughters, Ayo and Dara, and they are the reason for this and many other books. Sometimes when the grand currents and themes of history are analyzed, the most frequently undervalued influences are those that motivate us each and every day. We can tell our children what our grandfathers told our mothers, what their great-grandmothers left behind to tell yet-unborn great-great-grandsons. In telling each other the things we need to know, we strengthen the chain. It is because of all that so many others have said and done, been and become, that we can share this day through this page in history. Happy birthday to all of our children!

Tuesday, November 2, 1971, New York, U.S.A.–Saint Eustatius
Family   **Empowerment**

NOVEMBER 3

On November 3, 1992, Carol Moseley-Braun became the first African-American woman elected to the U.S. Senate and the second Black senator of the twentieth century. Her victory came in an election year that also increased the numbers of women in Congress in the aftermath of Supreme Court Justice Clarence Thomas's Senate confirmation hearings. The hearings had elicited the shameful "Clarence Thomas–Anita Hill" spectacle in which two political constituencies—"Blacks" and "women"—were publicly disgraced by the skillful maneuvering of a 98-percent white male Senate over the issue of sexual harassment. It was a perfect "divide and conquer" scenario as old as the nation itself, when supporters of abolition (a "Black rights" issue) and supporters of suffrage (a "women's rights" issue) were historically pitted against one another (see March 31, June 21, August 7).

During her fourteen-year rise to national political acclaim, Carol Moseley-Braun had made her reputation as a coalition builder. For the election of 1992, she would build the coalition of a lifetime around her two distinct sociopolitical identities. Professionally and personally, as a "Black + woman" with solid credentials in law and politics, Carol Moseley-Braun was the right fusion candidate at the right time.

The *New York Times* quoted her as saying that the Thomas hearings had not only brought her to Congress but had also shattered her vision of the Senate as "a Valhalla where decisions were made by serious men—instead we saw they were just garden-variety politicians making bad speeches." The time for speeches was over. "Blacks" and "women" faced the all-important query: How serious are you about ending the twin evils of racism and sexism? Together, they represented a minimum of 60 percent of the population, a handy majority that could carry any vote. Just as the coalition had led to Moseley-Braun's victory, it had the potential to rewrite the national agenda completely.

Tuesday, November 3, 1992, Illinois, U.S.A.

Leadership   **Respect for Use of Power**

NOVEMBER 4

Actor-humorist Bill Cosby once said, "I do not know the secret of success, but I know the secret of failure: try to please everybody." On November 4, 1988, Bill and Camille Cosby opted for success. In an act of giving unprecedented in the history of American education, they gave one gift of $20 million to one school—Spelman College in Atlanta, Georgia. African-America's preeminent philanthropic family would build and endow the Camille Olivia Hanks Cosby Center. It was the largest donation ever to a historically Black institution and the largest single-source gift to any American college.

Two days after the announcement of the gift, Bill Cosby spoke at the inaugural gala for Spelman's new president, Dr. Johnnetta B. Cole, the college's first African-American woman president in its then 107-year history (see April 24). As the father of five children, four of whom are daughters, Cosby was sensitive to the unique issues surrounding the education of Black women—the greatest being an education in their own history. His gift to Spelman had been inspired by an incident related by one of his daughters while she was attending Spelman. In the library at her own school, she couldn't research a paper on the legendary civil rights leader Fannie Lou Hamer, one of the foremost Black women of the twentieth century. Cosby believed in reinvesting wealth in our greatest renewable resource—education. For years, the Cosbys had donated annual gifts to a range of educational institutions. Now, with this one dramatic donation, the spotlight was placed directly on saving historically Black colleges—the schools still responsible for graduating the greatest number of Black students.

Said Cosby, an alumnus of the Philadelphia projects turned superstar and multimillionaire, "I found a vein of gold in the side of the mountain." By investing it in education, his wealth and that of others would help mine our shared resources into pure "Black gold" for generations to come.

Friday, November 4, 1988, California–Georgia, U.S.A.

Philanthropy   **Vision**

NOVEMBER 5

Maya Lin—the architect who designed the Vietnam War Memorial in Washington, D.C., when she was only twenty-one—was about to accept a commission to design the Civil Rights Memorial in Montgomery, Alabama, for the human rights activist-attorney Morris Dees and his Southern Poverty Law Center (SPLC). En route, she read a quote from Dr. King: "We will not be satisfied until justice rolls down like waters and righteousness like a mighty stream." At that moment, she knew her design would be about that "mighty stream" of people who made up the civil rights movement. The words inspired an image—a waterfall streaming over an etched chronology of people and events. Only when Lin saw the mother of the martyred teen Emmett Till at the dedication of the memorial on November 5, 1989, did she know the power of her own design. "Emmett Till's mother was touching his name beneath the water and crying, and I realized her tears were becoming part of the memorial."

The first part of the memorial is a nine-foot wall carved with the quotation from Dr. King's speech. The second is a spill of water falling on a granite wheel twelve feet in diameter, incised with fifty-three milestone events and martyrs of the civil rights era, ending with Dr. King's assassination on April 4, 1968.

As Mrs. Mamie Till Mobley said at the dedication, "we are men and women of sorrow, and we are acquainted with grief. But we sorrow not as those who have no hope. We know that we were chosen to be burden bearers. Emmett's death was not a personal experience . . . it was a worldwide awakening that would change the course of history."

Lin herself was one of those so awakened. "I was horrified to realize that many of [the] murders had taken place during my lifetime and . . . it hadn't been taught to me in school. . . . And I thought, if you stop remembering, you can quickly slide backward into prejudicial ways." With the memorial, the names and their meaning are firmly etched in stone.

Sunday, November 5, 1989, Alabama, U.S.A.

Civil Rights Movement   **Awakenings**

NOVEMBER 6

With election results counted well into the night, on November 6, 1968, the nation awakened to the dawn of a new day—in life and politics. As a direct legacy of the Voting Rights Act of 1965, community organizers had succeeded in forging the civil rights agenda into a national election platform. In one voting day, ninety-seven Blacks were elected to state legislatures, seven were elected mayor, and four hundred were elected to local governments in the former Confederate states where voting rights had been thwarted for so long.

But nowhere was the victory more concentrated than on Capitol Hill. In a series of historic triumphs, the number of Blacks topped a record held since 1877—nine: eight in Congress and one in the Senate. Joining Senator Edward Brooke of Massachusetts were two new and six returning African-American members of the Ninety-first Congress.

New York's Shirley Chisholm became the first Black woman ever elected to Congress. The new men were Louis Stokes of Ohio and William Clay of Missouri. The returnees included Charles Diggs (Michigan), Augustus Hawkins (California), Robert Nix (Pennsylvania), and William Dawson (Illinois), the elder statesman of the group who couldn't even find a hotel in which to sleep when he first came to Congress in 1943.

Most significantly, Harlem voters reelected and vindicated their long-term congressman, the Reverend Adam Clayton Powell, Jr. As a twenty-four-year veteran of the House, the ranking majority leader, third in the line of succession to the presidency, Powell's congressional censure on trumped-up charges of slandering a numbers runner by calling her a "bag woman" was suspicious on its face, as the Supreme Court would later confirm. By rallying behind Powell, Harlem championed the right of every district—regardless of ethnicity or demography—to elect the qualified candidate of its choice.

Wednesday, November 6, 1968, U.S.A.

Politics   **Respect for Use of Power**

NOVEMBER 7

In 1841, as the story of the Amistad Mutiny (see August 24, November 27) drew to a close, a second successful mutiny aboard the slave ship *Creole* fueled an international incident that brought Britain and the United States to the brink of war.

On November 7, 1841, the *Creole* was en route from Hampton, Virginia, to the slave mart of New Orleans, Louisiana. In a successful mutiny led by Madison Washington, a member of its total "cargo" of 134, the rebels overpowered their captors and sailed to New Providence, Nassau, in the Bahamas where slavery had already been abolished. Because of that prohibition and the fact that the trafficking of slaves violated international law, the mutineers were granted political asylum and restored to freedom. Infuriated by the subversion of its proslavery laws, the United States threatened to go to war with Britain. As the war debate heated up, free Blacks who as a class had fought in every American war faced an unusual dilemma. An editorial in the *Colored People's Press*, later reprinted in the April 1, 1842, issue of *The Liberator*, asked:

> If war be declared, shall we fight with the chains upon
> our limbs? Will we fight in defense of a government
> which denied us the most precious right of citizenship?
> Shall we shed our blood in defense of the American slave
> trade? Shall we make our bodies a rampart in defense of
> American slavery?
>
> We asked these questions, because there is no law in
> existence which can compel us to fight, and any fighting
> on our part, must be a VOLUNTARY ACT. The States
> in which we dwell have twice availed themselves of our
> voluntary services, and have repaid us with chains and
> slavery. Shall we a third time kiss the foot that crushes
> us? If so, we deserve our chains.

Over the course of American history, the number of times this debate has been waged can only be called astounding.

Sunday, November 7, 1841, Louisiana, U.S.A.–Bahamas
Military   **Racial Dignity**

NOVEMBER 8

When Morehouse College's beloved president, Dr. Benjamin E. Mays, recalled his earliest memory, it was this one, an event that occurred when he was four years old:

> I remember a crowd of white men who rode up on horseback with rifles on their shoulders. I was with my father when they rode up, and I remember starting to cry. They cursed my father, drew their guns and made him salute, made him take off his hat and bow down to them several times. Then they rode away. . . . I have never forgotten them. . . . They were one of the mobs associated with the infamous Phoenix Riot which began in Greenwood County, South Carolina, on November 8, 1898, and spread terror throughout the countryside for many days thereafter. . . . Several Negroes were lynched on the ninth and others on subsequent days.

When asked what goaded him to high professional achievement from a life of "respectable poverty" as a farmer's son, he cited this story. And it is with this event that he begins his autobiography. Years later, he read a newspaper account of the period and found this editorial in the *Greenwood Index:*

> The action of the white people of South Carolina, and the determination with which the men went into the Phoenix episode, demonstrated above all things else that the white people of this country will not entertain even a suggestion of Negro domination. It is a basic principle in our unwritten law that the white man must rule. . . . It is a painful fact, however, that in order to enforce this law harsh measures are sometimes necessary.

These memories and the nurturing he received as the youngest child in a family of eight children created the grounding for his life as a world-respected educator, president of Morehouse College, mentor to Dr. King, counsel to presidents, international human rights advocate, and respected theologian—in short, as a tireless crusader for the triumph of the spirit over great adversity.

Tuesday, November 8, 1898, South Carolina, U.S.A.

Beginnings **Human Rights**

NOVEMBER 9

On November 9, 1779, Amos Fortune bought Violate, the love of his life. The next day they were married. On their wedding day, Amos was nearly seventy years old, Violate was perhaps ten years younger, and their twenty-two year marriage offered them the time of their lives. They even adopted a daughter, Celyndia.

When we wander among the grave markers in the old church burial ground of Jaffrey, New Hampshire, a town history emerges from the weather-worn script. But few stories are more perfectly preserved or more poignantly and succinctly told than the one of these two lovers. Twin black slate headstones inscribed with carved urns and epitaphs read:

SACRED	SACRED
to the memory of	to the memory of
AMOS FORTUNE,	VIOLATE,
who was born free in	by sale the slave of
Africa, a slave in America,	Amos Fortune, by Marriage
he purchased liberty,	his wife, by her
professed Christianity,	fidelity his friend and
lived reputably,	solace, she died his widow.
and died hopefully.	Sept. 13, 1802.
Nov. 17, 1801.	

Little is known of their earliest days. Born somewhere in Africa around 1710, Amos was captured and shipped to slavery in America. Freed in 1769, he made payments on himself for another year as a tanner so skilled that his bound books still survive. He bought a homestead and a wife, Lydia, who soon died. Later, he purchased, freed, and married Violate.

The ages of Amos and Violate Fortune when they married offer unique insights on freedom. Many of the slaves allowed their freedom were older people at the time of their manumission. Thus, freeing the slave actually freed the slave owner of an unproductive laborer. As for Amos and Violate Fortune, they took the life that was left them, and made the most of it.

Tuesday, November 9, 1779, New Hampshire, U.S.A.

Family   **Love**

NOVEMBER 10

On November 10, 1981, a Black sergeant staggered drunkenly across a darkened platform, mumbling to himself in the glare of a single light, "They'll still hate you! They still hate you." With his laugh muffled by the midnight mud, he was shot. With that, Charles Fuller's harrowing drama, *A Soldier's Play*, opened on the stage of New York's Theater Four.

The drama disturbed both its Black and white audiences. The intricate distortions of a harsh history uncovered a plot much more sinister than expected. The drunken sergeant, as it turned out, was not killed by the KKK as the audience was comfortably led to believe. He was killed by a Black enlisted man avenging the play's true victim, a young man named "C.J.," raised to be a "good colored boy" on the sick southern soil of the 1940s; a bulky, friendly young man raised to make himself appear less threatening to forever-threatening whites by grinning his way to survival. The sergeant's own self-hatred pushed C.J. to suicide. C.J.'s death was avenged by his friend. And as that friend was betrayed by another, the audience was left wondering when the legacy of torment would ever end.

The play won the Pulitzer Prize for 1982 and was made into a movie two years later. Moviegoers, like the playgoers, would ask the same disbelieving question: Was Fuller blaming Blacks for their own torment? Where was the demonstration of white complicity in all of this? Fuller seemed to be saying that when you see yourself as the problem, you can see yourself holding the key to its solution. Fuller's "morality tale" continues to challenge audiences, and every night *A Soldier's Play* plays anywhere is a night to remember.

Tuesday, November 10, 1981, New York, U.S.A.

Theater   **Responsibility**

NOVEMBER 11

One of the earliest milestones en route to the awe-inspiring small-band jazz of the 1950s was Louis Armstrong's first "Hot Five" and "Hot Seven" recordings of November 11, 1925.

The Louis Armstrong whom most people remember was the stage performer of international renown from his later years. But this was the same Louis Armstrong who at the beginning of his career earned the name "Pops" as one of the finest cornetists of all time. The flexibility and the range of textures that he brought to the cornet moved it into the forefront as a solo improvisational instrument, and it would dominate the hard, driving individualism of the small-band jazz that came to prominence in the 1950s.

Today, the Louis Armstrong House in Queens, New York, is a historic site preserved and open to the public. Its archive of Armstrong's private record collection is, perhaps, one of the world's finest for the period of his life. It also reveals thousands of handwritten pages of Armstrong's private hours as a diarist. Taken as an amazing whole, it all goes to show the depth of his singular talent—which charted new musical ground for fifty years.

Wednesday, November 11, 1925, New York, U.S.A.
Music   **Vision**

NOVEMBER 12

"It is Calm & Warm. Sierra Leone Looks Natural," wrote Paul Cuffe on November 12, 1811, as news spread that, at the helm of his own seventy-five-foot brig, the *Traveller*, the son of a long-lost African had come home at last.

Cuffe began his career as a fourteen-year-old seaman, one of the most dangerous occupations in an America torn by the Revolutionary War. Sailing by night to avoid capture—from both the British and the American sides—he broke blockades and embargoes in a time when all commerce was by sea and a trip between Boston and the off-shore island of Nantucket was an incursion into enemy waters. He survived more than one pirate raid, and whites, angry at the success of a Black captain and his all-Black crew, regularly attempted to kidnap and sell him into slavery.

En route to success as an international shipping magnate and the first African-American entrepreneur, he traded everything—except his identity as the son of a Native American Wampanoag mother and an African father kidnapped into slavery. With Black capitalism his currency and Pan-Africanism his philosophy, and with his superior skills of negotiation and international diplomacy, he became one of the wealthiest men of his day. But his experiences made him prey to the jealousy of others. Even on his long-anticipated journey to Africa, soon after the end of the slave trade, a French schooner tried to take him and his crew captive. But the gods and nature were on his side. As his biographer Lamont Thomas describes it, "within minutes a great squall providentially brought driving rain, high winds, and heavy seas. In the commotion the captain ordered extra sails aloft and the *Traveller* escaped certain seizure."

Navigating hostile tides throughout his career, his voyage and reception were all the more triumphant as he sailed into port in Sierra Leone, West Africa, on this day in 1811 and charted a route for the Back-to-Africa movement.

Tuesday, November 12, 1811, Massachusetts, U.S.A.– Sierra Leone

Business   **Excellence**

NOVEMBER 13

In documenting the twentieth-century freedom fight, the production team for *Eyes on the Prize* came across more stories of everyday courage and heroism than they could possibly retell. Thankfully, this anecdote survives in Juan Williams's companion book to the television series (see January 22):

While the history of the civil rights movement features nationally prominent leaders and organizations, the movement would have been impossible without a network of nameless heroes and grassroots organizations that knew every feature of their local terrain. In Selma, Alabama, that local group was the Dallas County Voters League, founded in the 1930s. As one of the few Black registered voters of the time, Amelia Platts Boynton, an active registration advocate, was posted at the polls to vouch for new registrants—most of whom were clearly of higher character and ability than the registrars seeking to block their rights.

On one occasion, a registrar had difficulty reading the questions to a Black teacher and would-be registrant. After several uneasy moments listening to the bumbling of the registrar, the teacher finally said, "Those words are 'constitutionality' and 'interrogatory.'" As the registrar reddened with anger, Ms. Boynton tells us, "[the teacher] flunked the test and was refused her registration certificate." Little wonder civil rights workers sang:

> *I know one thing we did right*
> *Was the day we began to fight*
> *Keep your eyes on the prize*
> *Hold on, hold on.*

And hold on they did until, within months of this incident, the passage of the 1965 Voting Rights Act outlawed all literacy, knowledge, and character tests as qualifications. Extended in 1990, that act is still considered the most effective civil rights legislation passed to date.

Friday, November 13, 1964, Alabama, U.S.A.

Civil Rights   **Milestones**

NOVEMBER 14

As early as 1934, Romare Bearden, a young artist and scholar, wrote, "Art should be understood and loved by the people. It should arouse and stimulate their creative impulses. . . . The best art has been produced in those countries where the public most loved and cherished it. . . . We need some standard of criticism then, not only to stimulate the artist, but also to raise the cultural level of the people."

Decades later, seventy-two years old and one of the twentieth century's most highly regarded and highly priced African-American artists, Bearden brought forth an exhibit of his watercolors, *Rituals of the Obeah*, on November 14, 1984.

To Romare Bearden, the poet Derek Walcott wrote in 1984:

> *How you have gotten it! It's all here, all right. . . .*
> *Dawn bleeds without a sound*
> *In all religions sacrifices matter,*
> *but to these rituals we ascribe malign reasons,*
> *and primitive dreams, but as was the lamb*
> *to Isaac, the ram to Abraham, all tribes have laid*
> *on the threshold of heaven, cocks, ewes, horned rams*
> *to the force that has made the fountain of the blood*
> *in which we are born, and the harvest of our mortal seasons,*
> *for a shadow comes towards us all, with its clean blade.*

Holding back the harvest a little longer, Bearden's watercolors aroused the spirits of the obeah, the Afri-Caribbean religion deeply grounded in ancient Ashanti roots. His paintings combined secrets of color and intonation only a Caribbean garden could know. His obeah was ceremonial, ritualistic, and reverent to the ancestors. Over the years he had spent much of his time in the countryside of the Caribbean islands, where the people had come to love him. At the time of his death he was collaborating with Harry Henderson on the definitive *History of African-American Artists: From 1792 to the Present*, resurrecting the riches of countless other harvest seasons.

Wednesday, November 14, 1984, New York, U.S.A.

Art   **Rituals**

NOVEMBER 15

Some 3,500 years ago, 150 years before the birth of King Tut (see November 29), Hatshepsitou lived and ruled in ancient Egypt, the first known ruling queen and the first to have openly challenged notions of male supremacy. Hatshepsitou was first named co-leader by her father, Thotmes I, when paralysis hampered his ability to rule. While he had two sons, he recognized in his daughter not only her loyalty but also her leadership abilities.

In addition to the performance of her duties as regent, she won the hearts of her people with two obelisks with dazzling peaks of silver and gold in which she had these words engraved:

> O ye people, who shall see my monument in the ages to come, beware of saying, "I know not, I know not why this was made and a mountain fashioned entirely from gold." These two obelisks My Majesty hath wrought that my name may abide, enduring in this temple forever and ever.

Still the men around her railed and tried to unseat her. After years of dissent, she finally found a solution to the problem: she declared herself a man! She wore men's clothing, changed her name from Hatshepsitou to Hatshepsut, declared herself of virgin birth, said that while Thotmes was thought to have been her father, her real father was the Great God, Amen Ra himself, who appeared to her mother "in a flood of light and perfume." From then on all portraits of her are those of a man, and the birth scene depicted in her tomb is that of her as a boy child. And as she then wrote of herself, "she is living Ra, eternally. He hath selected her for protecting Egypt, for rousing bravery among men. . . . I rule over this land like the son of Isis; I am mighty like the son of Nu. I shall forever be like the stars which changeth not." As was the custom, she began preparing her burial tomb, which she located not with Egypt's queens but in the Valley of Kings—an end that Hatshepsitou/Hatshepsut did not reach until she had ruled Egypt for a total of thirty-three years!

1500 B.C., Egypt

Women   **Pragmatism**

NOVEMBER 16

Nancy Gardner Prince wrote, "I left America, November 16th, 1840, in the ship *Scion, Captain Mansfield*, bound for Jamaica, freighted with ice and machinery for the silk factory. There were on board a number of handicraftsmen and other passengers. We sailed on Monday afternoon, from Charlestown, Massachusetts. It rained continually until Saturday."

In short, nothing happened on November 16, 1840. This fact has been preserved in book form 160 years later because the writer of the narrative was an African-American woman. She was married to Nero Prince, a cofounder with Prince Hall of the first African-American order of Freemasons (see May 6) and one of only twenty Black members of the Russian court in two hundred years. They met and married in Boston in February 1824. Two months later they returned to Russia where they lived for the next nine years until the climate forced her return to America in 1833. In 1840, widowed, ill, and sicker still of racism, she greeted news of emancipation throughout the West Indies in August 1838 with these thoughts: "My mind was bent upon going to Jamaica. A field of usefulness [as a teacher and missionary] seemed spread out before me."

In the perspective on African-American life shaped by a history burdened with adversity, there is a tendency for distortion to trade places with normalcy. The distorted condition of American slavery, so fundamentally unnatural to nature's plan that it required extreme levels of torture to sustain it, forms our view of the everyday normal Black life. The normal order of things, in which babies are born to mothers and fathers, families live as a unit, and people go about their daily lives and loves, is somehow projected as the distorted life of an exceptional few. And so it is with our perspective refreshed and righted that we recall this day and its legacy as a beacon of *normalcy* for African-Americans. On November 16, 1840, nothing happened, and Nancy Gardner Prince lived to write about it in her book, *A Black Woman's Odyssey Through Russia and Jamaica.*

Monday, November 16, 1840, U.S.A.–Jamaica–Russia
Adventure   **Self-Determination**

NOVEMBER 17

There is a mystery about the man who may have been the first and only person of African descent in Idaho for much of his life. Today, a simple marker in the Oakley, Idaho, pioneer cemetery tells of his death: "Gobo Fango, Died Feb. 10, 1886. Aged 30." But what of his life?

At some unknown date in 1856, perhaps this one, Gobo Fango was born in South or West Africa, depending on the source. Before the age of five, he was orphaned, or captured, and placed in the care of Mormon missionaries. In 1861, when that family returned to the United States, he was smuggled into the country between the mother's skirt folds and her apron. It was a dangerous time for a Black child in those days. One group wanted to capture him under anti–slave trade laws, while others were anxious to kidnap him into slavery as a rare, prized commodity. Crossing the country by wagon train, he was further endangered by Confederate soldiers searching for escaped slaves. When the family arrived in Utah, he was treated with the indifference reserved for the enslaved. Forced to sleep in an unheated barn on cold winter nights, he suffered frostbite in his feet and hobbled for the rest of his life. As a young man, he worked as a sheepherder. Then one night in 1886, while he was on watch, the growing dispute over grazing rights between the area's sheep men and cattlemen escalated into the "war" that claimed Gobo Fango's life. A man named Bedky rode into camp that night pretending to be his friend, and shot him. Mortally wounded, Fango crawled miles unaided until he reached the home of a friend. There, it is said, just before he died he wrote a will with a twig and his own blood leaving his $500 estate to charity, less the cost of a marker for his grave.

What was the measure of Gobo Fango's lonely life? Even those closest to him didn't note its details. And perhaps that is the miracle of it all: an innocent life, alone from infancy and mired in other people's wars and troubles, still left this world determined to leave his mark.

Sunday, November 17, 1861, Idaho, U.S.A.

Social History   Identity

NOVEMBER 18

When 1,800 delegates and nearly 18,000 observers and foreign guests assembled in Houston, Texas, on November 18, 1977, for the three-day National Women's Political Conference, the American women's movement came of age—in large measure because women of color had vowed, as one conferee put it, to "keep the proceedings honest!"

Financed with a $5 million congressional allocation, the task of the NWPC was to present recommendations to President Jimmy Carter for use in formulating new programs to be submitted to Congress. In a movement dominated by white middle-class women, the original platform negated crucial concerns for women of color. No mention of the assault on affirmative action appeared in the education plank. Minority interests were marginalized in programs (such as the Small Business Administration) enacted for their benefit. Forewarned, Black women came armed with an eighteen-page Black Women's Action Plan. From this base a coalition was built with other women of color: the United Minority Caucus.

The caucus's plank would have to be brought up for vote from the floor. In a brilliant strategy, word went out: "Watch Maxine Waters [then a California assemblywoman]; wherever she runs, rush the other minority plank speakers up behind her." Waters ran the length of the hall to microphone number four and was recognized. "Minority women share with all women the experience of sexism as a barrier to their full rights," she began, and deferred to the caucus member behind her. "Madam Chair, for Hispanic women," and this member deferred to a well-crooned alto: "Madam Chair, I rise on behalf of the Black Women's Caucus of the National Women's Political Conference." When the convention recognized the voice of Coretta Scott King (Dr. King's widow), it was stunned into listening to her every word. Then the crowd went wild, passing the full caucus plank by acclamation and leading the first major coalition of women across racial lines in American political history.

Friday, November 18, 1977, Texas, U.S.A.

Events   Leadership

NOVEMBER 19

When educators gathered in Chicago on November 19, 1992, for the annual National Association of Black School Educators (NABSE) convention, their keynoter, Dr. Adelaide Louvenia Hines Sanford, was expected to stir the group to action. What wasn't expected was that this New York State regent's speech, "Educational Excellence: Revisited and Reclaimed," would bring them to tears.

As she reminded her audience, the scholars of ancient Africa were the priests. "Educational excellence is part of a totality that includes cultural excellence—the temples, pyramids, sacred writings. For people of African ancestry there can be no educational excellence that is separated from cultural excellence." To educate those who have been so miseducated means recognizing potential "in spite of the lack of observable achievement." She went on:

> Now, in reality I don't know my name. I don't know the name that my ancestors would have given me. I can never go home, for I don't know where home is. I can never go to the town or village that is home. . . . I look at you and I wonder, was it your mother who was separated from my grandmother on the shores of West Africa?. . .
>
> But I am not beaten or broken by that. Rather I seek to make all of us into the perfect formation of the flying geese. Always going in the same direction, but willing to substitute the leader. Looking for a leader who breaks the current of air so that it doesn't beat heavily on the followers behind. And when that leader becomes fatigued, that leader flies to the end, but the formation doesn't change. The next leader comes up; it's his turn to lead and my turn to follow. And I would say to you that though the leader changes and the follower changes, the formation and the direction must never change.

With that, Dr. Hines guided her audience of educators—and all who share and understand a uniquely African-American human bond—back on course.

Thursday, November 19, 1992, Illinois, U.S.A.

Education   **Purpose**

NOVEMBER 20

Sixty years after the first land-grant colleges opened their doors, the concerns of school administrators matured as a result of a job well done. The original need to educate ex-slaves in basic skills had grown into mature institutions from which graduated a majority of the nation's Black college population. Having passed a succession of important hurdles, the historically Black colleges now faced the challenge of building scholarly library collections. On November 20, 1930, Fisk University played host to the three-day Negro Library Conference.

Although Hampton Institute had convened a conference of Black librarians in March 1927, only two of the presenters in the group assembled were Black; all the rest were white. Clearly the first order of business for the association was to attract more Blacks to the profession. The next order of business had to be the tackling of another critical issue: the lack of accessibility of library facilities for the general Black community at a time when Jim Crow law barred Black use of public libraries. The next agenda point was Fisk's own collection. Its new library had opened just six weeks earlier, showcasing Aaron Douglas's inspiring murals, and now Fisk president Charles S. Johnson wanted to expand the collection to equal its surroundings in quality. One month after the conference, one special attendee was approached and appointed curator, Arturo A. Schomburg—the noted bibliophile whose own personal collection was acquired by New York City in 1927.

Under Schomburg's tutelage, Fisk identified its mission and made the first strides in the acquisition of a globally based rare-book archive of African-American history.

Thursday, November 20, 1930, Virginia, U.S.A.

Libraries   **Continuity**

NOVEMBER 21

It is November 1840, the start of winter's chill; soon the first snow of the season will fall. Coming through the woods this winter's night, a woman's voice sings at the edge of the quarter, "When that old chariot comes, who's going with me?" And in the distance, another voice answers, "When that old chariot comes, I'm going with you!" It's a sign, and the woman singing is "Moses" herself, Harriet Tubman, recruiting passengers for the next trip headed up the line. The chariot will roll just before the first Saturday night storm, when the snow will cover the tracks of escaping slaves.

Somewhere in the dark a stranger says, "You travel late, neighbor." Another answers, "It's a dark night. Shall I bring a lantern?" "Don't bother, the North Star is bright." For freedom-bound slaves, the North Star was a code word and a guide.

When you run, follow nature's laws:

The handle of the Big Dipper points a heavenly route to the North Star.

On dark, cloudy nights, feel the trees for moss, which grows on the cooler, shadier, north side of the bark.

For shelter, nature provides caves, the undersides of cliffs, huge rocks, felled logs covered with brush.

Bent branches on your way, beware. The softer the exposed bark, the more recent the bend. Tread lightly, someone else is near.

Thunder is nature's trumpet, a sign of oncoming rain that can wash away your footprints of escape.

As a child, Harriet Tubman noticed that brooks near the Maryland plantation on which she grew up had a northward current. This knowledge aided her escape as an adult and was just one of the lessons she and others used for survival in helping thousands to freedom. When slave owners laughed at "superstitious" slaves, they did not realize that some of their best "jokes" came from those bound for freedom via their wits, knowledge of the laws of nature, and the codes of the Underground Railroad.

November 1840, Maryland, U.S.A.

Freedom   **Choices**

NOVEMBER 22

On November 22, 1987, the *Oracle of Truth* was dedicated at Mount Zion Baptist Church in Seattle, Washington—one of the more unusual sculptures by a most unusual sculptor, James Washington. A huge boulder perched at the church entrance, "the top of which is shaped into a large, fuzzy-coated, supine lamb whose body includes many ancient symbols," as described by Bearden and Henderson in their *History of African-American Artists*.

One of the things we most take for granted in this world is the medium in which Washington works—stone. But James Washington knows that from stone comes the wisdom of the ages. He must not impose his vision on the stone; his role is to bring from its texture and spirit the message it chooses to evoke. And as the prophetically titled *Oracle of Truth* was dedicated, the name seemed as much a measure of the work as the man.

At the ceremony that had attracted the prominent figures of the Northwest region, all eager to have their pictures taken with the artist and his work, Washington was concerned that the excitement was obscuring the work's main function: to make the ancient symbols speak to children. "Let the children come up here. It's for the children," Washington commanded. "The primary concern of the home, church, and the school should be to help each child find him or herself. . . . Our young people are trapped in this drug-infested society, and just to tell them to say 'No' to drug pushers is an uncouth cop-out."

The words were classic James Washington, the man who had written that children who are not stimulated to unleash their creativity early in life are not likely to do so as adults. "What I am trying to say with my sculptures is that each one of us has something within us waiting to be released, and the something is spiritual, the spirit being the universality of life itself." An oracle, indeed.

Sunday, November 22, 1987, Washington, U.S.A.

Art   **Substance**

NOVEMBER 23

From the island they call the "Gray Whale" comes the story of its first Black whaling captain and its premier African-American family. On November 23, 1751, a Nantucket, Massachusetts, slave owner wrote this declaration: "Boston, a Negro Man lately my servant is a free man & not a slave but hath liberty to trade & trafick with anybody & to go where he pleaseth." The owner had freed husband and wife, Absalom and Maria Boston, but their six children were to remain enslaved "until they arrive to twenty Eight years of age." Because of the stipulation of the children's gradual man-umission, we know their names and dates of birth.

Because the Quaker religion predominated on Nantucket, the island was openly opposed to slavery. The Quakers had held the historic "Germantown Protest" of 1688 in Pennsylvania by which they became the first organized reli-gion to formally denounce slavery. That not only helped free the Boston family; it also attracted a small Black community to the island where it began to grow and flourish.

Sprinkled about the island of Nantucket is the history of this early free Black community in America. The early-nineteenth-century African Free School still stands, and a trip to the island's Historical Society brings one face-to-face with the por-traits of the island's distinguished whaling captains. Among them is a third-generation member of the Boston family. From this island launch, Absalom F. Boston became the first Black whaling captain in 1822. His ship, the *Industry*, was manned entirely by Black officers and crew.

From that first document, the story of an early Black com-munity begins to emerge, putting a personal face on the social history of African-Americans. As each of us go about our daily lives, our family histories provide important links in the chain of life for our descendants. We are each of us, after all, their ancestors.

Tuesday, November 23, 1751, Massachusetts, U.S.A.
Social History   **Principles**

NOVEMBER 24

As handbills were passed out to teachers on November 24, 1841, the critical item at the top of their agenda the next day was this:

Brethren come! The cause of Education calls loudly upon you to come. Hundreds of children that are now shut out from the blessings of Education, call loudly upon you to come. If there was ever a time that called for united action, it is now. If there was ever a time for colored freemen to show their love of liberty, their hatred of ignorance, and determination to be free and enlightened, it is now!

As early in our history as 1841, the Association of Colored Teachers existed in New York. It had its own publication, *The New York Journal of Education and Weekly Messenger*, and meetings like the one being announced in the handbill were regularly held to protect their interests as professionals, to uphold the interests of the Black child, and to reunite with a community of adults for the purpose of guaranteeing Black children a quality education.

The handbill went on:

To the Colored Freemen of Long Island, for a convention to be held at Jamaica, Queen's County, November 25th, 1841 at 10 o'clock A.M. for devising means more effectually to advance the cause of education and temperance, and also for cooperating with our disfranchised brethren throughout the State in petitioning for the right of suffrage. . . . Let a general rally be made, and let there be a delegate from every town and village, and from every society [of Long] Island. Remember that the first county convention held in this State was held on the Island. . . . Let none refuse but those who are enemies of the prosperity and happiness of their people.

As teachers gather under the auspices of similar associations today, they are carrying on the tradition of a proud heritage and acknowledging a vital truth: it takes a whole village to raise a child.

Wednesday, November 24, 1841, New York, U.S.A.

Education   **Initiative**

NOVEMBER 25

An advertisement in the *New Orleans Bee* of November 25, 1843, announced, "J. Lion is prepared to take likenesses by the Daguerreotype or Lithographic process, at his rooms on St. Charles Street. Mr. Lion is an artist of superior merit."

Listed in the city directory of New Orleans for 1851 as Jules Lion, "f.m.c.," Lion was a free man of color, and it was he who introduced the daguerreotype, the earliest photographic ancestor, to New Orleans. To see mid-nineteenth-century Louisiana photographically unfold before us is to owe a great deal of thanks to Jules Lion. With his daguerreotypes, Lion preserved individual portraits, as well as such classic building and street scenes as his "The Cathedral, New Orleans" (1842) and "View of Canal Street" (1846).

As an "artist of superior merit," Lion was hardly immodest. The son of an African-American mother and white father who openly raised him, he was educated in Paris where Paris salon catalogs of the 1830s list his works among those exhibited and mention the fact that he received "honorable mention" for his lithograph "Affût aux Canards." And it is with his later pastel masterpiece, *Ashur Moses Nathan and Son*, that he stopped the show at the Metropolitan Museum exhibit *Selections of Nineteenth-Century Art* in 1976, 130 years after the work was painted. For there on canvas was the figure of the obviously loving Ashur Nathan and his biracial son.

Whether exacting his portraits by daguerreotype, oil, or pastels, Lion's medium was the truth of mid-nineteenth-century American life.

Saturday, November 25, 1843, Louisiana, U.S.A.

Art   **Truths**

NOVEMBER 26

Dr. King often remarked, "Eleven o'clock Sunday morning is the most segregated hour in America." Enduring vehement segregation in white churches, separation became a trend whose time had come with one Sunday morning in November 1786. As Richard Allen, first bishop of the AME Church, later recalled, Philadelphia's free Blacks set the trend toward independent worship with this incident:

> When the colored people began to get too numerous in attending the church . . . the sexton stood at the door . . . and told us to go in the gallery. We had not been long upon our knees before I heard considerable scuffling and low talking. I raised my head up and saw one of the trustees having hold of the Reverend Absalom Jones, pulling him off of his knees, and saying, "You must get up—you must not kneel here." Mr. Jones replied, "Wait until prayer is over." [The trustee said,] "No, you must get up now, or I will call for aid and force you away." Mr. Jones said, "Wait until prayer is over, and I will get up and trouble you no more." With that . . . one of the other trustees went to pull him up. By this time prayer was over, and we all went out of the church in a body, and they were no more plagued with us in the church.

And indeed, these African-American congregants never came back. Within months, the Free African Society of Philadelphia had been formed, leading to the creation of a new denomination, the African Methodist Episcopal Church. And by 1794, Richard Allen had saved enough to buy the property on which his church, Mother Bethel AME Church, still stands—the oldest continuously Black-owned property in America.

Sunday, November 26, 1786, Pennsylvania, U.S.A.
Religion   **Foundations**

NOVEMBER 27

On November 27, 1841, nearly three years after the ordeal of their capture began, the thirty-seven surviving heroes of the Amistad Mutiny (see August 24) were finally at sea, sailing their way back home.

From the time they reached the coast of Long Island in June 1839, they were considered "murderers and pirates" for denying their captors' right to sell them into slavery. For the next eighteen months, they were imprisoned while former president John Quincy Adams successfully defended their case for freedom before the Supreme Court. Finally, on March 12, 1841, they were freed. But they were still foreigners in a hostile land with no means of support or way to return home. For the next eight months, they toured and lectured throughout the North to raise funds for the trip home. Finally, after years of incidents that continually threatened their lives, a ceremony was held for them in Farmington to which guests came from towns throughout the Northeast. Prayers were offered and a final collection yielded $1,300 in pledges.

On November 27, 1941, the Amistad mutineers departed the United States at last on a ship chartered for their fifty-two-day voyage home. As they sailed, their true identity reemerged: they were the people of Mendi. Arriving in Freetown, West Africa, in January 1842, however, the heroes' welcome that they were certainly due was not to be theirs. Their villages had been so decimated by slave traders that most of their families had been captured and sold into slavery throughout the United States. Only their own daring mutiny had saved them from a shared fate. In the United States, their fight laid the legal ground for the abolition of slavery. Instead, the country chose to fight a war that the Amistad mutineers had long before won.

Saturday, November 27, 1841, U.S.A.–Sierra Leone
Maritime History   **Determination**

NOVEMBER 28

"Paul Robeson is a football genius," exclaimed the *New York Herald* headline on November 28, 1917. It was early testimony to the qualities of a young man who would excel in sports, law, film, theater, music, the cause of human rights, and in the defense of his own rights during an infamous encounter with the House Un-American Activities Committee (see June 12).

At seventeen Paul Robeson scored the highest marks ever attained on New Jersey statewide high school exams. That credit earned him an academic scholarship to Rutgers in the fall of 1915. Within weeks he made varsity as a substitute tackle. By November 20, he was starting at right guard. By his sophomore year, he had grown to six feet one inch tall, weighed 210 pounds, and—as his mightiest foes on and off the field soon found—there was no stopping him.

Along the way to world renown, he was hardly spared racist hurdles. While at Rutgers, he was sidelined for the benefit of white players refusing to engage in a fair contest with Blacks, but this only put Robeson on the bench . . . not out of the game. It helped build the character of a man who, as *Ebony* publisher John H. Johnson later recalled, refused to go anywhere or do anything as a celebrity that he could not go to or do as a Black man.

At the height of his career, renowned in film, theater, and on the concert stage, Robeson sacrificed the applause for justice. He paid dearly for his convictions; so did his audiences. He lost income and time; we lost his talents as an artist. As in his student years, he was sidelined by the 1950s political witch-hunt known as McCarthyism. Officially "blacklisted" at home and unable to work, the government seized his passport, denying him the possibility of seeking work abroad. Benched but hardly out of the game, Robeson "appeared" at one foreign concert by phone. To the end, as a world-class performer on history's stage, Robeson remained a genius and a giant with few peers.

Wednesday, November 28, 1917, New Jersey, U.S.A.

Heroes   **Integrity**

NOVEMBER 29

By a strange quirk of history, on November 29, 1922, one of Egypt's least known kings became one of its most famous. On that day, eight years of research by a one-hundred-member team yielded the twentieth century's most important archaeological find. There, at the base of sixteen newly uncovered steps, was a sealed doorway leading to a thirty-foot passageway behind which another sealed doorway bore the name of its royal occupant in ancient calligraphy: Tutankhamen, Egypt's boy-king. Less than twenty years old when he died, "King Tut" had ruled for less than a decade. With his premature death, there had been no time to prepare his tomb in his lifetime as would have been the case for a longer-reigning ruler. King Tut's tomb was, therefore, carved out beneath the more elaborate tomb of Ramses II. Tutankhamen's tomb had been hidden, undisturbed since his death and the sealing of the tomb 3,250 years earlier.

"With trembling hands," archaeologist Howard Carter wrote, "I inserted the candle and peered in. . . . I could see nothing, the hot air escaping from the chamber causing the candle flame to flicker, but presently as my eyes grew accustomed to the light, details of the room emerged slowly from the mist, strange animals, statues, and gold—everywhere the glint of gold."

In the four-room burial chamber were the treasures of a lifetime. A sculpture of the king's head as a boy, a folding bed, his boomerang, a floral bouquet, his state chariot covered in gold and semiprecious stones, his boat—a total of over seven hundred separate objects in all. And at the back of the formal burial chamber was King Tut himself—his masked and mummified body wrapped in nineteen layers of linen in its three-layered coffin, stone sarcophagus, and the outer gold and jeweled shrine covered with sacred texts from the *Book of the Dead* and the *Book of the Divine Cow*. Over the next ten years, this 3,250-year-old treasure trove would be meticulously preserved and moved to the National Museum in Cairo, providing blinding evidence of the amazing wealth that is our African legacy.

Wednesday, November 29, 1922, Egypt

Archaeology   **Knowledge**

NOVEMBER 30

When the Order of Saint Luke gathered for its testimonial for Maggie Lena Walker on November 30, 1924, it was a long-awaited chance to honor the life and work of the first African-American woman banker.

She was born in 1867, two years after the end of the Civil War, when newly free men and women were bonding into organizations that would help them survive the transition from slavery to freedom. Among those was the Grand United Order of Saint Luke. Founded in Baltimore by an ex-slave, Mary Prout, it aimed to meet the social, medical, and cooperative insurance needs of Black families. It was as a member of the order's Richmond, Virginia, hometown chapter that Maggie Walker, a married woman with three children and post–high school courses in accounting and salesmanship, took an eight-dollars-per-month job as executive secretary-treasurer in 1899. Shuttling between the order's branches in the new era of Jim Crow, she recognized the need for Black businesses to have their own cooperative ventures.

Under the umbrella of the order, she gradually tested the waters in insurance, banking, and a short-lived cooperative department store. At the time of her testimonial at Richmond's City Auditorium twenty-five years later, the order had grown to one hundred thousand members under her direction, owned a building then worth $100,000, had an emergency fund of $70,000, published a newspaper, *The Saint Luke Herald*, employed fifty-five clerks, 145 field workers, had 15,000 children enrolled in thrift clubs, and Maggie L. Walker was president of the Saint Luke Bank and Trust Company, which she had founded as a "penny savings bank."

In symbiotic support with her community, her work with the order exemplified the "do-for-self" businesses Blacks built from the ground up despite official antagonism. Significantly, her bank is still operating today as one of the biggest African-American banks, the Consolidated Bank and Trust Company.

Sunday, November 30, 1924, Virginia, U.S.A.

Business   **Attitude**

DECEMBER

Front page, *Frederick Douglass' Paper* (December 9, 1859). Reprinted courtesy of the author. For more information see October 16, December 2, December 3.

DECEMBER 1

On December 1, 1955, in a now-legendary moment, Rosa Parks refused to render her bus seat to racism and thus made a place for herself in history. As mythmakers tell it, her feet were tired that day, too tired to move. Every inch of Rosa Parks was tired that day, tired of Jim Crow laws conscripting her to life at the back of the bus. Her act moved her people to launch the Montgomery bus boycott, the city of Montgomery to end segregated bus travel, the Supreme Court to overturn long-standing laws upholding segregated interstate travel, and the nation to enact civil rights legislation outlawing segregation in all public accommodations (see December 20).

The bus driver on that day had previously insisted she get up for a white person and reboard at the rear of the bus, only to drive off leaving her in the street without refunding her fare. This time, however, Parks didn't move to the back, she simply slid over to make room. The driver barked a threat. She sat still. Police were called. She was arrested.

Rosa Parks had not planned her protest in advance. Nor was she the first to refuse and be arrested. What made her protest so moving was Parks herself—a quiet, dignified, disciplined forty-three-year-old warrior-woman. After bailing her out of jail, E. D. Nixon, a former NAACP chapter head, asked if she would agree to be a test case. Parks was a former NAACP youth organizer. Nixon was a man with an idea whose time had come, and the community swung into action in support. Women's Political Council leader Jo Ann Robinson (see May 21) stayed up all night churning out flyers, students passed out leaflets, ministers took to pulpits in support. And on Monday, December 5, as Mrs. Parks went to court, the Montgomery bus boycott became a historic reality. When it was done, Mrs. Parks had earned our respect and gratitude as the Mother of the Civil Rights Movement. (See June's lead photograph of Mrs. Parks at the 1968 Poor People's Solidarity March.)

Thursday, December 1, 1955, Alabama, U.S.A.

Desegregation   **Conscience**

DECEMBER 2

On December 2, 1859, six weeks after his heroic blow for abolition at Harper's Ferry, West Virginia, John Brown passed this note to a guard as he was led to a wagon bearing his empty coffin. "Charlestown, Va., 2d, December, 1859. I, John Brown, am now quite certain that the crimes of this guilty land: will never be purged away; but with Blood." To his surprise on this brilliant clear day, thousands of soldiers awaited his emergence from the jail. "I had no idea that Governor Wise considered my execution so important," Brown exclaimed. He was helped onto the carriage, seated on the empty coffin, driven to the scaffold, forced to wait over the trapdoor a full twelve minutes as the immense regiment positioned itself, and then he was hanged.

At a nearby hotel, his wife awaited the now-weighty coffin that would soon be on its way to their Adirondack mountain farm in upstate New York. As the train bearing the funeral cortege moved on, in towns along the entire length of the route, "solemn church bells rang out," wrote biographer Barrie Stavis. On the last leg of the trip, John Brown was given an honor guard at the Elizabethtown, New York, courthouse where he lay in state for the night. Then, on December 8, 1859, Brown was laid to rest, just as he had requested, in the shadow of a great granite rock on his family's farm in North Elba, New York. Orator and abolitionist Wendell Phillips delivered this eulogy:

"History will date Virginia Emancipation from Harper's Ferry. True, the slave is still there. . . . John Brown has loosened the roots of the slave system; it only breathes—it does not live—hereafter."

As Phillips predicted, less than two years would pass before the tempestuous "war for liberation," the Civil War. (For Frederick Douglass's headline of the execution, see December's lead illustration.)

Friday, December 2, 1859, West Virginia, U.S.A.

Heroes   **Commitment**

DECEMBER 3

On December 3, 1847, an escaped slave and self-taught man, Frederick Douglass, founded his own newspaper. Its title was offered as a beacon of hope to others. During his escape, its namesake had been his own guiding light, the *North Star*. Working with him as coeditor and copublisher was Dr. Martin R. Delany, a freeborn physician. As ardent abolitionist, Underground Railroad conductor, and Back-to-Africa crusader, Delany demonstrated his total commitment to heal all that ailed the wounded souls of Black folk.

The Liberator, founded by Douglass's mentor William Lloyd Garrison, had served well as an abolitionist newspaper, and for both Garrison and Douglass, publishing the *North Star* was more than competition; it was a rift between father and son. It was Garrison, a white abolitionist, who had helped launch Douglass's career as a lecturer. Because of Garrison, Douglass had achieved a notoriety that he might not have otherwise held. But it was because of Douglass that Garrison's work found credence and a tone of authenticity that it, too, might not otherwise have known. The rift that formed between Douglass and Garrison signaled the fundamental difference between the slave and the advocate for the slave; the difference between Black and white in America. It was time for Douglass and Garrison to grow separately. Both believed in the total abolition of slavery. But Garrison could afford to wait. Douglass could not.

"[Our] Anti-Slavery Journal has resulted . . . from the sincere and settled conviction that such a Journal, if conducted with only moderate skill and ability, would do a most important and indispensable work, which it would be wholly impossible for our white friends to do for us." So began a new publishing venture and a new era in the cause of African-American liberation. Over the next years, the paper's office was threatened and even burned out. Like its founders, it returned to fight again, and from 1851 to 1860 it survived as *Frederick Douglass' Paper* (see December's lead illustration).

Friday, December 3, 1847, New York, U.S.A.

Journalism   **Freedom**

DECEMBER 4

For the dance season of 1987, the newest thing on the scene was the work of seventy-eight-year-old dancer-choreographer-anthropologist Katherine Dunham. In a series of fourteen reconstructed works performed across two evenings, starting on December 4, 1987, Alvin Ailey's American Dance Theater returned to its spiritual, cultural, and intellectual roots with *The Magic of Katherine Dunham*.

"I have a strong sense of wanting to be original," Dunham had told the dancers as rehearsals began. It was an ironic comment from one so steeped in legacy. Yet, true to her word, audiences would be transported across the landscape of her creative vision like trailblazers to a new frontier. Among the milestones would be "Shango," evoking the ancient rites of *Vaudoisie* (voodoo); "Choros," with its variations on a nineteenth-century Brazilian quadrille; "Cakewalk," based on the high-strutting competitions from the turn of the century; "Field Hands"; "Plantation Dances"; and so much more.

There would be long-lasting lessons for the dancers. "Don't work to get outside muscles. Work to have the strength come from within so that even in a simple thing like lifting your arms you will see strength." And most of all there would be an exuberance only those who have seen as much through times as good and bad as Ms. Dunham could truly know.

With *The Magic of Katherine Dunham* the Ailey company was revisiting work that had captivated audiences of the 1940s and 1950s and that was deeply steeped in the diaspora. But Ailey was also taking a first step in tapping into and exhibiting treasures from a rediscovered gold mine.

Friday, December 4, 1987, New York, Diaspora–U.S.A.
Dance   **Passion**

DECEMBER 5

Mary McLeod Bethune knew the value of organization and the power of organizations. She knew how to push and pull an idea and a group of people through. What she did not know was why anyone would need another factionalized group of women, no matter how energetic. What Blacks needed during the depths of the Depression was clout, and that meant numbers.

On December 5, 1935, the woman who had been saying that the last thing anyone needed was another organization founded a new organization, but one with a difference. The National Council of Negro Women (NCNW) was to be an organization of member organizations. As its president and primary lobbyist, Bethune represented a coordinated roster of twenty-two member organizations and eight hundred thousand women.

It was a vision she had actually had as president of the National Association of Colored Women (NACW), which had dedicated its new Washington, D.C., headquarters seven years earlier. But the membership of that organization seemed more interested in decentralized regional activities. When she and the NACW no longer shared the same vision, Bethune created the NCNW. The new organization gave its newly enfranchised female membership political clout.

Even in the midst of the Depression—even in a Jim Crow era—her votes may not have been able to elect the group's own slate of candidates, but they could certainly help those platforms in need of support. Bethune's strategy was an important step toward Black political visibility.

Thursday, December 5, 1935, Washington, D.C., U.S.A.

Organizations   **Wisdom**

DECEMBER 6

When people protest about the number of books and magazine articles written promoting a racist agenda, the response of the publishers has always been that they are in the business of making money. As such, it is particularly refreshing to find that the publisher of *The Sporting News* was willing to risk that very same business objective on a matter of principle. The following excerpt on baseball was published on December 6, 1923:

> It matters not what branch of mankind the player sprang from with the fan, if he can deliver the goods. The Mick, the Sheeney, the Wop, the Dutch, and the Chink, the Cuban, the Indian, the Jap, or the so-called Anglo-Saxon—his "nationality" is never a matter of moment if he can pitch, or hit, or field. In organized baseball there has been no distinction raised—except tacit understanding that a player of Ethiopian descent is ineligible—the wisdom of which we will not discuss except to say by such rule some of the greatest players the game has ever known have been denied their opportnity.

As young men and women struggle with such imaginary opponents as "proving one's manhood," "being a real woman," and "patience," it is helpful to note the little known "glory days" like this one in 1925. With Black college enrollment at a record high, the 1920s were the "Golden Decade of Sports," and in Black college baseball, 1925 was a pretty good year. The traditional season high point, the Easter Monday game, saw Wilberforce and Livingstone set the diamond aglitter as the game set an all-time college baseball attendance record of ten thousand!

Within weeks of that, another record was set on the field as the pure contest of sport pitted racial pride against international affairs. The new team in town had just beaten Harvard, Yale, and Princeton. Now it was Howard University's turn to meet the touring squad of Japan's Meiji University. With the pride of U.S. college baseball resting on Howard's shoulders, in ten tense innings, Howard beat Meiji, 4–3.

These are the moments and inspirations worth remembering and acting upon.

Thursday, December 6, 1923, U.S.A.

Sports/Journalism　　　　　　　　　　　　　　　　　　**Truth**

DECEMBER 7

Announcing the 1993 Nobel Prize for literature, the Swedish Academy named author Toni Morrison, "a literary artist of the first rank.... She delves into the language itself, a language she wants to liberate from the fetters of race. And she addresses us with the luster of poetry." She was the first Black woman so honored in almost a century of Nobel laureates.

In twenty-four years, Morrison had given the world six extraordinary novels alive with the lifeblood of African-American enslavement and segregation. In resurrecting the African concept that "it takes a whole village to raise a child," she had achieved the artist's most difficult task: to cause readers to reread themselves. Now, she was taking her place in the literary pantheon with her "village" in clear sight. "I was thrilled that my mother is still alive and can share this with me," said Morrison. "I can claim representation in so many areas. I'm a Midwesterner, and everyone in Ohio is excited. I'm also a New Yorker, and a New Jerseyan, and an American, plus I'm an African-American, and a woman.... I'd like to think of the prize being distributed to these regions and nations and races."

On December 7, 1993, Toni Morrison mesmerized the international audience of her acceptance speech with a parable on the vitality and vulnerability of language. A wise elder is approached by village children to tell them if a bird they hold is alive or dead. She is blind and cannot see it. She does not know if they are innocently seeking a way to determine the bird's condition or if they are mocking her. "It's in your hands," she says. In Morrison's parable, the bird is language. It is the acts, ideas, and power that language represents. She is wary of those who would endanger us with coded language meant to manipulate and misinform. What we do with our language is in all of our hands. And with her metaphor of the bird, Toni Morrison left us to ponder the fate and scope of so many things that are, indeed, in our hands.

Tuesday, December 7, 1993, Sweden–U.S.A.

Literature   **Excellence**

DECEMBER 8

For three days in New York City, beginning on December 8, 1991, the mavens of African-American popular culture gathered for a symposium entitled "Discussions in Contemporary Culture," cosponsored by the Studio Museum in Harlem and Dia Center for the Arts in SoHo in New York. The conference was conceived by writer Michele Wallace to explore the growing politicization of popular culture, to explore the nature of Black community participation in contemporary culture, and to critique contemporary expressions of that culture.

Among the participants were Houston A. Baker, Jr., Angela Davis, Henry Louis Gates, Jr., bell hooks, Julianne Malveaux, Manning Marable, Cornel West, and Sherley Anne Williams. In five seminars, they presented papers on such topics as "Gender, Sexuality, and Black Images in Popular Culture," "The Urban Context," "The Production of Black Popular Culture," and, taking a cue from the theme of Spike Lee's then-recent film, "Do the Right Thing: Postnationalism and Essentialism."

The conference was stimulating enough, as can be seen in the book *Black Popular Culture*, in which the papers and transcripts of the panel discussions were published. But with such events one always wonders: where do we go from here? With this event, the question was answered distinctively. For this was one of the few documented occasions when the experts on Black people were Black people themselves. They had come with experiences born of the diaspora. And their range and indeed their "multiple personalities" had been framed by their multidimensional and multi-Black-cultural experiences. More to the point, because they were coming from so many different places, their forum—which was both scholarly and street-wise—was singularly authoritative in its reflection of the contemporary scene.

Sunday, December 8, 1991, Diaspora–New York, U.S.A.
Culture   **Pan-AfricanWorld**

DECEMBER 9

During his tenure as the first African-American governor, P. B. S. Pinchback didn't leave much of a record — because he didn't have much time to be governor! Only thirty-five days: from December 9, 1872, to January 13, 1873.

In the rollicking era of Reconstruction, it was probably safest for him not to try to hold his seat as white politicians struck terror into southern whites with threats of Black domination and as one by one, every Black elected official was removed from office by fraud, terror, or political maneuvering.

Such was the case with Pinchback. As a prominent publisher of the *New Orleans Louisianian,* his journalistic platform provided him a degree of visibility. In 1871, he was elected president pro tempore of the state senate. When the lieutenant governor died, by constitutional order of succession he filled the post. And when the governor was suspended under threat of impeachment a year later, Pinchback became acting governor. While he had support for his candidacy, it was considered "best" that he make a deal to withdraw gracefully. His opponent would be named, and Pinchback would be appointed to a six-year term in the U.S. Senate instead. Within a short time, even this arrangement was contested, and Pinchback was denied the promised Senate seat. But he was, at least, voted the equivalent of his salary for the equivalent period of time.

Sardonically, one would like to say thank heaven for Virginia's former governor Douglas Wilder! But the fact that in two hundred–plus years of American history there have been only three Blacks elected to statewide office — one governor and two senators — is no laughing matter.

Monday, December 9, 1872, Louisiana, U.S.A.

Reconstruction   **Injustice**

DECEMBER 10

December 10: Among the Nobel Peace Prize laureates of African birth or descent honored on or around this day—Chief Albert Luthuli (1960), Dr. Martin Luther King, Jr. (1964), Bishop Desmond Tutu (1984), South African president Nelson Mandela (1993)—the least known and the first was Ralph Bunche on December 10, 1950. As undersecretary to the United Nations, he was awarded the prize in 1950 for his work in negotiating the Middle East crisis of 1949.

The ongoing hostilities over the partitioning of the Middle East to found Israel as a modern-day state and the assassination of its lead mediator severely tested the United Nations and Dr. Bunche himself. Bunche faced the possibility of renewed war in the midst of a fragile cease-fire. Through six weeks of skillful and intensive negotiations, Bunche structured the "Four Armistice Agreement" strategy for which he was honored with the Nobel Prize. Through that agreement, all immediate violence ceased.

Dr. Bunche joined the U.N. at its inception in 1947, and his tenure preceded the success of the independence movement on the African continent. As a result, second only to Ethiopia's emperor Haile Selassie, he was the most prominent African or African-American of his day in international affairs. And of all the members of the United Nations' international diplomatic corps, as undersecretary general, Ralph Bunche was the highest-ranking American.

Sunday, December 10, 1950, Norway
International Affairs   **Presence**

DECEMBER 11

On December 11, 1981, as the dismantling of affirmative action began, historian Nell Irvin Painter's confession in the *New York Times* spread nationwide. "Affirmative action helped me," she divulged. It was a reckless thing to do, with the notion of "reverse racism" in its infancy.

In 1965, the first southern president since Reconstruction, Lyndon B. Johnson, issued Executive Order No. 11246. Under that directive, the federal government prioritized an end to discrimination. Government contractors were required to take "affirmative action" to fill job opportunities without regard to race or sex. It took into account these fairly consistent U.S. demographics:

Whites: 70 percent (males = 34 percent; females = 36 percent)
Blacks and other ethnic groups: 30 percent

"Affirmative action" set minimums or "quotas" at roughly 10 percent of all hiring. In other words, the 66 percent of the nation that is female and people of color were entitled to 10 percent of the opportunity; 34 percent, white males, retained 90 percent. Amazingly, 90 percent was not good enough.

Attempts to dismantle affirmative action began as soon as its ink was dry. The 1978 Supreme Court *Bakke* decision held that affirmative action quotas had squeezed out a white male. Soon, 90 percent was being projected as unfair to "qualified" applicants. Affirmative action became the "stigma" women and people of color had to overcome. The new "victims" were projected as white males denied their place in a tightening job market. Said Dr. Painter, with historical perspective on her side, "Without affirmative action, it never would have occurred to any large white research university to consider me for professional employment, despite my [Harvard] degree, languages, publications, charm, grace, despite my qualifications. I wish I could take [naysayers] back to the early sixties and let them see that they're reciting the same old white-male-superiority line, fixed up to fit conditions that include a policy called affirmative action."

Friday, December 11, 1981, North Carolina, U.S.A.

Labor   **Opportunity**

DECEMBER 12

After a three-year legal battle, the case of *Missouri ex rel. Gaines v. Canada, Registrar of the University of Missouri,* finally reached the Supreme Court in October 1938.

Lloyd Gaines, a Black student, was a graduate of Lincoln University whose undergraduate academic career fully qualified him for admission to the State University of Missouri School of Law as a state resident. He was specifically denied admission, however, on the grounds that his acceptance would be "contrary to the constitution, laws and public policy of the State to admit a Negro as a student in the University of Missouri." The goal of Gaines's soon-to-be-filed NAACP-sponsored lawsuit was certainly total desegregation. But his denial of admission was even a violation of the laws of segregation that decreed "separate but equal" facilities. Because the state of Missouri had no Black law school, the policy had usually been to send the student to an out-of-state school at state expense.

The state court upheld a finding that Gaines could attend law school out-of-state because such neighboring states as Illinois, Iowa, Kansas, and Nebraska did admit Blacks. Gaines's lawyers countered that the nearby states did not provide an education on in-state Missouri law. That factor, they argued, would have denied Gaines the opportunity to study specific Missouri case law, prevented him from observing the state courts in which he would be practicing, and denied him the prestige of the school most highly regarded by his potential clients.

Hearing all the arguments presented, the Supreme Court came down on the side of common sense. The very fact that a white student would be admitted to a state school while a Black student whose taxes equally subsidized operation of the school was denied was—on its face—unequal. On December 12, 1938, the decision of the state superior court was overturned. Lloyd Gaines had won.

Sadly, Gaines won a victory for every Black student but himself. Following the decision, Gaines disappeared and was never located.

Monday, December 12, 1938, Missouri, U.S.A.

Education   **Precedents**

DECEMBER 13

To witness the powerful performances of Dr. Bernice Johnson Reagon with Sweet Honey in the Rock is to witness a part of history. Bernice Johnson's exposure to music as a toddler in her father's church, where congregants sang a cappella to an accompaniment of hands and feet, was good preparation for her civil rights movement days. As one of those arrested with the Albany movement demonstrators in Georgia on December 13, 1961, Bernice Johnson knew the relationship between music and survival.

Taken to jail with the second wave of demonstrations, the leader of the first group, Slater King, asked her to sing a song. She told the story in *Eyes on the Prize:*

> If Slater said, "Bernice, sing a song," he wasn't asking for a solo, he was asking me to plant a seed. The minute you start the song, the song is created by everybody there. There is really almost a musical explosion. . . . Songs were the bed of everything, and I'd never seen or felt songs do that [before]. . . . In the movement all the words sounded different. "This Little Light of Mine, I'm Going to Let It Shine," which I'd sung all my life, said something very different. We varied the verses: "All in the street, I'm going to let it shine. All in the jailhouse, I'm going to let it shine."
>
> The voice I have now I got the first time I sang in a movement meeting after I got out of jail. I did the song "Over My Head I See Freedom in the Air," but I had never heard that voice before. I had never been that me before. And once I became that me, I have never let that me go. . . . A transformation took place inside of the people. The singing was just the echo of that. . . . Sometimes the police would plead and say, "Please stop singing." And you would just know that your word was being heard, and you felt joy.

While every generation of African-Americans has had its music and its pain, hopefully each generation will also come into the meaning of its joy.

Wednesday, December 13, 1961, Georgia, U.S.A.

Music   **Power**

DECEMBER 14

On the night of December 14, 1820, at his home in Kennet Township, Pennsylvania, John Read was too uneasy to sleep. He got up and made a fire, but the uneasiness remained. About midnight, he thought he heard people outside. Before coming to Pennsylvania as a freeman, he'd had firsthand knowledge of slave catchers attempting to kidnap him into slavery, and the fear of being kidnapped had never left him. He was at all times armed to protect himself, and when someone finally knocked at his door that night, he was prepared. He asked what was wanted and was told of a search warrant for stolen goods. Believing the men to be kidnappers, Read told them that he had no stolen goods, that they should leave and come back in the morning when they would be permitted to search the house. As his attackers stormed the door, he warned that he would shoot if they came in. As they pried the door off its hinges, Read heard a pistol click. He called out, "It is life for life!" to which the answer came, "Damn the Negro, he won't shoot." As the first entered, Read shot. When the next one rushed in, he clubbed him and seized his gun. Running to the home of a neighbor, Read explained that kidnappers had attacked him, that he had killed them, that he was afraid of being hunted, and that he needed additional gunpowder. Making no attempt to escape, he waited to be arrested. When officials searched his home, they found the two white bodies, pistols, handcuffs, a whip, and a rope.

At the trial, Read was charged with manslaughter in the kidnapper-agent's death and convicted. The state sought the death penalty; instead, he was sentenced to nine years in prison.

Even in a free state, there was no justice for a Black man. At least Read lived to tell the tale. Today, when judges and prosecutors cite precedent for their charges and rulings, the precedent itself may be the problem.

Thursday, December 14, 1820, Pennsylvania, U.S.A.
Human Rights   **Self-Defense**

DECEMBER 15

By 1863, the Civil War was known by Blacks everywhere as the "war for liberation." They hoped this was the war that would finally put an end to slavery. Yet Blacks had every reason not to join in the effort. Since the nation's founding, every pledge to end slavery and the mistreatment of free Blacks had been betrayed. African-Americans had shared every one of the nation's battles, much to our own detriment. Now, with everything to gain and many lives to lose, Blacks determined to make the war our "freedom fight." During the war years, two hundred thousand enlisted in the Union Army, thirty thousand in the navy, and over 250,000 Black men and women worked (and sometimes died) as military nurses, cooks, boat pilots, builders, and scouts.

One of the leading doubter-turned-advocates was Dr. Martin R. Delany, Harvard's first Black medical school graduate. His plan to stem Ontario, Canada's, cholera epidemic saved thousands of lives in 1856. Similarly, his pledge to help alleviate societal ills motivated him as an Underground Railroad conductor and copublisher (with Frederick Douglass) of the abolitionist *North Star* newspaper. It had been Delany's lifelong dream to found a repatriated African homeland, but on December 15, 1863, he joined the war effort, seeing in it a chance to bring about the greatest immediate good.

On December 15, Dr. Delany wrote War Secretary Edwin M. Stanton to offer his services as a recruiter: "We are able, sir, to command all the effective Black men, as agents, in the United States, and . . . to recruit colored troops in any of the southern or seceded States." As Delany knew, this was a risky proposition. In May, the Confederacy had declared all Black troops criminals, denying them prisoner-of-war status and condemning them, upon capture, to death or slavery. Risking all, Dr. Delany accepted a commission as major in the Union Army Quartermaster Corps, the highest rank assigned any Black man, and led the way for Black officers in the military.

Tuesday, December 15, 1863, Illinois, U.S.A.

Civil War   **Purpose**

DECEMBER 16

From Portland, Maine, this notice appeared on December 16, 1836, in the antislavery journal *The Liberator:*

George Potter and Rosella his wife, would take this opportunity to express their gratitude to God, and under him, to the benevolent individuals who generously contributed in aiding them to redeem their two children from Slavery. They have the unspeakable happiness of informing the generous donors that, on the 12th inst. they received their children, aged eleven and seven years, raised from the degradation of slavery to the rank of Freemen.

Free Blacks often raised public appeals for money to buy a loved one's freedom. Equally poignant and impressive is the knowledge that other African-Americans, with little money and often with relatives of their own in bondage, shared the costs of each other's freedom.

Today's grandparents, extended families, and strangers are still aiding those among today's children who are in need of rescue, in an African-American tradition that was established long ago. A simple notice in the newspaper is all it takes to start, and we have certainly had our contemporary share of bad press. Those who have answered the call have earned our collective esteem.

Friday, December 16, 1836, Maine, U.S.A.

Family   **Responsibility to Youth**

DECEMBER 17

On December 17, 1814, Andrew Jackson, the future president, wrote a special proclamation in honor of the two African-American battalions that joined him in defeating the British in the Battle of New Orleans in the War of 1812:

> TO THE MEN OF COLOR. Soldiers! From the shores of Mobile I collected you to arms; I invited you to share in the perils and to divide the glory of your white countrymen. I expected much from you. . . . I knew that you could endure hunger and thirst and all the hardships of war. I knew that you loved the land of your nativity, and that like ourselves, you had to defend all that is most dear to you. But you surpass my hopes. I have found in you, united to the qualities, that noble enthusiasm which impels to great deeds.

How often we have pledged our lives for the good of the country, only to find that it was not for the good of us! Jackson's goal in the War of 1812 was unpublicized but clear: to eliminate Florida as a "perpetual harbor for our slaves." In sharing the perils and glory of their white countrymen, Black soldiers had unwittingly acted against the Seminoles who had long adopted Blacks into their nation. They and other Native Americans regularly helped escaping slaves flee to freedom. While still a general, Jackson led a clandestine war to destroy the Seminoles, which included burning the Black Seminole village of Fowltown. As president in 1835, Jackson prohibited distribution of abolitionist mail in post offices across the South. That year he also sanctioned the plan to expel Cherokees from their homelands. That trek of indigenous men, women, and children from Georgia to Oklahoma in the dead of winter would later be known as the "Trail of Tears."

With knowledge of these facts, Jackson's praise for our soldiers seems tarnished indeed. But what our men and women in the military have done in the name of loyalty and trust can never be dishonored, no matter the source.

Saturday, December 17, 1814, Louisiana, U.S.A.

Military   **Truths**

DECEMBER 18

Minister Louis Farrakhan is a respected classical violinist, but when he delivered his first New York address in nearly twenty years on December 18, 1993, it was on the heartstrings of African-America that he so adeptly played. Thirty-two thousand people had gathered to experience the live event at the Jacob Javits Convention Center, and it was beamed to a national audience of millions more.

For days the media inflamed the air with the familiar rhetoric that always flares when Blacks gather in large numbers. The tension surrounding the event was explosive. Matchbooks, lighters, juice bottles, and all manner of potential weaponry were checked at the door and returned after the event. And these were just the "visible" signs of security that ensured safety. This was a time for clarity, for African-American unity. People across the spectrum of Black life had come together for this moment, including actor Wesley Snipes, radio host Gary Byrd, *Essence* magazine's Susan Taylor, National Black Theater founder Barbara Ann Teer (see December 28).

The contrapuntal sounds of thirty-two thousand people in cheers and tears is an amazing thing. Into the center of this emotional circle came Louis Farrakhan. But the adulation was actually—as he himself would say—for all those New who had gone through so much to brave an appearance that day and for those who had endured so much for centuries to make it possible. In a two-hour oratory of electric brilliance, his storytelling was complex, his message plain. "There is power in God and the word," he said. "Crack the word like a whip," "be responsible to your word," and "love yourselves." Impassioned by the clouds of fear and sorrow swarming the land (see January 25), he asked men to stand in commitment to themselves and their community. Minister Louis Farrakhan had orchestrated a rare moment in which deeply maligned Black men and Black women took the time and space to honor each other en masse as men and women of the storm. It was history—an inspired, healing moment.

Saturday, December 18, 1993, New York, U.S.A.

Religion   **Healing**

DECEMBER 19

African-America's premier portrait painter, Joshua Johnston, portrayed himself this way in his first ad in the *Baltimore Intelligencer* of December 19, 1798:

> The subscriber, grateful for the liberal encouragement which an indulgent public have conferred on him, in his first essays in PORTRAIT PAINTING, returns his sincere acknowledgements. He takes liberty to observe, That by dint of industrious application, he has so far improved and matured his talents, that he can ensure the most precise and natural likenesses. As a self-taught genius, deriving from nature and industry his knowledge of the Art; and having experienced many insuperable obstacles in the pursuit of his studies, it is highly gratifying to him to make assurances of his ability to execute all commands, with an effect, and in a style which must give satisfaction. He therefore respectfully solicits encouragement. Apply at this House, in the Alley leading from Charles to Hanover Street, back of Sears's Tavern.

There is so much that we don't know about Johnston. The little we do know has been unearthed to prove his "race"—an issue that would never have been raised but for the quality of his work. With the biases of his and our times, he speaks in duly guarded fashion of his "insuperable obstacles." Among his paintings are fine oils of the prominent Blacks of his day. He was listed in the 1817 Baltimore city directory as a "free householder of color." And as one scholar has put it, "to have listed a white man as a Negro would have been a serious matter." In fact, it would have been grounds for a libel suit. Sadly, the debate over Johnston is fueled by the assumption that he was "too good" to be Black. And was he really good? He was fabulous. See for yourself in books like Bearden and Henderson's *History of African-American Art* and in numerous collections, from the Abby Aldrich Rockefeller Folk Art Center of the Williamsburg Museum in Virginia to various folk art museums around the country.

Wednesday, December 19, 1798, Maryland, U.S.A.

Art   **Heritage**

DECEMBER 20

On the night of December 20, 1956, the African-American community of Montgomery, Alabama, unanimously voted to end its historic 385-day bus boycott.

To those who had confronted centuries of slavery and segregation by participating in the self-affirming community-wide action, the Montgomery bus boycott was a profound act of empowerment. In the 385 days following Rosa Parks's decision to keep her now-historic seat (see December 1), untold strengths were tapped to sustain the most timid souls across vast land mines of terror and fear. As empty buses roamed streets in search of former prey, men, women, and children en route to freedom left an indelible footprint as they hopped aboard a 100 percent effective citywide bus boycott.

Five weeks earlier, news of a Supreme Court–backed desegregation order had reached weary boycotters. Still they held on until the order was in hand. Finally in receipt of the order on December 20, that night they ended the boycott by unanimous vote.

For those who lost lives and livelihoods demanding equal service for equal payment; those who put their cars into service for the greater good; those who ran interference in courts of law and public opinion; those who secured insurance abroad when opposition forces corrupted underwriters nationwide; those who told the story; and even to those hell-bent on destroying it, the Montgomery bus boycott was a bold feat of courage and tenacity—a model of community organizing that launched a national civil rights movement and prodded a newly ordained twenty-seven-year-old strategist—the Reverend Dr. Martin Luther King, Jr.—to world renown and a Nobel Peace Prize.

Thursday, December 20, 1956, Alabama, U.S.A.

Rights   **Unity**

DECEMBER 21

Every year on this date, December 21, Alvin Ailey's dance theater masterpiece, *Revelations*, is performed someplace in the world. And whenever *Revelations* is performed, history repeats itself—gloriously and graciously. For what makes this work so special and so loved is its foundation in the life of the Black church, as Ailey knew it growing up in Rogers, Texas.

In three movements—"Pilgrim of Sorrow," "Take Me to the Water," and "Move, Members, Move"—each consisting of ten dances based on spirituals, Ailey tells the social history of people in the segregated Southwest.

First performed in 1960, *Revelations* has been the signature piece for the main company as well as the touring company Ailey founded in 1974. In nearly forty years, it has never been retired from either company's repertoire. Ailey tried once while on tour in Europe to take it off the program, but the audience and the dancers wouldn't permit it. To witness *Revelations* is to "go down to the river and be baptized," as our people would say.

Wednesday, December 21, 1996, Texas, U.S.A.

Dance   **Spirit**

DECEMBER 22

With passage of the Fugitive Slave Law endangering the lives of freemen and self-emancipated slaves alike, the winter of 1850 marked one of the greatest periods of exodus to Canada. Today, the story of the life African-Americans made in Canada is preserved at the North American Black Historical Museum in Amherstburg, Ontario.

Traveling to Ontario to see the museum is well worth the trip—particularly in the winter, when everything is knee-deep in snow. For only in winter can one fully appreciate the hardships our ancestors endured to make the story the museum portrays possible. Each of Harriet Tubman's nineteen Underground Railroad rescue missions was made in the winter. And with the Fugitive Slave Law's passage in the fall of 1850, refugees left for Canada soon after, escaping—usually on foot—in the winter when the trip was most difficult and most necessary. In the years 1800–60, over fifty thousand slaves made the pilgrimage to Canada. The settlements such as North Buxton, Dawn, and Nova Scotia absorbed daily arrivals, and still the refugees survived and they prospered.

But the Blacks didn't just move to Canada and stay there. With loved ones left behind in the United States, they had a special bond here. When the Civil War began, these émigrés who endured so much to leave the United States returned in major numbers to fight alongside the first Black volunteers. When the war ended, those communities sent back to the States a majority of the first Black professionals. Living in Canada, while it was not entirely free of discrimination, had at least allowed them to get an education from the elementary grades through college and professional schools of law and medicine.

All of this is preserved at the museum because of the vision of one man, Melvin Simpson, who was so filled with his dream that he inspired a community to make it a reality in September 1981.

Sunday, December 22, 1850, Ontario, Canada

Social History   **Continuity**

DECEMBER 23

The love of Kente cloth has swept African-Americans nationwide. This is the story of Ghana's own "home-spun" treasure:

During the days of Africa's colonization by Europe, Africa's natural raw resources were grown by Black hands but "owned" by the European colonizers. Once harvested, the raw materials would be shipped to European factories for manufacturing, and then Africans would have to buy back their own goods from Europe at steeply inflated prices. In 1957, the Gold Coast took its independence from England and resurrected itself as the modern nation of Ghana. The country's newly elected president, Kwame Nkrumah, knew that his young nation's ability to take control of its resources, manufacturing, and production of marketable assets was critical to its future. Ghana was rich in gold, cocoa, timber, coffee, rubber, diamonds, bauxite, and more. It was also rich in a long tradition of art and textiles. To symbolize Ghana's ability to profit by its own hands, Nkrumah helped to revive as an industry the weaving of the cloth traditionally worn by Ghanaian royalty. Woven into its distinctive patterns is the history of a people, preserved across the ages.

Today, the African-American desire to celebrate a continuity with the African past has resulted in poor-quality copies of the Kente-patterned cloth coming to the United States from sources other than Ghana. But preserving the quality of the heritage and the economic independence of Africa demands that the true celebrant of African culture demand true authenticity.

Friday, December 23, 1960, Ghana

Business/Art   **Understanding**

DECEMBER 24

No one knows when the so-called Underground Railroad officially began, but the first soul hailing a ride surely must have cried out during that historic arrival at Jamestown in 1619 (see August 1). And for the next 250 years, a private network of people in strange and distant places answered that call to help the victims of slavery to freedom. Filled with that purpose, many of the network's most active practitioners had no idea that others had given their work a name. Among those least aware of the term "Underground Railroad" were the members of the network's most unheralded group of agents and conductors—slaves themselves. In a group filled with heroes, these people deserve particular notice because they used their considerable knowledge of the routes to freedom not for themselves but for others. Resisting their own obvious opportunities for escape, they remained enslaved to help others on their way.

Most of these names will never be known, but thankfully Arnold Cragston's has survived to represent them all. On this December night, he and hundreds of other like-minded liberators could be found plying their secret trade.

A fugitive stealing through the plantation slave quarters throughout the South could hear the refrain, "One more river to cross." But from 1859 until emancipation in 1863, when that spiritual was raised in the quarters of Mason County, Kentucky, for fugitives in need, the person most likely to meet them "Down to the River Jordan" (the Ohio River) and row them across was Arnold Cragston. For four years, this enslaved man rowed hundreds, and perhaps thousands, of fleeing slaves across the river on moonless nights.

Years later, when he was asked about the Underground Railroad and his role in it, Cragston would confirm what others have long said: "We didn't call it that then. I don't know as we called it anything. We just knew there was a lot of slaves always a-wantin' to get free, and I had to help."

Saturday, December 24, 1859, Kentucky, U.S.A.

Heroes   **Life's Work**

DECEMBER 25

On Christmas Day, 1828, Anne Hampton and Solomon Northup pledged that their love would stand the test of time, not knowing that fate would put them to the test. For thirteen years they lived as free persons of color in their native New York. In January 1841, Solomon was offered a job as a part-time violinist with a traveling band. It was a trick. He was kidnapped, beaten, shipped to New Orleans, and sold into slavery. Solomon wrote Anne telling her what had happened, but he was unable to give his whereabouts to aid his rescue. Solomon was sold and resold. He tried to escape but failed. For the next eleven years, Anne tried to trace him, but she, too, failed each time. Finally, in September 1852, Solomon sent a second letter. This time, the postmark gave the missing clue: Marksville, Avoyelles Parish, Louisiana.

On November 19, 1852, Anne Northup petitioned the governor of New York to aid her husband's rescue: "Your memorialist [petitioner] and her family are poor and wholly unable to pay the expenses of restoring his freedom. . . . Your excellency is entreated to employ such agents deemed necessary to effect the return of Solomon Northup. . . . And your memorialist will ever pray." In January 1853, twelve years after his kidnapping, Solomon came home to Anne, a free man.

As the Northup love story shows, the greatest test of all may be in convincing others that we are telling the truth. But no matter the obstacle, we must first see ourselves as worthy of the defense. Harder still may be believing it ourselves. After eleven years, Solomon still gave his impossible dream a try. After eleven years in pursuit of a "lost cause," Anne's petition was no minor act of faith. Once home, Solomon published his story, *Twelve Years a Slave*, to such acclaim that the publicity helped capture his kidnappers. Today, five hundred years after the earliest families were torn apart by slavery, the story of the Northups provides rare insight into the trauma that Africans endured—struggling to find and recover lost loves.

Saturday, December 25, 1852, New York–Louisiana, U.S.A.
Family   **Hope**

DECEMBER 26

In 1966, Maulana Ron Karenga was a University of California Ph.D. candidate in political science. As a visionary scholar, he used the lessons of African civilization to create Kwanza, a seven-day annual cultural celebration for people of African descent, lasting from December 26 through January 1. Condensing the message of those lessons into seven principles—in Swahili, the *Nguzo Saba*—each of the seven days was dedicated to one of the seven principles. The word *Kwanza* means "first fruits," and thus this season is a time to honor the gifts of heritage and of life itself:

December 26: *Umoja* (Unity)—To strive for and maintain unity in the family, community, nation, and race

December 27: *Kujichagulia* (Self-determination)—To define ourselves, create for ourselves, and speak for ourselves, instead of being defined, named, created for, and spoken for by others

December 28: *Ujima* (Collective work and responsibility)—To build and maintain our community together, to make our sisters' and brothers' problems our problems, and to solve them together

December 29: *Ujamaa* (Cooperative economics)—To build and maintain our own stores, shops, and other businesses and to profit from them together

December 30: *Nia* (Purpose)—To make as our collective vocation the building and developing of our community in order to restore our people to their traditional greatness

December 31: *Kuumba* (Creativity)—To do always as much as we can in whatever way we can in order to leave our community more beautiful and beneficial than when we inherited it

January 1: *Imani* (Faith)—To believe with all our hearts in our people, our parents, our teachers, our leaders, and the righteousness and victory of our struggle

Thursday, December 26, 1996, U.S.A.

Kwanza: Umoja   **Unity**

DECEMBER 27

December 27: Kwanza day two. The annual day of *Kujichagulia*, self-determination. As Dr. Maulana Ron Karenga envisioned it (see December 26), this is a day "to define ourselves, create for ourselves, and speak for ourselves." In the winter of 1834, students at Cincinnati's first free school wrote essays on the topic, "What do you think most about?" Their essays were presented at the Ohio Antislavery Convention of 1835. Among them, these excerpts survive:

"Dear school-master, . . . what we are studying for is to try to get the yoke of slavery broke and the chains parted asunder. . . . O that God would change the hearts of our fellow men." (Age twelve)

"In my youthful days dear Lord, . . . bless the cause of abolition. We trust that it may be the means of moving mountains of sin off all the families. My mother and stepfather, my sister and myself were all born in slavery. The Lord did let the oppressed go free." (Age eleven)

"Dear Sir. . . . I have two cousins in slavery who are entitled to their freedom. They have done everything that the will requires and now they won't let them go. They talk of selling them down the river. If this was your case what would you do? Please give me your advice." (Age ten)

"I can't see how the Americans can call this a land of freedom where so much slavery is." (Age sixteen)

In their ability to speak for themselves so eloquently, these children also spoke for millions of others unable to attend school. With their voices and their drive, they provided the success stories propelling the movement to educate the children of ex-slaves.

Saturday, December 27, 1834, Ohio, U.S.A.

Kwanza: Kujichagulia   **Self-Determination**

DECEMBER 28

December 28: Kwanza day three. The day of *Ujima*, collective work and responsibility. As envisioned by Dr. Maulana Ron Karenga (see December 26), this is the day "to build and maintain our community together, to make our sisters' and brothers' problems our problems, and to solve them together."

For an African-American community of artists seized by the meaning and passion of 1968—the civil rights and Black Power movements, the murder of Dr. King, rebellion in the streets—a problem they all shared was a lack of their own financial base from which to express themselves through the arts. And without the voice of artists, the community itself was silenced. Fredrica Lila Teer expressed the need this way: "Artists can own and operate their own Institutions; create their own art forms, . . . develop, produce and manage their own businesses. . . . They are the visionaries who will provide the leadership for future generations to come." And in 1968, her sister and veteran actress, Barbara Ann Teer, founded the National Black Theater (NBT) on the principles that Fredrica, an "institution builder" to the core, had outlined.

Today, in the spirit of Ujima, we honor the leadership of Barbara Ann Teer and others who have made magic with their art. One of its greatest creations is the revitalization of its once-depressed Harlem neighborhood at the corner of 125th Street and Fifth Avenue.

In 1983, after a catastrophic fire destroyed the building out of which it had been operating for fifteen years, NBT literally rose from the ashes. Using her creativity and enterprise, Teer has since raised a $12 million facility in a neighborhood that insurance companies and banks wrote off and in which businesses refused to grow. Now her building houses twelve commercial tenants, the theater, its Institute of Action Arts, and the largest collection of sacred Yoruba art in the United States. Her motto, with which she has raised buildings and spirits: "Keep Soul Alive!"

Saturday, December 28, 1996, U.S.A.
Kwanza: Ujima　　　　　**Collective Work and Responsibility**

DECEMBER 29

December 29: Kwanza day four. The annual day of *Ujamaa*, cooperative economics. As Dr. Maulana Ron Karenga envisioned it (see December 26), this encourages us "to build and maintain our . . . own businesses and to profit from them together." In December 1959, thirty-year-old Berry Gordy was at the wheel of his Cadillac with nineteen-year-old Smokey Robinson. Their progress was frustrated by the snow and their status in the record business. It was the wisdom of the younger Smokey Robinson that convinced the more seasoned Berry Gordy that what they needed—and should dare to do—was to start their own record company.

From that prophetic trip, Motown was launched. It was a hazardous undertaking, coming as it did right after the "payola" scandals of the 1950s revealed the depth of corruption in the record industry. But coming through it ensured Berry Gordy's future not only as the independent record producer he already was but as the impresario of the "Motown Sound." He launched the careers of a roster of talent so young and so impressive that almost forty years later their music still dominates the charts: Ashford and Simpson, the Commodores, Marvin Gaye, Gladys Knight, the Jacksons (the Jackson Five, Michael Jackson, and Janet Jackson), the Pointer Sisters, Lionel Richie, Smokey Robinson and the Miracles, Diana Ross, the Supremes, the Temptations, and Stevie Wonder.

While Motown's primary legacy is music, it must also be appreciated as a business. The company rose from a community base in the "motor-town" of Detroit when vehement segregation was the rule, major record companies relished blocking Black ownership for breakfast, and promoters suddenly became disinterested in Black talent when it was under Black management. Motown was not the first Black record company (see March 24), but its existence forged a breakthrough. With its success, Motown nurtured ancillary careers in record and film production, promotion, management, and distribution.

Tuesday, December 29, 1959, Michigan, U.S.A.

Kwanza: Ujamaa   **Cooperative Economics**

DECEMBER 30

December 30: Kwanza day five. The annual day of *Nia*, purpose. This is a time "to make as our collective vocation the building . . . of our community . . . to restore our people to their traditional greatness."

In the latter part of the eighteenth century, the political and intellectual voice of the nation had come together in Philadelphia, the nation's first capital. The Declaration of Independence and the Constitution had been forged there. But instead of bringing about slavery's end, each new document left the institution better off than ever. Just before the dawn of the nineteenth century, free Blacks rallied in Philadelphia with their own declaration: Stop the slave trade! On December 30, 1799, seventy-five men, including AME Church founders Richard Allen and Absalom Jones, put their names on the line for freedom. Allen, Jones, and the others risked their all with this petition to the president, Senate, and House of Representatives:

> The Petition of the People of Colour, free men, within the City and Suburbs of Philadelphia, humbly showeth . . . In the Constitution and the Fugitive Slave Bill, no mention is made of black people, or slaves: therefore, if the Bill of Rights, or the Declaration of Congress are of any validity, we beseech, that as we are men, we may be admitted to partake of the liberties and unalienable rights therein held forth; firmly believing that the extending of justice and equity to all classes would be a means of drawing down the blessing of Heaven upon this land, for the peace and prosperity of which, and the real happiness of every member of the community, we fervently pray.

The support gathered for this petition built vital alliances in the movement to outlaw the slave trade, and the necessary legislation finally became law in 1808 (see January 1), leading the way for abolition, state by state, in the North.

Monday, December 30, 1799, Pennsylvania, U.S.A.

Kwanza: Nia   **Purpose**

DECEMBER 31

December 31: Kwanza day six. The day of *Kuumba,* Creativity: "to do always as much as we can in whatever way we can in order to leave our community more beautiful and beneficial than when we inherited it." Now, on December 31, 1862, the eve of freedom, people prepared for the magnitude of a day 243 years in the making—freedom day! The day of Jubilee! They also prepared for the very real possibility that it might not happen at all; that freedom might once again elude their grasp. In Boston, the Emancipation Proclamation's chief strategist, Frederick Douglass, awaited the decree with a crowd of thousands:

> An immense assembly convened in Tremont Temple to await the first flash of the electric wires announcing the "new departure." Two years of war, prosecuted in the interest of slavery, had made free speech possible in Boston, and we were now met together to receive and celebrate the first utterance of the long-hoped-for-proclamation, if it came, and if it did not come, to speak our minds freely; for, in view of the past, it was by no means certain that it would come. . . . Eight, nine, ten o'clock came and went, and still no word. A visible shadow seemed falling on the expecting throng. . . . At last, when patience was well-nigh exhausted, and suspense was becoming agony, a man with hasty step advanced through the crowd, and with a face fairly illumined with the news he bore, exclaimed in tones that thrilled all hearts, "It is coming!" "It is on the wires!". . . the first step on the part of the nation in its departure from the thraldom of ages.

When we think of all that our people have lived and done, there is no doubt that as individuals and together as one, we are a mighty soul indeed. As it says in the spiritual, "How I got over/My soul looks back in wonder/How I got over." On the eve of freedom for our ancestors, on the eve of a new year for us, there is history, there is heritage, and there is hope.

Wednesday, December 31, 1862, Massachusetts, U.S.A.
Kwanza: Kuumba   **Creativity**

SELECTED BIBLIOGRAPHY

Archives, Libraries, and Private Collections
Hampton University Archives, Hampton, Virginia.
Mme. C. J. Walker Mfg. Co. Archives, Tuskegee, Alabama.
Nantucket Historical Society ("Diary of Visits of F. Douglass to Nantucket" and "Absalom F. Boston, His Family and Nantucket's Black Community"), Nantucket, Massachusetts.
New Bedford Library and Genealogical Archives, New Bedford, Massachusetts.
Oberlin Public Library, Oberlin, Ohio.
Stamford Law Library, Stamford, Connecticut.

Books
Aaron, Hank, and Lonnie Wheeler. *I Had a Hammer: The Hank Aaron Story.* New York: HarperCollins, 1991.
Adams, Janus. *A Journey to the Moon and Beyond.* Wilton, Conn.: BackPax International, 1987.
———. *Underground Railroad: Escape to Freedom.* Wilton, Conn.: BackPax International, 1988.
Anderson, Jervis. *This Was Harlem: A Cultural Portrait.* New York: Farrar, Straus & Giroux, 1982.
Aptheker, Herbert. *A Documentary History of the Negro People in the United States.* 7 vols. New York: Citadel Press, 1951–1994.
Ashe, Arthur R., Jr. *A Hard Road to Glory: A History of the African-American Athlete.* 3 vols. New York: Amistad Press, 1988.
Bardolph, Richard. *Civil Rights Record: Black Americans and the Law: 1849–1970.* New York: Crowell, 1970.
Barrett, Leonard. *The Rastafarians.* New York: Beacon Press, 1977.
Bates, Daisy. *The Long Shadow of Little Rock.* New York: David McKay, 1962.
Beals, Melba Patillo. *Warriors Don't Cry.* New York: Pocket Books, 1994.
Bearden, Romare, and Harry Henderson. *A History of African-American Artists: From 1792 to the Present.* New York: Pantheon, 1993.
Bennett, Lerone, Jr. *Before the Mayflower: A History of Black America.* Chicago: Johnson Publishing Company, 1962, 1988.
Benson, Mary. *The African Patriots.* Chicago: Encyclopedia Britannica Press, 1964.
Bentley, Eric. *Thirty Years of Treason: Excerpts from Hearings Before HUAC 1938–1968.* New York: Viking, 1971.
Berlin, Ira, and Barbara Fields, et al., eds. *Free at Last.* New York: New Press, 1992.
Braithwaite, Fred, Jr. *Fresh Fly Flavor.* Stamford, Conn.: Longmeadow Press, 1992.
Branch, Taylor. *Parting the Waters: America in the King Years 1954–63.* New York: Simon & Schuster, 1988.
Butterfield, L. H., et al., eds. *The Book of Abigail and John: Selected Letters of the Adams Family 1762–1784.* Cambridge: Harvard University Press, 1975.
Cantor, George. *Historic Landmarks of Black America.* Detroit: Gale Research, 1991.
Carruth, Gorton. *Encyclopedia of American Facts and Dates.* New York: Harper & Row, 1987.
Carson, Clayborne, et al., eds. *Eyes on the Prize Civil Rights Reader.* New York: Viking Penguin, 1991.

Collins, Charles, et al., eds. *The African Americans.* New York: Viking Studio Books, 1993.

Collins, Marva, and Civia Tamarkin. *Marva Collins' Way.* Los Angeles: Jeremy Tarcher, 1982.

Columbus, Christopher. *Log of Christopher Columbus,* trans. Robert H. Fuson. Camden, Maine: International Marine Publishing, 1987.

Cullen, Countee. *My Soul's High Song: Collected Writings.* New York: Doubleday, 1991.

Dash, Julie. *Daughters of the Dust.* New York: New Press, 1992.

Davis, Edwin Adams, and William Ransom Hogan. *The Barber of Natchez.* Port Washington, N.Y.: Kennikat Press, 1972.

Driskell, David C. *Two Centuries of Black American Art.* New York: Los Angeles County Museum of Art/Knopf, 1976.

Drotning, Phillip T. *An American Traveler's Guide to Black History.* New York: Doubleday, 1968.

DuBois, Shirley Graham. *DuBois: A Pictorial Biography.* Chicago: Johnson Publishing Company, 1977.

Equiano. *The Interesting Narrative of the Life of Olaudah Equiano, or Gustavus Vassa, the African.* England: 1789.

Giddings, Paula. *When and Where I Enter: The Impact of Black Women on Race and Sex in America.* New York: William Morrow, 1984.

Harding, Vincent. *There Is a River.* New York: Vintage/Random House, 1983.

Harris, M. A. *A Negro History Tour of Manhattan.* New York: Greenwood Press, 1968.

Harris, Middleton A. et al., eds. *The Black Book.* New York: Random House, 1974.

Hill, Daniel G. *The Freedom-Seekers: Blacks in Early Canada.* Agincourt, Canada: Book Society of Canada Ltd., 1981.

Himes, Chester. *The Quality of Hurt.* New York: Paragon House, 1989.

Hine, Darlene Clark, et al., eds. *Black Women in America: An Historical Encyclopedia.* New York: Carolson Publications, 1993.

Jefferson, Isaac. *Memoirs of a Monticello Slave: As Dictated to Charles Campbell in the 1840s by Isaac, One of Thomas Jefferson's Slaves* Charlottesville, Va.: University of Virginia Press, 1951.

Jefferson, Thomas. *Jefferson Writings.* New York: Library of America, 1984.

Johnson, James Weldon. *Along This Way.* New York: Viking Press, 1968.

———. *Black Manhattan.* New York: Atheneum, 1969.

Johnson, John H. *Succeeding Against the Odds.* New York: Amistad Press, 1989.

Kaplan, Sidney. *The Black Presence in the Era of the American Revolution 1770–1800.* Greenwich, Conn.: National Portrait Gallery/New York Graphic Society, 1973.

Katz, William Loren. *Black West.* Seattle: Open Hand, 1987.

———. *Eyewitness: The Negro in American History.* Belmont, Calif.: David S. Lake Publishers, 1974.

Kent, George E. *A Life of Gwendolyn Brooks.* Lexington, Ky.: University Press of Kentucky, 1990.

Lecky, Sheryle, and John Lecky. *Moments: The Pulitzer Prize Photographs.* New York: Crown Publishers, 1978.

Lerner, Gerda. *Black Women in White America: A Documentary History.* New York: Random House, 1972.

Lewis, David Levering. *W. E. B. DuBois: Biography of a Race 1868–1919.* New York: Henry Holt, 1993.

Lewis, David Levering, ed. *Harlem Renaissance Reader.* New York: Viking Penguin, 1994.

Life and Adventures of Nat Love Better Known in the Cattle Country as Dead Wood Dick, by Himself. California: 1907.

Logan, Rayford, and Michael Winston. *Dictionary of American Negro Biography.* New York: W. W. Norton, 1988.

MacNeil, Robert, ed. *The Way We Were: 1963, the Year Kennedy Was Shot.* New York: Carroll & Graf, 1988.

Makeba, Miriam, and James Hall. *Makeba: My Story.* New York: Plume/NAL, 1987.

Mays, Benjamin. *Born to Rebel.* New York: Charles Scribner's Sons, 1971.

Metzger, Linda, et al., eds. *Black Writers: A Selection of Sketches from Contemporary Authors.* Detroit: Gale Research, 1989.

Moutoussamy-Ashe, Jeanne. *Viewfinders.* New York: Writers & Readers, 1993.

Myers, Walter Dean. *Malcolm X: By Any Means Necessary.* New York: Scholastic, 1993.

Patterson, Lindsay. *International Library of Afro-American Life and History: Anthology of the Afro-American in the Theatre.* Cornwells Heights, Pa.: Publisher's Agency, 1976.

Ploski, Harry A., and James Williams, et al., eds. *Negro Almanac.* Detroit: Gale Research, 1989.

Prince, Nancy. *A Black Woman's Odyssey Through Russia and Jamaica.* New York: Markus Wiener, 1990.

Rampersad, Arnold. *The Life of Langston Hughes.* Vol. 2, *1941–1967, I Dream a World.* New York: Oxford University Press, 1988.

Robeson, Paul. *Here I Stand.* New York: Othello Associates, 1958.

Robeson, Susan. *The Whole World in His Hands: A Pictorial Biography of Paul Robeson.* Secaucus, N.J.: Citadel, 1981.

Robinson, Jack Roosevelt. *I Never Had It Made.* New York: Putnam, 1972.

Rogers, J. A. *World's Great Men of Color.* Vols. 1 and 2. New York:Collier/ Macmillan, 1972.

Rose, Phyllis. *Jazz Cleopatra: Josephine Baker in Her Time.* New York: Doubleday, 1989.

Sammons, Vivian Ovelton. *Blacks in Science and Medicine.* New York: Hemisphere Publishing, 1990.

Schoener, Allen. *Harlem on My Mind: Cultural Capital of Black America 1900–1978.* New York: Dell Publishing, 1968, 1979.

Shenkman, Richard, and Kurt Reiger. *One Night Stands with American History.* New York: Quill, 1982.

Sinnette, Elinor DesVerney. *Arthur A. Schomburg: Black Bibliophile and Collector.* Detroit: New York Public Library and Wayne State University Press, 1989.

Southern, Eileen. *The Music of Black Americans: A History.* New York: W. W. Norton, 1971.

Spruill, Dorothy Redford. *Somerset Homecoming: Recovering a Lost Heritage.* New York: Anchor/Doubleday, 1988.

Story, Rosalyn M. *And So I Sing: African American Divas of Opera and Concert.* New York: Warner Books, 1990.

Stowe, Harriet Beecher. *Uncle Tom's Cabin.* Reprint, New York: Washington Square Press, 1966.

Studio Museum in Harlem. *Harlem Renaissance: Art of Black America.* New York: Harry N. Abrams, 1987.

Sullivan, Charles, ed. *Children on Promise: African-American Literature and Art for Young People.* New York: Harry N. Abrams, 1991.

Taylor, Susie King. *Reminiscences of My Life: A Black Woman's Civil War Memoirs.* New York: Markus Wiener, 1988.

Thomas, Lamont D. *Paul Cuffe: Black Entrepreneur and Pan-Africanist.* Urbana, Ill.: University of Illinois Press, 1988.

Van Peebles, Melvin. *Sweet Sweetback's Baadasssss Song.* New York: Lancer Books, 1971.

Van Sertima, Ivan. *They Came Before Columbus: The African Presence in Ancient America.* New York: Random House, 1976.

Van Sertima, Ivan, ed. *Blacks in Science: Ancient and Modern.* New Brunswick, N.J.: Transaction Books, 1983.

Walker, Alice. *In Search of Our Mothers' Gardens.* New York: Harcourt Brace, 1983.

Walker, Margaret. *How I Wrote Jubilee and Other Essays on Life and Literature.* New York: Feminist Press, 1990.

Wallace, Michele, ed. *Black Popular Culture.* Seattle: Bay Press, 1992.

Ward, Geoffrey C., and Ken Burns. *Baseball: An Illustrated History.* New York: Knopf, 1994.

Washington, James Melvin. *Conversations with God: Two Centuries of Prayers by African Americans.* New York: HarperCollins, 1994.

Washington, Margaret, ed. *Narrative of Sojourner Truth.* New York: Vintage, 1993.

Weisbrot, Robert. *Father Divine and the Struggle for Racial Equality.* Urbana, Ill.: University of Illinois Press, 1983.

Williams, Juan. *Eyes on the Prize.* New York: Viking, 1987.

Periodicals and Other Sources

Cleaver, Kathleen. "A Dreadful Absurdity." Diss., Yale University Law School, 1988.

Colloquium Journal: First World Festival of Negro Arts, Society of African Culture. UNESCO/Senegalese Government, 1966.

International Review of African American Art 7, no. 1.

Jackdaw No. 124—Tutankhamun and the Discovery of the Tomb.

Karenga, Maulana Ron. "Nguzo Saba: The Seven Principles."

Metropolitan Museum of Art. "Selections of Nineteenth Century Afro-American Art." Exhibition catalog.

GENERAL INDEX

INDEX OF SUBJECTS

INDEX OF INSPIRATIONAL THEMES